Seaforth

WORLD NAVAL REVIEW

2014

Seaforth

WORLD NAVAL REVIEW
2014

Editor
CONRAD WATERS

Seaforth
PUBLISHING

Frontispiece: Warships from the United States Navy and other
Pacific fleets seen alongside at Pearl Harbor in July 2012
during the biennial RIMPAC exercises. The Pacific region
remains a focal point for world naval activity. *(US Navy)*

The editor welcomes correspondence and suggestions from readers.
Please contact him via Seaforth at **info@seaforthpublishing.com**.
All correspondence should be marked **FAA: Conrad Waters**.

First published in Great Britain in 2013 by
Seaforth Publishing
An imprint of Pen & Sword Books Ltd
47 Church Street, Barnsley
S Yorkshire S70 2AS

www.seaforthpublishing.com
Email info@seaforthpublishing.com

British Library Cataloguing in Publication Data
A CIP data record for this book is available from the British Library

ISBN 978-1-84832-182-3

Typeset and designed by Stephen Dent
Printed and bound in China

CONTENTS

Note on Tables: Tables are provided to give a broad indication of fleet sizes and other key information but should be regarded only as a general guide. For example, many published sources differ significantly on the principal particulars of ships, whilst even governmental information can be subject to contradiction. In general terms, the data contained in these tables is based on official information updated as of June 2013, supplemented by reference to a wide range of secondary and corporate sources, such as shipbuilder websites.

1 OVERVIEW

INTRODUCTION

'A collision at sea can ruin your entire day' is a truism frequently attributed to the Ancient Greek historian and Athenian general Thucydides but now claimed to be a 1960s creation of US Navy Captain W B 'Bill' Hayler. Whatever the statement's origins, it most likely reflected the thoughts of the officers and crew of the US Navy mine warfare vessel *Guardian* (MCM-5) when their ship became stranded on the Tubbataha Reef in the Philippines on 17 January 2013 after a port call to Subic Bay. It proved impossible to salvage the minesweeper without significant damage to the protected World Heritage Site. She was subsequently decommissioned and broken up *in situ*.

Whilst *Guardian*'s loss has negligible impact on the world naval balance, her grounding and subsequent disposal does reflect two themes of broad significance. One is the US Navy's increased presence in the waters of the Western Pacific as part of the so-called 'Pivot to the Pacific' that was amongst the key priorities set out in the US Presidential Strategic Guidance issued in January 2012. Widely seen as an attempt to counter the growing influence of an increasingly assertive China, the rebalancing of United States' military assets towards the Asia-Pacific region continued during 2013. Most notably, newly-appointed Secretary of Defense 'Chuck' Hagel announced during the annual Asian security conference known as the Shangri-La Dialogue that sixty per cent of overseas US Air Force capabilities are now devoted to the region. This parallels a similar US Navy force allocation confirmed during 2012. At the same time, the United States is stepping-up its efforts to boost links with the militaries of other countries that share its concern over China's regional ambitions, which have already resulted in high profile territorial disputes with the Philippines and Japan.[1] The widely publicised deployment of the lead littoral combat ship *Freedom* (LCS-1) to Singapore – the first of eleven to be sent to the Asia-Pacific region by the early years of the next decade – is just one of a range of initiatives taken to reinforce regional alliances.

An unanswered question is the likely response to the United States' overtures by the many Asia-Pacific countries that fear China's growing influence but also rely on it as a major trading partner. This ambivalence is reflected in Australia's new *Defence White Paper* of 3 May 2013.[2] This – in contrast to the preceding 2009 document – specifically asserted that Australia '…does not approach China as an adversary…' but still supported the United States' rebalancing as being beneficial to regional security and prosperity. It remains a matter of conjecture whether Australia's vision of '…the most likely future as one in which the United States and China are able to maintain a constructive relationship encompassing both competition and cooperation' is a logical analysis of economic fundamentals or mere wishful thinking. Certainly, there is much concern in China that the United States' current approach places more emphasis on containment than collaboration.

The other notable aspect of *Guardian*'s stranding was the US Navy's apparent ready willingness to accept the loss of one of a limited fleet of mine warfare assets. This may simply have been due to the impracticality of completing a successful salvage operation without unacceptable environmental damage. Equally, it may also reflect a hard-headed decision to avoid expenditure on recovering and repairing a ship which was already due for replacement with new technology – in the form of mine-countermeasures modules deployed on littoral combat ships – within the next few years. After spending a lengthy period in

Table 1.0.1: COUNTRIES WITH HIGH NATIONAL DEFENCE EXPENDITURES – 2012

RANK	COUNTRY	TOTAL: US$	SHARE OF GDP: %	CHANGE 2011–12
1	United States	685.0bn	4.4%	-5.6%
2	China	166.0bn	2.0%	7.8%
3	Russian Federation	90.7bn	4.4%	16.0%
4	United Kingdom	60.8bn	2.5%	-0.8%
5	Japan	59.3bn	1.0%	-0.6%
6	France	58.9bn	2.3%	-0.3%
7	Saudi Arabia	56.7bn	8.9%	12.0%
8	India	46.1bn	2.5%	-0.8%
9	Germany	45.8bn	1.4%	0.9%
10	Italy	34.0bn	1.7%	-5.2%
	World	**1,753bn**	**2.5%**	**-0.4%**

Information from the Stockholm International Peace Research Institute (SIPRI) – http://milexdata.sipri.org
The SIPRI Military Expenditure Database contains data on 172 countries over the period 1988–2012.

Notes:
1 Spending figures are at current prices and market exchange rates.
2 Figures for China, Germany, Italy and the Russian Federation are estimates.
3 Data on military expenditure as a share of GDP (Gross Domestic Product) relates to GDP estimates from the IMF World Economic Outlook, October 2012.
4 Change is real terms change, i.e. adjusted for local inflation.

Two images of the US Navy mine-countermeasures vessel *Guardian* (MCM-5) aground on the Tubbataha Reef in the Philippines in January 2013. The ship was decommissioned and recovered in pieces when salvage proved impossible. *(US Navy)*

denial about the likely extent of budget reductions, the US military is starting to come to terms with the probability that the sequestration process mandated in the 2011 Budget Control Act will significantly curtail defence spending over the remainder of the decade.[3] As demonstrated by Table 1.0.1, the United States is likely to retain the world's largest defence budget by a big margin. Nevertheless, there is inherent friction between protecting current force structures and finding enough money for adequate investment in tomorrow's systems. The United States appears to be dealing with this quandary by combining incremental improvements to existing designs with reliance on technological innovation in a number of key areas. At the same time, costly 'legacy assets' are being withdrawn to preserve money for new investment.

A key development in this regard during 2013 were the successful trials of the X-47B demonstration unmanned combat air vehicle from the aircraft carrier *George H W Bush* (CVN-77) off the Virginia coast. These saw the first ever carrier-based catapult

The People's Liberation Army Navy Type 054A frigate *Chang Zou* on a goodwill visit to Sydney, Australia in December 2012. The United States sees Australia as an important ally in its efforts to counter growing Chinese influence but Australia's recent defence white paper suggests a degree of ambivalence. *(Royal Australian Navy)*

Table 1.0.2: MAJOR FLEET STRENGTHS 2012-2013

COUNTRY	USA		UK		FRANCE		ITALY		SPAIN		RUSSIA[2]		INDIA		CHINA[2]		JAPAN		S KOREA	
Year[1]	2012	2013	2012	2013	2012	2013	2012	2013	2012	2013	2012	2013	2012	2013	2012	2013	2012	2013	2012	2013
Aircraft Carrier (CVN/CV)	11	10	–	–	1	1	–	–	–	–	1	1	–	–	–	1	–	–	–	–
Support Carrier (CVS/CVH)	–	–	1	1	–	–	2	2	1	–	–	–	1	1	–	–	2	2	–	–
Strategic Missile Sub (SSBN)	14	14	4	4	4	4	–	–	–	–	15	10	–	–	3	3	–	–	–	–
Attack Submarine (SSGN/SSN)	58	58	7	7	6	6	–	–	–	–	20	20	1	1	5	5	–	–	–	–
Patrol Submarine (SSK)	–	–	–	–	–	–	6	6	3	3	20	20	14	14	55	55	16	16	12	12
Battleships/Battlecruisers (BB/BC)	–	–	–	–	–	–	–	–	–	–	1	1	–	–	–	–	–	–	–	–
Fleet Escort (CGN/CG/DDG/FFG)	107	102	19	19	17	17	15	15	10	11	30	25	21	23	55	60	40	39	20	22
Patrol Escort (DD/FFG/FSG/FS)	2	3	–	–	15	15	8	5	–	–	55	55	8	8	25	20	6	6	21	21
Missile Attack Craft (PGG/PTG)	–	–	–	–	–	–	–	–	–	–	50	50	12	12	75	75	6	6	9	9
Mine Countermeasures (MCMV)	14	13	15	15	14	14	10	10	6	6	45	40	7	7	20	20	30	30	9	9
Major Amph (LHD/LPD/LPH/LSD)	28	30	6	6	4	4	3	3	3	3	1	–	1	1	3	3	3	3	1	1

Notes:

1 Data refers to fleet strengths as of mid-year 2012 and 2013.

2 Figures for Russia and China are approximate.

launch of an unmanned aerial vehicle (UAV) on 14 May 2013 and the first touch-and-go landing on a carrier deck three days later. Current thinking envisages the deployment of an operational unmanned carrier-launched airborne surveillance and strike system (UCLASS) around the turn of the decade, potentially dramatically increasing the efficiency and cost-effectiveness of carrier operations. UAVs are also seen as having a significant role to play in ensuring efficient maritime surveillance operations. The maiden flight of the MQ-4C Triton took place on 22 May 2013, paving the way for the type to enter service as the key element of the broad area maritime surveillance system from 2016. Interestingly, both these aircraft have been developed by Northrop Grumman, which – along with its leadership of the MQ-8B/C unmanned helicopter programme – appears to be building a strong market position in the development of autonomous maritime aircraft.

Technological innovation is also making itself felt in other ways. Concerns relating to the proliferation of ballistic missiles have been given additional impetus by North Korea's nuclear weapons programme and associated bellicose rhetoric. Naval-based ballistic missile defence (BMD) systems are seen as one of the major elements of the antidote.[4] The introduction of increasing numbers of sophisticated air defence escorts in 'Western' fleets is driving interest in adapting these new ships to a BMD role, although only the United States and Japan have deployed fully-fledged naval capability in this area to date. However, the pace of development is accelerating. For example, the Royal Netherlands Navy's 2011 decision to modify its *De Zeven Provinciën* class frigates to support a ballistic-missile detection and tracking capability has been followed by the British Royal Navy's plans to embark on missile defence trials with the US Navy in the second half of 2013 during the lead Type 45 destroyer *Daring*'s circumnavigation of the globe.

FLEET REVIEWS

Current estimates of fleet strengths for the leading navies are set out in Table 1.0.2. Clearly, there has only been a limited amount of material change

An X-47B demonstrator UAV performs a touch-and-go landing on the deck of the US Navy aircraft carrier *George H W Bush* (CVN-77) on 17 May 2013. US reliance on technological innovation to balance pressure on fleet numbers is a key theme in naval trends. *(US Navy)*

A view of the first flight of the Northrop Grumman-built MQ-4C Triton unmanned surveillance aircraft on 22 May 2013. Northrop Grumman is playing a leading role introducing UAVs into US Navy service, also being responsible for the X-47B demonstrator and the MQ-8B/C series of Fire Scout unmanned helicopters. *(Northrop Grumman)*

Two views of the British Royal Navy's new *Queen Elizabeth* aircraft carrier, the components of which are being built at shipyards around the country prior to transport to Rosyth for assembly. The Royal Navy is making meaningful progress in recovering from the cutbacks imposed in 2010 but further pressure on the defence budget remains a threat. *(Aircraft Carrier Alliance)*

year-on-year, although the following observations are pertinent.

- The slow numerical shift from the traditional 'Western' naval powers towards the fleets of the new economic powerhouses of the Asia Pacific region that has been a continuing theme of the *Seaforth World Naval Review* series shows no sign of abating. It is also worth noting that the data does not adequately reflect a similar trend in the qualitative balance towards the developing fleets, albeit the American and European fleets still maintain a significant technological edge.

- 2013 data is notable in reflecting the commissioning of China's first carrier, *Liaoning*, in September 2012. This marks a major step forward in the country's 'blue water' ambitions. Conversely, the US Navy's carrier force has temporarily dipped to ten vessels with the deactivation of the veteran *Enterprise* (CVN-65) in December of the same year. The overall number of countries in the 'carrier club' has remained unchanged following the premature decommissioning of Spain's *Principe de Asturias* in February 2013 as an economy measure. However, Spain retains a fixed-wing naval aviation capability in the form of the LHD-type amphibious assault ship *Juan Carlos I*, which was designed with a secondary carrier role.

- The numerical decline in certain Russian fleet categories is the result of an increasing trend towards decommissioning technological obsolescent Soviet-era warships that have only limited serviceability and would be costly to modernise. Whilst significant investment is being made in constructing replacement ships, lack of technical capacity in the Russian military shipbuilding and equipment sector continues to hinder this process. By way of contrast, China is successfully replacing large numbers of obsolete surface vessels and submarines with modern units.

This year's Fleet Reviews focus on two Commonwealth Navies. Ross Gillett's description of the recent trajectory of the Royal New Zealand Navy makes an interesting comparison with last year's overview of the Irish Naval Service. His review demonstrates how adherence to a long-term policy framework is steadily increasing New Zealand's ability to ensure regional stability in spite of a limited budget. Meanwhile, Richard Beedall returns to examining the British Royal Navy, now midway between the 2010 and 2015 Strategic Defence Reviews (SDRs). Progress is being made towards rebuilding a credible and balanced fleet in line with the broader 'Future Force 2020' strategic vision after

A view of the German Type 212A submarine *U-34*. The class's successful adoption of PEM fuel cell-based air independent propulsion has helped Germany retain its traditional leadership in submarine design. *(German Navy)*

the cost-driven cutbacks of 2010/11. However, a significant mismatch between commitments and resources, exacerbated by uncertainty caused by the 2014 referendum on Scottish independence, threatens to overshadow this progress.

SIGNIFICANT SHIPS

Meanwhile, the theme of technological innovation referenced in the opening remarks has been a key influence on the selection of significant ships for detailed review. The development of air-independent propulsion, in particular, has provided the underwater flotillas of mid-sized navies with access to submerged endurance previously available only to the handful of naval powers fielding nuclear-powered submarines. HDW's Type 212A design, equipped with PEM fuel cells, has been in the forefront of demonstrating this technology's potential, thereby maintaining Germany's historic leadership in submarine design. However, innovation can also achieve results through adapting existing know-how. This is demonstrated by Scott Truver's review of the US Navy's new fast intra-theatre transport, *Spearhead* (JHSV-1). Here a commercial catamaran design has been modified to bridge the gap between high-capacity, slow-speed sealift and swift but costly airborne transport.

The combination of these approaches is typified by Guy Toremans' review of the Royal Danish Navy's *Iver Huitfeldt* class. These frigates marry cutting-edge technology in the form of Thales Nederland's APAR and SMART-L radars with modified commercial shipbuilding techniques. This has enabled Denmark to afford a maritime air-defence capability on a par with larger European fleets. Denmark has also been a leading member of the US-led coalition in the 'war against terror' and the new ships reflect a shift towards expeditionary operations that has been a feature of many European fleets in the post-Cold War era. The Japan Maritime Self Defence Force (JMSDF) is another allied navy that is adapting to provide more flexible capabilities. First-time contributor Tomohiko Tada's chapter on the *Hyuga* (DDH-181) helicopter-carrying destroyers outlines the JMSDF's typical evolutionary approach. In this case, the basic design philosophy behind the first generation of anti-submarine orientated DDH-type vessels has been expanded to produce a through-deck helicopter carrier that can conduct a wider range of missions. Two larger vessels are currently under construction. It has been mooted that the more assertive foreign policy of new Japanese Prime Minister Shinzo Abe may result in these being equipped with F-35B Joint Strike

Fighter variants, providing a fixed-wing naval aviation capability for the first time since the Second World War.[5]

TECHNOLOGICAL DEVELOPMENTS

An expanded concluding section on technological developments commences with David Hobbs' usual wide-ranging review of the past year's news with respect to naval aviation. Inevitably, the ongoing progress with fielding UAVs features prominently. Norman Friedman, meanwhile, delves underneath the waves with an overview of a number of factors that are influencing current and future torpedo design. Our concluding chapter returns to the theme of the British Royal Navy's Type 45 destroyer design, which featured prominently in the first *Seaforth World Naval Review*. Looking at the subject from a new perspective, new contributors Ian Johnston and Paul Sweeney describe how construction of the class proved the catalyst for significant modernisation of the historic shipbuilding on the River Clyde, successfully driving a block building approach which has subsequently been used on a much larger scale with the *Queen Elizabeth* class aircraft carriers.

SUMMARY

In summing up the world naval scene as of mid-2013, it seems appropriate to refer back to the analysis contained in the introduction to the initial *Seaforth World Naval Review 2010*, which was published some five years ago. As was the case then, the United States Navy's position as the dominant blue-water power remains essentially unchallenged. Although there are many dissenting voices, strategic choices such as the decision to combine the continued construction of evolved variants of tried-and-tested designs such as the *Arleigh Burke* (DDG-51) class destroyers with focused investment in new technologies such as UAVs, BMD defence and the modularised littoral combat ship concept appear to have been generally sound. In spite of the concerns expressed in the 2010 edition, therefore, an adequate match between numbers and technology has seemingly been achieved. Additionally, some previous 'problem children' such as the littoral combat ship and F-35 programmes seem to have been placed on a sounder footing. More broadly, progress has been made in building a network of regional alliances in an approach that has resonances with the British Royal Navy's attempt to balance

The US Aegis-equipped cruiser *Lake Erie* (CG-70) fires a SM-3 Block 1B missile during a successful interception of a ballistic missile target on 15 May 2013. The US Navy has managed to achieve a successful balance between evolving the capabilities of tried-and-tested designs with focused investment in new technologies. *(US Navy)*

limited resources and growing threats in the run-up to the First World War.[6] The new challenge is the combination of contradiction and paralysis that has infected the current US political process, disrupting efforts to implement long-term plans.

Elsewhere, the ongoing march of new Asia-Pacific economies in the 'Pacific Century' has been made more evident by Europe's ongoing financial difficulties, continuing the eastwards shift in international commerce and trade. The relative decline of the traditional European powers therefore remains a clear, if somewhat leisurely, trend brought into focus only occasionally by events such as the major cutbacks inflicted on the British Royal Navy in the 2010 SDSR. Equally, the growth of naval shipbuilding in the principal Asian countries referenced in *World Naval Review 2010* has become steadily more apparent, particularly with respect to China, South Korea and Singapore. Given also continued political tensions in Asian waters, it seems likely that the region will remain the prime area of focus for the student of naval affairs over the coming five years.

ACKNOWLEDGEMENTS

As always, prime place amongst acknowledgements must be taken by those to publishing editor Robert Gardiner, designer Steve Dent and illustrator John Jordan, all of whom have made an indispensable contribution over *Seaforth World Naval Review*'s five-year history. Their efforts have been supported by the consistently high-quality contributions of a distinguished list of writers, some of whom have made their debut with the annual this year. I would also like to reference the generosity of Derek Fox, Bruno Huriet, Arne Lütkenhorst, Mrityunjoy Mazumdar, Chris Sattler and Devrim Yaylali in supplying photographs, supplementing the assistance of a considerable number of defence and industry officials. The assistance of Solen Dupy of DCNS, Ester Benito Lope of Navantia, Captain Atsushi Minami of the JMSDF, Ragna Oxenløwe of DALO, Craig Taylor of Rolls Royce and Frank van de Wiel of Thales Nederland is worthy of particular acknowledgement. My family's continued patience in accepting the considerable time commitment required to produce this book, as well as my wife Susan's help with initial proof-reading, remains an ongoing cause for gratitude.

In closing, I would like to acknowledge the enduring influence of my father, Anthony Joseph Waters (13 April 1926 – 23 March 2013), who strongly encouraged my early forays into naval journalism and showed immense patience rearranging the itineraries of many of my childhood holidays to allow me to photograph the latest new or unusual warship.

Conrad Waters, Editor
30 June 2013

Notes

1. Both these stories have been widely reported, for example in Kathrin Hille's 'US boosts military ties in southeast Asia', *The Financial Times* – 1 June 2013 (London: Pearson Plc, 2013). *Guardian*'s transit of Philippine waters is itself a reflection of an agreement to allow US forces to utilise the port facilities at Subic Bay on a rotational basis, thereby re-establishing a tentative US presence at what was formerly one of its largest overseas bases.

2. For further detail see *Defence White Paper 2013* (Canberra: Commonwealth of Australia, 2013). A copy can be found at http://www.defence.gov.au/whitepaper2013/docs/WP_2013_web.pdf

3. More detail on the impact of the ongoing US budget debate on the country's military can be found in the introduction to Chapter 2.1.

4. An overview of the development of United States maritime BMD systems is contained in Norman Friedman's 'Ballistic Missile Defence and the USN', *Seaforth World Naval Review 2013* (Barnsley: Seaforth Publishing, 2012), pp.184–91.

5. Whilst the flight deck of the *Hyuga* class is not designed to withstand the jet exhausts from STOVL aircraft, there have been reports that the follow-on 22-DDH class may be able to operate the F-35B. For more on this and a range of other capabilities the Japanese Self Defence Forces may consider acquiring, see Paul Kallender-Umezu's 'Japan Plans More Aggressive Defense', *Defense News* – 26 May 2013 (Springfield VA:, Gannett Government Media Corporation, 2013).

6. The British experience in the early twentieth century has been referenced by a number of US writers, including by Andrew F Krepinevich, Simon Chin and Tod Harrison in *Strategy in Austerity* (Washington DC: Center for Strategic & Budgetary Assessments, 2012). An online copy can currently be found at http://www.csbaonline.org/publications/2012/06/strategy-in-austerity/. They are less positive than *Seaforth World Naval Review*'s editor with respect to the progress the United States military has made in responding to current challenges.

Author:
Conrad Waters

2.1 REGIONAL REVIEW

NORTH AND SOUTH AMERICA

INTRODUCTION

The main influence on naval developments in the Americas over the past year has undoubtedly been the broader debate over the future direction of the United States defence budget.[1] The FY2013 presidential budget proposals released early in 2012 laid plans for a significant but balanced reduction in spending plans over the decade ahead. However, they failed to take account of the potential imposition of further automatic reductions under the sequestration process mandated by the 2011 Budget Control Act. After months of denial, the US Department of Defense finally initiated plans in December 2012 to accommodate the increased likelihood of sequestration-imposed cutbacks being implemented. These reductions became a reality in March 2013, shaving US\$41bn off the initially proposed US\$614bn FY2013 total.[2] Whilst the full impact of the shortfall is not yet apparent, immediate implications for the US Navy included a halving of the carrier presence in the Persian Gulf, cancellation of other planned deployments and a reduction in the readiness of units not actively engaged in operations.

The FY2014 Presidential Budget Request submitted in April 2013 essentially attempts to reset base defence spending to that originally planned for FY2013, ignoring the requirements of sequestration. However, it seems unlikely these plans will be approved by a political process that is close to paralysis. In this regard it is noteworthy that, for the past three years, the Department of Defense has commenced each financial year without an autho-

rised budget. This potentially leaves the US military facing the worst of both worlds; they face long-term cutbacks in resourcing but are unable to plan effectively for them. Efforts are being made to mitigate this problem. In late May 2013, Pentagon officials were directed to draw up a range of planning scenarios for FY2014 onwards that encompass sequestration reductions.[3] These are linked to a Strategic Choices Management Review (SCMR) initiated by Defense Secretary Hagel that will determine the extent to which the budgetary backdrop will force changes to the direction of the January 2012 Presidential Strategic Guidance. The overall impact of full-scale sequestration on the US Navy is likely to be painful; for example, a March 2013 report by the Congressional Budget Office laid out options that would reduce warship numbers by between ten and thirty per cent.[4]

Whatever the SCMR's outcome, it seems likely that the priority given to rebalancing United States forces towards the Asia-Pacific region, as well as to the Gulf, will remain unaltered. This plays out in the US Navy's (and US Air Force's) favour, as it means that maritime capabilities are back in vogue following a decade where the priority was prosecution of largely land-based campaigns in Iraq and Afghanistan. As the Introduction noted, US Navy assets are already in increasing use to establish 'forward presence' in the Pacific. The 'poster-boy' amongst these is undoubtedly the new littoral combat ship *Freedom* (LCS-1), which commenced a ten-month deployment to South East Asia on 1 March 2013.[5] She docked at

Singapore's Changi Naval Base, her forward operating station for the mission's duration, on 18 April against a backdrop of press coverage not seen since the arrival of the British Royal Navy's Force Z in December 1941. Although marked by a number of the teething troubles that are common in lead vessels of new classes, the deployment should serve to demonstrate the growing maturity of a programme that has previously received more than its fair share of criticism.

Meanwhile, whilst US budgetary issues are a cause for concern, those experienced by the *Armada Argentina* are in an entirely different league. In October 2012, the sail training vessel *Libertad* was impounded in Ghana by hedge fund Elliott Management Corporation over unpaid debts relating to Argentina's 2002 default on sovereign debt. She was finally released when the United Nations ruled she had immunity from court action as a military vessel. The MEKO 140A corvette *Espora* was also stranded in South Africa around the same time, in her case awaiting payment for generator repairs. Finally, the veteran destroyer *Santisma Trinidad* sank at her moorings in January 2013 after a lengthy period in reserve. Although Argentina's defence budget has actually been increasing in recent years, this has been insufficient to counter the impact of a growing salary bill and years of previous neglect. As such, the Argentine government's continued rhetoric over the Falkland Islands is not yet matched by its military capabilities.

Table 2.1.1 provides a summary of major fleet strengths in the Americas as of mid-2013.

The US Navy littoral combat ship *Freedom* (LCS-1) pictured in late February 2013, shortly before commencing a ten-month deployment to South East Asia. Of particular note is her camouflage pattern, which is derived from the wartime Measure 32 scheme. Colours are understood to be FS36173 Ocean Gray, FS36270 Haze Gray, FS36373 Light Gray and Black. *Freedom*'s use of camouflage is reported to have been an initiative taken by her commanding officer and is its first appearance on a US Navy ship above patrol vessel size since the Second World War ended. *(US Navy)*

Table 2.1.1: FLEET STRENGTHS IN THE AMERICAS – LARGER NAVIES (MID 2013)

COUNTRY	ARGENTINA	BRAZIL	CANADA	CHILE	ECUADOR	PERU	USA	VENEZUELA
Aircraft Carrier (CVN/CV)	–	1	–	–	–	–	10	–
Strategic Missile Submarine (SSBN)	–	–	–	–	–	–	14	–
Attack Submarine (SSN/SSGN)	–	–	–	–	–	–	58	–
Patrol Submarine (SSK)	3	5	4	4	2	6	–	2
Fleet Escort (CG/DDG/FFG)	4	9	15	8	2	9	102	6
Patrol Escort/Corvette (FFG/FSG/FS)	9	5	–	–	6	–	3	–
Missile Armed Attack Craft (PGG/PTG)	2	–	–	6	3	6	–	6
Mine Countermeasures Vessel (MCMV)	–	6	12	–	–	–	13	–
Major Amphibious Units (LHD/LPD/LPH/LSD)	–	1	–	1	–	–	30	–

MAJOR NORTH AMERICAN NAVIES – CANADA

The Canadian National Shipbuilding Procurement Strategy announced in October 2011 marked a further stage forward in plans for a major fleet recapitalisation, but this has yet to translate into firm orders. Pending new construction, Canadian yards are being kept busy with upgrades of existing vessels. The combined *Halifax* Class Modernisation / Frigate Life Extension (HCM/FELEX) is now well underway on both the east and west coasts. The Atlantic-based *Halifax* will be the first modernised ship to return to operational service following commencement of post-refit trials towards the end of 2012, followed closely afterwards by Pacific-based *Calgary*. Both frigates featured prominently in publicity for the new Canadian naval ensign announced at the start of May 2013, which swaps the national flag for the flag formerly used as the jack.[6] In addition to modernised radars, electronics and command systems, the images released also clearly showed the installation of a transom flap in similar fashion to those adopted by British Royal Navy surface escorts to improve fuel efficiency.

The long hiatus in Canadian naval construction since the *Halifax* frigates were completed in the middle of the 1990s means that a number of new projects await implementation. Amongst the most pressing of these is a requirement for replacements for the two existing *Protecteur* class replenishment oilers, with up to three (two replacements and one option) new JSS joint support ships planned. On 2 June 2013 it was announced that licensed construction of ThyssenKrupp Marine Systems' Type 702 *Berlin* class had been preferred over a new design developed by BMT Fleet Technology, largely due to the greater certainty with respect to cost and delivery provided by a proven ship. The new vessels will be built by Seaspan's Vancouver Shipyards on Canada's west coast under a planned C\$2.6bn (US\$2.5bn) contract. However, Seaspan has also been allocated icebreaker construction for the Canadian Coast Guard and doubts have emerged as to whether both contracts can be handled simultaneously. It is not yet known which project has the higher priority, nor whether the option for a third JSS-type vessel will be exercised.

The other Canadian shipyard earmarked for large naval construction contracts is Halifax's Irving Shipbuilding. It will fulfil a requirement for between six to eight ice-strengthened Arctic patrol vessels before commencing work on a single class surface

The *Halifax* class frigate *Calgary* is the first of the Royal Canadian Navy's Pacific-based frigates to complete the HCM/FELIX modernisation and life extension package. This photograph dates from 5 May 2013 and shows key external elements of the modernisation package, including a Thales SMART-S radar on top of the bridge, additional communications equipment and a stern transom flap. She flies the new Canadian naval ensign that was introduced at the start of the month. The inset provides a detailed view of the new Royal Canadian Navy ensign. It is the flag previously used as the navy's jack. *(Canadian Forces Combat Camera)*

Table 2.1.2: CANADIAN NAVY: PRINCIPAL UNITS AS AT MID 2013

TYPE	CLASS	NUMBER	TONNAGE	DIMENSIONS	PROPULSION	CREW	DATE
Principal Surface Escorts							
Destroyer – DDG	**IROQUOIS**	3	5,100 tons	130m x 15m x 5m	COGOG, 29 knots	280	1972
Frigate – FFG	**HALIFAX**	12	4,800 tons	134m x 16m x 5m	CODOG, 29 knots	225	1992
Submarines							
Submarine – SSK	**VICTORIA** (UPHOLDER)	4	2,500 tons	70m x 8m x 6m	Diesel-electric, 20+ knots	50	1990

combatant to replace the current *Iroquois* and *Halifax* class escorts. The yard was awarded a c. C$290m (US$285m) detailed design contract for the patrol vessels in early 2013 prior to planned commencement of construction in 2015. Delivery of the first ship – already deferred by three years – is expected in 2018 but this schedule, as well as the estimated cost of C$3.1bn (US$3.0bn), will only be confirmed once design work has been completed.

Another project suffering significant delays is that for the new Sikorsky CH-148 Cyclone helicopter. A contract for twenty-eight Cyclones was signed in 2004 for delivery from November 2008. However, none of the rotorcraft have been formally accepted to date, even in interim configuration. A number of interim variants have now reached Canada for ground-based training of support personnel under Sikorsky ownership but the company has admitted that it will be unable to meet revised delivery schedules. Recent reports suggest that it will be at least 2015 before a fully-operational Cyclone is available. The result is inevitable strain on the remaining fleet of CH-124 Sea Kings, which first entered service in the early 1960s.

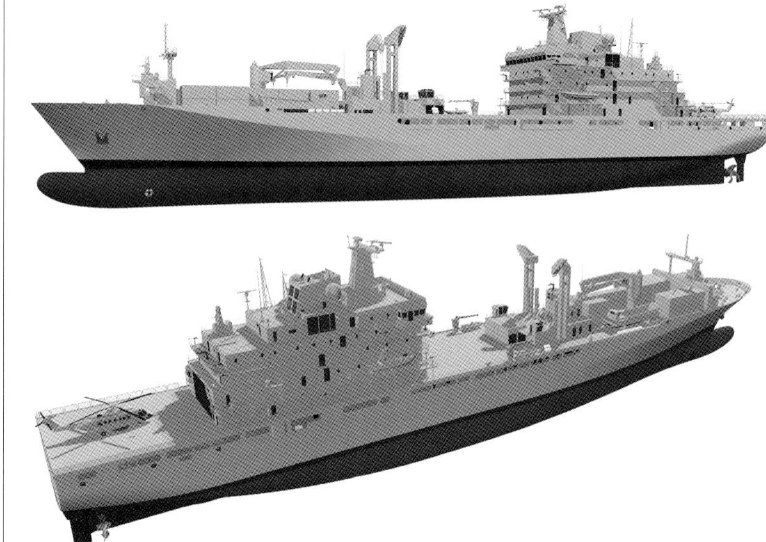

Two images of Thyssen Krupp Marine Services' winning design for the new Canadian JSS joint support ship. The chosen design is a slightly modified version of the firm's Type 702 *Berlin* class combat support ship, three of which have been built for the German Navy. The new ships will be built at Seaspan's Vancouver yard in line with Canada's 2011 National Shipbuilding Procurement Strategy. *(Blohm & Voss, ThyssenKrupp Marine Systems)*

There continues to be generally better news with respect to the previously troubled *Victoria* (former British Royal Navy *Upholder*) class submarines, although plans to have three boats ready for operations have yet to be achieved. *Victoria* herself is fully operational on the west coast and sank the decommissioned US auxiliary *Comfort* (T-AFS-5) with a Mk 48 torpedo in July 2012 during the RIMPAC war games. Meanwhile *Windsor* has returned to sea on the east coast following completion of a docking period during 2012 but has been subjected to a temporary limitation on allowed mission profiles until a defective generator is repaired. *Chicoutimi* should also commence post-refit trials before the end of 2013, allowing the damaged *Corner Brook* to enter deep maintenance and begin repairs. Progress is also being made in achieving the required 372-strong full complement of qualified submariners, with seventy-eight sailors training to fill forty-six vacant positions as of February 2013.

The Royal Canadian Navy's submarine *Victoria* (formerly the British Royal Navy's *Unseen*) pictured berthing at Pearl Harbor during the RIMPAC 2012 exercises. *Victoria* was Canada's only fully operational submarine as of mid-2013 but progress is being made returning others to service. *(Canadian Forces Combat Camera)*

The US Navy's nuclear-powered aircraft carrier *Nimitz* (CVN-68) and amphibious assault ship *Essex* (LHA-2) lead a group of warships participating in the RIMPAC 2012 issues on 27 July 2012. Whilst the US Navy's force structure plans continue to target a fleet of over 300 ships, budget constraints suggest operations in partnership with other fleets are going to become increasingly important. *(US Navy)*

MAJOR NORTH AMERICAN NAVIES – UNITED STATES

The ongoing debate with respect to the US defence budget makes any analysis of the US Navy's future trajectory particularly difficult, as there is currently a significant disconnect between official government plans and likely levels of funding. The official position is set out in the new Navy Combatant Force Structure Requirement that was released in January 2013.[7] This establishes a revised target of 306 vessels compared with the previous formal 313-ship requirement that was first assessed in 2005 and more recent references to a goal of around 300 combatants. The differences can largely be explained by strategic changes emanating from the 2012 Presidential Strategic Guidance and greater use of forward deployment. For example, the decision to base four Aegis-equipped destroyers at Rota in Spain will allow a presence to be retained in European waters with fewer vessels, whilst the ultimate number of littoral combat ships has fallen from fifty-five to fifty-two due to a reduced emphasis on Africa.

The ongoing problem is that the planned future balance of construction and decommissionings suggest that – even under official plans – the required number of warships is unlikely to be achieved in the short to medium term, as Table 2.1.3

Table 2.1.3: REVISIONS TO PROJECTED US NAVY BATTLE FORCE LEVELS: FY2013 PLAN COMPARED TO FY2014 PLAN

SHIP TYPE FY2013 Plan/**FY2014 PLAN**[2]	PLAN[1]	FY2014		FY2015		FY2016		FY2017		FY2018		FY2019		FY2020	
		2012	**2013**	2012	**2013**	2012	**2013**	2012	**2013**	2012	**2013**	2012	**2013**	2012	**2013**
Aircraft Carrier (CVN)	11 (11)	10	10	11	10	11	11	11	11	11	11	11	11	11	11
Strategic Submarine (SSBN)	12 (12)	14	14	14	14	14	14	14	14	14	14	14	14	14	14
Attack Submarine (SSGN/SSN)	48 (52)	59	59	58	59	57	57	54	54	55	56	55	56	52	53
Fleet Escort (CG/DDG)	88 (94)	78	85	78	78	80	82	82	83	84	84	86	86	87	87
Patrol Escort / MCMV (FFG/LCS/MCMV)	52 (55)	30	26	26	23	30	27	32	29	35	33	39	38	37	37
Amphibious Vessels (LHA/LHD/LPD/LSD)	33 (33)	29	31	28	28	29	29	30	30	31	31	31	31	31	31
Other	62 (56)	59	57	61	58	63	60	62	62	62	62	64	64	63	62
TOTAL	306 (313)	279	282	276	270	284	280	285	283	292	291	300	300	295	295

Notes:
1 Plan figures relate to the Force Structure Requirement released in January 2013. The plan figures in brackets relates to the 313-ship requirement identified in the 2005 Force Structure Assessment and revalidated in 2010.
2 These figures are derived from the Long Range Plan for Construction of Naval Vessels produced for FY2013 and FY2014.

makes clear. Indeed, it is unlikely that the US Navy will reach the targeted figure of 306 vessels until FY2037. It is also noteworthy that a comparison of historic construction plans and force structures reveals an almost consistent reduction in procurement quantities and force sizes as forward plans became a reality.[8] This reflects oft-repeated criticism from the Congressional Budget Office and others that the actual cost of future procurement has been underestimated and is unlikely to be affordable.

In fairness, the five-year shipbuilding plan announced in the FY2014 budget shows broad stability compared with previous plans, as illustrated by Table 2.1.4. The main changes from FY2013 are the addition of a second *Virginia* (SSN-774) class attack submarine in the current year's request to maintain a production 'drumbeat' of two boats p.a. and further deferral of the planned replacement dock landing ship beyond FY2018. Sequestration has impacted the timing of an order for the additional, third *Arleigh Burke* (DDG-51) class destroyer authorised in the final FY2013 budget approval and – if not modified – will certainly impact planned procurement in FY2014 and beyond.

Current fleet numbers have fallen to just over 280 vessels, within the range of around 280–290 ships that has been maintained over the last decade.

A more dramatic fall has been temporarily averted by a congressional veto of plans for the early decommissioning of *Ticonderoga* (CG-47) cruisers and *Whidbey Island* (LSD-41) class dock landing ships, although the US navy seeks to overturn this refusal in the FY2015 budget. Greater detail of recent developments with respect to specific ship categories is provided below.

Aircraft Carriers: The US Navy's carrier force has temporarily fallen to just ten units with the deactivation of the veteran *Enterprise* (CVN-65) in December 2012. Her replacement, *Gerald R Ford* (CVN-78) remains under construction at Huntington Ingalls Industries' (HHI's) Newport News yard. Her launch has been delayed from July to November 2013 due to earlier construction delays. This will, in turn, push back planned delivery from September 2015 to the first half of 2016. However, good progress appears to have been achieved over the last year, with the distinctive island structure lifted into position in January 2013 and primary structural completion being achieved at the start of May. Around US$4bn in advanced funding has already been spent on her sister *John F Kennedy* (CVN-79) prior to a formal contract expected later in 2013. It was confirmed that a third planned vessel

– due to be ordered in FY2018 – will be named *Enterprise* (CVN-80) during her namesake's deactivation ceremony.

Surface Combatants: There is currently something of a pause in the delivery of surface combatants to the US Navy. This is due to the gap between termination of *Arleigh Burke* (DDG-51) destroyer production and the decision to restart construction, as well as to the transition between prototype and series production with respect to the littoral combat ship programme.

The final ship of the original sixty-two strong *Arleigh Burke* programme, *Michael Murphy* (DDG-112) was delivered on schedule on 6 October 2012, whilst production of vessels under the follow-on programme has now commenced. Previous orders for four continuation destroyers were supplemented by orders for a further nine ships on 3 June 2013 under a multi-year procurement agreement covering planned requirements for FY2013 to FY2017. Five of the ships have been allocated to HHI under contracts valued at US$3.3bn, with the other four being constructed by General Dynamics' Bath Iron Works yard for US$2.8bn. The agreement with Bath Iron Works also encompasses an option for the third destroyer approved under the FY2013 budget, which will be firmly contracted if the sequestration-related shortfall in funding can be resolved. Whilst all the orders are initially in 'Flight IIA' configuration, it is still planned to construct three of the later ships according to the Air and Missile Defence Radar (AMDR) equipped 'Flight III' design. There is still some scepticism as to whether the basic DDG-51 hull can be stretched to meet the requirements of the new system and it is still possible alternatives may be examined. Interestingly, HHI has suggested the *New Orleans* (LPD-17) class design could be configured for the ballistic missile defence role that is one of the key missions envisaged for the Flight IIIs.

Meanwhile progress continues with the three-ship *Zumwalt* (DDG-1000) programme that was curtailed in favour of renewed DDG-51 production on cost grounds. The lead ship's massive composite deckhouse structure was successfully installed in December 2012 and launch is scheduled for the second half of 2013. The keel of the second ship *Michael Monsoor* (DDG-1001) – already under fabrication since October 2009 – was formally laid on 23 May 2013.

Table 2.1.4: USN FY2014 FIVE YEAR SHIPBUILDING PLAN (FY2014-FY2018)

SHIP TYPE	FY2013: ACTUAL	FY2014: REQUEST	FY2015: PLAN	FY2016: PLAN	FY2017: PLAN	FY2018: PLAN
Aircraft Carrier (CVN-78)	1	Nil (Nil)	Nil (Nil)	Nil (Nil)	Nil (Nil)	1 (1)
Attack Submarine (SSN-774)	2	2 (1)	2 (2)	2 (2)	2 (2)	2 (2)
Destroyer (DDG-51)	3	1 (1)	2 (2)	2 (2)	2 (2)	2 (2)
Littoral Combat Ship (LCS-1/2)	4	4 (4)	4 (4)	2 (2)	2 (2)	2 (3)
Amphibious Assault Ship (LHA-6)	Nil	Nil (Nil)	Nil (Nil)	Nil (Nil)	1 (1)	Nil (Nil)
Dock Landing Ship (LSD-X)	Nil	Nil (Nil)	Nil (Nil)	Nil (Nil)	Nil (Nil)	Nil (1)
Joint High Speed Vessel (JHSV-1)	1	Nil (Nil)	Nil (Nil)	Nil (Nil)	Nil (Nil)	Nil (Nil)
Mobile Landing Platform (MLP-1)	Nil	1 (1)	Nil (Nil)	Nil (Nil)	Nil (Nil)	Nil (Nil)
Replenishment Oiler (TAO(X))	Nil	Nil (Nil)	Nil (Nil)	1 (1)	Nil (Nil)	1 (1)
Fleet Tug (TAFT)	Nil	Nil (Nil)	Nil (Nil)	0 (2)	2 (Nil)	1 (1)
Total	11	8 (7)	8 (8)	7 (9)	9 (7)	9 (11)

Notes

1 Figures in brackets relate to previous FY2013 Budget Request and Shipbuilding Plan.

2 Figures relate to Ship Battle Forces – other ships are not included.

3 The original FY2013 budget request was increased by one additional DDG-51 when the budget was authorised.

4 The FY2014 MLP mobile landing platform ship will be built as an afloat forward staging base (AFSB) variant.

The third littoral combat ship *Fort Worth* (LCS-3) was commissioned in September 2012, whilst *Coronado* (LCS-4) has commenced builders' trials.[9] Orders for a further pair of each variant were placed with Lockheed Martin and Austal USA in March 2013, covering LCS-13 through to LCS-16.[10] Production of the earlier series ships is well underway but the first, *Milwaukee* (LCS-5), will not join the fleet before 2015. As such, numbers of small surface combatants will continue to fall as 'legacy' *Oliver Hazard Perry* (FFG-7) class frigates are decommissioned in steadily increasing numbers. *Underwood* (FFG-36), *Crommelin* (FFG-37), *Curts* (FFG-38), *Klakring* (FFG-42) and *Carr* (FFG-52) have all been withdrawn from service over the last year and the process will accelerate in the year ahead. In the meantime, considerable effort is being expended developing the anti-surface, anti-submarine and mine countermeasures modules that will form the heart of the new littoral combat ships' capabilities. A modified version of the anti-surface package was installed for *Freedom*'s Asia-Pacific deployment whilst *Independence* (LCS-2) is heavily involved in testing the mine countermeasures system.

Amphibious Shipping: The amphibious shipping force has been boosted by continued completion of *New Orleans* class amphibious transport docks. *Arlington* (LPD-24) was delivered from her builders HHI at the end of 2012 prior to ceremonial commissioning in April 2013; her sister-ship *Anchorage* (LPD-23) was accepted in September 2012 before commissioning on 4 May. The ninth ship of the class, *Somerset* (LPD-25) is also well advanced. Her arrival during 2014 will allow the withdrawal of the veteran *Denver* (LPD-9), now the oldest active ship in the fleet and the last of the *Austin* (LPD-4) class to serve in her original role. The new amphibious assault ship *America* (LHA-6) should also be accepted within the next twelve months, paving the way for *Peleliu* (LHA-5) to be retired during FY2015.

A second-line amphibious fleet is also starting to develop in accordance with previous plans. The first two *Spearhead* (JHSV-1) class high speed transports were delivered during the last twelve months, whilst the tenth and final vessel was ordered in December 2012.[11] May 2013 saw acceptance of the lead mobile landing platform *Montford Point* (T-MLP-1). She is the first of at least three innovative vessels intended

The lead *Gerald R Ford* (CVN-78) class aircraft carrier's primary construction is now complete following the completion of the last of some 162 lifts of constituent blocks in early May 2013. These images show the carrier's distinctive island structure being lifted into place in January 2013 and the completion of the forward flight deck three months later. *(Huntington Ingalls Industries)*

The tenth US Navy *Virginia* class submarine, *Minnesota* (SSN-783), was delivered nearly eleven months ahead of schedule by Huntington Ingalls Industries in June 2013. Current US Navy shipbuilding plans continue to envisage the class being built at the rate of two units p.a. *(Huntington Ingalls Industries)*

to act as a transit point for the offloading of stores and equipment from joint high speed vessels and other transports prior to onward transfer by ship to shore connectors such as the landing craft air cushion (LCAC) as part of the wider sea-basing concept. The existing LCAC fleet is set for replacement by the new ship-to-shore connector (SSC), which is being developed by a team headed by Textron under a US$212m contract awarded on 6 July 2012. The new craft will have similar dimensions to the current LCAC so as to ensure compatibility with existing amphibious ships but will be able to carry a higher payload.

Submarines: The US Navy submarine fleet has remained in a broadly stead state condition over the past year. *Minnesota* (SSN-783), the last Flight II variant of the *Virginia* class nuclear-powered attack submarines, was handed over nearly eleven months early on 6 June 2013, maintaining a recent track record of early deliveries. She is scheduled to commission in September, bringing the class up to ten units and counterbalancing the planned withdrawal of the *Los Angeles* (SSN-668) class submarine *Dallas* (SSN-700) during FY2014. Thereafter, attack submarine numbers will start to fall as deliveries of Flight III *Virginia* class boats will be outpaced by *Los Angeles* class withdrawals until the doubling of the former's construction to two units p.a. stabilises the situation.

The next major submarine programme is the SSBN(X) replacement for the existing *Ohio* (SSBN-726) class strategic missile submarines. Although procurement for the first of a planned class of twelve vessels is not expected until FY2021, more than US$2.5bn has already been expended on research and development funding, which is currently running at over US$1bn p.a. The lead boat is expected to cost a total of US$12bn in develop-

Table 2.1.5: UNITED STATES NAVY: PRINCIPAL UNITS AS AT MID 2013

TYPE	CLASS	NUMBER	TONNAGE	DIMENSIONS	PROPULSION	CREW	DATE
Aircraft Carriers							
Aircraft Carrier – CVN	**NIMITZ** (CVN-68)	10	101,000 tons	340m x 41/78m x 12m	Nuclear, 30+ knots	5,700	1975
Principal Surface Escorts							
Cruiser – CG	**TICONDEROGA** (CG-47)	22	9,900 tons	173m x 17m x 7m	COGAG, 30+ knots	365	1983
Destroyer – DDG	**ARLEIGH BURKE** (DDG-51) – Flight II-A	34	9,200 tons	155m x 20m x 7m	COGAG, 30 knots	380	2000
Destroyer – DDG	**ARLEIGH BURKE** (DDG-51) – Flights I/II	28	8,800 tons	154m x 20m x 7m	COGAG, 30+ knots	340	1991
Frigate – FFG	**OLIVER HAZARD PERRY** (FFG-7)	18	4,100 tons	143m x 14m x 5m	COGAG, 30 knots	215	1977
Littoral Combat Ship – FS	**FREEDOM** (LCS-1)	2	3,100 tons	115m x 17m x 4m	CODAG, 45+ knots	‹50[1]	2008
Littoral Combat Ship – FS	**INDEPENDENCE** (LCS-2)	1	2,800 tons	127m x 32m x 5m	CODAG, 45+ knots	‹50[1]	2010
Submarines							
Submarine – SSBN	**OHIO** (SSBN-726)	14	18,800 tons	171m x 13m x 12m	Nuclear, 20+ knots	155	1981
Submarine – SSGN	**OHIO** (SSGN-726)	4	18,800 tons	171m x 13m x 12m	Nuclear, 20+ knots	160	1981
Submarine – SSN	**VIRGINIA** (SSN-774)	9	8,000 tons	115m x 10m x 9m	Nuclear, 25+ knots	135	2004
Submarine – SSN	**SEAWOLF** (SSN-21)	3[2]	9,000 tons	108m x 12m x 11m	Nuclear, 25+ knots	140	1997
Submarine – SSN	**LOS ANGELES** (SSN-688)	42	7,000 tons	110m x 10m x 9m	Nuclear, 25+ knots	145	1976
Major Amphibious Units							
Amph Assault Ship – LHD	**WASP** (LHD-1)	8[3]	41,000 tons	253m x 32/42m x 9m	Steam, 20+ knots	1,100	1989
Amph Assault Ship – LHD	**TARAWA** (LHA-1)	1	40,000 tons	250m x 32/38m x 8m	Steam, 24 knots	975	1976
Landing Platform Dock – LPD	**SAN ANTONIO** (LPD-17)	8	25,000 tons	209m x 32m x 7m	Diesel, 22+ knots	360	2005
Landing Platform Dock – LPD	**AUSTIN** (LPD-4)	1	17,000 tons	171m x 25m x 7m	Steam, 21 knots	420	1965
Landing Ship Dock – LSD	**WHIDBEY ISLAND** (LSD-41)	12[4]	16,000 tons	186m x 26m x 6m	Diesel, 20 knots	420	1985

Notes:

1 Plus mission-related crew. **2** Third of class, SSN-23 is longer and heavier. **3** LHD-8 has many differences. **4** Includes four LSD-49 HARPERS FERRY variants.

ment and construction costs; the following submarines will average between US$4.9bn and US$5.4bn each. There are therefore concerns about the impact of the project budget on other US Navy construction, which may be reflected in the removal of the four SSGN strike submarines from the revised Force Structure Requirement. The SSBN(X) programme is closely linked to the British Royal Navy's 'Successor' strategic submarine replacement, sharing a common missile compartment and similarities in nuclear reactor technology.

Operationally, the US Navy has maintained a high tempo of activity in spite of the sequestration-related cut backs to specific deployments. In addition to the Asia-Pacific region, the Persian Gulf remains a key focal point of activity, where the day-to-day hazards of extended deployments were demonstrated by a collision between the destroyer *Porter* (DDG-78) and the Japanese-owned tanker M/V *Otowasan* in the Strait of Hormuz on 12 August 2012. *Porter* was temporarily patched up in Dubai before returning home for permanent repairs and a BMD upgrade that could cost as much as US$65m.[12] The Gulf is also to see the US Navy's first deployment of a laser weapon system, when a solid-state laser is installed on the interim afloat forward staging base *Ponce* (AFSB(I)-15) in 2014. The weapon has already been successfully tested at sea against aerial targets onboard the destroyer *Dewey* (DDG-105) and offers the prospect of a new defensive system with a virtually infinite magazine capacity and a minimal cost per shot.

The US Coast Guard continues to recapitalise its surface fleet. The sixth *Bertholf* (WMSL-750) class national security cutter, *Munro* (WMSL-755), was ordered under a US$487m contract on 30 April 2013; two other vessels are in the course of construction with HII at Ingalls Shipbuilding in Pascagoula, Mississippi and long-lead items for a seventh, *Kimball* (WMSL-756) were contracted in June 2013. This ends fears the eight-ship programme would end at six ships. Twenty-five intermediate offshore patrol cutters are also planned and tenders for a preliminary design contract closed in January 2013. Up to three proposals may be taken to the design stage prior to selection of a final contactor around the end of 2015. Smaller fast-response cutters are already been turned out in rapid order, with sixth unit *Paul Clark* (WPC-1106) the latest of five vessels delivered in the last year.

A prototype laser weapon system pictured whilst temporarily installed on the destroyer *Dewey* (DDG-105) in the summer of 2012, when it successfully destroyed a number of aerial targets. An operational deployment on board the afloat forward staging base *Ponce* (AFSB(I)-15) is scheduled for 2014. *(US Navy)*

The US Coast Guard's smaller units are being replaced by the *Bernard C Webber* (WPC-1101) class fast response cutters, which are referred to as the 'Sentinel' class by the service. Six of these cutters – which are based on the Damen Stan Patrol 4708 design – had been delivered by mid-2013. *(US Coast Guard)*

Twelve further vessels of a planned total fifty-eight ship class have been ordered. Increased activity in the Arctic has also produced renewed interest in the Coast Guard's icebreaking capabilities and the heavy icebreaker *Polar Star* (WAGB-110) has been reactivated after over six years in caretaker status. An entirely new ship is planned in the next few years. It will possibly be built in collaboration with the Canadian Coast Guard's requirement for a similar vessel.

OTHER NORTH AND CENTRAL AMERICAN NAVIES

The *Armada de México* remains the only other major navy amongst the North and Central American countries, although it remains preoccupied with the internal war against the drug cartels. Whilst Mexico's new president, Enrique Peña Nieto, has pledged to demilitarise the campaign through creation of a new gendarmerie, the navy's marines remain far less tainted than the other security forces by allegations of corruption by the drugs gangs. As such, it seems their interior policing role will continue for a while yet. Naval construction remains focused on constabulary and relief missions, with a second *Montes Azules* class logistic support ship *Libertador* launched by ASTIMAR's yard in Oaxaca in September 2012. The United States has offered to transfer the FFG-7 class frigates *Curts* (FFG-38) and *McClusky* (FFG-41) to modernise the small and obsolescent force of front-line surface escorts but there are doubts whether Mexico sees this as a priority. It may alternatively decide to resume construction of *Oaxaca* class offshore patrol vessels, which has been stalled since delivery of the fourth member of the class, *Revolución*, in November 2010. Local construction is continuing of smaller patrol vessel types, including Swedish 'Polaris' CB-90 type fast assault craft and Damen Stan Patrol 4207 coastal patrol vessels. Two of the latter type were delivered during 2012 and a contract for a third was signed in May 2013.

Also making use of Damen designs is the Royal Bahamas Defence Force, with a letter of intent for a wholesale modernisation of the country's fleet and naval bases being signed with the Dutch company in April 2013. The so-called 'Sandy Bottom' programme includes the construction of nine new ships, including a Stan Lander 5612 landing craft, four Stan Patrol 4207 patrol vessels and four smaller Stan Patrol 3007 types. The contract also includes provision for mid-life upgrades of the two existing *Bahamas* class offshore patrol vessels, which were delivered by VT Halter Marine around the turn of the Millennium.

MAJOR SOUTH AMERICAN NAVIES – ARGENTINA

Current Argentine fleet strength is set out in Table 2.1.6. There has been no change to principal fleet units year-on-year but overall serviceability has been reported as low. A number of ships are effectively laid up due to lack of maintenance and spare parts and funding for operational deployments has been restricted. The depressed current state of affairs also extends to refit and refurbishment activities, with return to service of both the TR-1700 type submarine *San Juan* and the icebreaker *Almirante Irizar* badly delayed. Similarly, the new construction programme for German Fassmer-designed OPV80 offshore patrol vessels announced as long ago as 2010 appears to be stalled. A bad year has been capped by the October 2012 resignation of the Chief of Naval Staff Admiral Carlos Alberto Paz, who resigned over the crisis resulting from Ghana's impounding of the training vessel *Libertad*.

MAJOR SOUTH AMERICAN NAVIES – BRAZIL

The *Marina do Brasil* remains the largest and most potent of the Latin American navies, as reflected in Table 2.1.7 of principal fleet constituents. It is also one of only a few regional fleets that is seemingly achieving tangible success with ambitious modernisation plans, at least in part.

The last year has seen significant progress with the PROSUB (*Programa de Desenvolvimento de Submarinos*) project. This will see four 'Scorpène' type patrol submarines designed by France's DCNS and a nuclear-powered variant incorporating a Brazilian developed power plant assembled in a newly-built local facility at Itaguaí, south of Rio de Janeiro. The huge new complex – incorporating a component manufacturing hall, a shipyard, a submarine maintenance facility with two dry docks, and an operating base – is reported to cost c. US$4bn. It is being completed in stages, with the 55,000m^2 manufacturing hall being formally opened by Brazilian President Dilma Rousseff on 1 March 2013. The hall will fabricate sections for the submarines, although a significant part of the first will be partly assembled by DCNS' Cherbourg yard. Named *Riachuelo*, she is expected to be delivered by the end of 2015 and become operational by 2017. Her three sisters will follow at eighteen-month intervals, whilst construction of the nuclear submarine will commence in 2016 for completion in 2023 and commissioning in 2025. Although this will be sufficient to replace the existing submarine flotilla on a one-for-one basis, more submarines are likely to be built in the longer term. The nuclear-powered boat has a high profile in Brazilian political circles, being seen as reinforcing the country's aspirations for permanent membership of the United Nations Security Council.[13]

Table 2.1.6: ARGENTINE NAVY: PRINCIPAL UNITS AS AT MID 2013[1]

TYPE	CLASS	NUMBER	TONNAGE	DIMENSIONS	PROPULSION	CREW	DATE
Principal Surface Escorts							
Destroyer – DDG	**ALMIRANTE BROWN** (MEKO 360)	4	3,600 tons	126m x 14m x 4m	COGOG, 30 knots	200	1983
Frigate – FSG	**ESPORA** (MEKO 140)	6	1,800 tons	91m x 11m x 3m	Diesel, 27 knots	100	1985
Corvette – FSG	**DRUMMOND** (A-69)	3	1,200 tons	80m x 10m x 3m	Diesel, 24 knots	95	1978
Submarines							
Submarine – SSK	**SANTA CRUZ** (TR 1700)	2	2,300 tons	65m x 7m x 7m	Diesel-electric, 25 knots	30	1984
Submarine – SSK	**SALTA** (Type 209)	1	1,200 tons	54m x 6m x 6m	Diesel-electric, 22 knots	30	1974

Notes:

1 A number of units have doubtful serviceability.

Table 2.1.7: BRAZILIAN NAVY: PRINCIPAL UNITS AS AT MID 2013

TYPE	CLASS	NUMBER	TONNAGE	DIMENSIONS	PROPULSION	CREW	DATE
Aircraft Carriers							
Aircraft Carrier – CV	SÃO PAULO (FOCH)	1	33,500 tons	265m x 32/51m x 9m	Steam, 30 knots	1,700	1963
Principal Surface Escorts							
Frigate – FFG	GREENHALGH (Batch I Type 22)	3	4,700 tons	131m x 15m x 4m	COGOG, 30 knots	270	1979
Frigate – FFG	NITERÓI	6	3,700 tons	129m x 14m x 4m	CODOG, 30 knots	220	1976
Corvette – FSG	INHAÚMA	4	2,100 tons	96m x 11m x 4m	CODOG, 27 knots	120	1989
Corvette – FSG	BARROSO	1	2,400 tons	103m x 11m x 4m	CODOG, 30 knots	145	2008
Submarines							
Submarine – SSK	TIKUNA (Type 209 – modified)	1	1,600 tons	62m x 6m x 6m	Diesel-electric, 22 knots	40	2005
Submarine – SSK	TUPI (Type 209)	4	1,500 tons	61m x 6m x 6m	Diesel-electric, 22+ knots	30	1989
Major Amphibious Units							
Landing Ship Dock – LSD	CEARÁ (LSD-28)	1[1]	12,000 tons	156m x 26m x 6m	Steam, 22 knots	345	1956

Notes:

1 The dock landing ship *Rio de Janeiro* was decommissioned on 15 June 2012.

Brazil is building a huge new submarine manufacturing and operating base at Itaguaí, south of Rio de Janeiro. The submarine assembly hall and associated ship lift are located towards the right of this digital image, with two covered dry docks seen immediately to its left. Base facilities encompass much of the rest of the foreground. In the background, towards the mountains is the 55,000m² manufacturing hall opened by Brazil's President on 1 March 2013. It is connected to the assembly hall and base by a road network and tunnel that cuts through the intervening mountain. The tunnel entrance can be seen immediately behind the dry docks. *(DCNS)*

Although construction of major surface units has taken second place to the new submarine programme, Brazil continues to acquire offshore patrol vessels. These images show the British-built *Port of Spain* class vessel *Amazonas* on sea trials in UK waters in July 2012 and the smaller French-designed but locally-constructed *Macaé* at Rio de Janeiro in November of the same year. *(Alexander Waters / Bruno Huiret)*

The huge investment in the submarine programme, as well as slower growth prospects for the Brazilian economy, is seemingly delaying other naval projects, notably the PROSUPER (*Programa de Obtenção de Meios de Superfície*) surface fleet recapitalisation plan. Severn countries have registered an interest in supporting the local construction of five surface escorts, five offshore patrol vessels and a replenishment ship that the plan requires but there have been growing rumours of likely postponement. Some of the pressure for new patrol vessels has been eased by the opportunistic acquisition of Trinidad and Tobago's three cancelled *Port of Spain* class ships from British builder BAE Systems. The renamed *Amazonas* and *Apa* (the former *Scarborough*) have already arrived in Brazil, whilst *Araguari* (formerly *San Fernando*) was handed over at Portsmouth on 21 June 2013. The Brazilian Navy is also looking to start construction of a modified version of the corvette *Barroso*, with the current plan being to start fabrication of up to four new ships before the end of 2014. Other plans include further orders of the licensed-built CMN 'Vigilante 400' type *Macaé* class. The first two of these are now fully operational and a further five are under construction. Up to another twenty are required to police Brazil's long coastline but funding is a problem. Recent reports suggest that discussions have been held with the state development bank to provide the necessary cash under a long term lease arrangement.

MAJOR SOUTH AMERICAN NAVIES – CHILE

The *Armada de Chile* completed a major modernisation programme over the previous decade and the current fleet is relatively modern by South American standards, as reflected in Table 2.1.8. Recent naval

Table 2.1.8: CHILEAN NAVY: PRINCIPAL UNITS AS AT MID 2013

TYPE	CLASS	NUMBER	TONNAGE	DIMENSIONS	PROPULSION	CREW	DATE
Principal Surface Escorts							
Frigate – FFG	**ALMIRANTE WILLIAMS** (Batch II Type 22)	1	5,500 tons	148m x 14m x 5m	COGOG, 30+ knots	260	1988
Frigate – FFG	**ALMIRANTE COCHRANE** (Type 23)	3	4,800 tons	133m x 16m x 5m	CODLAG, 28 knots	185	1990
Frigate – FFG	**CAPITÁN PRAT** (L class)	2	3,800 tons	131m x 15m x 4m	COGOG, 30 knots	200	1986
Frigate – FFG	**ALMIRANTE RIVEROS** (M class)	2	3,300 tons	122m x 14m x 4m	CODOG, 30 knots	160	1992
Submarines							
Submarine – SSK	**O'HIGGINS** ('Scorpène')	2	1,700 tons	66m x 6m x 6m	Diesel-electric, 22 knots	30	2005
Submarine – SSK	**THOMSON** (Type 209)	2	1,400 tons	60m x 6m x 6m	Diesel-electric, 22 knots	35	1984
Major Amphibious Units							
Landing Platform Dock – LPD	**SARGENTO ALDEA** (FOUDRE)	1	12,000 tons	168m x 24m x 5m	Diesel, 20 knots	225	1990

Table 2.1.9: PERUVIAN NAVY: PRINCIPAL UNITS AS AT MID 2013

TYPE	CLASS	NUMBER	TONNAGE	DIMENSIONS	PROPULSION	CREW	DATE
Principal Surface Escorts							
Cruiser – CL	**ALMIRANTE GRAU** (DE RUYTER)	1[1]	12,200 tons	187m x 17m x 7m	Steam, 32 knots	950	1953
Frigate – FFG	**CARVAJAL** (LUPO)	8	2,500 tons	112m x 12m x 4m	CODOG, 35 knots	185	1977
Submarines							
Submarine – SSK	**ANGAMOS** (Type 209)	6[2]	1,200 tons	54m x 6m x 6m	Diesel-electric, 22 knots	30	1980

Notes

1 *Almirante Grau* remained in commission as of mid-2013 but is understood to be no longer sea-going.

2 Peru operates both T209/1100 and T209/1200 submarines. Details refer to the Type 209/1100 variant

procurement has therefore focused more on upgrades to existing assets or the purchase of incremental capabilities rather than entirely new acquisitions. These have included surplus United States AAV7 armoured amphibious vehicles for operations from the amphibious transport dock *Sargento Aldea* (formerly the French *Foudre*) and further frigate upgrades. An exception is renewed construction of Fassmer OPV80 offshore patrol vessels following completion of repairs to the tsunami-damaged ASMAR yard at Talcahuano. The keel of *Comandante Marinero Fuentealba*, third in the series of Chilean vessels, was laid on 13 December 2012 following commencement of fabrication in July. She is due for launch in the second half of 2013 prior to delivery in 2014. Two further ships are planned. Longer-term purchases may involve the acquisition of France's *Siroco* to join her sister *Foudre*. Replacements may also be sought for the aging Type 209 submarines, as well as for the two small flotillas of fast attack craft that guard the country's northern and southern extremities. One of the latter's northern quartet, the former German Type 148 class *Guardiamarina Riquelme*, was retired at the end of 2012, leaving three units serving in each command.

MAJOR SOUTH AMERICAN NAVIES – PERU

The *Marina de Guerra de Perú* is another South American fleet that has essentially marked time recently, with the main development in 2012–13 being the arrival of the first two of seven new Griffon 2000TD hovercraft for operation in the Amazon region.[14] However, the last year has also seen the announcement of a major contract with local shipyard SIMA-Peru for new support and patrol assets. The US$300m agreement encompasses the acquisition of two 7,000-ton logistic support vessels; four offshore and six coastal patrol vessels;

and a sail training ship. Reports suggest that Korea's Daewoo Shipbuilding and Marine Engineering (DSME) will provide design and technical assistance for the programme, with the support vessels likely based on the Indonesian Navy's *Makassar* class amphibious transport dock. Peru continues to have a requirement for the modernisation of its six-strong submarine fleet, with which DSME is also likely to be involved.

Table 2.1.9 summaries Peru's major naval units and shows no change from last year's position.

OTHER SOUTH AMERICAN NAVIES

The *Armada de la República de Colombia* remains by far the most ambitious of the smaller South American navies, with a programme of domestic construction being supplemented by acquisitions of second-hand units from overseas, as well as by the

An image of the veteran Peruvian cruiser *Almirante Grau* – the former Dutch *De Ruyter* – alongside at Callao Naval Base in February 2013. Although maintained in commission and in good condition she is unlike to be deployed again except in an emergency. *(Guy Toremans)*

refurbishment of existing vessels.[15] The most significant development over the past year has been confirmation of previous rumours of the purchase of decommissioned Type 206 German submarines, with both *Intrépido* (formerly *U-32*) and *Indomable* (the former *U-33*) transferred at Kiel on 28 August 2012 after completion of tropicalisation work. They join two larger Type 209 submarines of similar vintage that are being modernised by local shipyard COTECMAR in conjunction with Germany's HDW. Press reports suggest the submarines will play a key role combatting drugs traffickers' use of semi-submersible vessels to smuggle contraband.

The surface fleet has been boosted by completion of modernisation work on the four *Almirante Padilla* class frigates. The upgrades have been carried out by Thales in conjunction with COTECMAR and have

The Colombian Navy's newly modernised *Almirante Padilla* class frigate *Antioquia* seen training with the US Navy in September 2012. Thales has recently headed a major mid-life upgrade programme for the four units in the class, which has encompassed weapons systems and electronics. Amongst these are installation of a new SMART-S radar and a modernised 76mm main gun. *(US Navy)*

included the installation of Thales SMART-S and Terma Scanter 2001 radars; electronics and fire control upgrades; and new engines. COTECMAR is also involved in the ongoing construction of Fassmer OPV-80 vessels, with *7 de Agosto*, the second of up to six ships already well advanced. However, local fabrication of the smaller Fassmer CPV40 type appears to have been abandoned in favour of a South Korean STX design. This decision may well have been influenced by South Korea's gift of the decommissioned *Donghae* class corvette *Anyang*, which may be the first of several such transfers.[16]

Elsewhere in South America, Ecuador is seeing modernisation of its two Type 209 submarines make good progress at Chile's ASMAR. Work on *Shyri* was completed towards the end of 2012, whilst *Huancavilca* will be redelivered during 2014. Venezuela's upgrade of its own pair of Type 209 boats is also drawing to a conclusion, although previous plans to acquire new Russian submarines have yet to produce a contract. The introduction of Spanish-designed 'BVL' type littoral patrol vessels is another project coming to fruition with the official keel laying for the fourth and final unit *Tamanaco* at the local Dianca yard on 3 August 2012. Construction has been stalled due to a dispute between designer Navantia's reservations about the local builder's technical ability to complete the ship and, although Venezuela appears to have won the argument, it is notable that eleven out of the ship's twelve constituent blocks have been fabricated in Spain. Meanwhile, *Warao*, one of the quartet of larger 'POVZEE' type oceanic patrol vessels delivered under the same contract, has been seriously damaged after grounding on a reef off northern Brazil in August 2012 whilst on exercises with the *Marina do Brasil*. She was subsequently transferred by heavy lift ship to Rio de Janeiro, where repairs will be carried out.

Notes:

1. The debate has its origins in heated political disagreement within the United States' political establishment – somewhat beyond the scope of this book – as to how best to control the large government deficit and the appropriate balance between spending and taxes. The 2011 Budget Control Act attempted to chart a path towards a more sustainable position. It agreed immediate reductions to the planned rate of growth in government spending and put in place an automatic mechanism – sequestration – for substantial additional cuts if alternative deficit reduction measures were not agreed. From a defence perspective, this process resulted in the announcement of significant cutbacks – a little under US$500bn over ten tears – compared with previous plans in the FY2013 budget. However, no plans were made at the time to deal with a broadly similar level of cuts mandated under sequestration on the assumption that an alternative agreement would be reached. This assumption proved to be overly-optimistic and sequestration-related reductions took effect from March 2013. The US military also had to live without an agreed FY2013 defence budget from October 2012 due to political disagreement but this was resolved by enactment of Public Law 11306 on 26 March 2013.

2. Of this amount, c. US$525bn related to core funding and the balance to overseas contingency operations, relating to extra funds allocated to live missions such as the war in Afghanistan. The sequestration-related reduction in US Navy funding amounts to c. US$11bn from total approved funding of US$174bn, of which US$160bn reflects core expenditure.

3. For further detail, refer to Marcus Weisgerber's 'FY15 Guidance Takes Sequester Into Account', *Defense News* – 30 May 2013 (Springfield VA: Gannett Government Media Corporation, 2013).

4. See *CBO: Approaches for Scaling Back the Defense Department's Budget Plans* (Washington DC: Congressional Budget Office, 2013).

5. Amongst the voluminous press coverage of Freedom's deployment, Grace Jean's 'Briefing: *Freedom* Unleashed', *Jane's Defence Weekly* – 3 April 2013 (Coulsdon: IHS Jane's, 2013), pp 24–8 provides a good overview of US Navy expectations at the start of the deployment.

6. The Royal Canadian Navy provides a helpful guide on the history and positioning of flags on its warships at http://www.navy.forces.gc.ca/cms/3/3-a_eng.asp?id=936.

7. The new requirement is set out in *Report to Congress: Navy Combatant Vessel Force Structure Requirement – January 2013* (Washington DC, US Navy, 2013). The publicly-available document is only four pages long but was supplemented by a classified briefing. Reference should also be made to the *Report to Congress on the Annual Long-Range Plan for Construction of Naval Vessels for 2014* (Washington DC: US Navy, 2013) released in May 2013 for information on how the requirement will be implemented.

8. Some excellent analysis on the extent to which requirements and plans match is contained in Ronald O'Rourke's *Navy Force Structure and Shipbuilding Plans: Background and Issues for Congress* (Washington DC: Congressional Research Service), which is regularly updated. Mr O'Rourke – the CRS's specialist in naval affairs – prepares a number of other regularly updated on key naval programmes, including the CVN-78, SSN-774, DDG-51 and littoral combat ship classes. The reports are not made directly available to the public but many are hosted by the Federation of American Scientists at http://www.fas.org/sgp/crs/.

9. *Coronado*'s trials were temporarily halted by minor fires that occurred in the ship's diesel exhausts during a full-power demonstration in April 2013. Although seized upon by detractors of the littoral combat ship programme, the damage caused was apparently minor and should not delay delivery.

10. The two Lockheed Martin ships have been named *Wichita* (LCS-13) and *Billings* (LCS-15). The Austal variants are *Manchester* (LCS-14) and *Tulsa* (LCS-16).

11. The *Spearhead* class are described by Scott Truver in Chapter 3.3.

12. More coverage of the *Porter* collision and repair is contained in Grace Jean's 'Damaged US destroyer to be repaired and given BMD upgrade', *Jane's Defence Weekly* – 8 May 2013 (Coulsdon: IHS Jane's, 2013), p.11.

13. The Portuguese language Poder Naval website at www.naval.com.br continues to remain an excellent source of information on this and other Brazilian naval developments and often contains links to official navy presentations.

14. Riverine operations have significance to a large number of South American navies and hovercraft are being increasingly seen as a means of supporting such activities. In addition to Peru, Colombia has also acquired the Griffon GT2000, signing a contract for eight in January 2013.

15. Further information on the smaller South American navies can be found on the Spanish language Base Naval website at www.basenaval.com. *Janes's Defence Weekly* has also recently provided an overview of regional procurement programmes as part of Inigo Guevara's 'The Latin beat' – *Janes's Defence Weekly* – 20 March 2013 (Coulsdon: IHS Jane's, 2013), pp.24–36.

16. Colombia was originally going to receive the slightly more modern *Po Hang* class corvette *Kun San*. However, a report by Forecast International suggests a Colombian Navy delegation that visited South Korea in February 2013 opted for the older vessel.

Author:
Conrad Waters

2.2 REGIONAL REVIEW

ASIA AND THE PACIFIC

INTRODUCTION

The background to naval events in the vast Asia-Pacific region continues to be driven by disputes over maritime boundaries, notably in the East and South China Seas. These are often simplistically seen as a product of an increasingly assertive China seeking to grab resources whilst bolstering national prestige. However, the underlying picture is more complicated. Indeed, there are a myriad of competing claims over the region's waters, as evidenced by continued diplomatic spats between Japan and South Korea over the Dokdo islets in the Sea of Japan and friction between Taiwan and both Japan and the Philippines over regional fishing rights.

Nevertheless, it is China's actions that are making the headlines. An increasingly heated dispute over claims to the Japanese-administered Senkaku Islands (Diaoyutai to China) some 200 miles southwest of Okinawa has produced frequent confrontations between the Japan Coast Guard and Chinese surveillance ships. There have also been major anti-Japanese demonstrations in Chinese cities. The situation resulted in new Japanese Prime Minister Shinzo Abe explicitly threatening the use of force to repel any Chinese landing on the uninhabited island group in a statement to Japan's parliament on 23 April 2013.[1] Abe and his Liberal Democratic Party are, themselves, taking a more assertive stance towards Japan's global profile, most notably through a debate on revisions to Article 9 of the Japanese Constitution. Drafted under United States' influence after Japan's wartime defeat, this outlaws the country's recourse to

war as a means of settling disputes and, by implication, places significant restrictions on the activities of its military.[2] Amendment would give Japan more flexibility in determining future military acquisitions, particularly with respect to offensive weapons such as fixed-wing aircraft carriers, and allow it to play a larger role on the world stage. Equally, it could revive past fears of Japanese militarism at a time when some revisionist right wing politicians are attempting to downplay the country's responsibility for its wartime actions. Meanwhile, a revised FY2013 defence budget has seen the first – albeit modest – increase in Japan's military spending for eleven years. This was, in part, justified by the need to beef-up the security of the southern islands in the current environment.

The Senkaku confrontation has distracted attention from the territorial disagreements in the South China Sea, where China's 'nine-dash line' claim potentially sets it add odds with Brunei, Indonesia, Malaysia, Taiwan, the Philippines and Vietnam.[3] The dispute between China and the Philippines, encompassing Scarborough Shoal and the Spratly Islands, has been particularly contentious. This resulted in the Philippines asking for international arbitration under the 1982 UN Convention on the Law of the Sea in January 2013. Unsurprisingly, China has refused to support the arbitration process. More practically, the Philippine government has continued to strengthen its renewed alliance with the United States, whilst bolstering its armed forces with new assets that may include its first missile-armed ships.

This approach confirms a trend of real-terms growth in defence expenditure across the region; a process arguably driven by China itself. According to SIPRI, Chinese military expenditure rose by 175 per cent between 2003 and 2012; the fastest amongst any of the world's fifteen highest-spending military powers.[4]

An added complication to this potent mix of territorial disagreements and increasing military expenditures – to say nothing of renewed American regional engagement – is represented by the continued unpredictability of North Korea's behaviour. The country's ongoing tests of nuclear warheads and ballistic weapons have been met with tighter sanctions, in turn provoking further aggressive rhetoric towards South Korea, the United States and their allies. These culminated in a bizarre threat in March 2013 to launch a pre-emptive nuclear strike against the United States itself. As previously, this bellicose language was not combined with physical action and tensions have since eased. Although there is consensus that the North's military capabilities do not match its verbal aggression, its threats are driving further investment in countermeasures that will have a marked impact on naval procurement; both regionally and beyond. For example, South Korea is actively considering the acquisition of Standard SM-3 anti-ballistic missile (ABM) interceptors for its Aegis-equipped destroyers in similar fashion to the United States and Japan. Moreover, the events have provided further impetus for the broader global adoption of sea-based ABM technology that is likely to become increasingly evident as time progresses.

The modernised People's Liberation Army Navy Type 052 destroyer *Harbin* on exercise with NATO forces in the Indian Ocean in April 2013. The increasing extent of China's maritime reach – combined with fears over the extent of its territorial ambitions – is driving regional naval procurement. *(NATO)*

Table 2.2.1: FLEET STRENGTHS IN ASIA AND THE PACIFIC – LARGER NAVIES (MID 2013)

COUNTRY	AUSTRALIA	CHINA	INDONESIA	JAPAN	S KOREA	SINGAPORE	TAIWAN	THAILAND
Aircraft Carrier (CV)	–	1	–	–	–	–	–	–
Support/Helicopter Carrier (CVS/CVH)	–	–	–	2	–	–	–	1
Strategic Missile Submarine (SSBN)	–	3	–	–	–	–	–	–
Attack Submarine (SSN)	–	5	–	–	–	–	–	–
Patrol Submarine (SSK/SS)	6	55	2	16	12	6	4	–
Fleet Escort (DDG/FFG)	12	60	6	39	22	6	26	8
Patrol Escort/Corvette (FFG/FSG/FS)	–	20	24	6	21	6	–	11
Missile Armed Attack Craft (PGG/PTG)	–	75	9	6	9	–	c.30	6
Mine Countermeasures Vessel (MCMV)	6	20	11	30	9	4	10	6
Major Amphibious Units (LHD/LPD/LSD)	1	3	5	3	1	4	1	1

Notes: Chinese numbers approximate; Some additional Indonesian patrol gunboats are able to ship missiles; Taiwan's submarines are reported to have limited operational availability.

The Royal Australian Navy's *Collins* class submarine *Dechaineux* leads class members *Waller* and *Sheean* during training exercises in Cockburn Sound in March 2013. Improvements to Australian support arrangements should result in three of the six-strong fleet being available for ninety per cent of the time within the next three years. *(Royal Australian Navy)*

MAJOR REGIONAL POWERS – AUSTRALIA

A summary of Australia's current major warships is provided in Table 2.2.2. The medium-term direction for Australia's armed forces was determined by the release of the new defence white paper on 3 May 2013. So far as the Royal Australian Navy is concerned, force structure plans remain essentially unaltered from those set out in the previous defence white paper of 2009. As before, the main question remains the extent to which an ambitious programme of new construction will be affordable. The 2013 Australian budget, subsequently delivered on 14 May 2013, unexpectedly restored much of the previous cut to defence spending announced in 2012 that had taken the budget to a post-war low of c. 1.6 per cent of GDP. Expenditure is now planned to rise in the years ahead, although a commitment to restore the budget to a targeted two per cent only remains a longer-term aspiration.

A major factor influencing the success of Australia's plans will be whether or not new projects can be delivered on budget. Amongst the most significant of these is the long-term plan to expand the current submarine fleet from six to twelve boats that is estimated to cost as much as A\$36bn (US\$35bn) over the project's life. The white paper announced that previous consideration of the 'off-the shelf' purchase or modification of existing types from DCNS, HDW and Navantia had been abandoned. This narrows options to an evolution of the existing *Collins* class boats or construction of an entirely new design. Whilst there is some logic in this approach given none of the existing classes have been designed for oceanic operations, the choice inevitably adds to project risk and complexity and will also extend the lead-in time to construction. The life of the existing *Collins* class will therefore be extended by one docking period (taking service lives from between 2024 and 2031 to between 2031 and 2038) to

Table 2.2.2: ROYAL AUSTRALIAN NAVY: PRINCIPAL UNITS AS AT MID 2013

TYPE	CLASS	NUMBER	TONNAGE	DIMENSIONS	PROPULSION	CREW	DATE
Principal Surface Escorts							
Frigate – FFG	**ADELAIDE** (FFG-7)	4	4,200 tons	138m x 14m x 5m	COGAG, 30 knots	210	1980
Frigate – FFG	**ANZAC**	8	3,600 tons	118m x 15m x 4m	CODOG, 28 knots	175	1996
Submarines							
Submarine – SSK	**COLLINS**	6	3,400 tons	78m x 8m x 7m	Diesel-electric, 20 knots	45	1996
Major Amphibious Units							
Landing Ship Dock – LSD	**CHOULES** ('Bay')	1	16,200 tons	176m x 26m x 6m	Diesel-electric, 18 knots	60	2006

Canberra, the first of two new Australian *Juan Carlos I* type amphibious assault ships, is close to commencing sea trials after conclusion of fitting-out work in BAE System's yard at Melbourne. These images show the island structure being installed on top of the ship's hull, which was delivered by barge from Navantia in Spain in October 2012. *(BAE Systems)*

compensate for the likely delay. The first stage of Project SEA 1439 Phase 3.1, which will upgrade the platform management systems on the class, was announced on 14 June 2013. Further steps are also being taken to increase the reliability of the existing fleet by changing the docking cycles of the current boats in line with the conclusions of the final phase of the Coles Review made public in December 2012.[5]

Meanwhile, good progress has been made with existing Australian shipbuilding projects. The hull of *Canberra*, the first of two new *Juan Carlos I* type amphibious assault ships, arrived from Spain's Navantia in October 2012 for installation of the island structure and final fitting-out by BAE

Systems' yard at Williamstown near Melbourne. This work is now well-advanced and sea trials are scheduled for the second half of the year prior to planned delivery in the first quarter of 2014. Her sister-ship *Adelaide* was launched by Navantia at Ferrol in July 2012; she will arrive at Williamstown early in 2014 and will be delivered in 2016. The amphibious fleet will also be supplemented by the dock landing ship *Choules* (the former *Largs Bay*), which has completed repairs to defective transformers and will now be kept in the fleet when the new assault ships commission. 2016 will also see the delivery of the first *Hobart* class destroyer, which saw its keel laid in a formal ceremony at ASC in Adelaide in September 2012. As of mid-2013, fifteen of the ship's thirty-one constituent blocks had been assembled, with all the remainder already delivered to the yard. Construction of the two follow-on ships is also underway.

The defence white paper dashed hopes that the option for a fourth *Hobart* class destroyer would be exercised. The next major construction programme will therefore be for the new future frigates that will eventually replace the current eight *Anzac* class vessels on a one-for-one basis. The United Kingdom is heavily promoting its Type 26 Global Combat Ship concept for the new class, which are likely to incorporate a development of the Australian designed CEAFAR phased-array radar currently been retrofitted to the existing ships. The decision not to exercise the *Hobart* option produces a gap in Australian shipbuilding construction around the turn of the decade. This may have influenced the announcement that a replacement for the existing *Armidale* class patrol boats will be brought forward. The intention is to use an existing, proven design, thereby deferring the previous plan to procure a flexible multi-role ship that could also fulfil mine countermeasures and survey roles. Given previous selection of Spanish technology, Navantia's 'BAM' type offshore patrol vessel might be a leading contender. The white paper also indicated that the existing replenishment vessels *Sirius* and *Success* would be replaced at the earliest possible opportunity. Adelaide's ASC has subsequently proposed the construction of three replenishment ships to BMT's Aegir 18A design to meet the resulting SEA 1654 Phase 3 requirement. Two of these would be completed by Korea's Daewoo Shipbuilding & Marine Engineering (DSME), with the third built in Australia.

MAJOR REGIONAL POWERS – CHINA

Recent developments in the People's Liberation Army Navy (PLAN) have continued to be headlined by steady progress with its aircraft carrier programme. The former Russian Project 1143.5/6 *Varyag* was commissioned as *Liaoning* on 25 September 2012 at a ceremony at the Dalian shipyard which had carried out its refurbishment, the importance of the event being marked by the presence of outgoing Chinese President Hu Jintao. The ship subsequently carried out initial take-off and landing exercises during November before deploying to the PLAN's new North Sea Fleet base at Dazhu Shan near Qingdao in February 2013.[6] Flight operations were conducted by Shenyang J-15 jet fighters which have been reported as derivatives of Russia's Sukhoi Su-33, an assertion criticised as being '… groundless and sour' by China's Xinhua news agency. Their successful carrier debut was marred by the demise of the head of the Shenyang Aircraft Corporation, Luo Yuang, who died from a heart attack after watching the exercises. China has confirmed that it plans the domestic construction of further ships to supplement *Liaoning* but has denied reports that further carriers are already being assembled.

Whilst China's carrier programme has attracted most attention, it is the more rapid modernisation of the rest of the PLAN's fleet that has most immediate relevance. As Table 2.2.3 makes clear, previous reliance on largely obsolescent designs is increasingly been overcome by the introduction of new construction.[7] Major developments with respect to key ship categories are highlighted below:

Major Surface Combatants: Recent surface-ship construction has been dominated by the mass production of the new Type 056 'Jiangdao' littoral warfare corvettes. The first of these was delivered in February 2013 before being commissioned as *Bengbu* on 12 March. Displacing a little under 1,500 tons at full load, she has a balanced armament that includes a 76mm gun, surface-to-air and surface-to-surface missiles, anti-submarine torpedo tubes and close-in-weapons systems, as well as a flight deck to support helicopter or UAV operations. Falling between the Type 022 'Houbei' class catamarans and Type 054A 'Jiangkai II' frigates in size and capability, the new ships are intended as replacements for the older Type 053 'Jianghu' frigates and Type 037 'Hainan' patrol vessels and have drawn comparisons with the US

Navy's larger littoral combat ships. By mid-2013 as many as six of the class had been delivered from four different shipyards. Additionally, more than ten further vessels were under construction. Commentators have suggested that the corvettes will be used for offshore patrols in the disputed waters of the South and East China Seas, releasing the PLAN's larger ships for true 'blue water' operations.

The Type 054A 'Jiangkai II' frigates remain in series production at both the Hudong-Zhonghua and Huangpu shipyards as the PLAN's principal 'blue water' surface escort. Around fifteen of the class have now been delivered and a final total of at least twenty is expected. They increasingly appear to be the vessel of choice for China's overseas deployments, possibly because of the range and economy offered by their CODAD propulsion. The Black Sea and Malta are just some of the new shores visited by the class over the past year.

'High-end' production is focused on the Type 052C 'Luyang II' destroyer and the improved Type 052D variant. Production of the second, four-ship batch of Type 052Cs is now drawing to a close and all should be in service by early 2014. The follow-on Type 052D is estimated to be slightly larger than its predecessor with a length of 160m (155m) and beam of 18m (17m) but features new, flatter phased array panels, a revised vertical launch system and larger gun. Two of the new ships had been launched by the end of 2012 and additional units are variously reported under construction or planned.

Submarines: News flow on the PLAN's submarine force has continued to remain limited. The US Department of Defense's annual report to Congress on the Chinese military provides little information not already in the public domain on the nuclear-powered attack (Type 093 'Shang') and strategic (Type 094 'Jin') submarines, although it does support previous contentions that there may be a transition to new Type 095 and Type 096 designs.[8] There have certainly been few reports of new construction, suggesting previous rumours of difficulties with existing designs, both conventional and nuclear-powered, may have some foundation. Recent suggestions that China may be negotiating the acquisition of Russian 'Lada' type AIP-equipped submarines lend credence to this thesis with respect to the current generation of diesel-electric boats, as a major reason for the purchase would be the access to new technology it would provide. It is also worth

The Chinese Type 903 fleet tanker *Qian Dao Hu* undertook a port visit to Sydney, Australia in December 2012. Whilst media attention has been focused on deliveries of the new carrier *Liaoning* and further escort vessels, construction of additional replenishment vessels has equal relevance for China's ability to project 'blue water' naval power. *(Royal Australian Navy)*

Table 2.2.3: PEOPLE'S LIBERATION ARMY NAVY: PRINCIPAL UNITS AS AT MID 2013

TYPE	CLASS	NUMBER	TONNAGE	DIMENSIONS	PROPULSION	CREW	DATE
Aircraft Carriers							
Aircraft Carrier – CV	Project 1143.5/6 **LIAONING** (Kuznetsov)	1	60,000 tons	306m x 35/73m x 10m	Steam, 32 knots	Unknown	2012
Principal Surface Escorts							
Destroyer – DDG	Type 051C **SHENYANG** ('Luzhou')	2	7,100 tons	155m x 17m x 6m	Steam, 29 knots	Unknown	2006
Destroyer – DDG	Type 052C **LANZHOU** ('Luyang II')	5	6,500 tons	154m x 17m x 6m	CODOG, 28 knots	280	2004
Destroyer – DDG	Type 052B **GUANGZHOU** ('Luyang I')	2	6,000 tons	154m x 17m x 6m	CODOG, 29 knots	280	2004
Destroyer – DDG	Project 956E/EM **HANGZHOU** (Sovremenny)	4	8,000 tons	156m x 17m x 6m	Steam, 32 knots	300	1999
Destroyer – DDG	Type 051B **SHENZHEN** ('Luhai')	1	6,000 tons	154m x 16m x 6m	Steam, 31 knots	250	1998
Destroyer – DDG	Type 052 **HARBIN** ('Luhu')	2	4,800 tons	143m x 15m x 5m	CODOG, 31 knots	260	1994
Plus c.10 additional obsolescent destroyers of Type 051 **JINAN** ('Luda') class							
Frigate – FFG	Type 054A **XUZHOU** ('Jiangkai II')	15	4,100 tons	132m x 15m x 5m	CODAD, 28 knots	190	2008
Frigate – FFG	Type 054 **MA'ANSHAN** ('Jiangkai I')	2	4,000 tons	132m x 15m x 5m	CODAD, 28 knots	190	2005
Frigate – FFG	Type 053 H2G/H3 **ANQING** ('Jiangwei I/II')	14	2,500 tons	112m x 12m x 5m	CODAD, 27 knots	170	1992
Frigate – FSG	Type 056 **BENGBU** ('Jiangdao')	6	1,500 tons	89m x 12m x 4m	CODAD, 28 knots	60	2013
Plus c.10-15 additional obsolescent frigates of Type 053 H/H1/H1G/H2 **XIAMEN** ('Jianghu') classes							
Submarines							
Submarine – SSBN	Type 094 ('Jin')	2+	9,000 tons	133m x 11m x 8m	Nuclear, 20+ knots	Unknown	2008
Submarine – SSBN	Type 092 ('Xia')	1	6,500 tons	120m x 10m x 8m	Nuclear, 22 knots	140	1987
Submarine – SSN	Type 093 ('Shang')	2+	6,000 tons	107m x 11m x 8m	Nuclear, 30 knots	100	2006
Submarine – SSN	Type 091 ('Han')	3	5,500 tons	106m x 10m x 7m	Nuclear, 25 knots	75	1974
Submarine – SSK	Type 039A/Type 041 ('Yuan')	8+	2,500 tons	75m x 8m x 5m	AIP, 20+ knots	Unknown	2006
Submarine – SSK	Type 039/039G ('Song')	13	2,300 tons	75m x 8m x 5m	Diesel-electric, 22 knots	60	1999
Submarine – SSK	Project 877 EKM/636 ('Kilo')	12	3,000 tons	73m x 10m x 7m	Diesel-electric, 20 knots	55	1995
Plus c.20 obsolescent patrol submarines of the Project 033 ('Romeo' class) and Type 035 ('Ming' class) designs. A Type 039B/Type 43 'Qing' trials submarine has also been commissioned.							
Major Amphibious Units							
Landing Platform Dock	Type 071 **KULUN SHAN** ('Yuzhao')	3	18,000 tons	210m x 27m x 7m	CODAD, 20 knots	Unknown	2007

noting that the PLAN's flotillas of conventional submarines have already seen significant upgrades over the past decade, perhaps allowing other construction to be prioritised. It is also apparent that China is paying particular attention to the logistic, maintenance and training facilities required to support effective 'blue water' submarine operations, attempting to learn lessons from Russian Cold War failures in this regard.[9]

Other Warships: Modernisation of China's front-line surface forces is being balanced by further investment in secondary vessels. The increasing tempo of international deployments has put particular pressure on the small fleet of replenishment vessels and two additional Type 903 auxiliary supply vessels were close to completion by mid-year to supplement the earlier pair. The pace of development of indigenous amphibious vessels has been less marked, with construction of the Type 071 'Yuzhao' amphibious transport docks seemingly suspended after completion of the third ship in September 2012. This might possibly indicate a transition to fabrication of a long-rumoured amphibious assault ship class. In the interim, amphibious capabilities are being strengthened by the introduction of giant Ukrainian Zubr hovercraft, with four being acquired under a reported US$315m contract. The latter pair will be built in China under Ukrainian supervision, opening up the possibility of further domestic production in due course.

A key feature of recent territorial confrontations has been the active role taken by ships belonging to China's various paramilitary maritime agencies as opposed to front-line PLAN warships. Significant investment is being made in such constabulary assets and steps have recently been taken to adapt their command structure to a more homogenous model. In March 2013, it was announced that an enlarged National Oceanic Administration overseen by the Ministry of Land and Resources would add the China Coast Guard forces of the Public Security Ministry; the Fisheries Law Enforcement Command; and the maritime anti-smuggling police of the General Administration of Customs to its existing responsibility for China Marine Surveillance. The new unified Coast Guard will have over 50,000 personnel and is likely to assume a similar role to that carried out by counterparts in the United States, Japan and elsewhere. In addition to providing improved efficiency, the new structure is

reported to be intended to enhance the protection of China's maritime rights and interests. As such, it is likely to continue playing a key role in China's pursuit of its various territorial claims.

MAJOR REGIONAL POWERS – JAPAN

The Japan Maritime Self Defence Force is currently approximately midway through implementation of the 2011–15 Japanese Mid-Term Defence Programme, which is linked to the longer-term, ten-year National Defence Programme Guidelines. These plan for a fleet of forty-eight surface escorts (of which four will eventually be carrier-like heli-copter-carrying destroyers) and twenty-two submarines, as well as support and minor war vessels. Given limited funds for new construction, considerable attention is being focused on the modernisation and life extension of existing classes. The recent change in Japan's political administration resulted in the announcement of a review of these plans in December 2012, although any changes have yet to be announced. A revised budget request did, however, incorporate increased orders

for SH-60K anti-submarine and MCH-101 minesweeping helicopters.

Principal constituents of the current fleet are set out in Table 2.2.4. There are currently forty-seven escorts and sixteen submarines in service, as well as three additional destroyers and two submarines in reserve roles. The number of destroyers has temporarily slipped below the targeted threshold as only one of the new *Akizuki* (DD-115) class destroyers was delivered over the past year but two of the old *Hatsuyuki* (DD-122) class destroyers have been decommissioned. The situation should be restored in the years ahead as two further *Akizuki* class vessels ordered under the FY2009 budget are scheduled for delivery in early 2014, whilst the life extension programme referenced above should slow the rate of withdrawals there-after. As such, the planned 48-ship force should be in place by 2020. There have also been reports that up to four of the *Hatsuyuki* class will be transferred to the Japan Coast Guard, which has found its resources severely stretched by the ongoing Senkaku islands dispute.

A flotilla of JMSDF escort vessels pictured during a public 'sea day' in 2012 headed by the first of four '19DD' destroyers *Akizuki*. Long-term plans call for the JMSDF to maintain a force of forty-eight frontline surface escorts, including four helicopter carriers. *(Rolls-Royce)*

The FY2013 defence budget provides funding for three new vessels.[10] The most significant of these is a new 5,000-ton (standard displacement) destroyer that will cost a total of 76bn Japanese yen (c. US$730m) including 5.8bn Japanese yen in non-recurrent, first-of-class costs. Images suggest the new ship will be based on the existing *Akizuki* class design but she will be optimised towards anti-submarine warfare and incorporate an innovative COGLAG (combined gas-electric and gas) propulsion system. The budget also encompasses continued production of *Soryu* class AIP-equipped submarines; with an order for a ninth boat envisaged at a cost of 53.1bn Japanese yen (c. US$500m). Although the submarine flotilla is a long way below its targeted level, numbers should start to creep upwards from 2015 onwards as the existing *Oyashio* class benefit from life-extensions and further *Soryu* class boats are delivered. The required force structure

Another view of the new Japanese destroyer *Akizuki* (DD-115). Powered by four Rolls-Royce Spey gas turbines, she displaces a little under 7,000 tons in full load condition and has a maximum speed of c. 30 knots. She is primarily intended for the local air defence of the JMSDF's surface flotillas, leaving the Aegis-equipped vessels to focus on the ABM role. *(Japan Maritime Self Defence Force)*

therefore appears achievable from 2020, when there should be eleven submarines of each type in commission. Meanwhile, the budget also included the usual annual allocation for a new mine-counter-measures vessel, maintaining the fleet at around thirty units.

MAJOR REGIONAL POWERS – SOUTH KOREA

An overview of the Republic of Korea Navy's major units is set out in Table 2.2.5. The last year has seen delivery of the third and final KDX-III destroyer, *Ryu Sung-ryong*, on 30 August 2012 and the lead FFX patrol frigate, *Incheon*, on 17 January 2013. Further members of the *Incheon* class are under construction but orders for larger surface vessels are likely to be deferred for the time being. This is a reflection of the renewed focus on littoral warfare that has resulted from ongoing tensions in the Korean peninsula, leaving South Korea's 'blue water' naval ambitions to take second place to investment in equipment better placed to counter the North's asymmetrical capabilities. There has been a particular emphasis on improving anti-submarine capabilities, as demonstrated by a firm contract for Lynx Wildcat helicopters from the United Kingdom and

Table 2.2.4: JAPAN MARITIME SELF-DEFENCE FORCE: PRINCIPAL UNITS AS AT MID 2013

TYPE	CLASS	NUMBER	TONNAGE	DIMENSIONS	PROPULSION	CREW	DATE
Support and Helicopter Carriers							
Helicopter Carrier – DDH	**HYUGA** (DDH-181)	2	18,000 tons	197m x 33m x 7m	COGAG, 30 knots	340	2009
Principal Surface Escorts							
Helicopter Destroyer – DDH	**SHIRANE** (DDH-143)	2	7,500 tons	159m x 18m x 5m	Steam, 32 knots	350	1980
Destroyer – DDG	**ATAGO** (DDG-177)	2	10,000 tons	165m x 21m x 6m	COGAG, 30 knots	300	2007
Destroyer – DDG	**KONGOU** (DDG-173)	4	9,500 tons	161m x 21m x 6m	COGAG, 30 knots	300	1993
Destroyer – DDG	**HATAKAZE** (DDG-171)	2	6,300 tons	150m x 16m x 5m	COGAG, 30 knots	260	1986
Destroyer – DD	**AKIZUKI** (DD-115)	2	6,800 tons	151m x 18m x 5m	COGAG, 30 Knots	200	2012
Destroyer – DDG	**TAKANAMI** (DD-110)	5	5,300 tons	151m x 17m x 5m	COGAG, 30 knots	175	2003
Destroyer – DDG	**MURASAME** (DD-101)	9	5,200 tons	151m x 17m x 5m	COGAG, 30 knots	165	1996
Destroyer – DDG	**ASAGIRI** (DD-151)	8	4,300 tons	137m x 15m x 5m	COGAG, 30 knots	220	1988
Destroyer – DDG	**HATSUYUKI** (DD-122)	5 (3)	3,800 tons	130m x 14m x 4m	COGOG, 30 knots	200	1982
Frigate – FFG	**ABUKUMA** (DE-229)	6	2,500 tons	109m x 13m x 4m	CODOG, 27 knots	120	1989
Submarines							
Submarine – SSK	**SORYU** (SS-501)	5	4,200 tons	84m x 9m x 8m	AIP, 20 knots+	65	2009
Submarine – SSK	**OYASHIO** (SS-590)	11	4,000 tons	82m x 9m x 8m	Diesel-electric, 20 knots+	70	1998
Submarine – SSK	**HARUSHIO** (SS-583)	0 (2)	3,300 tons	77m x 10m x 8m	Diesel-electric, 20 knots+	75	1990
Major Amphibious Units							
Landing Platform Dock – LPD	**OSUMI** (LST-4001)	3	14,000 tons	178m x 26m x 6m	Diesel, 22 knots	135	1998

Note: Figures in brackets refer to trials or training ships.

Pictured shortly before commissioning on 17 January 2013, *Incheon* is the prototype of what is intended to be a numerous class of small frigates intended to replace existing smaller escorts. Displacing a little less than 3,000 tons in full load condition, the frigates pack a powerful armament that includes a 127mm gun, RAM and Phalanx CIWS, surface-to-surface missiles, anti-submarine torpedoes and facilities to embark and operate a light helicopter. *(Hyundai Heavy Industries)*

The Republic of Korea Navy's KDX-III type destroyer *Yulgok Yil* was a participant in the RIMPAC 2012 exercises. It seems likely that Korea will fit an ABM capability to these three Aegis-equipped ships, but there has to be doubt whether sufficient funding is available to satisfy navy aspirations for a further three class members. *(US Navy)*

reports of a planned purchase of up to twenty maritime patrol aircraft to replace the existing squadron of Lockheed Martin P-3C Orions. Boeing's P-8 Poseidon seems to be the leading contender for the new contract, although Airbus Military's C-295 and Lockheed Martin's SC-130J Sea Hercules may also be in contention.[11]

The emphasis on littoral warfare is also seen in continued construction of PKX fast attack craft, of which nine are already in service. STX Offshore & Shipbuilding and Hanjin Heavy Industries have both launched batches of three additional ships over the past year. An order for a final trio is expected to meet a total requirement of eighteen. Images of the latest Hanjin vessels suggest modifications from earlier class members, including improved communications and installation of the latest 76mm Oto Melara gun. The combined construction of FFX and PKX vessels should allow further withdrawals of the obsolescent *Po Hang* class corvettes, some of which are being offered for transfer to foreign fleets.

There does, however, remain a significant school of thought within the Republic of Korea Navy that retains ambitions for a more expeditionary force structure, perhaps influenced by the capabilities of the rival JMSDF. This will have been provided with some consolation from the most notable contract of the year, viz. the December 2012 news that DSME had won a US$1.6bn order to construct the first two KSS–III submarines. These will follow the current Type 214 assembly programme for delivery by 2022. In contrast with previous Korean submarine construction, which has been based on license-built German designs, the new boats are of entirely indigenous origin, albeit some key equipment is still being sourced from overseas. Whilst little detailed information has been released, their reported displacement of c. 3,000 tons makes them much larger than South Korea's existing submarines, presumably to assist capacity for extended deployments. It would also seem likely they will incorporate a vertical launch system for submarine-launched cruise missiles and an AIP propulsion plant.

Table 2.2.5: REPUBLIC OF KOREA NAVY: PRINCIPAL UNITS AS AT MID 2013

TYPE	CLASS	NUMBER	TONNAGE	DIMENSIONS	PROPULSION	CREW	DATE
Principal Surface Escorts							
Destroyer – DDG	KDX-III **SEJONGDAEWANG-HAM**	3	10,000 tons	166m x 21m x 6m	COGAG, 30 knots	300	2008
Destroyer – DDG	KDX-II **CHUNGMUGONG YI SUN-SHIN**	6	5,500 tons	150m x 17m x 5m	CODOG, 30 knots	200	2003
Destroyer – DDG	KDX-I **GWANGGAETO-DAEWANG**	3	3,900 tons	135m x 14m x 4m	CODOG, 30 knots	170	1998
Frigate – FFG	FFX **INCHEON**	1	3,000 tons	114m x 14m x 4m	CODOG, 30 knots	140	2013
Frigate – FFG	**ULSAN**	9	2,300 tons	102m x 12m x 4m	CODOG, 35 knots	150	1981
Corvette – FSG	**PO HANG**	21	1,200 tons	88m x 10m x 3m	CODOG, 32 knots	95	1984
Submarines							
Submarine – SSK	KSS-2 **SON WON-IL** (Type 214)	3	1,800 tons	65m x 6m x 6m	AIP, 20+ knots	30	2007
Submarine – SSK	KSS-1 **CHANG BOGO** (Type 209)	9	1,300 tons	56m x 6m x 6m	Diesel-electric, 22 knots	35	1993
Major Amphibious Units							
Amph Assault Ship – LHD	LPX **DOKDO**	1	18,900 tons	200m x 32m x 7m	Diesel, 22 knots	425	2007

In the medium term, the navy would like to see renewed construction of major surface vessels, including a further trio of KDX-III type vessels and a class of as many as nine, smaller Aegis-equipped destroyers, referred to as KDX-IIA. It seems highly unlikely that sufficient funding will be found to meet all these aspirations whilst continuing construction of smaller warships. However, the mooted upgrade of the existing Aegis-equipped ships to provide an ABM capability would seem quite likely given the growing threat posed by North Korea's nuclear weapons programme.

OTHER REGIONAL FLEETS

Burma (Myanmar): Myanmar's growing re-engagement with the international community is shedding more light on the activities of its navy, which is evolving from a coastal and riverine force to one with greater seagoing abilities. China – which remained a key ally during the country's estrangement with the Western Powers – remains a key supplier of external equipment, including two surplus PLAN 'Jianghu II' Type 053H1 frigates delivered during 2012. However, Myanmar also has a significant indigenous shipbuilding capability. Two indigenous missile-armed *Anawratha* class corvettes were built in the first decade of the millennium and these are now being followed by a series of larger *Aung Zeya* class frigates. India, ever keen to counter Chinese influence in its neighbouring seas, is reportedly supplying radars and sonar for the new ships. The two countries also conducted their first ever bilateral naval exercises in the Bay of Bengal during March 2013, reflecting an equal desire on Myanmar's part to increase interaction with local navies. Whilst a dispute with Bangladesh over maritime boundaries was resolved during 2012, there remains concern over the rapid modernisation of Bangladesh's own fleet that closer links with the regional superpower might help to alleviate.

Indonesia: The Indonesian Navy is continuing to make slow but steady progress towards building a modern fleet capable of ensuring the security of its vast territorial waters. Given inevitably limited resources, the broad approach is to combine construction of a small number of 'high-end' units with much larger numbers of cheaper ships, such as fast attack and patrol craft, as well as amphibious and transport shipping. In order to support local economic development – and for reasons of cost –

Years of international sanctions have resulted in the Myanmar Navy developing its own naval construction capability, although China has also been a major supplier. This image shows the recently transferred 'Jianghu II' Type 053H1 frigate *Mahar Bandoola,* the former PLAN *Anshun. (Mrityunjoy Mazumdar)*

The Indonesian Navy is pursuing a policy of supplementing a small force of 'high-end' submarines, light frigates and corvettes with much greater numbers of inexpensive patrol vessels to police the country's extensive territorial waters. This image shows one of the 'high-end' vessels, the 'Sigma' 9113 type corvette *Frans Kaisepo* on exercises with the JMSDF's air defence destroyer *Shimakaze* (DDG-172) in September 2012. *(Royal Australian Navy)*

An artist's impression of the new Damen Schelde 'Sigma' PKR 10514 light frigate. Two vessels are being assembled in Indonesia from components that are largely imported from Europe. A larger development of the earlier quartet of Dutch-built 'Sigma' 9113 *Diponegoro* class corvettes, they feature an enhanced sensor and weapons fit and are similar to the Royal Moroccan Navy's 'Sigma' 10513 type. *(Thales Nederland)*

An image of the domestically-built Indonesian fast attack vessel *Kujang*, the second member of the KCR-40 *Klurit* class, in May 2013. Armed with two Chinese C-705 surface-to-surface missiles and lighter weapons, she has a reasonable anti-surface capability but can be cheaply built. The four planned members of the class are the smallest of three types of fast attack craft currently under construction. *(Guy Toremans)*

there is a strong preference for local construction. At the same time, design expertise and equipment for the more complex vessels is inevitably sourced from overseas.

The core of the 'high-end' surface fleet is currently formed by the four 'Sigma' type *Diponegoro* class corvettes completed by Damen in the Netherlands at the end of the last decade, supplemented by the six, much older former Royal Netherlands Navy *Van Speijk* class frigates. A contract for local assembly of the enlarged Sigma PKR 10514 design was signed in June 2012 and an option has subsequently been exercised for construction of a second vessel. Each ship will be assembled from six separate blocks, at least some of which will be fabricated in Damen's European yards before transfer to PT PAL's yard in Surabaya for integration. The current schedule envisages the first ship being handed over in January 2017, with the second being delivered in the following October. It has also been reported that Indonesia is in negotiations to acquire the three BAE Systems-built *Nakhoda Ragam* class corvettes originally ordered by Brunei but never delivered. A potential sticking point is the Indonesian Navy's desire to replace their Seawolf missile system with alternative surface-to-air missiles.[12]

Underneath the waves, the contract signed with Korea's DSME for three 1,400-ton modified Type 209 submarines appears to be progressing well, with the final design signed off by the Indonesian Navy. Equipment selections include a variant of the Kongsberg MSI-90U combat management system found in the HDW Batch 1 Type 212A submarines, Indra ESM systems and a range of Korean-sourced equipment. Deliveries should occur at two-yearly intervals from around 2015, with the last unit being assembled domestically at newly-expanded facilities at PT PAL.

Extensive local construction of 'low-end' units is headlined by no less than three different types of missile-armed fast attack craft, each assigned to a specific builder. The smallest are the KCR-40 vessels constructed by PT Palindo Marine in Batam, which has delivered three out of an initial order for four to date. Displacing around 250 tons and capable of speeds of up to 30 knots, armament comprises two Chinese C-705 missiles, a 30mm cannon and lighter weapons. Next in size is the KCR-60 class allocated to PT PAL, which displaces around 450 tons and substitutes a 57mm main gun for the KCR-40's

The Royal Malaysian Navy's *Kedah* class offshore patrol corvette *Kelantan* pictured sailing alongside the US Navy destroyer *Milius* (DDG-69) in early 2012. Malaysia is about to embark on construction of a larger and more heavily armed '*Kedah* 2' design based on DCNS's 'Gowind Combat' light frigate. The project is known as the littoral combat ship in Malaysian circles. *(US Navy)*

lighter weapon. Three units have been ordered, with the second laid down in April 2013. Top of the range is an innovative KCR trimaran built by PT Lundin at Banyuwangi in the east of Java, which features a wave-piercing hull form and laminated carbon fibre construction. *Klewang*, the first of a class of four, was successfully launched on 31 August 2012 but was totally destroyed by fire less than a month later. Local yards are also heavily involved in the construction of other vessels, including smaller patrol ships, replenishment tankers and a new class of tank landing ship.

Malaysia: The Royal Malaysian Navy is somewhat smaller than its Indonesian neighbour but comprises a more modern balance of vessels with a greater emphasis on more-capable, war-fighting units. This distinction is likely to increase further as progress is made with the '*Kedah* 2' patrol vessel project, which is widely reported as comprising six light frigates based on DCNS's 'Gowind Combat' design. A number of equipment awards have been announced throughout 2012-13, notably BAE Systems 57mm guns and Thales' SMART-S radar and Captas sonar, although a formal order with builders Boustead has yet to be placed. The six original *Kedah* class, corvette-like, offshore patrol vessels built to a German MEKO design are also likely to be upgraded. This will effectively give Malaysia a reasonably up-to-date and homogenous twelve-strong light frigate force by the early part of the next decade.

Future force requirements could encompass a renewed push to increase the 'high-end' frigate force above the two existing *Lekiu* class units; for which BAE Systems' Type 26 Global Combat Ship is a potential contender. Similarly, an increase in the submarine flotilla beyond the existing pair of 'Scorpènes' is also seen as a relatively high priority. However, support units have not been forgotten and 2013 will see the delivery of two new training vessels first ordered under a c. US$100m contract at the end of 2010 from NGV Tech and built with DSME assistance. Named *Gagah Samudera* and *Teguh Samudera*, the 77m vessels are lightly armed with a 30mm gun but feature a flight deck to support helicopter operations. They could form the basis of a more potent offshore patrol vessel.

New Zealand: A detailed review of recent developments related to the Royal New Zealand Navy can be found in Chapter 2.2A.

The Philippines: The Philippines' defence budget is expanding rapidly from a low base on the back of a resilient economy and increasing fears over China's territorial ambitions. This is encouraging all branches of the armed forces to draw up ambitious expansion plans. Mid-2012 newspaper reports suggested the navy was backing a 'Philippine Fleet Desired Force Mix' strategy calling for a fifteen-year, US$15bn acquisition plan built around six air-defence frigates, twelve anti-submarine corvettes, eighteen offshore patrol vessels and supporting units. Submarines and maritime patrol vessels were also on the 'wish list'.[13] In reality, immediate procurement is likely to be much more limited, with the current focus being on construction of new-build frigates after previous discussions to acquire second hand Italian ships proved abortive. A variant of South Korea's *Incheon* class is amongst the front-runners for a two-ship contract. Acquisition of multi-role strategic sealift vessels similar to Indonesia's *Makassar* class is also a relative priority. Meanwhile *Ramon Alcaraz*, the former US Coast Guard *Hamilton* (WHEC-715) class cutter *Dallas* (WHEC-716), finally sailed to join her sister in

The former US Coast Guard high-endurance cutter *Dallas* (WHEC-716) was transferred to the Philippines in May 2012. After a period of extensive maintenance and crew training she finally departed Charlestown SC on 10 June 2013 for the c. two month voyage to her new home. *(US Coast Guard)*

Philippine Navy service after an extended period of modernisation and training, in June 2013. It has been reported that she may be fitted with Harpoon missiles after arrival, thereby giving the Philippine Navy its first missile-armed ship.

Singapore: The Republic of Singapore Navy has completed modernisation of its submarine flotilla with the formal commissioning of its second upgraded *Archer* (former Swedish A-17 *Västergötland*) class boat, *Swordsman*, on 30 April 2013. The two new submarines will supplement the existing quartet of *Challenger* (A-12 *Sjöormen*) class boats, whilst providing an entirely new level of capability with their Stirling AIP equipment. The Singapore government intend to replace the older submarines with new construction in due course, providing Sweden with increased hopes that collaboration with respect to its new A-26 design will be possible. However, the most immediate requirement is a project to replace the eleven remaining *Fearless* class patrol vessels commissioned between 1986 and 1988 and which fall due for replacement by the end of the decade. On 30 January 2013 local firm ST Engineering announced that it had been rewarded a contract for eight replacement ships for delivery from 2016 onwards. The new ships are expected to be larger than the class they replace and may have similarity to the four 75m 'modified *Fearless*' class vessels ordered by Oman in 2012.

Taiwan: The ongoing saga that has been Taiwan's Republic of China Navy's programme to modernise its submarine flotilla took a new twist in early 2013 with reports that the indigenous design and construction of submarines was planned. The country has a longstanding requirement for eight new boats but has failed to make headway towards achieving this goal given the reluctance of the countries possessing the relevant technology to provoke mainland China. In the absence of a credible submarine force, the main maritime deterrent to a Chinese invasion currently comprises the large fleet of missile-armed 'Kuang Hua 6' fast attack craft, which have steadily replaced the older 'Hai Ou' type, based on Israel's 'Dvora' design. The handover was completed on 1 July 2012 when the remaining twenty 'Hai Ou' class craft were formally decommissioned. The prototype of a larger 'Hsun Hai' catamaran should be delivered during 2014. In the meantime, two refurbished former US Navy *Osprey* class minehunters were commissioned as planned in August 2012, taking the names of *Yung Jin* and *Yung An*. It also seems likely that Taiwan's existing complement of indigenously-built FFG-7 class frigates will be bolstered by transfers of decommissioned former US Navy vessels of the same type over the next few years. Any such transfers would facilitate replacement of the increasingly obsolescent *Chi Yang* (FF-1052 *Knox*) class.

Thailand: With its previous planned re-establishment of a submarine flotilla on the back-burner, the

The Republic of Singapore Navy's modernisation of its submarine flotilla was completed with the commissioning of the second modernised *Archer* class boat *Swordsman* on 30 April 2013. This image shows the submarine on her commissioning day. *(Republic of Singapore Navy)*

An image of the Royal Thai Navy's PF-103 type corvette *Tapi* in late 2010. Completed in the early 1970s, the two ships of this class face increasing obsolescence, with replacement by modern ships such as the *Port of Spain* class *Krabi* a relatively high priority. *(US Navy)*

Royal Thai Navy has turned its attention to renewal of its surface fleet. A c. US$1bn budget for two frigates reportedly brought bids from China, Germany and Spain but was eventually yet another contract won by South Korea's DSME. The successful DW-3000H design is said to based on the KDX-II destroyer and has a displacement of c. 4,000 tons. It features a prominent Thales integrated mast. The two new ships are intended to replace the existing pair of former US Navy *Knox* class frigates, which are scheduled for withdrawal around 2015. The navy is also considering acquisition of a pair of decommissioned US Navy FFG-7 frigates, although it is not known whether these will allow an expansion of the existing surface force or replace other older vessels.

Modernisation of the two existing *Naresuan* class frigates is also continuing, encompassing combat systems upgrades by Saab and installation of the Evolved Standard Sea Sparrow Missile (ESSM). Up to thirty-two of these will be quad packed in the ships' eight-cell Mk41 VLS launcher. However, the fact that Raytheon's announcement of the initial sale encompassed just nine missiles provides some indication of the problems often faced by second-tier fleets in affording the full capability of the systems installed on their ships.

The British-designed but locally built *Port of Spain* class offshore patrol vessel *Krabi* commenced sea trials in the spring of 2013. She is more heavily armed than the other ships of the class, with a 76mm gun, Thales Variant radar and Tacticos combat management system and may be followed by a second unit in due course.

Vietnam: The Vietnam People's Navy's plans to become the latest country in the region to establish a submarine flotilla are making good progress. The first pair of a total of six Russian-built Project 636 'Kilo' class submarines were launched in the second half of 2012, taking the names *Hanoi* and *Ho Chi Minh City*. They should both be delivered by the end of 2013, by which time a third will have been launched. The remaining boats will follow until early 2016. Orders for a second pair of Project 1161.1E 'Gepard' class like frigates have also been confirmed, with fabrication on the initial vessel already underway. Local construction of fast attack craft and patrol vessels also continues. A key priority is expanded surveillance capabilities over territorial waters and the rumoured acquisition of surplus United States P-3 Orion maritime patrol aircraft will provide a further counter to fears over Chinese maritime expansion.

Notes

1. Prime Minister Abe's statement was made following a number of provocations, most seriously the alleged illumination of a Japanese destroyer by a People's Liberation Army Navy's warship's fire-control radar in January 2013. His remarks were widely reported, for example in Rick Wallace's 'Shinzo Abe threat to use force if Chinese land on Senkakus', *The Australian* – 24 April 2013 (Sydney: News Corporation, 2013).

2. Article 9 states that land, sea and air forces, as well as other war potential, will never be maintained but has been interpreted to allow the maintenance of the Japan Self Defence Forces. Further English language commentary on the debate over Article 9's revision was provided by Richard Lloyd Parry's 'Time to make war on peace constitution imposed by the US, Japanese PM says', *The Times* – 18 April 2013 (London: Times Newspapers Ltd, 2013). The Prime Minister was quoted as saying that the current constitution '… was made, in a way, by an occupation army, and we have never made a constitution ourselves. To make a new constitution with our own hands – I believe that such a spirit will carve out a new era.'

3. The nine-dash or nine-dotted line claim is said to date from the late 1940s and is widely regarded as having questionable legitimacy, particularly with respect to the United Nations Convention on the Law of the Sea.

4. This figure is contained in Sam Perlo-Freeman, Elisabeth Sköns, Carina Solmirano and Helén Wilandh's *SIPRI Fact Sheet April 2013: Trends in World Military Expenditure 2012* (Stockholm: Stockholm International Peace Research Institute, 2013).

5. Conducted by British expert John Coles CB, FREng, the final *Study into the Business of Sustaining Australia's Strategic Collins Class Submarine Capability* (Canberra: Commonwealth of Australia, 2012) concluded that improvements to support and sustainment arrangements could restore *Collins* class availability to a level in line with international benchmarks in about three years. It targets two of the class being available 100 per cent of the time, three for 90 per cent of the time and four for 50 per cent of the time. Mr Coles' work was conducted in two stages and a number of his earlier recommendations have already been implemented. Refer to http://www.defence.gov.au/dmo/publications/coles.cfm, for a summary of his findings, which also contains a link to the full report.

6. For further detail on the new base, refer to Joseph S Bermudez Jr. and James Hardy's 'Liaoning makes home at new PLAN North Sea Fleet naval base', *Janes's Defence Weekly* – 13 March 2013 (Coulsdon: IHS Jane's, 2013), p.17.

7. As always, accurate information on the PLAN is difficult to obtain and the table needs to be regarded with more than the usual caution. Much of the information provided in this section is derived from web based sources, with the *China Air and Naval Power* blog at http://china-pla. blogspot. co.uk/ and the *China Defense Blog* at http://china-defense. blogspot.co.uk/ being particularly useful.

8. Please refer to Annual report to Congress: Military and Security Developments Involving the People's Republic of China 2013 (Washington DC: US Department of Defense, 2013). A web based version can be found at http://www. defense.gov/pubs/2013_China_Report_FINAL.pdf.

9. An interesting assessment of the PLAN's focus on building an effective submarine support structure, including the influence of US Navy practice, was provided by Lyle Goldstein and Shannon Knight in Sub Force Rising, *Proceedings* – April 2013 (Annapolis MD: US Naval Institute, 2013).

10. A copy of the annual Japanese defence budget, the *Defense Programs and Budget of Japan: Overview of FY2013 Budget* (Tokyo: Japanese Ministry of Defence, 2013) can be found at http://www.mod.go.jp/e/d_budget/pdf/250516.pdf. There is also a detailed annual white paper entitled the *Defense of Japan*; the latest version is located at http://www.mod.go.jp/e/publ/w_paper/2012.html.

11. This story was reported by Kang Seung-woo under the heading 'Korea to buy 20 anti sub aircraft' in *The Korea Times* – 26 May 2013 (Seoul: Korea Times, 2013).

12. Much useful information on the SE Asian navies can be found on the *Defense Studies* blog at http://defense-studies.blogspot.co.uk/. In addition, Dzirhan Mahadzir recently provided a useful overview of the region in 'Southeast Asian navies: Building capabilities' *Janes's Defence Weekly* – 1 May 2013 (Coulsdon: IHS Jane's, 2013), pp.26-31.

13. Further information on the 'Philippine Fleet Desired Force Mix' was quoted in an article by Jamie Laude entitled 'Philippine Navy needs P500B to upgrade war capability', *The Philippine Star* – 24 May 2013 (Manila:, PhilStar Global Corporation, 2013).

Author:
Ross Gillett

THE ROYAL NEW ZEALAND NAVY

The Best Small Nation Navy

Records of naval activities in New Zealand waters can be traced back to 1642 when the lightly-armed merchant vessels of the Dutch Abel Tasman visited the region. The subsequent visits of the famous explorer Captain James Cook and the eventual colonisation of New Zealand resulted in the deployment of vessels for local defence by the colonial government, supplemented by the more substantial forces of the British Royal Navy's (RN's) Australia Station. The Naval Defence Act of 1913 resulted in the formation of a New Zealand naval force, although this remained a division of the RN until the Royal New Zealand Navy (RNZN) was formally established during the middle of the Second World War on 1 October 1941. The post-war period saw the fleet gradually evolve from a force structure based on traditional cruisers to modern frigates, largely reflecting ongoing RN influences.[1]

The navy's development over the last decade has been heavily influenced by the Defence Policy Framework of 2000. This placed an increased emphasis on surveillance and transportation capabilities, principally in a regional stabilisation context. An important consequence was authorisation of the NZ$500m (c.US$425m) Project Protector, which resulted in the acquisition of six constabulary-orientated patrol ships and a multi-role patrol vessel from Australia's Tenix Defence. These ships form the core of the current RNZN fleet and provide a much-enhanced ability to contribute to regional security in the Pacific region and protect the country's economic zone from various threats, such as fisheries protection and border security. As a result of these acquisitions, therefore, the RNZN has become more adept at fulfilling a broad range of roles that have importance in the neighbouring waters of the South Pacific and Great Southern Ocean, albeit at the expense of the loss of some war-fighting capabilities.

The 2010 Defence White Paper – which attempts to plan for overall defence requirements out to 2035 – effectively builds on the framework established in 2000 whilst reprioritising expenditure towards essential capabilities. This will see ongoing capital investment in upgrading fleet capabilities, albeit at the cost of some reductions in personnel. The number of regular RNZN personnel has fallen below 2,000 as a result of these changes and the availability of some ships was impacted during 2012–13. The white paper is supported by the 2011 Defence Capability Plan – charting how military capabilities will be built out to 2020 – and by annually updated statements of intent. A key medium-term objective is the establishment of a Joint Amphibious Task Force (JATF) capable of projecting a limited combined military force across the South Pacific by 2015.[2]

CURRENT FLEET STRUCTURE

2014 will see the RNZN celebrate its seventy-third birthday as a naval force built around a reorganised group of eleven principal ships of varying shapes, sizes and capabilities. These are allocated between four main force components, viz.:

- The Naval Combat Force, focused on the *Anzac* class frigates *Te Kaha* and *Te Mana*.
- The Naval Patrol Force, comprising the offshore patrol vessels (OPVs) *Otago* and *Wellington*, plus the four inshore patrol vessels (IPVs) *Rotoiti*, *Hawea*, *Pukaki* and *Taupo*.
- The Logistics Support Force, with the fleet tanker *Endeavour* and the multi-role sealift/amphibious support vessel *Canterbury*.
- The Littoral Warfare Support Group, comprising the Operational Diving Team (ODT) embarked aboard the dive support vessel *Manawanui*, the Mine Countermeasures and Maritime Survey teams and two small aluminium jet-boats named *Takapu* and *Tarapunga*.

Principal details of these warships are provided in Table 2.2A.1, whilst more detailed descriptions follow below. All warships operate from the Devonport Naval Base on Auckland's north shore, which encompasses a full spectrum of support, training, administration and hospital facilities.

FRIGATES

The two *Anzac* class frigates are the major units of the current day RNZN. Commissioned in July 1997 (*Te Kaha*) and December 1999 (*Te Mana*), the frigates will serve for around thirty years each, with decommissioning scheduled in 2027 and 2029 respectively.

Designed in Germany as part of the successful MEKO 200 series of frigates, they were constructed in Australia alongside eight sister-ships ordered for

The current Royal New Zealand Navy comprises eleven principal warships of varying sizes and capabilities. This 2011 image shows the multi-role vessel *Canterbury* leading the tanker *Endeavour*, three *Anzac* class frigates – two from Australia and one from New Zealand – and two RNZN inshore patrol vessels into Auckland Harbour. *(Royal New Zealand Navy)*

Table 2.2A.1: ROYAL NEW ZEALAND NAVY COMPOSITION – MID 2013

TYPE	CLASS	NAME	TONNAGE	DIMENSIONS	CREW	PROPULSION	IN SERVICE DATE
Naval Combat Force							
Frigate (FFG)	ANZAC	**TE KAHA** (F77)	3,600 tons	118m x 15m x 4m	175	CODOG, 27 knots, 6,000nm	1997
Frigate (FFG)	ANZAC	**TE MANA** (F111)	3,600 tons	118m x 15m x 4m	175	CODOG, 27 knots, 6,000nm	1999
Armament: 1 x 8-cell Mk41 VLS for Sea Sparrow SAMs, 1 x 127mm gun, 1 x Phalanx CIWS, light weapons, 2 x triple Mk32 torpedo tubes, hangar and flight deck for 1 helicopter.							
Naval Patrol Force							
Offshore Patrol Vessel (OPV)	OTAGO	**OTAGO** (P148)	1,900 tons	85m x 14m x 4m	35[1]	Diesel, 22 knots, 6,000nm	2010
Offshore Patrol Vessel (OPV)	OTAGO	**WELLINGTON** (P55)	1,900 tons	85m x 14m x 4m	35[1]	Diesel, 22 knots, 6,000nm	2010
Armament: 1 x 25mm gun, light weapons, hangar and flight deck for 1 helicopter.							
Inshore Patrol Vessel (IPV)	ROTOITI	**ROTOITI** (P3569)	350 tons	55m x 9m x 3m	20[2]	Diesel, 25 knots, 3,000nm	2009
Inshore Patrol Vessel (IPV)	ROTOITI	**HAWEA** (P3571)	350 tons	55m x 9m x 3m	20[2]	Diesel, 25 knots, 3,000nm	2009
Inshore Patrol Vessel (IPV)	ROTOITI	**PUKAKI** (P3568)	350 tons	55m x 9m x 3m	20[2]	Diesel, 25 knots, 3,000nm	2009
Inshore Patrol Vessel (IPV)	ROTOITI	**TAUPO** (P3570)	350 tons	55m x 9m x 3m	20[2]	Diesel, 25 knots, 3,000nm	2009
Armament: Light weapons.							
Logistics Support Force							
Fleet Replenishment Tanker	ENDEAVOUR	**ENDEAVOUR** (A11)	12,500 tons	138m x 18m x 8m	50	Diesel, 14 knots, 10,000nm	1988
Armament: Light weapons, hangar and flight deck for 1 helicopter.							
Multi-role Vessel (MRV)	CANTERBURY	**CANTERBURY** (L421)	9,000 tons	131m x 23m x 5m	55[3]	Diesel-electric, 19 knots, 9,000nm	2007
Armament: 1 x 25mm gun, light weapons, hangar and flight deck for 2 helicopters (up to 4 helicopters can be embarked), 2 x LCM landing craft.							
Littoral Warfare Support Group							
Diving Support Vessel	MANAWANUI	**MANAWANUI** (A09)	900 tons	43m x 10m x 3m	25	Diesel, 11 knots, 5,000nm	1988 (1979)

Notes:

1 Plus space for 10 flight personnel, 4 from government agencies and 30 spare berths.

2 Plus space for 4 from government agencies and 12 spare berths.

3 Plus space for 10 flight personnel, 4 from government agencies and 7 army personnel. In addition up to 35 trainees and 250 troops can be accommodated for a total of c. 360 personnel.

the Royal Australian Navy (RAN). Prior to their integration into naval service, the RNZN had primarily been a four-frigate navy, built upon the original British Royal Navy Type 12 *Whitby* and *Rothesay* class frigate designs and the subsequent *Leander* class derivatives.

The *Anzac* class frigates are designed and equipped to operate in environments where military threats exist or could develop at short notice and where non-combat ships (such as the offshore patrol vessels and *Canterbury*) cannot go unless protected by a frigate. Since coming into service fifteen to seventeen years ago, the two ships have each steamed c. 500,000 nautical miles and operated the world-over on joint exercises, military diplomacy and operational roles. Their major deployments have included East Timor in 1999, the Solomon Islands during 2000–01 and various periods in the Middle East between 1999 and 2008.

A March 2013 view of the *Anzac* class frigate *Te Mana* in Australian waters. Over the last decade the RNZN has moved from a force structure based on war-fighting capabilities to one capable of undertaking a broader spectrum of missions. However, continued possession of two frigates allows the RNZN to operate where military threats exist. *(Chris Sattler)*

Mid-Life Upgrades: As the New Zealand Defence Force's (NZDF's) most important assets, the two frigates have undergone a number of upgrades to maintain their relevance in an ever-changing naval environment. Most significantly, a Frigate Platform Systems Upgrade (PSU) project approved in 2007 has provided for a mid-life upgrade including (i) stability enhancement and compartment changes (ii) power propulsion improvements (iii) a replacement integrated platform management system and (iv) a heating, ventilation and air-conditioning revisions.

Phase I of the PSU encompassed the first two elements of the project. This included installation of two new MTU 12V1163 TB93 diesel engines in each ship to replace existing life-expired units;

together with stability management enhancement and compartmental modifications, including the partial enclosure of the quarterdeck. Design manager for this work, carried out during scheduled maintenance periods at Devonport Naval Dockyard, was ThyssenKrupp Marine Systems Australia. Both frigates now boast a greater speed from their new, more-powerful diesels, as well as a small increase in range and economy of usage. Phase I has now been completed on both ships.

Phase II of the PSU completes the project. Siemens (NZ) Ltd has been contracted to focus upon both frigates' Integrated Platform Management Systems (IPMS), enhancing the ships' engine monitoring and automation, whilst Noske-

Kaesar NZ Ltd will improve their heating, ventilation and air-conditioning systems. *Te Mana* was to begin this Phase II upgrade early in 2012 but, although she underwent a period in dockyard hands lasting until the second half of the year, the actual upgrade was deferred. *Te Kaha* is therefore expected to be the first frigate to complete the work package around the end of 2013, with *Te Mana* subsequently re-entering maintenance to bring the mid-life upgrades to a conclusion. Meanwhile, she commenced a major deployment to East Asia, including Singapore, Vietnam, Hong Kong, China and Japan, in early 2013.

Weapons Systems Enhancements: PSU upgrades to the two frigates are also being supplemented by enhancements to the ships' weapon systems. The Phalanx 20mm close-in weapons system (CIWS) that forms the frigates' last-ditch defence against hostile aircraft, anti-ship missiles and fast (and small) inshore attack craft have already been modernised under a NZ$25m (c. US$20m) contract that was signed with Raytheon in November 2007. This enhances the Phalanx CIWS to the Block 1B configuration, providing an anti-surface capability against small vessel threats. *Te Mana* became the first frigate to be upgraded in October 2010, with *Te Kaha* completing her acceptance testing in late 2011.

Subsequently, in December 2012, Defence Minister Dr Jonathan Coleman announced that

The Royal Australian Navy's *Anzac* class frigate *Parramatta* seen on exercises with her New Zealand sister *Te Mana* and the FFG-7 type frigate *Melbourne*. New Zealand's two *Anzac* class frigates were built in Australia in the 1990s and are now undergoing a series of mid-life upgrades to permit a further fifteen years of service. *(Royal Australian Navy)*

The Royal New Zealand Navy's *Anzac* class frigates have recently completed upgrades to their Phalanx CIWS to Block 1B configuration as part of a programme of weapons enhancement. This November 2012 view of *Te Mana* provides a good view of the weapon on top of the helicopter hangar. *(Royal Australian Navy)*

tenders would be sought for a much more extensive upgrade of the self-defence and sensor capabilities of *Te Kaha* and *Te Mana*. 'The frigates are a vital part of our Defence Force but the weapons and sensor systems were designed in the late 1980s and require a mid-life upgrade,' Dr Coleman said.

The New Zealand cabinet subsequently approved the detailed business case, with the request for tender issued by the New Zealand Ministry of Defence in early 2013. The project will replace the hardware and software of the combat management systems on the ships, modernise their radars and electro-optic sensors, and replace the self-defence missile systems. This will address issues of obsolescence with the ships' technology, and ensure the vessels remain a credible capability to operate in the South Pacific and wider Asia-Pacific regions. This next tier of work will effectively complete the mid-life upgrade for both frigates, ensuring a further fifteen years of service life.[3]

One additional potential project is a modern torpedo replacement for use aboard the frigates, as well as for the Royal New Zealand Airforce's (RNZAF's) P-3K Orion anti-submarine patrol aircraft and the Kaman Seasprite helicopters operated by *Te Kaha* and *Te Mana* and other ships.

PATROL VESSELS

Whilst the RNZN's two frigates are purpose-built warships, the remainder of the fleet comprises vessels that, largely for reasons of cost, are based largely on commercial rather than on naval standards. The most significant of these are the two OPVs, *Otago* and *Wellington*, and the four IPVs *Rotoiti*, *Hawea*, *Pukaki* and *Taupo*. All of these ships were ordered in 2004 under Project Protector, which was intended to make good perceived deficiencies in New Zealand's constabulary patrol and sealift capabilities.

The Royal Australian Navy's *Anzac* class frigates are having new radar and combat systems installed as part of the Anti-Ship Missile Defence (ASMD) programme. This view of *Perth* shows the change in class profile resulting from the upgrade. It seems likely that New Zealand will order similar equipment for its own planned frigate self-defence upgrades. *(US Navy)*

Offshore Patrol Vessels: *Otago* and *Wellington* were both built in Australia by Tenix Defence (now part of BAE Systems) to a design by STX Canada Marine. They were finally accepted into service during 2010 after considerable delivery delays and significantly exceeded their intended weight. Displacing 1,900 tons each, the OPVs possess a very long endurance – c. 6,000 nautical miles – to patrol the full national Exclusive Economic Zone (EEZ). Each OPV crew consists of approximately thirty-five officers and sailors, although extra accommodation is provided for ten flight crew and specialist staff from other government agencies. As such, there are sufficient berths for seventy-nine personnel.

The OPV design is strengthened for operations in new-ice waters, a capability demonstrated to the full during February and March 2011 when *Wellington* sailed to the Ross Sea in the Antarctica. Sea conditions below 65° Latitude were among the worst ever encountered and proved the design's value. The ability to extend patrols to areas that have not been previously subject to regular oversight is one of the major benefits offered by the new class. At the other end of the spectrum, *Otago* operated in the much warmer South Pacific climate from May to June in the same year

The new OPVs can deploy and sustain an

A view of a Kaman SH-2G helicopter undergoing initial trials on the new offshore patrol vessel *Otago* during the spring of 2012. The trials, involving 161 landings and take-offs, demonstrated the new class's suitability for helicopter operations, vastly increasing their surveillance capabilities. *(Chris Weissenborn Royal New Zealand Navy)*

embarked helicopter and *Otago* undertook initial trials with an SH-2G Seasprite helicopter in April/May 2012. The Seasprite conducted 161 landings and take-offs, performed day and night, in varying wind and sea conditions in the Hauraki Gulf and the Bay of Plenty. The trials proved that the helicopter could conduct an airborne surveillance task from the OPV of up to two and a half hours duration, enabling 4,500 square nautical miles to be covered in a single sortie. During July 2012 *Otago* demonstrated another capability when she undertook a forward basing trial in Nuku'alofa, Tonga. This involved putting the ship into a maintenance period away from Devonport Naval Base, thereby proving the ship's capability to maintain patrols over a long period in the South Pacific. Overall, *Otago* spent 123 days at sea in 2012 and, as well, became the first RNZN ship to conduct fisheries inspections in the Southern Ocean that December. This deployment is set to become a regular (two-month-long) activity within the new Fleet plan.

Operating these very capable OPVs is intended to free up the larger multi-purpose *Anzac* class frigates for tasks further afield and for which their combat capabilities may be better suited. However, *Wellington*'s time at sea in 2012 was only ninety-six days as manpower constraints meant that she was laid up inactive from mid-year along with two of the smaller IPVs. The restricted use of such new vessels resulted in much controversy in the New Zealand media. *Wellington*'s reduced availability period (RAP) ended early in 2013 and she returned to sea shortly afterwards.

The inshore patrol vessel *Hawea* pictured early in 2011. The four inshore patrol vessels all entered service during 2009 and carry two RHIBs with diesel-powered three-stage jet units. Their armament comprises 12.7mm machine guns and small arms. *(Chris Sattler)*

Inshore Patrol Vessels: The second group of commercially-designed naval units are the four 340-ton, 55m long IPVs that now comprise the RNZN's key platforms for carrying out law enforcement, surveillance and homeland security tasks in coastal waters. As for the OPVs, these missions are routinely carried out with personnel from other branches of the government embarked and this is reflected in accommodation arrangements. As such, berths for a core crew of twenty are supplemented by accommodation for four personnel from government agencies, as well as twelve spare bunks.

Hawea, *Pukaki*, *Rotoiti* and *Taupo* were all constructed in Whangarei, New Zealand by Tenix Defence and delivered during 2009. Their designed range of c. 3,000 nautical miles is more than sufficient for their coastal duties and their constabulary mission is reflected in their armament of light machine-guns. The nominal availability level for sea patrols was initially set at 290 days, equating to around a total of 950 days actually at sea for the four-vessel force. However, manpower shortages have also impacted this target and *Hawea* and *Pukaki* were both laid up in RAPs due to a lack of available crews during 2012–13.

LOGISTIC SUPPORT SHIPS

The Royal New Zealand Navy's logistic support component comprises two ships, the veteran tanker *Endeavour* and the much more recently commissioned multi-role vessel, *Canterbury*.

Fleet Replenishment Tanker: The 25-year-old fleet tanker *Endeavour*, the navy's sole replenishment ship, was constructed in South Korea to a commercial design. As part of the building process a helicopter deck was added at the stern, plus rigs and fuel hoses for the underway replenishment of accompanying RNZN or allied warships. During 2008 work was undertaken on *Endeavour* to double-side the ship. Costing about NZ$2m some of the tanks were closed off, effectively giving it a double hull but reducing capacity by twenty-five per cent to 5,500 tons of fuel. Despite this work *Endeavour*'s non-compliance with International Maritime Organisation maritime pollution requirements from 2013 onwards was reflected in the 2010 New Zealand Defence White Paper, which outlined the RNZN's urgent need for a suitable replacement tanker able to undertake extended missions and with a double-hull to meet maritime regulations. The type of the ship the RNZN will acquire was outlined in April 2013 as a multi-purpose support vessel combining both replenishment and some amphibious capabilities. The new logistics ship will probably be a merchant ship design, but modified to the naval role.

Multi-Role Vessel: In June 2007 *Canterbury* became the first of the seven vessels ordered under Project Protector to be commissioned into the RNZN, the others being the patrol vessels already described. Intended to provide sealift and limited amphibious capabilities in non-combat scenarios, the multi-role *Canterbury* was completed with a Class 1C ice-strengthened hull for operations in and around new ice conditions in the sub-Antarctic region. The new 9,000-ton vessel was based on a Dutch roll-on roll-off, passenger-carrying ferry design intended for coastal use. Built by the Dutch Merwede yard under sub-contract to Tenix defence, she completed fitting out at the latter's Australian facilities. *Canterbury* can carry fifty-plus vehicles, 250 troops and more than thirty 20ft containers. For ship-to-shore movements, she also carries two 23m long Landing Craft Medium (LCM) and has the ability to embark and sustain helicopters.

During her initial years in service *Canterbury* was criticised for her reduced level of seaworthiness in higher sea states. At times, excessive pitching caused the propellers to exit the water. The placement of the ship's rigid-hulled inflatable boats (RHIBs) in open alcoves just 3.3m above the waterline was another major problem. Discussions with BAE Systems – the new owners of Tenix Defence – over the ship's warranty issues (and those related to other Project Protector ships) resulted in an agreement signed in January 2010 for the builder to incorporate additional ballast to the ship, repositioning the RHIB alcoves and the redesign/replacement of the LCM bow ramps. This remediation work was performed in stages, with the majority of the work completed by 2013.

Canterbury is a regular visitor to Australia for combined amphibious exercises with the RAN and in her earlier years operated in support of activities in East Timor and conducted relief efforts after the Samoan tsunami in 2009. When the large earth-

The fleet replenishment tanker *Endeavour* provides the Royal New Zealand Navy with the ability to conduct lengthy deployments: this March 2013 view was taken in the course of a voyage that included Singapore, Vietnam, China and Japan. She is a commercial design modified with replenishment equipment and a flight deck and hangar for helicopter operations. *(Chris Sattler)*

Above: A starboard quarter view of the multi-role vessel *Canterbury* in April 2011. Note the open stern door, the helicopter on the flight deck, the empty RHIB alcove and the LCM on davits. Further forward is the starboard side ramp in its raised position. *(Chris Sattler)*

Right: The entry into service of the multi-role vessel *Canterbury* has substantially increased the Royal New Zealand Navy's aviation capabilities. The ship is able to embark a wide range of helicopters: this view shows two Karman SH-2Gs on the flight deck. *(Royal New Zealand Navy)*

Below: The Royal New Zealand Navy's diving support vessel *Manawanui* is currently the sole sea-going ship allocated to its Littoral Warfare Support Force. This February 2011 shows her alongside at Devonport Naval Base near Auckland. *(Chris Sattler)*

quake struck Christchurch on 22 February 2011, *Canterbury* was docked at the nearby port of Lyttelton. To assist in the disaster region she was utilised as a command post in the immediate aftermath of the major quake.

LITTORAL WARFARE SUPPORT SHIPS

The purpose of the Navy's Littoral Warfare Support Force (LWSF) is to ensure access to and the use of harbours, inshore waters and associated coastal zones in New Zealand and wherever the ships and personnel of the NZDF are required to operate. Following the decommissioning of the hydrographic survey vessel *Resolution* from naval service at a formal ceremony in the Devonport Naval Base on 27 April 2012, the diving tender *Manawanui* is the sole seagoing ship allocated to the force. Current plans envisage both *Resolution* and *Manawanui* being replaced with a single littoral warfare support ship within the next five years.

In the interim, the LWSF has taken delivery of two of the RNZNs newest small craft; the aluminium jet-boats *Takapu* and *Tarapunga*. Built by Northland Spars and Rigging and delivered in

The Karman SH-2G Seasprite currently forms the core of the Royal New Zealand Navy's aviation capabilities, with five helicopters in service. They will be replaced by eight upgraded variants under a US$205m deal announced in April 2013. *(Royal Australian Navy)*

A Royal New Zealand Air Force NH90 helicopter pictured during flight testing in 2011. The new helicopters are now starting to arrive in New Zealand and undertook trials with the multi-role vessel *Canterbury* during 2012. *(Eurocopter)*

early 2013, these 9.2m-long craft were specially designed for operation by the LWSF. *Takapu* and *Tarapunga* are officially classified MCM/REA (Mine Counter-Measure / Rapid Environmental Assessment) boats. In service, they provide fast access to harbours and other shore areas to conduct anti-mine work, surveying, diving support, disaster relief and other similar operations.

As part of the contract, the boats were required to be carried aboard *Canterbury* as well as *Otago* and *Wellington*. Each craft has space for a crew of at least six, and feature a cabin with dry working conditions for two crew with notebook computers, a head, basic cooking facilities and fresh water, a winching/davit arrangement to lift objects up to 200kg from a depth of 60m and the ability to tow a 500kg submerged weight. Their endurance is six hours at 24 knots and twelve hours at 6 knots.

HELICOPTERS

The RNZN operates Seasprite helicopters from the two frigates, two offshore patrol vessels and the amphibious support ship *Canterbury*. The current force of five SH-2Gs was delivered from mid-2001 to February 2003. The helicopters are operated by 6 Squadron RNZAF, located at Whenuapai, a short distance from Auckland. This unit is responsible for the maintenance of naval aviation.

On 19 April 2013 the New Zealand Defence Minister Dr Jonathan Coleman announced the Government's approval for the purchase of a replacement Seasprite helicopter fleet. Eight helicopters (plus two spare airframes) would be acquired from Kaman Aerospace for NZ$242m (c. US$205m), including a training simulator, Penguin anti-ship missiles and additional components. Of the total NZ$147m (c. US$120m) was for the actual airframes. The upgraded SH-2G(I) model will be embarked in the same ships as the current helicopters but the available fleet will be increased by sixty per cent.

The new helicopters have been equipped with a modernised sensor, weapons and flight control systems. All were originally acquired by the Australian Defence Force (ADF). However, in 2009 the Australian Government cancelled the contract after questions had been raised about their suitability to meet ADF requirements. A key issue was the ADF need for the aircraft to be flown by a two-person crew and have a computer flight system that could fly the aircraft with 'no hands' on the controls. The NZDF will operate the helicopter with a three-person crew and the 'no-hands' requirement has not been adopted. The first three SH-2G(I)s are planned to arrive in New Zealand in late 2014, with the entire force operating in 2016.

The arrival of the RNZAF's new NH90 helicopters means that plans are also in hand to operate this helicopter from the amphibious ship *Canterbury*. During July 2012 the ship undertook first-of-class flying trials with an NH90. The NH90 trials proved the Defence Force's ability to land, stow and then relaunch the helicopter from *Canterbury*, with up to four of the helicopters capable of being stowed in the ship's hangar. As a result of this first trial, alterations required to the ship's aviation facilities to support NH90 operations were identified and will be performed during the ship's scheduled maintenance programme. *Canterbury* has also undertaken trials with the RNZAF's AW109 light utility helicopters in preparation for future deployments. This overall series of trials can be seen as the first stage of a process intended to fully integrate troop-carrying helicopter and ship operations – an important step towards the New Zealand Defence Force goal of establishing a Joint Amphibious Task Force (JATF) by 2015.[4]

PARTNERSHIPS

The RNZN's closest partner in the twenty-first century is still the RAN. The naval forces of both nations have operated together successfully for almost a century and continue to exercise together and, sometimes, deploy together. Both navies operate the same type of frigates, the *Anzac* class, whilst the ships acquired under Project Protector were supplied by an Australian contractor.

The Australian Minister for Defence and New Zealand Minister of Defence meet regularly each year to discuss their nation's viewpoints on both regional and global security issues and to identify areas of further defence, including naval, cooperation. In 2013, both Ministers considered progress to date with the implementation of the 2011 Review of the Australia New Zealand Defence Relationship, signed in January 2012. One important agreed issue was the increased collaboration between the two navies for sealift and afloat support.[5]

A more recent development has been the RNZN's growing re-engagement with the US Navy, including involvement in the RIMPAC 2012 exercises for the first time in twenty-eight years and the very successful Pacific Partnership deployment.[6] For the latter, a US Navy Commodore was embarked in

the amphibious ship *Canterbury* for this series of humanitarian missions. The United States so-called 'Pivot to the Pacific' is resulting in greater emphasis being placed on building relationships with potential local partners and past disputes over nuclear policy are therefore being downplayed.

New Zealand also retains a long-term connection with South East Asia through the 1971 Five Power Defence Arrangements that also involve the United Kingdom, Australia, Malaysia and Singapore. In addition, the South Pacific and its small sovereign island states remain a key sphere of influence and activity for the New Zealand Government. Indeed,

the 2012 Annual Report of the NZDF stressed the importance of the country's Pacific neighbourhood as the primary area of focus.

FUTURE DEVELOPMENTS

The most significant subject of immediate attention for the RNZN is probably its key role in the development of the new JATF capability, of which *Canterbury* is the most important element. The ship had performed well as a sealift vessel but the RNZN still needs fully to deliver upon the ship's potential in the area of amphibious operations. The work undertaken to rectify initial capability deficiencies is important in this regard, especially that relating to the operation of her two landing craft. The current intention is to provide an operational amphibious capability by 2015 which, although structured for the deployment of combat forces, is more likely to be involved in humanitarian and nation-building missions. However, the full development of the JATF capability will be staged over a number of years, with the long-term vision in the 2010 Defence White Paper charting a course out to 2035.

Meanwhile, from 2015 to 2020, the RNZN is expected to add to its existing capabilities through the acquisitions of a replacement for the support ship *Endeavour* and of the new littoral warfare support platform to perform mine counter-measures, military hydrography and diving operations. The former process commenced in April 2013, when a request for information was issued for a Maritime Projection and Sustainment Capability (MPSC) ship. Intended to be acquired by 2018, the new vessel will carry 8,000 tons of ship fuel, plus a minimum of 1,700 tons of aviation fuel. The latter figure is an impressive increase over the 150 tons currently carried by *Endeavour*. The new ship will also be capable of embarking the recently ordered SH-2G(I) Seasprite helicopters and the new NH-90 helicopters. In the traditional replenishment role she will refuel and sustain military forces both at sea and – from the sea – ashore.

A contract for the still-unnamed ship is expected in early 2015 for delivery to the RNZN in December 2017. To assist the logistic ship *Canterbury* the new vessel will also include a capability for lift-on/lift-off operations of embarked cargo. An upper deck stowage area will provide for vehicles and up to thirty-three, 20ft shipping containers, with below deck space for about 260 lane metres for additional vehicles. Two 65-ton landing

A French helicopter lands on the multi-role vessel *Canterbury* during an amphibious exercise also involving forces from Australia and some of the Pacific islands. The development of a basic indigenous capability to conduct amphibious operations is the New Zealand Defence Forces' principal short-term aim. *(Royal Australian Navy)*

The Royal New Zealand Navy offshore patrol vessel *Wellington* and the Royal Australian Navy minehunter *Gascoyne* alongside at Rabaul in Papua New Guinea in late 2011 during a Second World War ordnance disposal mission (Operation 'Render Safe'). The RAN remains the RNZN's principal partner in securing regional stability. *(Royal Australian Navy)*

craft (like those attached to *Canterbury*) will also be carried to ferry these loads ashore. To ward off the threat from pirates a small number of 12.7mm machine guns will protect the ship, with space and weight for a Phalanx CIWS included in the overall design. During her long career *Endeavour* has never carried weapons other than 5.56mm Steyr assault rifles and pistols. The navy said it was looking at following global trends to give the new ship the ability to fight off pirates, with measures that could include high-pressure water systems and barbed wire. The ship will therefore be more versatile than *Endeavour* with a limited sealift capacity but still retain its main function as a fleet tanker, helping sustain a task force with food, dry stores and fuel. Having such a capability is essential if the JATF is to operate independently in the Pacific.

New Zealand's new MPSC ship will be crewed by seventy personnel, with additional space for fifty passengers. Her range at 16 knots will be 8,000 nautical miles, rising to a top speed of 18 knots. RNZN authorities have advised that the ship will be designed for a service life of twenty-five years. She will be capable of annual operations in the waters of the Antarctica, as far south as the McMurdo Sounds, between December and March.

Beyond 2020–35 the strategic plan envisages the further strengthening of capabilities across the three services. It is later in this period that the frigates, the inshore and offshore patrol vessels and the amphibious sealift vessel are due to be replaced.

CONCLUSION

The RNZN in 2014 is, without doubt, a very effective small naval force. It employs a proper balance of seagoing and coastal, purpose-built and modified commercially designed vessels, each able to perform their full range of assigned tasks and responsibilities. Planned acquisitions will further enhance its ability to police the country's economic zone and contribute to regional stability across the vast waters of the Pacific and Great Southern oceans. It can claim with some justification to be meeting its vision 'to be the best small-nation navy in the world'.

Notes

1. A good review of the RNZN's post-war development can be found in Robert Gardiner (ed), *Conway's All the World's Fighting Ships 1947-1995* (London: Conway Maritime Press, 1995), whilst R J McDougall, *New Zealand Naval Vessels* (Auckland: GP Books, 1989) is another useful source.

2. The New Zealand Defence Force's website at http://www.defence.govt.nz/ provides links to all key publications mentioned in this chapter, including the *Defence White Paper 2010*, the *Defence Capability Plan 2011* and the annual NZDF Statements of Intent. Additional details of RNZN ship activities can be found at www.navy.mil.nz/visit-the-fleet/

3. Given that the Royal Australian Navy's *Anzac* class frigates are already undergoing a similar upgrade under the Anti-Ship Missile Defence (ASMD) programme, it seems likely that New Zealand might follow a similar path. This would include installation of the Australian-designed and built CEAFAR active phased array radar, associated CEAMOUNT illuminators and an updated combat management system.

4. In addition to embarked aviation forces, the key role of the RNZAF's six Orion P-3K maritime patrol aircraft in ensuring maritime surveillance and security should also be mentioned. Operated by 5 Squadron RNZAF, they are currently completing upgrades to a new 'K2' standard.

5. The availability of *Canterbury* to support potential sealift requirements has been particularly useful for the RAN prior to the introduction of the new amphibious assault ships *Canberra* and *Adelaide*.

6. Relations between the United States and New Zealand militaries had been strained since the mid-1980s, when New Zealand prohibited warships carrying nuclear weapons from visiting its ports. This resulted in the suspension of the ANZUS alliance and a ban on New Zealand warships visiting US bases. There has been a growing rapprochement in recent years, which has accelerated following the US–New Zealand Wellington and Washington declarations of 2010 and 2012. The US ban on New Zealand warship visits was lifted in September 2012.

7. In addition to the references above and various press releases published by the Defence Communications Group of the NZDF, the following sources provide additional reading:

– Gordon Arthur, 'The New Royal New Zealand Navy', *Asia-Pacific Defence Reporter* – August 2010 (Miranda NSW: Ventura Media Asia Pacific Pty Ltd, 2010).
– Gordon Arthur, 'Royal New Zealand Navy – "The Best Small-Nation Navy in the World"?', *Asia-Pacific Defence Reporter* – December 2011 (Miranda NSW: Ventura Media Asia Pacific Pty Ltd, 2011).
– Richard Jackson, Andrew Cutler and David McLoughlin (eds), *Navy Today* (Wellington: NZ, Defence Communications Group) – various issues 2010-13.

2.3 REGIONAL REVIEW

THE INDIAN OCEAN AND AFRICA

Author:
Conrad Waters

INTRODUCTION

The most notable maritime development in the Indian Ocean and Africa over the past year has been the accelerating decline in piracy off Somalia and in the Gulf of Aden. Just seventy-five ships reported attacks in the region during 2012 compared with as many as 237 during the previous year, contributing to a global five-year low in overall international maritime piracy. This trend continued in the first quarter of 2013, when the region recorded just nine reported incidents.[1] There are a number of factors explaining this significant level of progress, most notably proactive naval action against suspected pirate groups, improved security measures on merchant ships themselves and a steadily improving security position in mainland Somalia. However, like a many-headed Hydra, the threat of piracy is moving elsewhere in the region with the Gulf of Guinea, Nigeria and the Ivory Coast all recording an increase in violence. A number of local governments are increasing investment in naval patrol assets to counter the threat whilst the presence of European navies off West African shores is also more apparent. The threat from Islamist insurgents in countries such as land-locked Mali is a complicating factor. The United States is reportedly establishing bases for MQ-1 Predator and MQ-9 Reaper drones in the region and, as in the Indian Ocean, these could be used to undertake a maritime surveillance role.[2]

An interesting question is whether the tail-off in piracy will result in a reduced international naval presence in the Indian Ocean. Certainly, it seems unlikely that China will relinquish its naval footprint in waters that represent a key sea line of communication to resources in Africa and the Middle East that are seen as increasingly important for the country's commercial interests.[3] Similarly, from a Western perspective, the continued tensions arising from Iran's nuclear weapons programme and the associated threat to shipping passing through Strait of Hormuz will continue to command a significant regional naval presence. The first half of 2013 saw a number of exercises intended to test the ability of United States and allied forces to ensure freedom of transit in the Persian Gulf. Amongst the most prominent was the second International Mine Countermeasures Exercise – IMCMEX 2013 – in May, including the practice convoying of a LNG carrier through the Strait by an Anglo-American task force headed by the destroyers *Dragon* and *William P Lawrence* (DDG-110). Although the election of the moderate politician Hassan Rouhani as Iran's president on 15 June 2013 should help ease regional tensions, the ongoing civil war in Syria and continued Arab-Israeli tensions mean the Middle East is likely to remain in the headlines.

Events in Syria are having a significant impact on Russia's presence in the Middle East. Units of Russia's Black Sea Fleet are becoming an increasingly frequent sight in the Eastern Mediterranean as they shuttle to and from the Russian naval facility at the Syrian port of Tartus, reportedly carrying military supplies for President Assad's beleaguered regime. The deployment is clearly putting pressure on the elderly units that comprise the bulk of Russia's local naval forces. In May 2013, a significant flotilla of reinforcements from as far away as the main Pacific base in Vladivostok arrived via the Suez Canal to bolster the mission. The increased naval presence is also providing an opportunity for wider defence diplomacy. This included the first ever visit of a Russian warship to Israel when the landing ship *Azov* docked at Haifa on 1 May.

Elsewhere along the southern shores of the Mediterranean, something of a regional arms race is underway. *IHS Jane's* reports that defence expenditure in the three main North African markets of Algeria, Egypt and Morocco is likely to grow by around a third in the four years to 2016. It is quite difficult to pin down any one specific reason for this largesse, although border tensions and internal security considerations in the aftermath of the Arab spring are obviously playing a part. In any event, all three countries' fleets are undergoing a major recapitalisation focused on new surface warships. The most recent development has been Egypt's reported order for a pair of new Type 209 submarines from HDW, apparently causing tensions with Israel whose *Dolphin* class have been constructed by the same Kiel yard. Whether the plan will survive the return of unrest in Egypt remains to be seen.

Table 2.3.1 provides an overview of the most significant regional navies as of mid-2013.

In spite of the disruption caused by the 'Arab Spring', something of a regional naval arms race is underway along the southern shores of the Mediterranean. This image shows the new Egyptian fast attack craft *S Ezzat*, the first of four 'Ambassador III' fast attack craft being built with US financial assistance at VT Halter Marine in Pascagoula, Mississippi, on sea trials in November 2012. *(VT Halter Marine)*

Table 2.3.1: FLEET STRENGTHS IN THE INDIAN OCEAN, AFRICA AND THE MIDDLE EAST – LARGER NAVIES (MID 2013)

COUNTRY	ALGERIA	EGYPT	INDIA	IRAN	ISRAEL	PAKISTAN	SAUDI ARABIA	SOUTH AFRICA
Support/Helicopter Carrier (CVS/CVH)	–	–	1	–	–	–	–	–
Attack Submarine (SSN/SSGN)	–	–	1	–	–	–	–	–
Patrol Submarine (SSK/SS)	4	4	14	3	5	5	–	3
Fleet Escort (DDG/FFG)	–	6	23	–	–	11	7	4
Patrol Escort/Corvette (FFG/FSG/FS)	6	4	8	6	3	–	4	–
Missile Armed Attack Craft (PGG/PTG)	12	30	12	24	10	8	9	4
Mine Countermeasures Vessel (MCMV)	–	14	7	–	–	3	7	4
Major Amphibious (LPD)	–	–	1	–	–	–	–	–

Notes:

1 Egyptian fast attack craft numbers approximate.

2 The South African attack craft and mine countermeasures vessels serve in patrol vessel roles.

INDIAN OCEAN NAVIES

Bangladesh: The last year has seen the Bangladesh navy achieve more success in attempting to transform itself into a modern, three-dimensional force but much work remains to be done. Modernisation of the surface fleet has moved forward with an agreement for the transfer of two 1980s vintage 'Jinaghu III' class frigates – reported as *Huangshi* and *Wuhu* - from China, thereby finally allowing withdrawal of the fleet's veteran British Royal Navy Type 41 frigates. The escort force has been further bolstered by the grant of the former US Coast Guard high-endurance cutter *Jarvis* (WHEC-725), which was officially handed over on 23 May 2013. Renamed *Somudro Joy*, she will be the largest of Bangladesh's five front-line surface escorts and the first to be powered by gas turbines.

Meanwhile patrol forces have received further enhancement with the construction of two large missile-armed patrol vessels by China's Wuchang Shipyard. Displacing 650 tons and with a top speed of 28 knots, the two 64m-long vessels are armed with guns and surface-to-surface missiles. A class of five smaller 50m patrol vessels are being built in Bangladesh's Khulna Shipyard with Chinese technical assistance. The first of these, *Padma*, was commissioned on 24 January 2013 by Bangladesh's Prime Minister, representing the country's first indigenously-built warship. Naval aviation capabilities are also progressing with the delivery of Dornier 228 NG maritime patrol aircraft from RUAG but the establishment of a submarine flotilla to complete the three-dimensional triad is further away. Whilst a number of new and second-hand options have been considered, cooperation with China seems to be the most effective way of achieving this ambitious objective.

India: Although India remains by far the most significant naval power in southern Asia, its ambition to develop a modern, effective fleet continues to be frustrated by delays to the delivery of new warships. Major fleet units are listed in Table 2.3.2. The current long-term 2012–27 Maritime Capabilities Perspective Plan places increased emphasis on fleet capacity rather than absolute numbers, reportedly confirming the requirement for an active carrier task group on both India's coasts and seeking improved surveillance potential across the Indian Ocean.[4] Nevertheless, an overall force level of at least 150–160 ships has long been regarded as an appropriate objective to secure regional maritime interests, representing a fifteen to twenty per cent increase on the current fleet. The use of indigenous yards has been the preferred route to achieve this objective. However, the state-owned companies that dominate the warship construction sector have consistently failed to rise to the challenge. Heavy reliance on Russia for key weapons systems – as well as some specific shipbuilding projects – has also not been a universal success. As such, the fleet has shown little change in overall size and composition over the last decade.

Looking forward, modernisation of facilities at the major state shipyards and the promotion of alliances with the private sector should yield some results. However, these will not become apparent until the next generation of ships are ordered. Consequently, the impact of India's slowing economy on future defence spending is an additional complicating factor. In the meantime, the current position with major warship categories is set out below:

Aircraft Carriers: The expected delivery of the refurbished carrier *Vikramaditya* (the former Russian *Admiral Gorshkov*) in December 2012 was delayed when defects in the fire-resistant insulation of the ship's eight boilers emerged during sea trials, requiring further refurbishment. New trials are expected to start in July 2013 prior to a revised November 2013 handover date. Work on the first indigenous carrier, *Vikrant*, is also progressing slowly, with commissioning now expected no earlier than 2017–18, at least four years later than originally planned. A formal launch ceremony is planned for August 2013.[5] The existing veteran carrier *Viraat* (the former British Royal Navy *Hermes*) has been in dockyard hands from December 2012 onwards for a refit intended to eke a few more years out of her veteran hull. However, lack of operational Sea Harrier jets limits her usefulness.

Major Surface Combatants: With the delivery of the third and final Project 17 *Shivalik* class frigate *Sahyadri* in July 2012, current construction of major surface warships is concentrated on the three Project 15A *Kolkata* class destroyers being built by Mazagon Dock in Mumbai. Fitting out of the lead ship was well advanced by mid-2013 and the Indian Navy – perhaps optimistically – hope to take delivery by year end. This represents a total building time of around ten years. Mazagon Dock is currently midway through a major modernisation programme

The Bangladesh offshore patrol vessel *Sangu* (the former British Royal Navy 'Island' class *Guernsey*) seen on exercises with the US Navy in September 2012. Bangladesh is supplementing purchases of second-hand warships with new-build Chinese and indigenous construction. *(US Navy)*

The new Russian-built Project 1135.6 frigate *Tarkash* stopped off at Portsmouth, UK in November 2012 on her delivery voyage to India. She features a number of differences compared with the first three ships of the class, including a simplified close-in weapons system. *(Conrad Waters)*

Table 2.3.2: INDIAN NAVY: PRINCIPAL UNITS AS AT MID 2013

TYPE	CLASS	NUMBER	TONNAGE	DIMENSIONS	PROPULSION	CREW	DATE
Aircraft Carriers							
Aircraft Carrier (CV)	**VIRAAT** (HERMES)	1	29,000 tons	227m x 27/49m x 9m	Steam, 28 knots	1,350	1959
Principal Surface Escorts							
Destroyer – DDG	Project 15 **DELHI**	3	6,700 tons	163m x 17m x 7m	COGAG, 32 knots	350	1997
Destroyer – DDG	Project 61 ME **RAJPUT** ('Kashin')	5	5,000 tons	147m x 16m x 5m	COGAG, 35 knots	320	1980
Frigate – FFG	Project 17 **SHIVALIK**	3	6,200 tons	143m x 17m x 5m	CODOG, 30 knots	265	2010
Frigate – FFG	Project 1135.6 **TALWAR**	6	4,000 tons	125m x 15m x 5m	COGAG, 30 knots	180	2003
Frigate – FFG	Project 16A **BRAHMAPUTRA**	3	4,000 tons	127m x 15m x 5m	Steam, 30 knots	350	2000
Frigate – FFG	Project 16 **GODAVARI**	3	3,850 tons	127m x 15m x 5m	Steam, 30 knots	315	1983
Corvette – FSG	Project 25A **KORA**	4	1,400 tons	91m x 11m x 5m	Diesel, 25 knots	125	1998
Corvette – FSG	Project 25 **KHUKRI**	4	1,400 tons	91m x 11m x 5m	Diesel, 25 knots	110	1989
Submarines							
Submarine – SSN	Project 971 **CHAKRA** ('Akula II')	1	9,500+ tons	110m x 14m x 10m	Nuclear, 30+ knots	100	2012
Submarine – SSK	Project 877 EKM **SINDHUGHOSH** ('Kilo')	10	3,000 tons	73m x 10m x 7m	Diesel-electric, 17 knots	55	1986
Submarine – SSK	**SHISHUMAR** (Type 209)	4	1,900 tons	64m x 7m x 6m	Diesel-electric, 22 knots	40	1986
Major Amphibious Units							
Landing Platform Dock – LPD	**JALASHWA** (AUSTIN)	1	17,000 tons	173m x 26/30m x 7m	Steam, 21 knots	405	1971

Delays to the construction of new submarines are a cause of concern for the Indian Navy and are leaving it increasingly reliant on the modernisation of existing types. *Sindhurakshak* – seen here in February 2013 – is the latest 'Kilo' class submarine to return from refit and upgrade in Russia. *(Conrad Waters)*

encompassing modular workshops, wet basins, additional stores and installation of a Goliath crane intended to make construction of the next generation of warships, the Project 15B destroyers (four units) and Project 17A frigates (seven units), more efficient. Construction of the latter will be shared with Kolkata's Garden Reach Shipbuilders & Engineers, which has also been modernised. It is currently completing a quartet of Project 28A *Kamorta* class anti-submarine corvettes. *Kiltan*, the third of the class, was launched on 26 March 2013, and trials of the first should commence in the second half of the year.

The slow headway made with indigenous construction has resulted in reliance on Russian yards to maintain fleet numbers, most notably through the orders for two batches of Project 1136.6 *Talwar* class stealth frigates. *Tarkash*, the second member of the second batch and fifth of the overall class, was delivered in November 2012 followed by final ship, *Trikand*, on 29 June 2013. Her arrival allowed withdrawal of the final *Nilgiri* (*Leander*) class frigate, *Taragiri*, two days earlier.

Submarines: Whilst progress with developing India's surface fleet has been frustratingly slow, the situation below the waves is likely to be giving the Indian naval command even more cause for concern. The construction of six Project 75 'Scorpène' class submarines at Mazagon Dock continues to be beset by delays. The latest reports suggest a further eighteen-month delay in the delivery of the first boat until around the end of 2016. This compares with a planned date of 2012 when the project was first launched in 2005. With no progress reported in allocating contracts for the follow on Project 75-I class, it seems likely that the current force of patrol submarines will suffer a lengthy depletion from its current level of fourteen boats as the existing 'Kilo' and Type 209 boats fall due for retirement. The former continue to receive sonar and weapons upgrades, including the capability to fire Club-S cruise missiles, with *Sindhurakshak* the latest to complete modernisation in January 2013.

On the plus side, delivery of the Russian-built Project 971 'Akula II' class attack submarine *Chakra* in April 2012 is providing useful experience with nuclear-powered underwater operations in advance of delivery of the country's first strategic missile submarine, *Arihant*. Local press reports indicated that the latter's nuclear reactor was set to go live around June 2013, paving the way for sea trials in the second half of the year. A twelfth, successful trial of the K-15 ballistic missile designed to equip the new boats was completed from a submerged pontoon in January 2013, bringing its initial development phase to a conclusion. Integration with the submarine will be the next step. Construction of a second strategic submarine, *Aridhaman*, is also progressing but reports of a 2012 launch have proved overly optimistic.

Other Warships: India's requirement for front-line

The first Indian P8-I Poseidon maritime patrol aircraft was handed over 'on site' during 2012, with deliveries to India commencing in 2013. Their arrival significantly strengthens India's ability to monitor activity in the Indian Ocean. *(Boeing)*

warships is supplemented by a need for second-line and support units, particularly patrol vessels for security and surveillance roles. January 2013 saw the commissioning of *Saryu*, the first of a class of new 105m offshore patrol vessels built by Goa Shipyard Ltd. Displacing over 2,200 tons she is armed with an Oto Melara 76mm gun and lighter weapons and incorporates a hangar and flight deck for a light helicopter. Endurance is some 6,000 nautical miles. Three other members of the class are being built at Goa, which has also gained an order for similar vessels from the Indian Coast Guard. Five further similarly-sized vessels for the Indian Navy were contracted with the private Pipavav yard in 2010. Other private construction includes a class of innovative catamarans designed for coastal hydrographic survey built by the Alcock Ashdown firm. Commercial yards may also be involved in the construction of further replenishment vessels, for which a request for information was released in April 2013. As many as five 40,000-ton ships are sought, each of which must be able to ship around 25,000 tons of fluid at speeds of up to 20 knots and be capable of embarking and operating a single helicopter.[6]

Operationally, India's main preoccupation is countering China's increased presence in the Indian Ocean, with reports of PLAN submarine activity a particular cause for concern. The arrival of India's first Boeing P-8I maritime patrol aircraft is seen as particularly significant in this context. The navy has again deployed units to the Pacific – including visits to the Philippines and Vietnam – in what many regard as a counter to China's Indian Ocean activities. Equally, it has reportedly shied away from joint manoeuvres with the United States and Japan to avoid unnecessary provocation. In line with the focus on capability rather than absolute numbers, efforts are being made to improve fleet network-centric capabilities, including considerable investment in satellite communications.

Pakistan: The main constituents of the current Pakistan Navy are set out in Table 2.3.3. The most significant development over the last year has been the commissioning of the fourth and final F-22P *Zulfiqar* class frigate *Aslat* on 18 April 2013. Unlike the three previous Chinese-built vessels she was assembled locally by Karachi Shipyard and Engineering Works (KSEW). KSEW has also been responsible for assembling the second Chinese-designed *Azmat* class missile-armed fast attack craft, *Dehshat*, which was launched on 16 August 2012.

Future developments will largely be driven by budgetary considerations that are not altogether promising. Priority in the defence budget will continue to be given to land-based forces focused on border and internal security, whilst transfers of surplus 'Western' equipment are less likely than previously. Given the deterioration in relations with the United States following the death of Osama bin Laden within Pakistan's borders and controversy over civilian casualties arising from American drone attacks on Islamist insurgents in the country, China looks increasingly likely to be the principal source of future naval equipment.[7] Subject to funding being made available, new patrol submarines and frigates are high priorities. The latter would replace the aging *Tariq* (British Royal Navy Type 21) class, which will start to be withdrawn soon. However, links with Turkey, which has also been an important supplier, are also strong. A contract has been signed with Turkey's government-owned electronics company Havelsan to upgrade the sole FFG-7 type frigate *Alamgir* with the GENESIS combat management system installed in Turkey's members of the class. Turkey's STM is also collaborating with KSEW on the construction of a new replenishment tanker.

AFRICAN NAVIES

Naval procurement in Africa has expanded over the past few years on the back of the better funding backdrop provided by an upturn in the commodity cycle, that now appears to be drawing towards a close, and an increasingly pressing need to improve maritime security. There has been significant investment in constabulary assets amongst the minor fleets of both East and West Africa. The equipment obtained has varied widely. At one end of the scale it encompasses elderly second-hand units such as **Ghana's** refitted former German Navy Type 143 *Albatros* class fast attack craft *Naa Gbewaa* (formerly *Albatros*) and *Yaa Asantewaa* (formerly *Bussard*). At the other, it includes the two (plus two options) brand new, 2,000-ton offshore patrol vessels ordered by an undisclosed West African state from India's Pipavav, as well as smaller vessels such as **Cape Verde's** Damen Stan Patrol 5009 *Guardião*. However, only a few navies at the northern and southern extremities of the continent have anything more than a localised offshore patrol capability.

So far as **South Africa** is concerned, the situation is largely positive. The replacement of the navy's fleet of patrol vessels under Project Biro is being accorded a high profile given the priority accorded to dealing with the pirate threat. The refurbishment of the naval base at Salisbury Island in Durban that will be used to support Indian Ocean patrols is progressing, whilst life extensions of three of the 'Warrior' class fast attack craft now used in the offshore patrol role are to be broadened to include a fourth vessel to fill the gap until the new ships arrive. Four 'River' class mine-hunters are also being used for patrols. More negatively, funding for annual 'hours at sea' is scheduled to fall by nearly a third from the current level of 35,000, although this may reflect a desire to return operations to a more sustainable level of activity following the recent upsurge in anti-piracy deployments.

Table 2.3.3: PAKISTAN NAVY: PRINCIPAL UNITS AS AT MID 2013

TYPE	CLASS	NUMBER	TONNAGE	DIMENSIONS	PROPULSION	CREW	DATE
Principal Surface Escorts							
Frigate – FFG	**ZULFIQAR** (F22P)	4	3,000 tons	118m x 13m x 5m	CODAD, 29 knots	185	2009
Frigate – FFG	**ALAMGIR** (FFG-7)	1	4,100 tons	138m x 14m x 5m	COGAG, 30 knots	215	1977
Frigate – FFG	**TARIQ** (Type 21)	6	3,600 tons	117m x 13m x 5m	COGOG, 32 knots	180	1974
Submarines							
Submarine – SSK	**HAMZA** (AGOSTA 90B/AIP)	1	2,100 tons	76m x 7m x 6m	AIP, 20 knots	40	2008
Submarine – SSK	**KHALID** (AGOSTA 90B)	2	1,800 tons	68m x 7m x 6m	Diesel-electric, 20 knots	40	1999
Submarine – SSK	**HASHMAT** (AGOSTA)	2	1,800 tons	68m x 7m x 6m	Diesel-electric, 20 knots	55	1979

The threat posed by piracy in West Africa is growing and many countries are upgrading constabulary patrol forces as a result. These images show the Cape Verde Island Coast Guard's Damen Stan Patrol *Guardião* on exercise with the British Royal Navy frigate *Argyll* in March 2013 and one of a new class of coastal patrol boat built by France's Radico Marine for Nigeria. *(Crown Copyright 2013 / Bruno Huriet)*

In northern Africa, the modernisation of **Morocco's** surface fleet is drawing to a close as new vessels are delivered. The completion of the three-ship programme for Damen Schelde 'Sigma' type frigates was achieved with commissioning of the final ship, the Sigma 9813 *Allal Ben Abdellah* on 8 September 212. She will be joined before the end of the year by the FREMM anti-submarine frigate *Mohammed VI* which commenced sea trials from DCNS' Lorient yard on 17 April 2013 and which was undergoing combat systems trials as of mid-year. **Algeria's** more ambitious recapitalisation programme is somewhat further from delivery, although work is underway at Kiel on the two (plus two options) MEKO A200 frigates ordered from ThyssenKrupp Marine Systems in 2012 and at Fincantieri's Riva Trigoso facility on the improved *San Giorgio* class amphibious transport dock which was started the same year. Reports suggest that she should be launched before the end of 2013 for delivery during 2014. Along the coast, **Egypt** awaits the arrival of the 'Ambassador III' fast attack craft from the United States, the first of which has now commenced sea trials. The reported purchase of two Type 209 submarines from HDW is a significant development which, if implemented, would bring a conclusion to lengthy Egyptian efforts to replace its obsolete flotilla of remaining Project 633 'Romeo' boats. However, the selection of the relatively mature Type 209 design is quite surprising given the potential availability of the more modern Type 214 boat equipped with air-independent propulsion.

MIDDLE EASTERN NAVIES

Developments amongst the Middle Eastern Navies continue to be heavily influenced by **Iran**, which has steadily built a potent asymmetrical maritime capability focused around a triad of midget submarines, fast attack craft and shore based anti-shipping missiles. Operated by both the regular navy and the Islamic Revolutionary Guards, this force structure aims to 'swarm' more sophisticated enemy units by sheer numbers and is having a significant impact on the tactics adopted by US and allied naval forces deployed to safeguard shipping in the region. Further deliveries of new equipment has taken place over the last year, including further 120-ton 'Ghadir' submarines that can do significant damage with their principal armament of two 533mm torpedo tubes. Iran also continues to introduce and modernise more conventional equipment. The 'Kilo'

The South African MEKO A200 'Valour' class frigate *Isandlwana* and the German Type 122 frigate *Lübeck* on exercise off the South African coast in the first half of 2012. The South African Navy has been worked hard to combat the threat of piracy spreading in the Indian Ocean but the latest budget envisages a return to a lower operational tempo. *(German Navy)*

Morocco will have entirely modernised her frontline surface fleet by the end of 2013, with four new frigates and corvettes delivered. This includes the Dutch-built 'Sigma'9813 light frigate *Allal Ben Abdellah*, pictured here during trials in the second half of 2012. *(Thales Nederland)*

The Royal Navy of Oman's first 'Khareef' class corvette *Al Shamikh* departing Portsmouth, UK for sea trials on 15 June 2013. This was to be her last voyage under the Red Ensign; she was delivered to her owners on 26 June 2013 soon after this this final set of builders' trials had been concluded. A series of problems meant that delivery was some three years later than initially envisaged. *(Conrad Waters)*

class submarine *Tareq* and the PF-103 class corvette *Bayandor* have both returned to the fleet after refurbishment, whilst a second indigenously-built 'Moudge' class frigate, *Velayat*, has been delivered at Bandar Anzali on the Caspian Sea. Her arrival takes place against a backdrop of increased tensions in the southern part of this land-locked sea in part arising from neighbouring Azerbaijan's close links with Israel as well as unsettled maritime boundaries in an area rich in natural resources. Iran has threatened to bolster its interests in the region through deployment of midget submarines, whilst Turkmenistan – essentially a bystander to the dispute – has been steadily modernising its own fleet through the acquisition of coastal patrol vessels from Turkey.[8] Meanwhile, Iran has also been active on the oceans, dispatching a fleet on a goodwill visit to China and suggesting the imminence of an Atlantic Ocean deployment, possibly to Cuba.

Back in the Gulf, the defence priorities of those countries feeling threatened by Iran's theocracy seems to be more focused on countering the threat posed by its missiles than on naval investment, possibly reflecting a view that the maritime dimension will be taken care of by the US Navy. As such, recent news has been more focused on deliveries under existing contracts rather than new orders. **The United Arab Emirates** has seen most activity in this regard, with the anti-submarine corvette *Abu Dhabi* and the smaller 55m long 'Falaj-2' stealth patrol vessel, *Ghantut*, both handed over in early January 2013, followed by the second 'Falaj 2', *Salahah*, in April. Work continues on the local assembly of heavily-armed *Baynunah* strike-corvettes at Abu Dhabi Ship Building, which has also been entrusted with construction of Phase II 'Ghannatha' class missile-armed patrol craft. A modification of the original 'Ghannatha' troop carriers, these have been lengthened to accommodate four box launchers for medium-range MBDA Marte Mk 2 surface-to-surface missiles. A total of twelve new vessels is envisaged, of which nine-will be subject to local build. Neighbouring **Oman** has finally seen progress with its Project Khareef programme, with lead ship *Al Shamikh* finally delivered by BAE Systems in Portsmouth on 26 June 2013, around three years later than initially envisaged. Two further ships should also be handed over before year-end, whilst four smaller offshore patrol ships are being built by ST Marine in Singapore. Regional defence giant **Saudi Arabia** also has ambi-

tious fleet upgrade plans but no further tangible progress with these is yet apparent.

The situation is somewhat different in **Israel**, which is making good headway with the expansion of its submarine force to meet the requirements of a much-rumoured 'second strike' strategic deterrent role. The fifth *Dolphin* class submarine, *Rahav*, was handed over at Kiel in April 2013 and will arrive in Israel once weapons integration and final trials are completed. One of the larger, second batch of three boats that are the largest submarines ever built by HDW, she incorporates fuel cell air-independent propulsion and has a larger than normal outfit of torpedo tubes, presumably to facilitate her strategic function. Funding has also been allocated for much-needed surface fleet modernisation, reflecting the current 1980s-1990s vintage of most existing units and the growing importance of the country's offshore gas industry. Up to four heavily-armed vessels of a broadly similar size to the existing 'Saar 5' design are envisaged, with a particular emphasis being placed on surface-to-air missile capabilities given the successful 2006 Hezbollah attack on *Hanit*. Local construction by Israel Shipyards seems likely when a contract is eventually awarded.

Two images of the new 'modified *Fearless*' type offshore patrol vessel being built by Singapore's ST Marine for the Royal Navy of Oman. *(ST Marine)*.

Notes

1. These figures were reported by the International Maritime Bureau, part of the International Chamber of Commerce's Commercial Crime Arm. The general trend was also reported by Chris Johnston in 'Piracy threat migrates to West Africa', *The Times* – 19 June 2013 (London: Times Newspapers Ltd, 2013).

2. The main reason for the United States' interest in drone operations in West Africa is to improve intelligence on Islamist insurgent groups in the Saharan region. However, drones deployed to the Seychelles and Djibouti have proved useful in combatting piracy in the Indian Ocean and could be assigned similar tasking in West Africa as they are released from operations in Afghanistan.

3. China itself seems still to be working out its most appropriate future strategic direction in the region. For example, see Ananth Krishnan's 'China details Indian Ocean strategy and interests', *The Hindu* – 9 June 2013 (Chennai: The Hindu Group, 2013). This describes a 'blue book' policy document prepared by Chinese academics in an attempt to bring clarity to the country's approach to regional engagement.

4. As far as the editor is aware, the Maritime Capabilities Perspective Plan has not been formally published, with

information on its contents being largely revealed by comments from serving navy officers. Some quoted objectives – including a near doubling in manpower from c. 60,000 to c. 100,000 – do not look realistic under any reasonable assumptions.

5. *Vikrant* had already been floated out previously in December 2011 to free her construction dock whilst she awaited the delivery of propulsion machinery and other equipment.

6. An excellent source for ongoing news on Indian naval developments is the Bharat Rakshak Consortium of Indian Military Websites at http://www.bharat-rakshak.com/. The editor also thanks Mr Mrityunjoy Mazumdar for the provision of information for this chapter.

7. A good overview of the range of equipment potentially being sought from China was contained in Usman Ansari's 'Pakistan's Dream Navy?', *Defense News* – 24 April 2013 (Springfield VA: Gannett Government Media Corporation, 2013)

8. The background to tensions in the Caspian Sea was explained by Jeremy Binnie in 'Iran threatens to deploy subs to the Caspian Sea', *Jane's Defence Weekly* – 15 August 2012 (Coulsdon: IHS Jane's, 2013).

2.4 REGIONAL REVIEW

EUROPE AND RUSSIA

Author:
Conrad Waters

INTRODUCTION

The outlook for Europe's fleets has changed little over the past year. The underlying theme remains an ongoing struggle to maintain capabilities and operational availability against a backdrop of continued downward pressure on budgets and new procurement. A good example of the current reality was provided by the new French white paper on Defence and National Security that was published by the new Hollande regime on 29 April 2013.[1] In a similar fashion to the previous British Strategic Defence and Security Review of 2010, this essentially asks the French armed forces to achieve the same objectives as previously with lower manpower and less equipment.

So far as naval forces are concerned, an interesting question raised by the budget squeeze is the extent to which Europe's warship-building industry can be maintained as orders diminish. When the current economic crisis commenced, state spending on shipbuilding was seen by many as a potential lever in the fight against rising unemployment. The accelerated order for the French amphibious assault ship *Dixmude* in April 2009 was typical of this approach. However, the current state of government finances makes this strategy less of an option. With export contracts facing increased competition from a new cohort of Far Eastern yards, prospects for many European shipbuilders look bleak. For example, Spain's Navantia currently has no government construction underway beyond the troubled programme for S-80 submarines at Cartagena. Similarly, the Dutch naval sector faces a five-year gap

in work for the Royal Netherlands Navy once the joint support ship *Karel Doorman* is delivered around 2014–15. The latter situation has resulted in the Netherlands Marine Building Consortium putting pressure on the government to reschedule contracts planned for the 2020 timeframe to allow maintenance of both R&D and workforce skills.[2]

The response of Europe's shipbuilders has been varied, based largely on national circumstances and policies. France and the United Kingdom are possibly the only countries that retain sufficiently large fleets to support a substantial naval construction sector from their own requirements. Accordingly, their overall approach shares similarities. Both have been downsizing facilities to reflect expected reductions in workload – for example, DCNS has focused its Brest operations entirely on fleet maintenance activities whilst BAE Systems has been involved in protracted discussions to close at least one of its three surface yards once the *Queen Elizabeth* carrier programme winds down – and both are placing greater emphasis on long-term, more predictable support business. The two companies are also exploring increased export opportunities to a greater or lesser extent, whilst DCNS also has developed activities in renewable energy and civil nuclear engineering.

Elsewhere, choices seem more severe. Most notably, Denmark experienced the effective termination of its shipbuilding capability with the closure of the Odense Steel Shipyard – largely devoted to merchant construction in any event – on completing work on the last *Iver Huitfeldt* class frigate. An inter-

esting 'halfway house' has been achieved by Germany's ThyssenKrupp, which finished restructuring its ThyssenKrupp Marine Systems shipbuilding business on 1 January 2013. Its new approach essentially leaves it as a 'virtual builder' of surface warships. It will retain design, engineering and procurement capabilities but sub-contract actual construction to other companies. These include previous group-owned facilities in Hamburg and Kiel now divested to third parties, as well as overseas yards signing collaboration agreements. The idea is to avoid the expense of production facilities whilst increasing flexibility to meet customer requirements by facilitating relationships with a wider range of contractors. Interestingly, however, HDW's submarine manufacturing operations in Kiel have been kept 'in house', reflecting the complexity of this activity.

Elsewhere, political changes in Russia involving the dismissal of former defence minister Anatoly Serdyukov have cast doubt on the use of foreign expertise to modernise Russia's shipbuilding industry. In particular, the wisdom of acquiring *Mistral*-type ships from France has been criticised and exercise of options for local construction of two further vessels has been postponed. This seems to be a retrograde step, as the involvement of the St Petersburg Baltic Shipyard in fabrication blocks for the first pair of ships seems to be going well, with the first stern unit floated out on schedule on 26 June 2013. By way of contrast, indigenous programmes still seem to be encountering problems, with a number of further, high-profile delays arising over the last year.

The fifth and final Navantia-built F-100 type frigate *Cristóbal Colón* (*Christopher Columbus*) seen on sea trials before delivery to the Spanish Navy on 23 October 2012. The impact of the sovereign debt crisis on the Spanish defence budget means that Navantia now has little ongoing work for the Spanish government. *(Navantia)*

TABLE 2.4.1: FLEET STRENGTHS IN WESTERN EUROPE – LARGER NAVIES (MID 2013)

COUNTRY	FRANCE	GERMANY	GREECE	ITALY	NETHERLANDS	SPAIN	TURKEY	UK
Aircraft Carrier (CVN)	1	–	–	–	–	–	–	–
Support/Helicopter Carrier (CVS/CVH)	–	–	–	2	–	–	–	1
Strategic Missile Submarine (SSBN)	4	–	–	–	–	–	–	4
Attack Submarine (SSN)	6	–	–	–	–	–	–	7
Patrol Submarine (SSK)	–	4	8	6	4	3	14	–
Fleet Escort (DDG/FFG)	17	13	13	15	6	11	17	19
Patrol Escort/Corvette (FFG/FSG/FS)	15	5	–	5	–	–	7	–
Missile Armed Attack Craft (PGG/PTG)	–	8	16	–	–	–	27	–
Mine Countermeasures Vessel (MCMV)	14	17	4	10	6	6	20	15
Major Amphibious (LHD/LPD/LPH/LSD)	4	–	–	3	2	3	–	6

Notes: **1** German K-130 corvettes now all in commission. **2** Greek mine-countermeasures vessels overstated in previous editions.

MAJOR REGIONAL POWERS – FRANCE

The future outlook for France's *Marine Nationale* has been given greater clarity with publication of the 2013 defence white paper; the first since 2008. This provides a strategic overview of defence priorities within a budgetary framework that envisages broadly unchanged defence spending in cash terms. However, full details of future procurement plans await publication of the *loi de programmation militaire (2014–19)*, which is due in the second half of 2013.

So far as the navy is concerned, the white paper continues to give a high priority to the strategic underwater nuclear deterrent. The planned force of nuclear-powered ballistic missile and attack submarines is scheduled to remain unchanged from the current level, comprising four and six boats respectively. This secures production of the new 'Barracuda' class submarines, the first three of which are currently under construction by DCNS at Cherbourg. The sole aircraft carrier *Charles de Gaulle* will also remain in service but longstanding plans for a second carrier have been officially abandoned. In addition, the decision to limit the country's total fast jet fleet to just 225 aircraft (300 were previously envisaged) could put pressure on the number of naval-variant Rafales operated by the *Aéronavale*.

Plans for the future surface fleet provide less good news, with the force of frontline surface escorts scheduled to be reduced from eighteen to fifteen units. There has been speculation that this will result in a reduction in orders for the new FREMM type multi-mission frigates from eleven to eight ships. However, recent statements by French defence minister Jean-Yves Le Drian indicate that the FREMM programme will retain its current scope, albeit with some slowdown in production. This suggests that some of the *La Fayette* class stealth frigates will be disposed of before FREMM production is completed. The white paper also provided further detail on the force of second-line surface ships, which will eventually comprise six light frigates and as many as fifteen offshore patrol vessels. A new class of *frégates de taille intermédiaire* (FTI) will eventually replace the existing *Floréal* type in the former role, presumably following-on from completion of the FREMM programme at Lorient. The offshore patrol vessels will be provided by the BATISMAR (*bâtiments de surveillance et d'intervention maritime*) programme, which may be built by the recently announced Kership alliance between DCNS and Piriou of Concarneau. The two companies collaborated on the construction of the innovative 'Gowind' type offshore patrol vessel *L'Adroit*, which may provide the prototype for the new class.

The amphibious flotilla also takes a hit with the decision not to acquire a fourth *Mistral* class amphibious assault ship. The three existing members of the class will be retained but the amphibious transport dock *Sirocco* will be decommissioned, possibly joining her sister *Foudre* in Chile. Although not specifically referenced, the pressing need to replace the remaining 'Batral' type light transports serving on colonial stations seems to be accepted and orders for three or four new 'B2M' (*bâtiments multi-missions*) are likely within the next few months. Similarly, whilst little is said about replacement of the remaining *Durance* class replenishment vessels, it seems likely that the 2014–19 programme will authorise their replacement by DCNS' BRAVE (*bâtiment ravitailleur d'escadre*) design.

Operationally, the navy's activities have been somewhat overshadowed by the intervention in land-locked Mali, which has largely been an army and air force affair. However, *Marine Nationale* 'Atlantique 2' aircraft were deployed to neighbouring Senegal in a surveillance role, whilst *Dixmude* was used to transport supplies to the region. Elsewhere, the ongoing programme to re-equip the strategic submarine fleet with the new M51 ballistic missile suffered a rare setback on 5 May 2013 when a test missile fired from the newly-refitted submarine *Le Vigilant* auto-destructed in flight shortly after launch from the Bay of Audierne off the Brittany coast. The cause of the failure, which occurred in the early propulsion phase of the firing, has not yet been announced.

Current fleet composition is set out in Table 2.4.2.

TABLE 2.4.2: FRENCH NAVY: PRINCIPAL UNITS AS AT MID 2013

TYPE	CLASS	NUMBER	TONNAGE	DIMENSIONS	PROPULSION	CREW	DATE
Aircraft Carriers							
Aircraft Carrier – CVN	CHARLES DE GAULLE	1	42,000 tons	262m x 33/64m x 9m	Nuclear, 27 knots	1,950	2001
Principal Surface Escorts							
Frigate – FFG	AQUITAINE (FREMM)	1	6,000 tons	142m x 20m x 5m	CODLOG, 27 knots	110	2012
Frigate – FFG	FORBIN ('Horizon')	2	7,000 tons	153m x 20m x 5m	CODOG, 29+ knots	195	2008
Frigate – FFG	CASSARD (FAA-70)	2	5,000 tons	139m x 15m x 5m	CODAD, 30 knots	250	1988
Frigate – FFG	GEORGES LEYGUES (FASM-70)	7	4,800 tons	139m x 15m x 5m	CODOG, 30 knots	240	1979
Frigate – FFG	LA FAYETTE	5	3,600 tons	125m x 15m x 5m	CODAD, 25 knots	150	1996
Frigate – FSG	FLORÉAL	6	3,000 tons	94m x 14m x 4m	CODAD, 20 knots	90	1992
Frigate – FS[1]	D'ESTIENNE D'ORVES (A-69)	9	1,300 tons	80m x 10m x 3m	Diesel, 24 knots	90	1976
Submarines							
Submarine – SSBN	LE TRIOMPHANT	4	14,400 tons	138m x 13m x 11m	Nuclear, 25 knots	110	1997
Submarine – SSN	RUBIS	6	2,700 tons	74m x 8m x 6m	Nuclear, 25+ knots	70	1983
Major Amphibious Units							
Amph Assault Ship – LHD	MISTRAL	3	21,500 tons	199m x 32m x 6m	Diesel-electric, 19 knots	160	2006
Landing Platform Dock – LPD	FOUDRE	1	12,000 tons	168m x 24m x 5m	Diesel, 20 knots	225	1990

Note: 1 Now officially reclassified as offshore patrol vessels.

The main change year-on-year is the delivery of the first FREMM, *Aquitaine*, on 23 November 2012.[3] Her arrival offset the withdrawal of the final FASM-67 type frigate, *De Grasse*, which was removed from operational service on 7 May 2013. The lead FASM-70 class frigate, *Georges Leygues*, is also scheduled for decommissioning shortly. She will be replaced by the second French FREMM, *Normandie*, which was launched on 18 October 2012.

MAJOR REGIONAL POWERS – ITALY

The principal units comprising Italy's *Marina Militare* as of mid-2013 are set out in Table 2.4.3. As for France, the main development has been the arrival of the navy's first FREMM, in Italy's case the general-purpose *Carlo Bergamini*. Handed over on 29 May 2013, she reflects significant design differences incorporated in the Italian ships. These include installation of the more powerful active phased-array variant of the EMPAR multifunction radar compared with the French ship's Herakles, a smaller initial missile capability through installation of only sixteen Sylver A50 vertical launch cells, a large hangar capable of housing up to two helicopters, an extended stern to facilitate operation of larger helicopters and an ability to accommodate a larger crew. The general purpose variant also ships a larger 127mm gun but lacks some of the specialised equipment installed in the Italian anti-submarine variant. A further five ships of the class are either undergoing trials or in the course of construction, with Fincantieri laying the keel of the sixth vessel, *Luigi Rizzo*, at Riva Trigoso on 5 March 2013. There are also increasing hopes for orders for a further two vessels (compared with an initial plan for a total of ten ships) to help sustain employment in Italian yards.

The ongoing delivery of the new frigates will partly compensate for a significant reduction in overall force levels, including withdrawal of the bulk of the *Maestrale*, *Artiglieri* and *Minerva* classes, as well as additional minehunters, replenishment and training vessels, by 2018. However, in overall terms, just eight new ships and submarines will replace thirty vessels that are being withdrawn from service. The navy is heavily promoting a new class of multi-role surface escort referred to as the *pattugliatore d'altura multimissione* or multi-role oceanic patrol ship to stem the decline. Displacing around 4,000 tons, the new frigate-sized vessels would have a basic armament of a 127mm and 76mm gun as well as a hull-mounted sonar and integrated mast but would

An image of DCNS' BRAVE (*bâtiment ravitailleur d'escadre*) design. The French Navy has a requirement for four ships of this type but confirmation of orders awaits publication of the forthcoming 2014–19 military programme. *(DCNS)*

The first Italian FREMM-type frigate *Carlo Bergamini* was commissioned in May 2013. A further five vessels are under construction and there are hopes that two more may be ordered shortly to maintain work at Fincantieri's shipyards along the Gulf of Genoa. *(OCCAR)*

Table 2.4.3: ITALIAN NAVY: PRINCIPAL UNITS AS AT MID 2013

TYPE	CLASS	NUMBER	TONNAGE	DIMENSIONS	PROPULSION	CREW	DATE
Aircraft Carriers							
Aircraft Carrier – CV	CAVOUR	1	27,100 tons	244m x 30/39m x 9m	COGAG, 29 knots	800	2008
Aircraft Carrier – CVS	GIUSEPPE GARIBALDI[1]	1	13,900 tons	180m x 23/31m x 7m	COGAG, 30 knots	825	1985
Principal Surface Escorts							
Frigate – FFG	CARLO BERGAMINI (FREMM)	1	6,500 tons	144m x 20m x 5m	CODLOG, 27 knots	145	2013
Frigate – FFG	ANDREA DORIA ('Horizon')	2	7,100 tons	153m x 20m x 5m	CODOG, 29+ knots	190	2007
Destroyer – DDG	DE LA PENNE	2	5,400 tons	148m x 16m x 5m	CODOG, 31 knots	375	1993
Frigate – FFG	MAESTRALE	8	3,100 tons	123m x 13m x 4m	CODOG, 30+ knots	225	1982
Frigate – FFG	ARTIGLIERE	2	2,500 tons	114m x 12m x 4m	CODOG, 35 knots	185	1994
Frigate – FS	MINERVA	5	1,300 tons	87m x 11m x 3m	Diesel, 25 knots	120	1987
Submarines							
Submarine – SSK	TODARO (Type 212A)	2	1,800 tons	56m x 7m x 6m	AIP, 20+ knots	30	2006
Submarine – SSK	PELOSI	4	1,700 tons	64m x 7m x 6m	Diesel-electric, 20 knots	50	1988
Major Amphibious Units							
Landing Platform Dock – LPD	SAN GIORGIO	3	8,000 tons	133m x 21m x 5m	Diesel, 20 knots	165	1987

Notes

1 Now operates largely as a LPH.

feature a modular structure allowing them to be adapted for various roles. The intention is to replace six classes of existing vessel ranging from the *De la Penne* air-defence destroyers to various lighter patrol vessels. The new Italian Navy Chief of Staff, Admiral Giuseppe De Giorgi, has been reported as seeking an ultimate total of twelve ships, of which six would be ordered in an initial batch.[4]

The case relating to the two San Marco Regiment marines held in India continues to drag on through the Indian legal system. They were arrested over the deaths of Indian fishermen seemingly mistaken for pirates when they approached the tanker *Enrica Lexie* that the pair were guarding in February 2012. Both have been allowed to return home on occasion but a major Indo-Italian diplomatic crisis was only narrowly averted in March 2013 when the Italian government initially refused to return them after they had been permitted to travel to Italy to participate in the country's general election. The case continues to raise significant questions over the rights and responsibilities of military personnel assigned to guard civilian ships.

MAJOR REGIONAL POWERS – SPAIN

Spain's ongoing financial crisis is having a greater and greater impact on the *Armada Española*, with the last twelve months proving particularly difficult. Previous rumours that the aircraft carrier *Principe de Asturias* would be decommissioned were proved correct and the former fleet flagship was withdrawn from service in February 2013. Several countries have reportedly expressed an interest in acquiring the 25-year-old ship but the need for a refit that was one of the consider-

ations behind her withdrawal would make this an expensive proposition. The navy retains a fixed-wing aviation capability through the amphibious assault ship *Juan Carlos I*, which can operate the navy's fleet of sixteen AV-8B Plus Harrier jets.

Some compensation for *Principe de Asturias'* withdrawal was provided by the commissioning of the fifth and final F-100 class frigate *Cristóbal Colón* on 23 October 2012 and the fourth BAM type offshore patrol vessel *Tornado* on 12 July of the same year. However, the financial situation means that a planned order for a sixth F-100 type frigate has been cancelled. Similarly, previously announced authorisations for further offshore patrol vessels have not materialised into further contracts. In April 2013, the Spanish defence minister Pedro Morenes confirmed that no further warship orders were envisaged for the

Table 2.4.4: SPANISH NAVY: PRINCIPAL UNITS AS AT MID 2013

TYPE	CLASS	NUMBER	TONNAGE	DIMENSIONS	PROPULSION	CREW	DATE
Principal Surface Escorts							
Frigate – FFG	ÁLVARO DE BAZÁN (F-100)	5	6,300 tons	147m x 19m x 5m	CODOG, 28 knots	200	2002
Frigate – FFG	SANTA MARIA (FFG-7)	6	4,100 tons	138m x 14m x 5m	COGAG, 30 knots	225	1986
Submarines							
Submarine – SSK	GALERNA (S-70/AGOSTA)	3	1,800 tons	68m x 7m x 6m	Diesel-electric, 21 knots	60	1983
Major Amphibious Units							
Amph Assault Ship – LHD	JUAN CARLOS I	1	27,100 tons	231m x 32m x 7m	IEP, 21 knots	245	2010
Landing Platform Dock – LPD	GALICIA	2	13,000 tons	160m x 25m x 6m	Diesel, 20 knots	185	1998

present, leaving local builder Navantia dependent on exports for further work. The navy's highest priorities are reported as being resurrection of the second batch of BAMs, as well as construction of new F-110 type frigates to replace the existing FFG-7 class.[5]

The only live domestic construction programme is for the four new S-80, *Isaac Peral* class submarines, which will be equipped with air independent propulsion. The €2.1bn (US$2.7bn) project hit a significant snag in May 2013 when it was announced that a design defect meant the first boat was up to 100 tons overweight, leaving it with insufficient buoyancy to surface safely. The Electric Boat subsidiary of the United States' General Dynamics has been called in to advise on a solution to the problem, which could involve lengthening the class's hull and delay delivery by between one and two years. The life of the existing *Agosta* class submarine *Tramontana* may need to be extended to maintain a credible submarine fleet if funding can be found. Her sister-ship *Mistral* is currently completing a similar life-extension, being returned to the water in April 2013 after an eighteen-month docking.

Table 2.4.4 lists current major fleet units. In spite of the difficult funding situation, the navy remains active internationally. For example, the BAM-type vessels *Rayo* and *Relámpago* have both made anti-piracy deployments to the Indian Ocean to support the European Union's Operation Atalanta, also spending considerable time off West Africa during their deployments. Additionally, the new replenishment tanker *Cantabria* has been operating with the Royal Australian Navy for much of 2013 as part of an agreement aimed at helping Australian sailors familiarise themselves with the new Spanish designed ships that will shortly commence delivery.

MAJOR REGIONAL POWERS – UNITED KINGDOM

A full review of recent developments with regard to the British Royal Navy is provided in Chapter 2.4A, whilst Table 2.4.5 provides an outline of core fleet constituents. In line with the Future Force 2020 structure set out in the 2010 Strategic Defence and Security Review, there has been no change in overall fleet numbers. However, there have been shifts in overall force composition. Most notably, nearly forty years of Type 42 destroyer operations with the fleet came to an end with the decommissioning of *York* and *Edinburgh*. The latter was the last of the class in service when she decommissioned on 6 June 2013.

The Spanish Navy's *Agosta*-type submarine *Mistral* was returned to the water in April 2013 after an eighteen-month docking period. The three remaining Spanish submarines of the type may have to remain in service longer because of problems with the follow-on S-80 programme. *(Navantia)*

The Spanish Navy's new replenishment tanker *Cantabria* has spent much of 2013 operating with the Royal Australian Navy to help train sailors earmarked for the latter fleet's new Spanish-designed vessels. This February 2013 image shows *Cantabria* passing the *Juan Carlos I*-type amphibious assault ship *Canberra*, which is close to completion at BAE Systems' Melbourne yard. *(Royal Australian Navy)*

The last operational Royal Navy Type 42 destroyer *Edinburgh* pictured departing Portsmouth Harbour on 6 May 2013 on the ship's final deployment, a 'flag waving' cruise around the UK. Some equipment had already been removed, most notably the Phalanx close-in weapons systems. She was decommissioned a month later on 6 June 2013 following her return. *(Conrad Waters)*

Australia, Malaysia, New Zealand and Singapore as part of the Five Power Defence Arrangements and attendance at the fleet review in Sydney celebrating the Royal Australian Navy's hundredth anniversary.

The submarine flotilla has seen a similar progression. The second *Astute* class submarine, *Ambush*, commissioned on 1 March 2013, counterbalancing the withdrawal of *Turbulent* in July 2012. However, the new class's entry into service has been far from straightforward and the lead boat has yet to be deployed operationally.

In addition to continued construction of the *Astute* class and preparatory work for the 'Successor' class strategic submarines, the main construction effort is currently focused on the new *Queen Elizabeth* class aircraft carriers. The lead ship has rapidly taken shape over the past year and came close to physical completion with the installation of the aft island structure on 28 June 2013. A major programme of refits also continues, most notably including installation of the prototype Type 997 Artisan radar on the Type 23 frigate *Iron Duke*. The new lightweight 3D system is claimed to be capable of tracking up to 800 targets at a range of 200km. It will increasingly become the principal radar for the bulk of the Royal Navy's surface fleet as production versions are delivered.

MID-SIZED REGIONAL FLEETS

Germany: The *Deutsche Marine* has enjoyed a broadly positive year. The commissioning of the three remaining K-130 *Braunschweig* class corvettes

Their replacements were the final two Type 45 destroyers *Defender* and *Duncan*, which provide an entirely different level of capability. *Defender* was formally commissioned on 21 March 2013, whilst *Duncan* was delivered the following day. The class are now being used extensively in support of operations, with *Dragon* being the third of the class to deploy to the Middle East to protect shipping in the Persian Gulf. Meanwhile *Daring* departed Portsmouth on 27 May 2013 for a global circumnavigation that was due to encompass missile defence tests with the US Navy, exercises with

Table 2.4.5: BRITISH ROYAL NAVY: PRINCIPAL UNITS AS AT MID 2013

TYPE	CLASS	NUMBER	TONNAGE	DIMENSIONS	PROPULSION	CREW	DATE
Aircraft Carriers							
Aircraft Carrier – CVS	**INVINCIBLE**[1]	1	22,000 tons	210m x 31/36m x 8m	COGAG, 30 knots	1,100	1980
Principal Surface Escorts							
Destroyer – DDG	**DARING** (Type 45)	6	7,400 tons	152m x 21m x 5m	IEP, 30 knots	190	2008
Frigate – FFG	**NORFOLK** (Type 23)	13	4,900 tons	133m x 16m x 5m	CODLAG, 30 knots	185	1990
Submarines							
Submarine – SSBN	**VANGUARD**	4	16,000 tons	150m x 13m x 12m	Nuclear, 25+ knots	135	1993
Submarine – SSN	**ASTUTE**	2	7,800 tons	93m x 11m x 10m	Nuclear, 30+ knots	100	2010
Submarine – SSN	**TRAFALGAR**	5	5,200 tons	85m x 10m x 10m	Nuclear, 30+ knots	130	1983
Major Amphibious Units							
Helicopter Carrier – LPH	**OCEAN**	1	22,500 tons	203m x 35m x 7m	Diesel, 18 knots	490	1998
Landing Platform Dock – LPD	**ALBION**	2	18,500 tons	176m x 29m x 7m	IEP, 18 knots	325	2003
Landing Ship Dock – LSD (A)	**LARGS BAY**	3	16,200 tons	176m x 26m x 6m	Diesel-electric, 18 knots	60	2006

Note: 1. Now operates as a LPH

in the early months of 2013 suggests that good progress has been made in resolving the type's technical difficulties and will ease the pressure on the aging fast attack craft currently used in support of the United Nations UNIFIL mission off Lebanon. Their arrival also compensates for the accelerating withdrawal of F-122 *Bremen* class frigates. *Köln* was decommissioned in July 2012 and both *Emden* and *Bremen* are scheduled for withdrawal over the next twelve months, leaving only four of the original class of eight in service.

The main surface construction effort remains the F-125 *Baden-Württemberg* class stabilisation frigates. The two separately-constructed halves of the first ship's hull were joined in Hamburg at the end of 2012 but unsubstantiated rumours in the German press suggest that construction difficulties have been encountered and the formal christening ceremony delayed. The keel of the second vessel, *Nordrhein-Westfalen*, was laid by Lürssen in Bremen on 24 October 2012 and the other two ships should follow at Hamburg at yearly intervals. Meanwhile, the third and final Type 702 *Berlin* class replenishment ship, *Bonn*, has also missed its planned delivery date and will be handed over during the summer of 2013. The delays suggest that ThyssenKrupp Marine Systems' new virtual construction model may still be bedding down. Elsewhere, the domestic Type 212A construction programme is drawing to a close with both Batch 2 boats scheduled for delivery before the end of 2014. A full review of this programme is contained in Chapter 3.4.

The navy suffered its first reported mutiny in 2013, when six sailors were charged over allegations they had seized a petty officer in his cabin, taped him to a table and wrote the phrase 'the retards live here' on his lower leg whilst the fast attack craft *Hermelin* was berthed in Beirut. If convicted, the crew members face up to five years in jail.

Greece: Long-standing national fears over Turkey mean that the Greek armed forces continue to receive a relatively high priority in terms of what limited government funding is available in spite of the country's challenging financial situation. However, there is no doubt that the economic crisis has brought significant dislocation to the military and the Hellenic Navy is no exception. In particular, existing domestic construction appears to be paralysed whilst longstanding plans for new orders have been stalled.

The hulk of the former Royal Navy aircraft carrier *Ark Royal* departed Portsmouth in suitably funereal weather on 20 May 2013 bound for the breakers in Turkey. Her premature withdrawal from service was one of the main consequences of the 2010 Strategic Defence and Security Review. *(Derek Fox)*

The two halves of the lead German F-125 stabilisation frigate *Baden-Württemberg* being manoeuvred into dock for integration in Hamburg during November 2012. Press reports suggest that the programme is facing some delays but launch of the new ship is expected soon. *(Blohm & Voss, ThyssenKrupp Marine Systems)*

Orders for new surface construction appear a particular priority given the un-modernised *Elli/Kortenaer* class frigates are now approaching the end of their service lives. *Bouboulina* was the first of the class to be decommissioned from Greek service on 18 February 2013; she will be used as a source of spare parts to support the rest of the class. The Greek government has reportedly been in discussions with France to lease *La Fayette* or FREMM class frigates to fill the gap; this would tie in with the recent defence white paper's plans to reduce the size of the French surface fleet. Meanwhile efforts are being made to resume stalled existing construction with signature of a draft agreement with Elefsis Shipyards to finish work on the three incomplete *Roussen* class fast attack craft being built to a BAE Systems design. Assembly of Type 214 class submarines by Hellenic Shipyards remains the other main outstanding construction contract but there has been no further news of developments in its regard.

The Netherlands: The Royal Netherlands Navy's main current focus is to bring the new *Holland* class offshore patrol vessels into operational service. Three of the class have now been fitted with the Thales IM-400 integrated mast that incorporates their main sensor suite, with *Friesland* due to complete the process in September 2013. They will be followed by the JSS joint support ship *Karel Doorman*, which will be transported to the

The Royal Netherlands Navy is steadily bringing the new *Holland* class offshore patrol vessels into operational service. They were initially delivered without their pyramidal integrated masts but most ships have now been fitted. This view shows second of class *Zeeland* in June 2013. *(Derek Fox)*

Netherlands in the second half of 2013 once basic structural work has been completed by Damen's Galati yard in Romania.

The next major project is the life extension of the existing four *Walrus* class submarines, which initially entered service in the early 1990s. The modernisation programme is being overseen by the Imtech Marine subsidiary of the Dutch Royal Imtech Group and will be carried out at the naval dockyard at Den Helder between 2013 and 2020. In addition to conservation and mechanical upgrades, improvements encompass a new combat management system, improved sonar, installation of an optronic mast and communications systems enhancements The aim is to keep the class operational until at least 2025, providing time for a decision to be made on a replacement class.

Turkey: The Turkish Navy has steadily developed into one of the leading naval powers in both the Eastern Mediterranean and Black Sea. Considerable emphasis has been placed on building an indigenous naval construction and equipment industry during this period of growth. The submarine flotilla and principal surface escorts still comprise vessels of foreign construction or design but this situation is slowly changing. Most notably, the leading 'Milgem' or 'Ada' class corvette, *Heybeliada*, is now fully operational, undertaking both Black Sea and Mediterranean deployments during the first half of 2013. Second of class *Büyükada* is expected to be delivered by Istanbul Naval Shipyard before the end of the year, whilst the RMK Marine subsidiary of local conglomerate Koç has been selected as the preferred bidder for series production of a further six

The prototype 'Milgem' class corvette *Heybeliada* pictured in August 2012. The most important indigenous Turkish naval programme, a further ship is under construction and contracts for a further six are expected soon. *(Devrim Yaylali)*

Units of the Irish Naval Service on exercise in June 2013, with the *Emer* class offshore patrol vessel *Aísling* seen in the foreground. The two older ships of the class will soon be replaced by new PV90 vessels being built by Babcock Marine in the United Kingdom. *(Irish Naval Service)*

vessels. This suggests the class will be reduced from an initial plan of twelve units, possibly due to increased priority being given to the long-delayed TF-2000 air-defence frigates that will be the next major construction programme. Up to eight of the frigates will be built in conjunction with a foreign builder; they will feature an indigenous multifunction radar being developed by local electronics company Aselsan. Given, however, the long timescale involved in realising the project, it is possible that additional FFG-7 type frigates will be transferred from the US Navy and modernised as an interim measure.

With the construction of new Type 214 submarines at a relatively early stage, other recent warship deliveries have been focused on minor vessels. These have included further examples of the *Tuzla* class coastal anti-submarine vessels that are broadly similar in concept to the British Royal Navy's 'Ford' class of the 1950s, as well as the first pair of four larger *Dost* class search and rescue vessels for the Turkish Coast Guard. Amphibious forces have been bolstered by the delivery of all eight *Ç-151* tank landing craft from the ADIK shipyard, which has now received the go-ahead to commence work on two much larger 5,000-ton tank landing ships. A much larger through-deck amphibious assault ship is also planned for which Navantia has been heavily promoting its proven *Juan Carlos I* design in competition with BMT and Chinese designs. A decision was imminent in mid-2013.[6]

OTHER REGIONAL FLEETS

Black Sea: Developments in the **Ukraine** dominate relatively sparse news flow from the Black Sea over the past year. The country's considerable efforts to return the Project 641 'Foxtrot' class submarine *Zaporizhzhya* appear to have met with success, with her first underwater dive after refit concluded on 18 July 2012. Further refurbishment work was carried out at a Russian dockyard in the first half of 2013, with repair work reported as being complete at the end of June. The Ukrainian media have also referenced the return of other ships to service as the navy attempts to make good two decades of post-Cold War neglect and play a more visible interna-

tional role. As part of this objective, the fleet flagship *Hetman Sagaidachny* is likely to be deployed on anti-piracy activities in the Indian Ocean around the end of the year. This follows a similar deployment by **Romania's** Type 22 frigate *Regele Ferdinand* (the former British Royal Navy *Coventry*) as part of the European Union's Operation Atalanta in late 2012.

Efforts at securing stability in the Black Sea have continued to see periodic activation of the Black Sea Naval Force, usually under Turkish or Russian leadership. Established back in 2001, this brings naval units from Bulgaria, Georgia, Romania, Russia, Turkey and the Ukraine together for regular exercises.

North Sea and Atlantic: The peripheral Eurozone countries bordering the Atlantic have been hard hit by the European financial crisis. However, the **Irish Naval Service's** modernisation plans have survived the country's economic difficulties. Delivery of the first of two new offshore patrol vessels built by Babcock Marine is scheduled for the first half of 2014 with a sister following a year later. They will replace the thirty-five year-old *Emer* and *Aoife* to maintain an eight-strong patrol vessel force. It has been reported that the names of the authors *Samuel Beckett* and *James Joyce* have been assigned to the new ships, the latter drawing criticism from Joyce's grandson on account of his relative's pacifist leanings.

Portugal's **Marinha Portuguesa** has experienced more mixed fortunes. It had committed funds for renewal of its frontline surface and submarine forces before the crunch hit but has found its plans for domestic construction of constabulary patrol vessels and support ships stalled. The reality of the situation was recognised in September 2012 when the Portuguese government revoked outstanding contracts for coastal patrol boats and all but the first two NPO2000 offshore patrol vessels placed with state-owned shipbuilder ENVC. The first NPO2000, *Vianio do Castelo*, has already been delivered, whilst funds have been found to complete work on the second ship, *Figueira da Foz*, by the end of 2013. The project's cancellation means that at least some of Portugal's six remaining corvettes will have to remain in service for a while yet even though

life-extensions of these elderly and labour-intensive ships may not be cost-effective.

Belgium has also contracted for new patrol vessels, placing a €27m (US$35m) order with French builder Socarenam for two 52m, 500-ton ready duty ships. They will be used for exclusive economic zone (EEZ) policing tasks, probably replacing the 1960s-vintage converted tugs *Albatros* and *Valcke*.

Scandinavia and the Baltic: The Scandinavian countries are continuing to make good progress in reconfiguring their navies towards more flexible structures better suited for international operations, whilst still keeping a watchful eye on Russian naval re-armament. The latter factor could well result in a move towards higher levels of defence spending and greater emphasis on territorial defence. The most proficient and best-funded local force is currently the **Royal Norwegian Navy**. This completed modernisation of its surface fleet over the past twelve months with the long-awaited deliveries of the two

final *Skjold* class fast attack craft. *Gnist* was handed over in November 2012 whilst *Skjold* herself followed on 26 April 2013, having been upgraded to the same configuration as the five production vessels. The *Skjold* class and five larger *Fridtjof Nansen* class frigates will be armed with the new Kongsberg NSM Naval Strike Missile. A successful series of 'at sea' test firings of the new missile has been conducted over the past year, concluding with a live firing against the decommissioned frigate *Trondheim* in early June 2013. Images suggest the missile performed entirely as designed, causing significant damage to the target ship. There is also a requirement for a new replenishment vessel to support the surface fleet, with a BMT design built by Korea's DSME currently the preferred option.

Norway's next major naval programme is modernisation of its submarine flotilla, which currently comprises six German-built *Ula* class boats commissioned between 1989 and 1992. The current choice appears to rest between modernisation of the existing class and acquisition of new submarines, for which six firms have responded to a request for information. A final recommendation on the way forward will be made in 2014 to allow the relevant project to commence in 2017. A strong contender is likely to be **Sweden**'s new A-26 class, for which design work is underway but for which planned orders for two units have yet to be placed. Sweden's main current effort remains the five *Visby* class stealth corvettes, which are steadily being upgraded to full operational standards and brought into service.

Elsewhere in the Baltic, **Denmark**'s progress with the introduction of the three new *Iver Huitfeldt* air-defence frigates is subject to detailed assessment in in Chapter 3.2. **Finland** is finally bringing the three new *Katanpää* class minehunters into service; the first arrived from Italy's Intermarine by heavy-lift vessel in July 2012. A new fleet of twelve waterjet-powered high-speed troop transports have also been ordered to help with coastal defence; armed with a remotely controlled turret housing a heavy machine gun or grenade launcher, they are capable of speeds in excess of 40 knots. Meanwhile **Poland**'s naval planning appears to be somewhat in disarray following the 2012 decision to cancel modernisation of the existing two FFG-7 class frigates and terminate the problematic MEKO A-100 'Gawron' corvette programme. However, there has subsequently been something of a change of heart. It now

The Belgian Naval Component is currently modernising its small force of patrol vessels, known locally as ready duty ships. These images show the existing *Stern* – a former Swedish Coast Guard vessel – and a computer-generated image of a new design ordered to replace two older vessels from France's Socarenam. Once delivered, the new ships will mainly operate in Belgium's exclusive economic zone in the North Sea. *(Conrad Waters / Belgian Maritime Component)*

The Royal Norwegian Navy carried out a successful test of its new Kongsberg NSM Naval Strike Missile on 5 June 2013. A single weapon was fired by the recently commissioned *Skjold* class fast attack craft *Gnist* at the decommissioned *Oslo* class frigate *Trondheim*. Reports suggest that the test firing was a success and these images certainly show that the target ship suffered significant damage. The surface-to-surface version of the NSM will be shipped by both the *Skjold* and larger *Iver Huitfeldt* types; whilst an air-launched variant is being developed to equip the Royal Norwegian Air Force's planned F-35A Joint Strike Fighters. *(Peder Torp Mathisen / Norwegian Armed Forces)*

appears that the sole MEKO A-100 hull will be completed as a lower specification offshore patrol vessel under the name *Ślązak* whilst at least one of the frigates will be refurbished to remain in service until the end of the decade. Medium term plans costed at around US$3bn appear to envisage a force structure built around three submarines and three offshore patrol vessels supported by smaller patrol vessels and minehunters by 2026. Discussions over supply of some of the smaller vessels are already underway. However, it is uncertain how far this plan is achievable given the low priority historically accorded to the navy within the overall Polish defence budget.

RUSSIA

The Russian Navy continues to be supported by apparently strong political will to rebuild a powerful fleet after its post-Cold War collapse. Frequent pledges to invest substantial funds constructing a wide range of warships are backed by plans to rebuild the shipbuilding industry and its support sectors under the leadership of the state-controlled United Shipbuilding Corporation. The reality, however, is one of much slower progress in the face of industrial fiefdoms, corruption and political disagreements as to how best to effect modernisation, most notably over the extent to which overseas companies should be used to accelerate the modernisation process. Although it seems that slow improvements are being made, news continues to be dominated by delayed projects, warships and submarines that reportedly fail to meet design specification and ongoing problems maintaining the operational availability of a very elderly fleet. The dismissal of the reformist Anatoly Serdyukov from the defence ministry in November 2012 is a retrograde step in this regard, as it is regarded as strengthening the position of vested industrial interests.[7] Nevertheless, there still seems to be recognition that some foreign involvement in regenerating capacity will be necessary. Successful delivery of the *Mistral* class project may give this impetus.

Table 2.4.6 shows little change in principal fleet constituents from previous years, reflecting the slow pace with which much-needed new equipment is being introduced. Detail on the major construction projects that are currently underway is provided below.

Submarines: Renewal of Russia's strategic underwater deterrent remains the highest priority against a backdrop of steadily shrinking availability of current ballistic missile submarines. Russia has committed to resuming continuous at-sea deterrent patrols after a collapse in activity following the end of Cold War. However, it appears that the remaining elderly force of 'Delta III' and 'Delta IV' strategic submarines is not sufficient to meet this requirement, with only five deterrent patrols concluded in the whole of 2012.[8] The key to any long-term improvement is introduction of the new generation of eight Project 955 and Project 955A 'Borey' class boats and their RSM-56 'Bulava' (NATO: SS-NX-30) ballistic missiles. The latter underwent a somewhat problematic development history but a successful series of

TABLE 2.4.6: RUSSIAN NAVY: SELECTED PRINCIPAL UNITS AS AT MID 2013

TYPE	CLASS	NUMBER[1]	TONNAGE	DIMENSIONS	PROPULSION	CREW	DATE
Aircraft carriers							
Aircraft Carrier – CV	Project 1143.5 **KUZNETSOV**	1	60,000 tons	306m x 35/73m x 10m	Steam, 32 knots	2,600	1991
Principal Surface Escorts							
Battlecruiser – BCGN	Project 1144.2 **KIROV**	1 (1)	25,000 tons	252m x 29m x 9m	CONAS, 32 knots	740	1980
Cruiser – CG	Project 1164 **MOSKVA** ('Slava')	3	12,500 tons	186m x 21m x 8m	COGAG, 32 knots	530	1982
Destroyer – DDG	Project 956/956A **SOVREMENNY**	c.5	8,000 tons	156m x 17m x 6m	Steam, 32 knots	300	1980
Destroyer – DDG	Project 1155.1 **CHABANENKO** ('Udaloy II')	1	9,000 tons	163m x 19m x 6m	COGAG, 29 knots	250	1999
Destroyer – DDG	Project 1155 **UDALOY**	c.8	8,400 tons	163m x 19m x 6m	COGAG, 30 knots	300	1980
Frigate – FFG	Project 1154 **NEUSTRASHIMY**	2	4,400 tons	139m x 16m x 6m	COGAG, 30 knots	210	1993
Frigate – FFG	Project 1135 **BDITELNNY** ('Krivak I/II')	c.4	3,700 tons	123m x 14m x 5m	COGAG, 32 knots	180	1970
Frigate – FFG	Project 2038.0 **STEREGUSHCHY**	3	2,200 tons	105m x 11m x 4m	CODAD, 27 knots[2]	100	2008
Frigate – FFG	Project 1161.1 **TATARSTAN**	2	2,000 tons	102m x 13m x 4m	CODOG, 27 knots	100	2002
Submarines							
Submarine – SSBN	Project 955 **YURY DOLGORUKY** ('Borey')	1	17,000+ tons	170m x 13m x 10m	Nuclear, 25+ knots	110	2010
Submarine – SSBN	Project 941 **DONSKOY** ('Typhoon')	1	33,000 tons	173m x 23m x 12m	Nuclear, 26 knots	150	1981
Submarine – SSBN	Project 677BDRM **VERKHOTURYE** ('Delta IV')	6	18,000 tons	167m x 12m x 9m	Nuclear, 24 knots	130	1985
Submarine – SSBN	Project 677BDR **ZVEZDA** ('Delta III')	3	12,000 tons	160m x 12m x 9m	Nuclear, 24 knots	130	1976
Submarine – SSGN	Project 949A ('Oscar II')	c.5	17,500 tons	154m x 8m x 9m	Nuclear, 30+ knots	100	1986
Submarine – SSN	Project 971 ('Akula I/II')	c.10	9,500 tons	110m x 14m x 10m	Nuclear, 30+ knots	60	1986
Submarine – SSK	Project 677 **ST PETERSBURG** ('Lada')	1	2,700 tons	72m x 7m x 7m	Diesel-electric, 21 knots	40	2010
Submarine – SSK	Project 877/636 ('Kilo')	c.20	3,000 tons	73m x 10m x 7m	Diesel-electric, 20 knots	55	1981

Notes:

1 Table only includes main types and focuses on operational units: bracketed figures are ships being refurbished or in maintained reserve.

2 Some sources state CODOG propulsion.

tests in the second half of 2011 apparently cleared the way for official adoption. However, there has subsequently been a surprising lack of further launches and sea trials of the second Project 955 submarine, *Aleksandr Nevsky*, had yet to include a missile firing as at mid-2013. In the interim, the lead Project 955 boat, *Yury Dolgoruky*, was officially accepted into service in January 2013 whilst trials of the third, *Vladimir Monomakh*, are expected to commence imminently. Looking further ahead, submarine-builder Sevmash formally laid the keel of *Knyaz Vladimir* (formerly *Svyatitel Nikolay*), fourth of the series and the first being built to the revised 955A specification, at a ceremony attended by Russian President Vladimir Putin on 31 July 2012. Recent press reports confirm that the modified design will retain the sixteen missile tubes of the first three boats but will incorporate a number of other, unspecified enhancements.

Construction of conventionally-armed but nuclear-powered attack submarines remains focused on the Project 885 'Yasen' class. The lead boat, *Severodvinsk*, which was originally laid down as long ago as the early 1990s, is expected to join the fleet before the end of 2013 after nearly two years of extensive trials that have included surfaced and submerged firings of cruise missiles. She is being followed on the production line by modified Project 885M variants which will eventually replace the Cold War 'Akula' and 'Oscar' types. The third leg of current submarine procurement – the Project 677 'Lada' diesel-electric type – appears to have survived the project's previous suspension. It was announced in July 2012 that *Sevastopol* and *Kronshtadt* the two currently incomplete boats, would be completed to a modified design. However, renewed construction of at least six upgraded Project 636.3 'Kilo' types is continuing to maintain overall patrol submarine numbers.

Aircraft Carriers & Amphibious Ships: Recent reports suggest that the major mid-life upgrade planned for Russia's sole aircraft carrier, *Admiral Kuznetsov*, has been put on hold. Instead, she will make a return deployment to the Mediterranean in the second half of 2013 to bolster Russia's growing maritime presence in the region. The deferral may be linked to delays completing the refit of India's *Virkamaditya*, which will not now depart the Sevmash yard until late 2013, a year later than planned. Meanwhile good progress is seemingly

The Russian Black Sea Fleet's Project 775 'Ropucha I' large landing craft *Kaliningrad* seen transiting the Bosphorus in February 2013 on return from a deployment to the Mediterranean. Her weather-beaten appearance gives some indication of the pressure placed on Russia's current small fleet of amphibious vessels by frequent shuttles to and from Tartus in Syria, reportedly carrying military supplies for President Bashar al-Assad's beleaguered dictatorship. (*Devrim Yaylali*)

being made with construction of the first *Mistral* class amphibious assault ship, *Vladivostok*, in spite of apparent politically-induced criticism of the design's suitability for operation in the severe weather conditions often faced by Russian ships. Current plans envisage her launch at STX Europe's Saint-Nazaire yard by the end of 2013 prior to arrival in Russia during 2014 for outfitting with additional Russian specified equipment. The keel of her sister-ship, *Sevastopol*, was laid at a ceremony in June 2013. The two ships are urgently needed by Russia's amphibious forces given the decision to decommission the last remaining Project 1174 *Ivan Rogov* large landing ship, *Mitrofan Moskalenko*, which has spent some years in reserve. The smaller landing ships assigned to the Black Sea Fleet are being heavily used on Mediterranean deployments and serviceability is being impacted as a result. At least some should eventually be replaced by the new Project 1171.1 *Ivan Gren* class, the prototype of which is being fitted out by the Yantar yard in Kaliningrad.

Surface Vessels: The Russian Navy's surface warship construction efforts remain dominated by the Project 2235.0 *Gorshkov* frigate and Project 2038.0 *Steregushchy* corvette programmes that are headed by St. Petersburg's Severnaya Verf. The lead ship of the former class is now close to completion and initial sea trials are scheduled for the autumn prior to delivery in 2014. Two other ships are currently

under construction and an order for a fourth is scheduled before the year end as part of plans to have between six and eight in commission by the early years of the next decade. The new ships will be 130m long, displace around 4,500 tons and have a combined diesel and gas power plant for speeds in excess of 30 knots. Principal armament will include two, eight-cell launch modules for surface-to-surface missiles and four, eight-cell launch modules for surface-to-air missiles which may be quad packed in the same fashion as the Evolved Sea Sparrow Missile (ESSM). Meanwhile, Project 2038.0 construction is somewhat further advanced, with, *Boiky*, the third of six ships handed over in mid May 2013. The lead ship, *Steregushchy*, is planned to take part in her first international deployment in the second half of the year when she participates in the annual four-way FRUSUK exercises off the coast of Brittany. Two modified and enlarged Project 20338.5 variants are also under construction but there has been criticism of the design's overall cost-effectiveness and original plans for an ultimate total of up to twenty seem unlikely to be realised.

Delays with the new generation of designs have resulted in adoption of India's modified 'Krivak III', Project 1135.6 *Talwar* class for Russian naval service. Designated Project 1135.6M, at least six of the modernised type are planned with lead ship *Admiral Grigorovich* currently scheduled for launch by Yantar in the summer of 2013. Pending delivery

The Russian Navy Project 1155 *Udaloy* class destroyer *Admiral Panteleyev* is one of a relatively small number of 'blue water' surface escorts the fleet can call on for international operations. With new construction programmes badly delayed, further Soviet era ships may be refurbished to ease the situation. *(US Navy)*

of new ships, operational tasking is dependent on the relatively small numbers of Project 1155 *Udaloy* and Project 956 *Sovremenny* that form the bulk of the current blue-water surface fleet. This continues to spur studies into the refurbishment of laid-up Soviet-era ships, most notably the Project 1144 *Kirov* class nuclear-powered battlecruiser *Admiral Nakhimov.* The ship has been laid up at the Sevmash yard in Severodvinsk for the last fifteen years and a number of announcements have been made of her planned return to service, none of which have yet been realised. The most recent reports suggest a contract has been signed that will see her enter dry dock in 2014 prior to completion of a major modernisation programme by 2018. Given Sevmash's previous track record with *Vikramaditya* hardly inspires confidence, there has to be scepticism as to the extent and timescale to which these plans are achievable.

Notes

1. A French language copy of the *Livre Blanc: Défense et Sécurité Nationale 2013* (Paris, Direction de l'information légale et administrative, 2013) can currently be found at http://www.gouvernement.fr/sites/default/files/fichiers_joints/livre-blanc-sur-la-defense-et-la-securite-nationale_2013.pdf.

2. The future construction gap faced by the Dutch naval sector was highlighted by Menno Steketee and Nick de Larrinaga in 'Dutch naval industry concerned by build flow', *Jane's Defence Weekly* – 17 April 2013 (Coulsdon: IHS Jane's, 2013), p.20.

3. A full review of the Aquitaine variant of the FREMM was contained in the editor's 'France's Aquitaine: First French FREMM heralds a Renaissance for its Surface Fleet', *Seaforth World Naval Review 2013* (Barnsley: Seaforth Publications, 2012).

4. A number of defence journalists have commented on the Italian Navy's plans, including Tom Kington in 'Italian Navy Chief Proposes New Dual-Use Vessel', *Defense Daily* – 20 May 2013 (Springfield VA: Gannett Government Media Corporation, 2013).

5. A good source of information on Spanish naval developments – as well as those in Latin America is the infodefensa.com website, which was the first to report the *Armada Española's* construction priorities.

6. Devrim Yaylali's *Bosphorus Naval News* blog at http://turkishnavy.net/ remains an excellent source of news on Turkish and wider regional naval developments.

7. It is salutary to note that, in addition to the Russian minister of defence, the Russian Navy's commander-in-chief, Admiral Vladimir Vysotsky, and the head of United Shipbuilding Corporation, Andrei Dyachkov, have both been dismissed over the last fifteen months.

8. This information was reported on the Federation of American Scientist's blog by Hans M Kristensen under the title 'Russian SSBN Fleet: Modernizing But Not Sailing Much' on 3 May 2013. A link was available as of mid-2013 at http://blogs.fas.org/security/2013/05/russianssbns/. The report relied on information released by US Naval Intelligence under a Freedom of Information Act Request. It concluded that the five deterrent patrols carried out during 2012 would not have been sufficient to maintain a continuous deterrent given that Russian patrols normally only have a duration of between forty and sixty days, shorter than the US Navy's equivalents.

Author:
Richard Beedall

2.4A Fleet Review

THE ROYAL NAVY Mind the Gaps

The last few years have been extremely difficult for the United Kingdom's Royal Navy. The Strategic Defence and Security Review of 2010 (SDSR 2010) cut the frontline strength of the Royal Navy by approximately twenty per cent, on top of a similar reduction since 2004. Overall, the Royal Navy and its supporting Royal Fleet Auxiliary (RFA) Service are about two-fifths of the size that they were at the end of the Cold War in 1990.

The downsized Royal Navy (RN) is having to meet its continuing world-wide commitments with no fixed-wing aircraft carrier, only four operational nuclear-powered fleet submarines (all well over twenty years old), and a total force of just nineteen frigates and destroyers. In addition, morale has been badly hit by redundancies – both voluntary and compulsory – that had reduced trained strength to just 24,400 officers and ratings (plus 6,900 Royal Marines and c. 2,000 civilians in the RFA) as of 1 April 2013. It is proving to be impossible to reconcile fully the mismatch between the demands still being placed on the Royal Navy, and its reduced means and the capability gaps that have been accepted by the government.

More positively, the RN is in the midst of a major re-equipment programme, with new destroyers, fleet submarines, tankers and helicopters all entering service. Perhaps most critically, good progress is being made with the construction of the two new aircraft carriers of the *Queen Elizabeth* class. Another Strategic Defence and Security Review will be held in 2015 (SDSR 2015) and working parties have already started to gather information, analyse options and prepare briefs. With the ending of the United Kingdom's (UK) military operations in Afghanistan, the RN is hopeful that SDSR 2015 will support an increased emphasis on flexible, sea-based, power projection, expeditionary warfare, and maritime security – money permitting.

The destroyer *Diamond* (D34) off the coast of Scotland during Exercise Joint Warrior in April 2013. The helicopter carrier *Illustrious* from the Response Force Task Group (RFTG) can be seen astern; the assault ship *Bulwark* was also in the vicinity. Amphibious operations were undertaken a few days later; note the early preparations on *Diamond* to provide gunfire supporting using its 4.5in Mk 8 mount. The Royal Navy has shrunk considerably in recent years but a major re-equipment programme involving ships such as the Type 45 destroyers gives hope for the future. *(Crown Copyright 2013)*

The deep cuts made by SDSR 2010 resolved a serious funding gap faced by the Ministry of Defence (MOD) and appeared even to give some headroom. However, this was removed when further cuts in the UK's defence budget were announced in December 2012, reducing the non-capital expenditure element of the 2013/14 budget by c. one per cent or £250m (c. US$375m) and the 2014/15 budget by two per cent or c. £500m (c. US$750m). Another reduction of around £250m p.a. was announced in the March 2013 Budget, leaving the 2014/15 budget at a little under £33bn (c. US$50bn) in cash terms. SDSR 2010 had assumed that the defence budget would start to grow again in real terms from 2015/16, but Treasury officials subsequently stated that they would be seeking further material cuts in non-equipment spending in that year; it still being anticipated that the MOD's equipment budget would continue to grow by one per cent a year in real terms from 2015/16 in order to fund programmes such as the

'Successor' strategic submarines. In the event, the Spending Review announced on 26 June 2013 – which covered just 2015/16 – produced a near flat cash settlement; better than some had expected.[1]

ORGANISATION

At the highest level, the MOD is headquarters for the RN. All major policy issues are referred to the Secretary of State of Defence, currently (mid-2013) Philip Hammond. The most senior military officer in the UK is the Chief of the Defence Staff (CDS), from July 2013 this will be General Sir Nick Houghton. The professional head of the Royal Navy is the First Sea Lord – Admiral Sir George Zambellas since April 2013 – who advises CDS on maritime strategy and policy.

Until April 2012 Commander-in-Chief Fleet (a 4* position, i.e. a full Admiral) was responsible for naval operations, but that has now been downgraded to a 3* post (Vice Admiral) entitled Fleet Commander and Deputy Chief of Naval Staff. The most important seagoing post is Commander UK Task Group (COMUKTG), a 2* rank (Rear Admiral). Before SDSR 2010 he was likely to fly his

Table 2.4A.1: ROYAL NAVY FLEET COMPOSITION – MID 2013

TYPE	CLASS	NUMBER	DATE[1]	NOTES
Carriers				
Helicopter Carrier – CVH	**INVINCIBLE**	1	1982	One ship, *Illustrious* (R06). Last survivor of three ships that first entered service in 1980; converted from a CVS to CVH/LPH role post SDSR 2010. To decommission 2014 when *Ocean* completes refit.
Principal Surface Escorts				
Destroyer – DDG	**DARING** (Type 45)	6	2008–13	*Daring* (D32), *Dauntless* (D33), *Diamond* (D34), *Dragon* (D35), *Defender* (D36), *Duncan* (D37). Last delivered in March 2013 but not commissioned as of mid-year.
Frigate – FFG	**NORFOLK** (Type 23)	13	1991–2002	*Argyll* (F231), *Lancaster* (F229), *Iron Duke* (F234), *Monmouth* (F235), *Montrose* (F236), *Westminster* (F237), *Northumberland* (F238), *Richmond* (F239), *Somerset* (F82), *Sutherland* (F81), *Kent* (F78), *Portland* (F79), *St Albans* (F83). Three additional ships disposed of early to Chile.
Submarines				
Submarine – SSBN	**VANGUARD**	4	1993–9	*Vanguard* (S28), *Victorious* (S29), *Vigilant* (S30), *Vengeance* (S31). To be replaced by 'Successor'.
Submarine – SSN	**ASTUTE**	2	2009 onwards	*Astute* (S119), *Ambush* (S120). Some sources quote pennants as S94 and S95. Five further boats under construction or planned. Not yet operational.
Submarine – SSN	**TRAFALGAR**	5	1985–91	*Tireless* (S88), *Torbay* (S90), *Trenchant* (S91), *Talent* (S92), *Triumph* (S93). Survivors of an original class of seven, will steadily be replaced by the new *Astute* class submarines.
Amphibious Ships				
Helicopter Carrier – LPH	**OCEAN**	1	1998	*Ocean* (L12). Currently in refit before replacing *Illustrious* as operational helicopter carrier.
Landing Platform Dock – LPD	**ALBION**	2	2003–05	*Albion* (L14), *Bulwark* (L15). Only one ship kept operational under SDSR 2010, *Bulwark* is currently fleet flagship, with *Albion* in reserve.
Landing Ship Dock – LSD(A)	**LARGS BAY**	3	2006–07	*Lyme Bay* (L3007), *Mounts Bay* (L3008), *Cardigan Bay* (L3009). *Largs Bay* sold to Australia post SDSR 2010 in 2011. Operated by RFA. Plans to reduce one to reserve not yet implemented.
Minor War Vessels				
Patrol Vessel – OPV	**TYNE** ('River')	3	2003	*Tyne* (P281), *Severn* (P282), *Mersey* (P283). Fishery Protection Squadron.
Patrol Vessel – OPV	**CLYDE** (Modified 'River')	1	2007	*Clyde* (P257). An upgraded 'River' used as Falkland Islands Patrol Vessel.
Patrol Vessel – OPV	**PROTECTOR**	1	2011	*Protector* (A173). Former Norwegian commercial ice breaker built in 2001. Antarctic Patrol Vessel.
Minehunter – MCMV	**SANDOWN**	7	1998-2002	*Penzance* (M106), *Pembroke* (M107), *Grimsby* (M108), *Bangor* (M109), *Ramsey* (M110), *Blyth* (M111), *Shoreham* (M112). Five earlier vessels sold to Estonia, laid up or used for static training.
Minehunter – MCMV	**BRECON** ('Hunt')	8	1980–9	*Ledbury* (M30), *Cattistock* (M31), *Brocklesbury* (M33), *Middleton* (M34), *Chiddingfold* (M37), *Atherstone* (M38), *Hurworth* (M39), *Quorn* (M41). Five other vessels sold or used for static training.

Notes

1 Date refers to the delivery date(s) of ships in the class remaining in service.

2 Other vessels include three survey ships of the *Scott* and *Echo* classes and sixteen inshore patrol vessels of the *Archer* and *Scimitar* classes. The Royal Fleet Auxiliary service also includes 2 x 'Wave' class fleet tankers; 2 x 'Rover' class small fleet tankers; the support tanker *Orangeleaf*; the auxiliary oiler and replenishment vessel *Fort Victoria*; 2 x *Fort Rosalie* class stores vessels; the forward repair ship *Diligence* and the casualty receiving ship *Argus*.

3 Front line Fleet Air Arm units include the Commando Helicopter Force with three squadrons (845, 846 and 848 NAS) of Sea King Mk 4 transport helicopters plus one squadron (847 NAS) of Lynx Mk 9A utility helicopters; three squadrons of Merlin Mk 1 sea control helicopters (814, 820 and 829 NAS); a single Lynx Mk 8 sea-control helicopter squadron (815 NAS); and two Sea King Mk 7 squadrons (854 and 857 NAS) for surveillance and control. These are supported by a number of trials, training and conversion and search and rescue units.

Bulwark (foreground) is pictured in the Mediterranean with the French ship Mistral during Exercise Corsican Lion in October 2012, testing the maritime element of the UK-French Combined Joined Expeditionary Force (CJEF). The RN's Response Force Task Group (RFTG) – its only major standing formation – was the main British component of this exercise. Collaboration between the two navies has increased dramatically since the Lancaster House Treaties of 2010, which provided for defence and security cooperation between France and the United Kingdom. (Crown Copyright 2012)

Royal Navy and allied ships moored at Bahrain in May 2013 prior to commencement of the International Mine Countermeasures Exercise (IMCMEX) 2013. RN ships pictured include the Type 45 destroyer Dragon, the amphibious transport dock Cardigan Bay, the 'Hunt' class minehunters Atherstone and Quorn, as well as one of the Sandown class. In recent years, the Commodore ranked posting of Commander UK Maritime Component in Bahrain has emerged as an important position, controlling all RN assets based East of Suez. (US Navy)

flag on an *Invincible* class aircraft carrier, but now normally uses the amphibious transport dock that is designated as the fleet flagship, currently *Bulwark*. This has rather sidelined the only other 2** seagoing appointment: Commander UK Amphibious Forces (COMUKAMPHIBFOR). In recent years, the 1* post (Commodore) of Commander UK Maritime Component (UKMCC) has emerged as an important position. Based in Bahrain in the Arabian Gulf, he controls all RN assets deployed East of Suez. Whilst not overly numerous, they can still represent a quarter of the RN's entire operational strength.

The fleet is divided between three naval bases; Devonport, Portsmouth and Clyde (commonly known as Faslane), all of which are badly under-utilised. If Scotland votes for independence in a referendum planned for September 2014, the ships and submarines based at Faslane will be moved south to Devonport and Portsmouth. Presumably Faslane would then become the main base of a newly formed Scottish Navy.

Current fleet composition is set out in Table 2.4A.1.

THE RESPONSE FORCE TASK GROUP

The Response Force Task Group (RFTG) is currently the RN's only major standing naval formation. Orientated towards amphibious warfare, it is at five days' notice to deploy anywhere in the world in response to events.

Until the end of 2014, the core of the RFTG will be the assault ship and fleet flagship *Bulwark*, and the helicopter carrier *Illustrious*. At least one Type 23 frigate (known as the Fleet Ready Escort) is always available as an escort. Other UK military assets can be assigned as necessary to provide air defence, ground forces, attack helicopters, additional sea lift, logistics, afloat support, land attack missiles and intelligence, As the RN currently lacks an aircraft carrier to provide air cover, the RFTG has to rely for this on allied aircraft carriers or Royal Air Force (RAF) aircraft operating from land bases. When

deployed, the RFTG is normally commanded by COMUKTG.

In 2016, a Combined Joint Expeditionary Force will be formed by France and the United Kingdom. This will be held at thirty days' notice to deploy to meet short-term international crises. The RFTG and the Royal Marines will provide much of the UK's contribution to this new formation.

OPERATIONS AND DEPOLYMENTS

After the Cold War, the Royal Navy developed a regular pattern of world-wide deployments to meet what were called 'directed tasks'. This approach became stretched as the number of RN frigates and destroyers dropped below thirty-one (in 2004), and effectively collapsed after SDSR 2010. The temporary remedies adopted in 2011 such as over working the remaining ships and crews are not viable long-term, and the RN is now meeting operational requirements with whatever assets are available. This is a very inefficient approach, and in November 2012 the then CDS, General Sir David Richards, made a speech in which he said he was particularly worried about the size of the fleet and suggested that a shortage of ships meant resources were being allotted to the wrong tasks. He highlighted the problem by stating, 'You get to this ridiculous situation where in Operation "Atalanta", off the Somali coast, we have £1bn [Type 45] destroyers trying to sort out pirates in a little dhow with RPGs [rocket-propelled grenades] costing $50, with an outboard motor [costing] $100 … That can't be good. We've got to sort it out.'

As of 2013, enduring RN deployments include:

- A *Vanguard* class submarine on continuous patrol, providing the UK's nuclear deterrence.
- Four mine countermeasures vessels plus a 'Bay' class RFA based at Bahrain, in the Arabian Gulf.
- One to two frigates or destroyers, plus a supporting RFA vessel, in the Arabian Gulf or Indian Ocean.
- One frigate or destroyer in the South Atlantic: Atlantic Patrol Task (South).
- One frigate or RFA in the West Indies for six months a year: Atlantic Patrol Task (North).
- One fleet submarine (SSN), 'East of Suez'.
- *Clyde*, deployed as the Falkland Islands Patrol Vessel.
- *Protector*, deployed to patrol the Antarctic between about September and April every year.
- Three patrol vessels on fishery protection duties in UK waters.
- Ocean survey ships, active around the world.

In addition, a pattern has emerged of the RFTG making a major deployment each year – Exercise Cougar – to the Mediterranean and beyond for exercises with the French and other allied navies.

EQUIPMENT: AIRCRAFT CARRIERS AND CARRIER STRIKE

Since 1998, the Royal Navy has been endeavouring to develop a greatly-enhanced carrier strike capability, defined by the MOD as being 'to provide an expeditionary offensive air capability to contribute to focused intervention, power projection and peace enforcement operations'. This resulted in the announcement in July 2007 of a planned order (confirmed in 2008) for two new 65,000-ton carriers – *Queen Elizabeth* and *Prince of Wales* – at an estimated total cost of £5.9bn (c. US$9bn). Each carrier will be able to operate up to thirty of the Short Take Off and Vertical Landing (STOVL) F-35B variant of the Lockheed Martin Lightning II Joint Strike Fighter (JSF).

The RN's last operational aircraft carrier, the 21,000-ton *Ark Royal*, was unexpectedly decommissioned in December 2010 as a result of SDSR 2010.[2] Subsequent experiences (e.g. Libya in 2011) have demonstrated that this has created a huge capability gap, and the regeneration of some form of RN carrier capability has become a high political and military priority.

Unexpectedly, SDSR 2010 enthusiastically embraced the strike carrier concept and proposed that one of the new carriers should be fitted with catapults and arrestor gear (commonly termed 'cat and trap') in order to enable the operation of more capable conventional carrier aircraft such as the F-35C carrier variant (CV), and permit greater cooperation with US and French carriers and naval jets. The initial estimate for the cost of this conversion was £800m (c. US$1.2bn) for one ship; unfortunately this was based on incomplete information and by early 2012 the estimate had risen to £2bn (c. US$3bn) for *Prince of Wales*, and another £3bn (c. US$4.5bn) if *Queen Elizabeth* was converted as well. To the disappointment of many in the RN it was decided that this was unaffordable and on 10 May 2012 the Defence Secretary, Philip Hammond, reversed the decision, telling Parliament that, 'The most cost effective route to deliver Carrier Strike by 2020 is now to switch [back] to the STOVL variant of the Joint Strike Fighter.' The £74m (c. US$110m) already spent on the redesign has been written off.

Construction and assembly of *Queen Elizabeth* passed the two-thirds mark in early 2013 and she will be launched (actually floated out of a dry dock) during 2014. It is expected that the naming cere-

Mersey , one of the three 'River' class OPVs that comprise the Fishery Protection Squadron, which enforces UK and EU fisheries legislation. In addition, they are now the only warships on permanent patrol around the UK. The three ships were originally leased, but were purchased outright from BAE Systems by the MOD in September 2012 for £39m. *(Crown Copyright 2013)*

An image of *Queen Elizabeth* at sea. The twelve JSF's on her flight deck (plus one on a lift) represents the maximum that she is likely to regularly embark. Note the potential risks to deck-parked aircraft of a F-35B landing from astern using the proposed shipborne rolling vertical landing (SRVL) technique. *(Aircraft Carrier Alliance)*

mony will be performed by Her Majesty Queen Elizabeth II, but this probably will not be officially confirmed until shortly beforehand. Final fitting-out of the ship and builders' sea trials will then follow, with her in service date currently scheduled for the fourth quarter of 2017, although it will be the end of 2020 before she will be operational with fixed wing aircraft. Construction of *Prince of Wales* has also started; she is about three years behind her sister and due to enter service in December 2020.

SDSR 2015 will decide whether the RN will operate both of the new carriers or just one – the other being sold or placed in extended reserve (in practice, likely a source of spare parts for the operational carrier). Having both will ensure that a carrier is available 100 per cent of the time rather than sixty per cent of the time at the cost of only a further £25m (c. US$38m) p.a., increasing to £60m (c. US$90m) a year for simultaneous operation – mostly related to additional personnel. The RN is seeking a robust rationale for the retention of both. The old 'carrier strike' justification has lost some credibility; instead the RN is repositioning the ships as the essential core of the RFTG and vital for successful expeditionary and amphibious operations by the UK – termed Carrier Enabled Power Projection. A *Queen Elizabeth* carrier with (for example) a Royal Marine Commando Group embarked and an air group consisting of a dozen F-35B's, Merlin 'Crowsnest' helicopters (see below), a squadron of troop-carrying helicopters, and a flight of British Army Apache gunship helicopters, will represent an impressive and versatile asset. It is possible to think of many scenarios where this type of capability would be useful – from Sierra Leone in 1999 to Syria in 2013. The *Queen Elizabeth* carriers

Queen Elizabeth under construction in a dry dock at Babcock Marine's Rosyth Dockyard on 15 April 2013. Assembly of the hull is nearly complete, and the forward island has been lifted in to place by the giant Chinese-built crane. Note that the forward launch ramp (ski-jump) is not yet fitted; this will be done at the end of 2013. The ship will be floated out of the dock in 2014, and assembly of *Prince of Wales* will then commence in the same dock a few months later. *(Aircraft Carrier Alliance)*

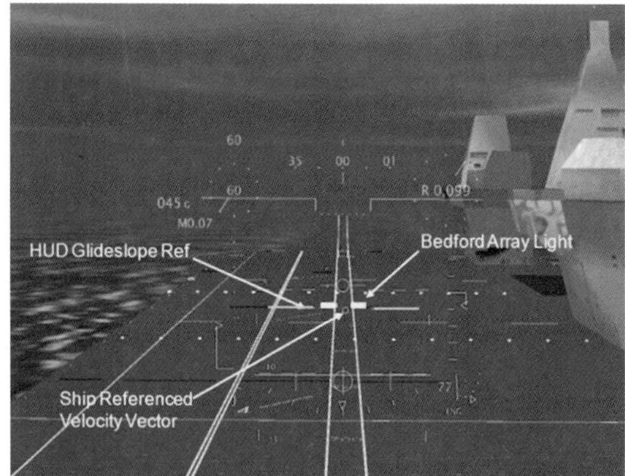

A simulated pilot's view of an F-35B about to land on a *Queen Elizabeth* class carrier using the shipborne rolling vertical landing technique. The Bedford Array Landing Reference System is prominently marked, and a series of symbols are presented in the pilot's Heads-Up Display (HUD). The need for a clear axial flight deck when landing is obvious. *(QinetiQ)*

The UK's first F-35B Joint Strike Fighter, serial ZM135, was delivered in July 2012. The MOD plans to buy forty-eight of the planes by 2022 for carrier and land-based operations. *(Lockheed Martin)*

thus will provide greatly increased capabilities compared to *Illustrious* and *Ocean*, and be similar in role to the new *America* (LHA-6) class amphibious assault ships being built for the US Navy.[3]

As already noted, the *Queen Elizabeth*s will be able to operate the F-35B JSF; SDSR 2010 stating the carrier would 'routinely have twelve fast jets embarked for operations'. The MOD now plans to buy forty-eight F-35Bs by 2022, including three already ordered trials-phase aircraft which may never be converted to operational configuration. In 2014, it is planned these aircraft will be formed into 17 Squadron (split 60:40 between RAF and RN personnel), based at Edwards Air Force Base in California USA for Initial Operational Test and Evaluation. The UK's first production standard F-35Bs will be ordered in late 2013 and 2014 at an expected cost of £100m (c. US$150m) each. These will be used to form the first front-line squadron – 617 Squadron – which will stand-up at the RAF's Marham airfield in 2016 with an eventual twelve aircraft (nine deployable). The squadron should become operational in 2018. A key task that year will be to start trials on the newly commissioned *Queen Elizabeth*, the carrier reaching operational status with the JSF in 2020/21.

Given the very small number of F-35B aircraft likely to be available in face of other competing commitments, the RAF considers that it will only be possible to provide a 'single figure' number of F-35B

aircraft for carrier operations a few weeks a few times a year; either for training purposes or for major exercises. A speculated compromise is the formation of a small Naval Strike Wing dedicated to carrier operations, but no official confirmation of this is likely before SDSR 2015.

A serious problem with the F-35B is its lack of a payload 'bring back' capability in the vertical landing mode, particularly in hot weather. Rather than having the aircraft jettison expensive ordinance before landing, the MOD is working with Lockheed Martin to develop a Shipbourne Rolling Vertical Landing (SRVL) technique that will increase bring back by at least 1,000kg (2,000lbs). Using SVRL, the F-35B will approach from aft of the ship on a 6° glide slope, land with a forward air speed of about 60 knots (40 knots relative to the deck) and stop using brakes only. This substantially increases the aircraft's payload bring-back capability, but introduces safety issues that aircraft carriers have not had to deal with since the advent of arrester gear and the angled deck. New landing aids such as the Bedford Array lighting system will help. However, during F-35B flight operations, an axial landing and take-off lane running the full length of the ship will need to be kept clear, and deck parking will be seriously constrained by the possibility of a landing F-35B drifting slightly off the landing lane or suffering a brake failure. Another problem will be the incompatibility of simultaneous F-35B SRVL

and helicopter operation: the ability to rapidly reconfigure the flight deck will be essential.

EQUIPMENT: HELICOPTERS AND CROWSNEST

The Fleet Air Arm (FAA) is in the midst of a period of major change. In particular its helicopter squadrons are being almost completely re-equipped by new or modernised types.

Rapid progress is now being made in replacing the current Lynx helicopter with upgraded AW159 Lynx Wildcats, manufactured by AgustaWestland. Four Lynx Wildcat Mk 1 attack helicopters will go into service with 847 Naval Air Squadron (NAS) from August 2014, replacing the Lynx Mk 9A, whilst twenty-eight of the Helicopter Maritime Attack (HMA) Mk 2 version will replace the Lynx Mk 8 for ship flight duties on frigates and destroyers. The first Mk 2 Wildcat was delivered to 700W NAS based at RNAS Yeovilton in early 2013, and the unit is now developing operational procedures. Front line squadrons will start to convert in 2015.

The Wildcat HMA Mk 2 will be able to carry the existing Sting Ray torpedo and Mk11 depth charge plus two new missile systems. The first is the Future Anti-Surface Guided Weapon – Light (FASGW-L), manufactured by Thales. This is a small missile with a range of up to eight kilometres (five nautical miles), and intended for use against small craft or fixed installations. The second new missile is the

Future Anti-Surface Guided Weapon – Heavy (FASGW-H) missile, a cooperative project with France. In RN service, FASGW-H will replace the venerable Sea Skua, which was first fired in anger during the 1982 Falklands War. The missile is being developed by MBDA and is intended to be able to disable warships of up to 1,000 tons. It was planned that the missile would enter service in 2015 but development delays driven largely by budgetary uncertainty in France mean that it probably won't be ready until 2016 at the earliest.

Also in 2014, the FAA's front-line Merlin Squadrons will continue replacing their existing AgustaWestland Merlin Mk 1 helicopters with thirty of the upgraded Mk 2 model, ordered in 2008 under an £850m (c. US$1.3bn) Merlin Capability Sustainment Programme managed by Lockheed Martin. Whilst still primarily a submarine hunter, the upgraded helicopters will have enhanced capabilities, and be easier to operate and maintain. A training squadron (824 NAS) had received five Mk 2s by May 2013, and the type is expected to be declared operational in June 2014.

The squadrons of the Commando Helicopter Force will begin in 2014 to replace their ancient Sea

A new AW159 Wildcat Mk 1 helicopter in British Army markings seen during field trials in 2012. The legacy Lynx will be replaced in the RM Commando Helicopter Force by the new Wildcat Mk 1 from August 2014. *(Crown Copyright 2012)*

King Mk 4 helicopters with Merlin HC3/3A helicopters transferred from the RAF. FAA personnel have been familiarising themselves with the new aircraft since 2012, and 846 NAS should become operational with them in 2015. The HC3/3A is unsuitable for ship-based operations and – funding permitted – will be gradually 'navalised' to the HC4 standard, which will enter service with 845 NAS in 2017.

For the FAA's other Sea King helicopter squadrons, the future is bleak. The two search and rescue flights will be disbanded in 2015, replaced by a commercial service provided by Bristow Group. The Sea King ASaC Mk 7 Airborne Surveillance and Control squadrons will also all be disbanded by 2016, without replacement – at least not immediately. Project Crowsnest has been launched to provide the RN with a new helicopter based airborne early warning capability. Two options are under consideration, a Thales proposal to integrate the existing Searchwater radars fitted to the Sea King Mk 7 with the Merlin Mk 2, and a Lockheed Martin/Northrop Grumman system named 'Vigilance' that could also be fitted to the Merlin Mk 2. The Thales solution may be favoured due to its low risk and low cost, if so ten modular systems are likely to be purchased, and these could be fitted or removed from a Merlin Mk 2 within a week. Assuming that a contract is awarded by 2015, trials will begin in 2018, an initial operational capability will be reached in 2020, and full capability delivered in 2022.

EQUIPMENT: SUBMARINES

The future of the RN's force of fleet submarines (attack submarines in American parlance) has been

The venerable Sea King helicopter is fast approaching the end of its Royal Navy service, with the search and rescue units being replaced by a commercial service provided by Bristow Group from 2015. *(Crown Copyright 2004)*

The second *Astute* class submarine, *Ambush*, is pictured leaving Barrow on her maiden voyage in September 2012; she commissioned on 1 March 2013. Serious design, construction and technical problems have dogged the class, and *Astute* had still not made an operational deployment nearly three years after her 'In-Service' date of July 2010. *(BAE Systems)*

invested in the new *Astute* class, and 2014 is likely to see the seventh and last of the class being ordered. The first of class, *Astute*, was commissioned on 27 August 2010, but as of mid-2013 she had still not deployed operationally. The tragic shooting and killing on the submarine in 2011 of Lieutenant Commander Molyneux received extensive press coverage, and despite significant remedial work the boat apparently still had serious technical defects several years after nominally entering service.[4] The situation was worsened by the sight of the second of class, *Ambush*, limping back to Faslane with a defect to her oil lubricating system a few days after commissioning on 1 March 2013. Getting these two boats operational is vital for the RN as only five *Trafalgar* class submarines remain in service – including *Tireless* whose service life has been temporarily extended due to delays with the *Astute*s – and they are all over twenty-three years old.[5]

Separately, development of a replacement for the *Vanguard* class ballistic missile submarines – termed 'Successor' – is in high gear. The programme gained 'Initial Gate' approval on 18 May 2011, and £3bn will be spent on a five-year Assessment Phase – this is where the concept and requirements are fleshed out and finalised into a detailed hull form and systems. Main Gate approval to order the first submarine is expected in 2016, and she will enter service in 2028. Three or four submarines will be ordered, at a cost of £11bn–£14bn (c. US$16.5bn–US$21bn) in 2006 prices. The 'Successor' submarines will be built by BAE Systems Maritime – Submarine at Barrow in Furness, utilise a Common Missile Compartment being developed in conjunction with the USA, and will have a new PWR3 nuclear propulsion plant manufactured by Rolls Royce but based on American technology. Almost no official UK information has been published on the 'Successor' design, but from American briefings it seems likely that the submarines will physically have twelve missile tubes, but only eight will actually be outfitted to carry Trident II D5 missiles.

The strategic nuclear-powered submarine *Vanguard* returning from a patrol. The significant investment required in the replacement 'Successor' programme will suck expenditure away from other badly-needed naval projects. *(Crown Copyright 2012)*

EQUIPMENT: DESTROYERS AND FRIGATES

A landmark moment occurred on 6 June 2013 with the decommissioning of the last Type 42 destroyer in RN service, *Edinburgh*. Fourteen were built for the RN, and eight were in service as recently as 2009. They have been replaced by the Type 45 *Daring* class, the sixth and last unit – *Duncan* – was delivered to the Royal Navy on 22 March 2013.

Potential upgrades to the Type 45s are being studied. They were expected to be fitted with a version of the US-developed Cooperative Engagement Capability (CEC), a real-time system that allows ships and aircraft to pool sensor data and have a greatly increased situational awareness of threats. This £500m project was cancelled in May 2012 but may be resurrected later in the decade. The fitting of Harpoon surface-to-surface missiles removed from decommissioned Type 22 frigates is a strong possibility for 2014. Also, the development of a UK Ballistic Missile Defence capability based on the Type 45 is being investigated – their SAMPSON radar and Sea Viper missile system may require few modifications to provide a basic level of protection. Finally, the Type 45s are being fitted with the Thales Vigile DPX electronic support measures system at a cost of £40m (US$60m), replacing capabilities lost when the Batch Three Type 22 frigates were decommissioned in 2011.

Thirteen Type 23 frigates also remain in service, eight of which have recently been fitted with the Thales UK Sonar 2087, a towed-array sonar system that enables them to hunt submarines at considerable distances. A continued programme of modernisation will see the class equipped with the new Artisan radar and replacement of Sea Wolf surface-to-air missiles with the new Sea Ceptor.

The Type 23 will be replaced by the new Type 26 Global Combat Ship (GCS) and BAE Systems

With the retirement of the final Type 42 destroyers *York* and *Edinburgh* during the last twelve months, the Royal Navy's fleet of surface escorts now comprises thirteen Type 23 frigates and six Type 45 destroyers, the final unit of the latter class being delivered in March 2013. The top two images show the Type 45 *Dragon* and the Type 23 *Monmouth* entering Portsmouth Harbour during 2012. The Type 23 frigates are being steadily modernised prior to replacement by the new Type 26 design from the start of the next decade. The bottom image is a computer-generated graphic of the new design dating from August 2012. *(Conrad Waters / Conrad Waters / BAE Systems)*

Computer generated graphics of some of the Royal Navy's next generation of warships, including the Type 26 Global Combat Ship (left) and the new 'Tide' class MARS tanker refuelling a Type 45 destroyer (right). *(BAE Systems / Defence Imaging & BMT Defence Services)*

received a £127m (c. U$188m) contract to conduct detailed design in 2010. The finalised design passed a key approval stage (Main Gate 1) in April 2012; in order to help keep costs down this is slightly smaller at 5,400 tons displacement and with a length of 148m (486ft) than the original 2010 concept. Thirteen units are planned at a cost of £250m–£350m (c. US$375m–US$525m) each, to be built at one a year. There will be five general-purpose units followed by eight units with enhanced anti-submarine (ASW) capabilities. Armament is expected to include a new medium-calibre gun and the Common Anti-Air Modular Missile being developed by MBDA (Sea Ceptor in RN service). Anti-ship or land-attack cruise missiles may also be carried. The ASW variant will also have a towed low-frequency sonar array. A Merlin or Lynx Wildcat Helicopter will be embarked, and a flexible mission space will allow for unmanned air, surface or underwater vehicles to be carried. The planned combined diesel-electric or gas (CODLOG) propulsion system is likely to centre on the Rolls Royce MT-30 gas turbine already adopted for the *Queen Elizabeth* class carriers.

An order for the first GCS is being delayed until after the 2014 Referendum on Scottish independence. If this fails then the class will be constructed by the two BAE Systems shipyards on the Clyde; if it passes then the BAE Systems shipyard at Portsmouth in England is likely to be upgraded to build the ships. Assuming an order for the first ship is placed in 2015, construction will start in 2016 and it will enter service in 2021.

EQUIPMENT: AUXILIARY SHIPS

The RFA flotilla is a civilian-manned fleet of ships. Its main task is to support the Royal Navy at sea with fuel, stores and ammunition. The RFA also supplies ships for aviation support, amphibious support, forward repair facilities and sea transport.

Since 2002 the Military Afloat Reach and Sustainability (MARS) project has been studying replacements for RFA's existing fleet. The urgent need to replace existing single-hulled tankers finally resulted in the MOD placing an order worth £452m (c. US$675m) with Daewoo Shipbuilding and Marine Engineering (DSME) of South Korea on 22 February 2012 for four 'Tide' class double-hulled fleet tankers which comply with the latest maritime environmental standards. The new tankers – to be called *Tidespring*, *Tiderace*, *Tidesurge* and *Tideforce* – are designed by BMT Defence Services in England, and will displace 37,000 tons with a length of 200.9m (660ft). A set of three abeam Replenishment and Supply (RAS) stations will be coupled with a hangar and flight deck for a medium helicopter, allowing simultaneous fuel and supplies transfers. The four vessels will replace the RFA's three remaining 'Rover' and 'Leaf' class tankers; equipment-sub-contracts indicate that only three of the new tankers will be operational with the RFA at any one time. Steel for *Tidespring* will be cut in June 2014; she will be delivered in late 2015 and enter service in 2016, followed by the three others at six-month intervals

The next output of the MARS programme will be three Fleet Solid Support (FSS) ships, to replace the RFA's two *Fort Rosalie* class ships, and *Fort Victoria*. An order is unlikely until late this decade. There were also plans for a Joint Sea-Based Logistics (JSBL) variant, and a fast tanker dedicated to supporting the *Queen Elizabeth* class but both ideas seem to have been dropped.

WHITE BOARD PROJECTS

The White Board is a MOD nickname for the Single Integrated Capability Priority List: equipment which the armed forces want but which is not yet funded. SDSR 2015 is the next major opportunity for the RN to get projects moved from the white board to the formal equipment programme.

The most likely success will be the purchase of new craft for the Royal Marines. A high priority requirement that emerged from operations in Iraq between 2005 and 2009 is the need for a Force Protection Craft that is fast, able to operate autonomously for several days, handle well the open sea and carry at least eight troops. Trials were conducted in 2011 with the Swedish-built CB90, but it was found to have several problems, in particular a lack of endurance. The requirement is for twelve craft entering service from 2017, these will replace some of the twenty-one LCVP Mk 5 landing craft acquired in 2001. Another requirement is for a 40-knot Fast Landing Craft (to be designated LCU Mk 11) able to land cargos of up to main battle tank size/weight. Two potential candidates were tested in 2010 but budgetary constraints have prevented any purchase so far.

The RN is also very keen to purchase ship-launched unmanned air systems able to operate from frigates, destroyers and RFAs. Compared to helicopters this would represent a very cost-effective surveillance asset in low threat situations, for example anti-piracy and drug patrols. It would also be able to track small, high-speed attack craft. Trials with the Boeing Insitu ScanEagle on a Type 23 frigate were conducted as long ago as 2005 and this finally resulted in a £30m order in June 2013.

In 2005, the MOD signed an agreement with BAE Systems, guaranteeing it a continuous stream of shipbuilding work until 2024. However a two-year gap has emerged between the completion of the fabrication of blocks for the *Queen Elizabeth* class carriers in 2015, and the likely ramping up of Type 26 frigate construction in 2017. To fill this gap, the MOD is considering an order for two Offshore Patrol Vessels (OPVs) at a cost of £150m (c. US$225m). These would be suitable for anti-piracy patrols and other maritime protection activities, and alleviate the pressures on the RN's small frigate and destroyer force. Funding the order is a major problem but BAE Systems is warning that it will have to close its Portsmouth Shipyard in 2014 without the order or equivalent subsidies. Mothballing of the shipyard is an alternative compromise. Since 2010 the MOD has been investigating options for a new Mine Countermeasure, Hydrographic, Patrol Craft (MHPC), displacing between 2,500 and 3,000 tons. However, this is not funded in the MOD's current Equipment Procurement Plan and the RN is very keen to get it incorporated in to SDSR 2015.

Finally, the Royal Navy is strongly supportive of efforts to resurrect the Maritime Patrol Aircraft (MPA) capability lost in 2010 with cancellation of the Nimrod MR4 and the earlier disbanding of the RAF's Nimrod MR2 squadrons. The MPA's combination of speed, range and surveillance capabilities has proved impossible to replace, and this has resulted in serious risks – including a limited ability to protect the *Vanguard* class submarines as they transit to/from their Faslane base. The purchase of up to eight American-built Boeing P-8 Poseidon MPAs to meet a future maritime surveillance requirement is a possibility for SDSR 2015 but the associated £1.5bn (c. US$2.25bn) price tag may result in a decision being deferred to the next review, presumably in 2020. The conversion of surplus RAF C-130J Hercules aircraft to an MPA role is an alternative, lower cost option being considered. Meanwhile, the RAF is endeavouring to maintain core MPA skills (Project Cornseed) by seconding personnel to the USA, Australia and other allies operating MPAs.

CONCLUSION

The Royal Navy has reluctantly adapted to the results of a decade of cutbacks, and the temporary 'gapping' of one of its core capabilities – fixed-wing aircraft carriers. However, the escort force is clearly too small, and the five remaining *Trafalgar* class submarines are struggling to cope with operational demands without the delayed *Astute* class boats. Also, spending on the 'Successor' submarines has already reached an estimated £600m (c. US$900m) a year, and will peak at about £1bn – sucking funding from every other naval equipment programme. Another serious challenge is how to maintain core expertise when the number of personnel in some branches and specialities has been reduced to double figures, making dedicated training infrastructure impossible to justify. This can be partly solved by sharing training facilities with the other UK armed forces, and seconding personnel to foreign navies, but neither approach is optimal. The forthcoming SDSR 2015 provides a real opportunity for a regeneration of the UK's maritime capabilities, but external events such as the Scottish Independence referendum planned for September 2014 and the possibility of further cuts to the defence budget after the next election overshadow the process.

Notes

1. A good overview of the outcome to the 2015/16 spending round is provided by Professor Malcolm Chalmers of the Royal United Services Institute (RUSI) in 'Respite from the Storm? Defence and the 2013 Spending Review Outcome', which was posted to the http://www.rusi.org/ website on 28 June 2013.

2. The remaining *Invincible* class carrier, *Illustrious*, was retained in service as a LPH type amphibious helicopter carrier prior to planned decommissioning during 2014.

3. The new carriers are essentially replacements for *Illustrious* and *Ocean* in the amphibious helicopter carrier role as well as providing fixed-wing capabilities. The *Queen Elizabeth* design is sufficiently flexible to deploy an embarked military force.

4. Major problems with *Astute*'s basic design and construction reported in *The Guardian* newspaper in November 2012, included a failure to achieve design speed; problems with instrumentation and circuit boards; unexpected corrosion and flooding during a routine dive. For more detail, see Nick Hopkins' 'Slow, leaky, rusty: Britain's £10bn submarine beset by design flaws', *The Guardian* –16 November 2012 (London: Guardian News and Media Ltd, 2012). The UK MOD's reluctance to issue detailed comments on the capabilities of the submarine flotilla makes it difficult to assess the extent to which the reported problems extend beyond routine teething problems, although RN leadership has publicly professed its contentment with the new class on many occasions.

5. Given the two *Astute* class submarines in commission are not yet fully operational and the *Trafalgar* class boat *Torbay* was completing a major docking period in the first half of 2013, the active nuclear-powered attack submarine fleet was reduced to a maximum of four boats. In practice this has been further reduced by defects in the increasingly elderly remaining submarines; for example *Tireless* has had to be docked for repairs following a coolant leak early in 2013.

6. The following sources provide worthwhile additional reading:

– The official website site of the Royal Navy can be found at www.royalnavy.mod.uk, and its official newspaper is *Navy News*, at www.navynews.co.uk. Whilst these both inevitably have a strong public relation and recruiting bias, they are still very useful for monitoring RN related news and current operations.

– A primary and revealing source on the progress of the UK's naval construction programme is the UK National Audit Office. Every year they publish the *Ministry of Defence: Major Projects Report*, plus occasional ad-hoc reports. Their website is at www.nao.org.uk.

– The House of Commons Library regularly publishes briefing papers and research on defence matters of interest to members. The library can be found on-line via www.parliament.uk.

– The Royal Navy annually publishes *Naval Force*, covering its achievements over the last year, strategy, operations, people and equipment. The on-line version can be found at www.royalnavy.mod.uk/News-and-Events/Reference-Library/Global-Force.

– Progress on the construction of the *Queen Elizabeth* class carriers can be followed at the Aircraft Carrier Alliance's web portal at www.aircraftcarrieralliance.co.uk.

– The Royal United Services Institute's *RUSI Journal is* an excellent source of well-informed criticism of UK defence policy. The Institute has a website at www.rusi.org.

Author:
Tomohiko Tada

3.1 SIGNIFICANT SHIPS

HYUGA CLASS DDH-TYPE DESTROYERS

Japan's New Through-Deck Surface Combatants

Through-deck surface combatants have recently re-appeared in Japan's maritime forces for the first time since the extinction of the Imperial Japanese Navy at the end of the Pacific War in 1945. These new surface combatants of the *Hyuga* class comprise *Hyuga* (DDH-181) and her sister *Ise* (DDH-182). The first ship was authorised in the Japanese Heisei 16 year (2004) budget, with the second ship being funded in the Heisei 18 year (2006) budget.[1] As such, they are also known as the 16DDH and 18DDH by the Japan Maritime Self Defence Force (JMSDF). They are classified as helicopter-carrying destroyers by the JMSDF but would be categorised as helicopter carriers in commonly-used terminology.

The advent of the *Hyuga* class is not the first time the JMSDF has operated carrier-like vessels. The three *Osumi* class LPD type amphibious dock transports that were commissioned between 1998 and 2003 feature a through deck of of c.160m in length. However, much of this deck – as well as the storage space below – is used to accommodate vehicles of the Japan Ground Self Defence Force (JGSDF) and

A picture of the Japanese helicopter-carrying destroyer *Hyuga* (DDH-181) at sea in March 2010, a year after delivery. *Hyuga* and her sister *Ise* (DDH-182) are the first JMSDF carrier-type vessels capable of sustained helicopter operations. *(Japan Maritime Self-Defence Force)*

helicopter operations are limited to two spots on the rear half of the through deck. Whilst, therefore, the *Osumi* class does have a through deck and are able to support limited amphibious operations, they are essentially transport vessels. As such, the *Hyuga* class are Japan's first aircraft carrier type vessels capable of sustained helicopter operations.

CLASS ORIGINS AND CONSTRUCTION

In the 1960s, during the height of the Cold War, the JMSDF recognised that the use of onboard sonar and torpedoes to detect and attack the Soviet Navy's high-speed nuclear submarines was no longer effective. It therefore developed plans to operate anti-submarine helicopters from ships in a similar fashion to other navies. After intensive discussions on the number of helicopters to be operated and the size of the ship, the JMSDF ordered two *Haruna* class helicopter-carrying destroyers that could each deploy three large anti-submarine helicopters. The lead ship, *Haruna* (DDH-141), was authorised in 1968, with *Hiei* (DDH-142) following in 1970. They commissioned in 1973 and 1974 respectively. With a full load displacement of 6,800 tons and a length of 153m, the *Haruna* class significantly improved the anti-submarine capabilities of the JMSDF. Subsequently, the need to meet the threat posed by anti-ship missiles in the 1970s, which could be launched from submerged submarines as well as surface vessels,

resulted in the development of an enlarged, more capable helicopter-carrying destroyer design. The resultant *Shirane* class design continued to ship three helicopters but featured a combat direction system that integrated the ships' anti-air, anti-surface and anti-submarine weapons systems. *Shirane* (DDH-143) was authorised in 1975 and commissioned in 1980, whilst a sister *Kurama* (DDH-144) was approved in 1976 for delivery in 1981.[2]

In 1977, the year following *Kurama's* authorisation, it was determined that all JMSDF new-built general-purpose destroyers would be capable of carrying one anti-submarine helicopter. This resulted in the development of the '8-8' fleet concept, under which each of Japan's four principal Escort Flotillas comprise eight warships carrying a total of eight helicopters.[3] This decision dramatically improved the anti-submarine capabilities of the JMSDF and the basic '8-8' structure has held good to the present day. At the same time, operational experience with the helicopter-carrying destroyers revealed limitations in handling three helicopters with only two landing spots and two sets of RAST (recovery, assist, securing and traversing) equipment. This experience influenced design deliberations when the first generation of helicopter-carrying destroyers were scheduled for replacement. This process resulted in plans to develop a through-deck type helicopter-carrying destroyer that was able to

A JMSDF escort flotilla on a demonstration exercise in 2012. The two *Hyuga* class destroyers are intended to provide both helicopter support and command and control facilities for two of the four JMSDF escort groups, each of which are built round an eight ship-eight ASW helicopter-operating concept. *(Royal Australian Navy)*

support the simultaneous take-off and landing of at least three large anti-submarine helicopters.

The *Hyuga* class that emerged was therefore built around this core requirement, although a number of other capabilities were also incorporated into the design. For example, the class incorporates a significant command and control potential and is also equipped to deal with asymmetric threats and to carry out humanitarian operations. They are therefore able to carry in excess of ten helicopters, with the precise air group embarked dependent on the particular mission situation. However, the through deck is not designed to withstand the high temperature produced by jet engine exhausts from STOVL (short take-off and vertical landing) aircraft. Thus, in spite of speculation to the contrary, the operation of fixed-wing aircraft is not envisaged.

The first ship, *Hyuga*, was laid down on May 2006 at IHI Marine United Inc.'s (now Japan Marine United Corporation's) Yokohama shipyard. She was launched on 23 August 2007 and commissioned on 18 March 2009. Her sister, *Ise,* was constructed by the same yard, being laid down on 30 May 2008, launched on 21 August 2009 and commissioned on 16 March 2011. The ships replaced *Haruna* and *Hiei,* which were decommissioned as soon as their replacements joined the fleet.

OVERALL DESIGN DESCRIPTION

Structural Configuration: The *Hyuga* class destroyers have a standard displacement of some 13,950 tons, increasing to 19,000 tons at full load. Overall length is 197m, beam 33m and draft 7m. The upper island structure is located to the starboard side of the flight deck, which is regarded as the ship's No. 1 deck.

The island is approximately 70m in length and has a c. 9m wide base. It has a five-layered structure comprising the flight deck level (No. 1 deck) and decks 01–04. The flight deck level includes waiting rooms and offices for aviation crew and flight deck personnel. Decks 01 and 02 are largely devoted to communications equipment. The bridge is located at the forward end of 03 deck, whilst air traffic control facilities are located to the rear, aft the funnels. The uppermost layer, 04 deck, is taken up with the fixed arrays for the FCS-3 multifunction radar and associated equipment. There is also a tower-type foremast, which is fitted with a variety of antennae, radar and electronic warfare systems.

The main hull has seven levels, descending from

The first-generation Japanese helicopter-carrying destroyer *Kurama* (DDH-144) seen in heavy weather with two SH-60 type anti-submarine helicopters on her flight deck. A desire to overcome the earlier destroyers' inability to operate more than two helicopters simultaneously was a key influence on the *Hyuga* class design. *(US Navy)*

No. 2 deck immediately below the flight deck to No. 7 deck. The flight deck is 195m in length and 33m in width and incorporates four take-off and landing spots.[4] There are two large elevators for aircraft and two smaller elevators for ammunition and supplies. The two aircraft elevators connect the flight deck to the hangar on No. 4 deck and have a maximum load capacity of 30s tons. The forward elevator, with dimensions of 20m x 10m, is slightly smaller than the rear (20m x 13m). The latter can handle a SH-60K anti-submarine helicopter with its main rotors extended. The flight deck also provides space for the forward Phalanx close-in weapons system (CIWS), a sixteen-cell Mk 41 vertical launch system (both located to starboard) and various items of communications equipment.

The foremost part of No. 2 deck houses mooring equipment. The rest of the deck is given over to a variety of uses, including the combat information

Pictured here shortly after her delivery on 16 March 2011, *Ise* (DDH-182) is the second of the two *Hyuga* class helicopter-carrying destroyers. This image emphasises her high freeboard and carrier-like design. *(Japan Maritime Self-Defence Force)*

A 2010 view of *Hyuga* (DDH-181) with five SH-60J/K helicopters on her flight deck. The 195m-long flight deck incorporates four take-off and landing spots for a nominal air group of one minesweeping and three ASW helicopters, although around ten aircraft can be operated in some comfort. *(US Navy)*.

A picture of *Ise* (DDH-182) operating at speed with other JMSDF escorts in November 2012. She has a two-shaft COGAG propulsion system that provides a design speed of 30 knots. *(US Navy)*

Hyuga (DDH-181) pictured in company with the US Navy carrier *George Washington* (CVN-73) and other JMSDF and USN ships. The command and control role is central to the *Hyuga* class design and the two ships incorporate a large combat information centre and excellent facilities for communication with both Japanese and other allied units. Note also the attention paid in terms of hull and island design minimising radar cross section. *(US Navy)*

centre (CIC), medical facilities, commander's office and wardroom. The two latter facilities are amongst those located in a gallery over the hangar. A port side catwalk can be approached from either the flight deck or No. 2 deck, whilst the aft Phalanx CIWS is located in an aft port sponson at this level. No. 3 deck encompasses a capstan compartment forwards and also includes officers' quarters and the sonar room. There are also a total of three recesses in the hull at this level for the stowage of the ship's motor launches.

No. 4 deck is dominated by the hangar, which is located between the two elevators and is c. 60m in length. There is a fire shutter in the middle of the hangar, which can divide the facility in two. Helicopter maintenance facilities are located aft of the rear elevator. The hangar deck can also be accessed by a side ramp on the starboard side to facilitate the boarding of personnel, stores and small vehicles when the ship is berthed. The lower decks are taken up with storage, crew accommodation, messes and galley facilities, as well as various equipment rooms. The combined machinery control room and damage control facility is located on No. 5 deck, whilst the lowest deck, No. 7, houses the engine rooms and auxiliary machinery. Control units for the two sets of fin-stabilisers are also housed at this level.

Propulsion System: The class is equipped with a combined gas and gas (COGAG) propulsion arrangement, with four GE LM2500 gas turbines driving two controllable-pitch propellers. No. 1 and No. 2 gas turbines are installed in the forward engine room and drive the port propeller shaft, whilst No. 3 and No 4. gas turbines are installed in the aft engine room and connected to the starboard shaft. Each gas turbine is installed in an enclosure on anti-vibration mounts as a sound reduction measure. There is also a Prairie-Masker system to shield and disguise noise generated by the propellers and hull.[5] Exhaust pipes from all four gas turbines are directed to the starboard of the hangar and vent via two funnels on the island structure.

Auxiliary power for ship services is provided by four electric generators, each driven by a dedicated gas turbine. They are housed in three dynamo rooms

Table 3.1.1.

HYUGA (DDH-181) PRINCIPAL PARTICULARS

Building Information:

Laid Down:	11 May 2006
Launched:	23 August 2007
Delivered:	18 March 2009
Builders:	IHI Marine United Inc. (IHI MU) at its Yokohama shipyard.

Dimensions:

Displacement:	13,950 tons standard displacement, 19,000 tons full load displacement.
Overall Hull Dimensions:	197m x 33m (maximum) x 7m. Depth is 22m.

Weapons Systems:

Aircraft:	An air group of around ten helicopters can be accommodated. There are four spots on the flight deck.
	A standard air group encompasses 3 x SH-60J/K anti-submarine helicopters and 1 x MCH-101 minesweeping helicopter.
Missiles:	2 x Mk 41 8-cell VLS modules for a total of 16 quad-packed ESSM surface-to-air missiles and 12 ASROC anti-submarine rockets.
Guns:	2 x 20mm Phalanx CIWS. Machine guns.
Torpedoes:	2 x triple HQS-303 324mm anti-submarine torpedo tubes for Mk 46 or Type 97 torpedoes.
Countermeasures:	NOLQ-3C electronic warfare suite. 6 x Mk 137 launchers for SBROC Mk 36. Type 4 towed decoy system.
Principal Sensors:	1 x FCS-3 multifunction radar. 1 x OPS-20C navigation radar. 1 x OQQ-21 integrated sonar suite.
Combat System:	OYQ-10 advanced combat direct system. Comprehensive communications system includes Links 11 and 16.

Propulsion Systems:

Machinery:	COGAG. 4 x GE LM2500 gas turbines rated at 75MW total produce 100,000shp through two shafts.
Speed:	Designed maximum speed is 30 knots.

Other Details:

Complement:	A typical crew comprises c.350 personnel. Accommodation is provided for c.480.
Class:	Two ships have been constructed: *Hyuga* (DDH-181) and *Ise* (DDH-182).

forward, between and aft of the engine rooms.

The gas turbines normally operate unattended under control from the bridge. Monitoring functions are carried out from a console in the combined machinery and damage control room, which can also be used for direct operation. The machinery control room also contains consoles to monitor the auxiliary machinery, the electrical distribution network and to carry out damage control functions.

Stealth Features: The class's high freeboard, about three times greater than a general-purpose destroyer, places it at a disadvantage in terms of its radar signature. Mitigating steps include actions to reduce the radar cross section (RCS), most notably in terms of the angles adopted for the hull and island structure. In addition, openings that might impact radar reflection such as the recesses for boat storage are covered by metal meshes or lids. Similar attention has been paid to life rafts, which are both inclined and fitted with meshes to reduce their signature.

ELECTRONIC AND COMMUNICATIONS SYSTEMS

The *Hyuga* class have been designed to carry out a leading command and control role in addition to their primary function as helicopter platforms. As such, they have been equipped with a range of sophisticated equipment to carry out this task, much of which has been newly developed.

Advanced Technology Combat System (ATECS): ATECS comprises a number of linked systems that collectively provide the heart of the *Hyuga* class's overall war fighting potential in similar fashion to the US Navy's Aegis. Amongst the most important of these are the OYQ-10 combat direction system, the FCS-3 fire-control system, the OQQ-21 sonar system, the NOLQ-3C electronic warfare system and the ship's various communications systems. ATECS essentially gathers information on the air, surface and underwater environment obtained by the ship's various sensors via its NOYQ-1 integrated network. The OYQ-10 combat direction system collates this information and identifies the appropriate weapons systems to respond to any

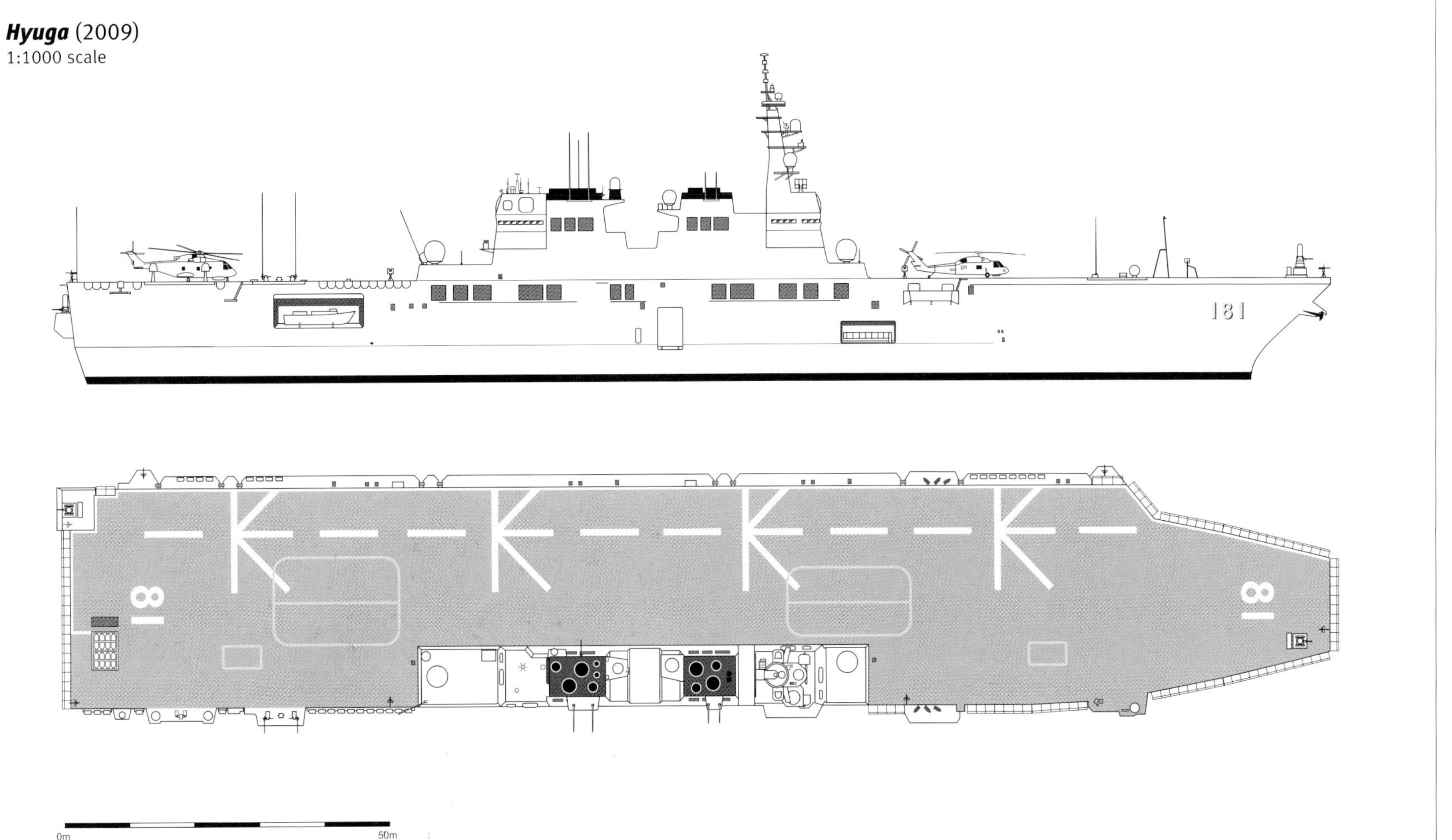

Hyuga (2009)
1:1000 scale

(Drawings © John Jordan, 2012)

Above: An overall view of the island on *Hyuga* (DDH-181), which has four principal levels. In addition to the multifunction radar, the various radomes shielding the communications antennae that are central to the class's command and control role are immediately apparent. *(Tomohiko Tada)*

Above: A detailed view of the upper forward island structure of *Ise* (DDH-182). Two radar arrays for the FCS-3 multifunction radar are mounted immediately above the bridge, with two jammers for the NOLQ-3C electronic warfare system located to port and starboard on top of the bridge structure. The large radome to starboard houses a NORA-1C communications antenna, whilst an OPS-20C navigation radar and ORQ-1C helicopter data link dome are on the centreline. The upper tiers of the mast house the ESM elements of the NOLQ-3C system and a large IFF ring. The whole is surmounted by a collar for the Link 16 communications system and an aircraft homing beacon. *(Tomohiko Tada)*

Left: A view of *Ise*'s (DDH-182) rear island, showing the bridge used to control air traffic operations and, above, the fixed arrays for the ship's FCS-3 multifunction radar. The large panels are 'C' band arrays primarily used for the surveillance and tracking of potential targets, with the smaller supplementary 'X' band arrays providing guidance for surface-to-air Evolved Sea Sparrow Missiles in an engagement's final stages. *(Tomohiko Tada)*

emergent threat on the basis of the overall data picture. The relevant response can be selected manually or implemented automatically on the basis of pre-programmed war-fighting rules (e.g. automated actions will be taken based on the threat's range, speed, bearing and/or altitude). Information gathered by ATECS is displayed on wall-mounted screens and multifunction consoles in the CIC, which is sufficiently large to support flotilla-wide command and control functions. Consequently, the CIC is also fitted with the latest MTA (Maritime Terminal Afloat) variant of the shipboard C2T (Command and Control Terminals) that are linked with the JMSDF's networked Maritime Operation Force (MOF) system. MTA is capable of two-way communication with the OYQ-10 combat direction system to provide a broader tactical picture than available from the ship's systems alone.

FCS-3 Fire-Control System: FCS-3 is a newly-developed Japanese electronically-scanned multi-function radar system. It is built around four fixed arrays mounted on the face and port side of the forward part of the island and on the rear and starboard side of the aft part of the island in an arrangement broadly reminiscent of the US Navy's *Ticonderoga* (CG-47) class. FCS-3 is used to direct the *Hyuga* class's RIM-162 Evolved Sea Sparrow Missile (ESSM) surface-to-air missiles, searching for and tracking targets, as well as controlling the missile engagement. It also carries out the role of a conventional air and surface search radar and is used for helicopter control purposes.

The basic research for FCS-3 started at the Technical Research and Development Institute (TRDI) of the Japan Defence Agency (JDA) in the 1980s, with the aim of developing an active phased-array radar at a time when the technology was still in its infancy.[6] A small research prototype was manufactured during FY 1986–8 and trials from a coastal site provided better-than-expected performance in detecting and tracking multiple targets flying over the sea. A subsequent developmental prototype constructed over FY 1990–4 was installed in the auxiliary trials ship *Asuka* (ASE-6102) for at-sea evaluation between 1995 and 1998, which confirmed the system's promise. It was adopted as the 'Type 00 FCS' in 2000. The operational system – first installed in *Hyuga* – was further refined from the prototype, taking advantage of ongoing

improvements in the size and weight of radar signal processors. It is particularly good at detecting and tracking low level targets, such as sea-skimming anti-ship missiles, in situations where there is heavy sea clutter.

FCS-3's primary arrays operate in the 4,000–8,000 MHz US Navy C (NATO G/H) band. Whilst these arrays are capable of identifying targets and of directing ESSM towards them, ESSM's use of semi-active homing technology means that it requires additional radar input in the later stages of an engagement. This is provided by the installation of four small supplementary fixed arrays operating in the 6,000–11,000 MHz USN X (NATO I/J) band next to the main arrays. These guide the missiles in this final phase through intermittent continuous wave illumination (ICWI) in a broadly similar fashion to the SPG-62 continuous wave illuminators used with Aegis.[7]

FCS-3's multifunction capabilities mean that the traditional separate air-search, surface-search and fire-control radars found on other Japanese surface combatants are no longer required in *Hyuga* and *Ise*. However, an OPS-20C navigation radar that is also used to undertake short-range surveillance of surface targets continues to be fitted.

OQQ-21 Sonar System: Responsible for detecting underwater threats in conjunction with the ship's anti-submarine helicopters, the OQQ-21 sonar system is housed in a huge bow dome. Developed by the TRDI and also trialled on *Asuka*, it incorporates both a cylindrical array for forward detection and a flank array for the identification of lateral threats. There is, however, no towed array. The sonar has both active and passive functionality and can operate in both modes simultaneously. It is capable of undertaking low frequency searches for distant targets and higher frequency searches for high resolution detection of small targets such as mines. The system's processors can also handle signals obtained by the anti-submarine helicopters as well as by the onboard arrays, thereby creating a comprehensive underwater picture.

NOLQ-3C Electronic Warfare System: The NOLQ-3C electronic warfare system fitted to the *Hyuga* class provides both electronic support measures (ESM) and electronic countermeasures (ECM) functions. The former detects communications and radar emissions from potentially hostile sources

whilst the latter can be used to transmit jamming signals. The ESM part of the system is mounted on top of the mainmast whilst the ECM element is located on top of the bridge, above the forward arrays of the FCS-3 radar. Like the ships' other war-fighting systems, NOLQ-3C is linked to the OYQ-10 combat direction system and integrated with other countermeasures, most notably the Mk 36 Super Rapid Blooming Off board Countermeasures (SRBOC) decoy launchers.

Three Mk 137 launchers for the Mk 36 SBROC are mounted slightly forward of the island structure to both the port and starboard of the flight deck facing forwards, outwards and aft. Each comprises six 130mm launching tubes mounted in two rows at a fixed angle of 45° or 60° to the deck. The combat direction system will assign firing orders to one of the launchers dependent on the direction of travel of the incoming threat. The launchers fire both radio wave distorting chaff and infrared decoys to combat different types of anti-ship missile.

Communications Equipment: The *Hyuga* class's command and control role means that a comprehensive outfit of communications equipment is an essential design feature. This is reflected in the particularly noticeable number of spherical radomes housing satellite communication antennae that have been fitted to the two helicopter carrying destroyers. Principal systems include the following communications outfits:

- NORA-1C: Two NORA 1-C antennae are installed on platforms fitted to the lower part of the mast and the aft of the forward funnel. NORA-1C uses transponders rented from SKY Perfect JSAT Corporation's Superbird B2 communications satellite, operates on the X band frequency and is also commonly fitted to other JMSDF ships. The Superbird B2 satellite was launched in February 2000 and covers the western Pacific, including Japan.
- NORA-7: Two NORA-7 broadband satellite communication antennae are housed in large spherical radomes on 01 deck level at the forward and aft ends of the island. Also operating in the X band, they use the Superbird D satellite launched in October 2000 and have a significantly higher data transmission rate than the NORA-1C system. Coverage extends through South East Asia as far as the Indian Ocean.

Although the *Hyuga* class destroyers have been equipped with a powerful suite of largely defensive systems, their principal war-fighting capability is provided by embarked SH-60J and SH-60K anti-submarine helicopters. They are modified variants of the US Navy's SH-60 Seahawk type licence-built by Mitsubishi Heavy Industries, with the improved SH-60K being introduced in 2005. This picture shows a SH-60J. *(US Navy)*

■ NORQ-1: The radome for the NORQ-1 satellite communication system is mounted on a platform to the port side of the rear funnel. It operates in the Ku band and uses the Superbird C2 satellite launched in the autumn of 2008. This provides faster and larger data-transmission capabilities than X band communication but is susceptible to adverse weather conditions.

■ USC-42: This system is installed to facilitate joint operations with the US Navy (USN) and links via its satellite network into the United States' Global Command and Control System-Maritime (GCCS-M). GCCS-M is the primary tactical command and control system used by the USN's operational commanders. One radome is located on the starboard side of the flight deck level midway between the island and the bow and the other at 01 deck level at the aft end of the island next to one of the NORA-7 domes.

■ NORC-4B: Two antennae for the Inmarsat commercial satellite system are mounted side by side on a platform to the starboard of the flight deck towards the stern. They provide voice telephone and data communications via Inmarsat's network of satellites.

■ ORQ-1C: This system provides a data link with the ship's helicopters. The two shipboard antennae are contained in radomes on platforms fitted to the higher part of the mast and to the forward face of the aft funnel.

The *Hyuga* class vessels are equipped with the standard Link 11 and Link 16 systems, which support transmission of information by tactical data link between ships and aircraft operating in concert. A number of rod antennae attached to the island and to the starboard side of the flight deck can be used

In addition to anti-submarine helicopters, *Hyuga* (DDH-181) and *Ise* (DDH-182) also regularly embark a minesweeping or transport helicopter of the MCH-101/CH-101 type, which is built by Kawasaki under licence from AgustaWestland. *(AgustaWestland)*

The Mk 41 VLS system installed on *Ise* (DDH-182). Comprising two, eight-cell units its nominal capacity is sixteen quad-packed ESSM and twelve ASROC anti-submarine rockets. Its location towards the aft of the flight deck uses space that would otherwise facilitate aircraft operations. *(Tomohiko Tada)*

The *Hyuga* class destroyers are fitted with two triple anti-submarine torpedo tubes for close-range defence. Located at No. 4 deck level, they are usually hidden within the hull by closed flaps that help limit the ship's radar signature. *(Tomohiko Tada)*

to support transmissions in HF (Link 11) and UHF (Link 11/16), although these can also make use of the satellite equipment installed. Link 11 was first introduced by the US Navy in the early 1960s as TADIL-A (Tactical Digital Information Link A) and is now showing its age in terms of the limited number of units that can share the network, speed of data transmission and vulnerability to jamming. The newer Link 16 or TADIL-J makes good many of these deficiencies but is limited to line of sight communication in UHF mode.

WEAPONS SYSTEMS

The new helicopter-carrying destroyers have been equipped with a relatively powerful suite of largely defensive weaponry given their principal role as aviation platforms. Principal weapons systems are as follows:

Mk 41 Vertical Launch System: Each *Hyuga* class destroyer is equipped with two eight-cell launch modules for the Mk 41 vertical launch system (VLS), which are located together at the starboard side of the flight deck close to the stern. The cells are used both for quad packed ESSM surface-to-air and ASROC (Anti-Submarine Rocket) missiles, with four cells being notionally allocated to a total of sixteen quad-packed ESSMs and twelve cells used for ASROC.

The short-range ESSM is a modernised version of the long-established series of RIM-7 Sea Sparrow missiles, which is itself derived from the AIM-7 Sparrow air-to-air missile. Weighing nearly 300kg and approximately 3.7m in length, its principal role is to provide point defence against anti-ship missiles. Equipped with a more powerful motor for greater speed, manoeuvrability and range than its ancestor, as well as thrust vector control and updated guidance technology, ESSM's effective range of at least 30km means it is also capable of carrying out the local area defence role previously performed by medium-range missiles. Four missiles can be accommodated in a Mk 25 launch canister, each of which is loaded into one of the Mk 41 launch cells.

ASROC is used to deliver anti-submarine torpedoes against targets operating at some distance from the ship where the range is too great for the destroyer's onboard torpedo launchers and attack by helicopter is not optimal. The system delivers a torpedo by rocket propulsion to a location near the target, after which it operates as a normal torpedo after splashdown. ASROC was originally introduced by the US Navy for launch from a bespoke, trainable eight-round launcher but a vertically launched modification was subsequently developed for use with the Mk 41 VLS, where it is installed in a Mk 15 canister. When used to deploy a standard US Mk 46 lightweight anti-submarine torpedo it weighs

750kg and is a little over 5m in length. Maximum firing range is variously reported as being between 10km and 20km. Although the system used on *Hyuga* and *Ise* currently uses the US Mk 46 torpedo, a variant of the Japanese Type 97 torpedo is likely to be installed in the near future.

Other Shipboard Anti-Submarine Equipment: Whilst prosecution of submarine targets identified by the OQQ-21 sonar system is largely in the hands of the ship's helicopters and ASROC, the class is also fitted with two triple HQS-303 torpedo tubes. These are installed in port and starboard torpedo rooms at No. 4 deck level to provide short-range anti-submarine defence.

Additional protection is provided by a Type 4 towed decoy system, which was developed domestically. This features an acoustic generator to confuse torpedoes closing on the ship. The system is fed through two openings in the port side of stern, from where it is towed when in operation.

Phalanx CIWS: Close-range defence against anti-ship missiles that have penetrated the protective barrier provided by ESSM is provided by two Phalanx Mk 15 Block 1B CIWS. These are located at the forward starboard end of the flight deck and in a sponson at the port side of the stern. The six-barrelled Gatling-type 20mm cannon units are

Left: *Hyuga* (DDH-181) seen operating with the Aegis-equipped guided missile destroyer *Kirishima* (DDG-174) in November 2011. Whilst the *Hyuga* class's ESSM and Phalanx CIWS mountings provide layered short-range defence, the helicopter-carrying destroyers would require the support of specialised JMSDF Aegis-equipped ships on operations where there was a high threat of air or missile attack. *(US Navy)*

fitted with Ku band search and tracking radars housed within their distinctive radomes that provide automatic fire-control solutions against any targets identified. The antennae unit rotates with the mount but both separate antennae can pivot and elevate independently. The mount is able to rotate 310° in bearing and can elevate between minus 25° and plus 80°. Rate of fire is 4,500 rounds per minute, whilst upgrades have increased the original effective range of c. 1.5km. The relevant oper-

Below: *Hyuga* (DDH-181) fuelling from the US Military Sealift Command's replenishment oiler *Walter S Diehl* (T-AO-193) in March 2011. The sponson for the port Phalanx CIWS mounting that projects from the ship's stern is a distinctive feature. *(US Navy)*

A picture of *Hyuga* (DDH-181) and *Ise* (DDH-182) operating together in July 2011. The image shows the location of the starboard Phalanx CIWS at the forward end of the flight deck. One of the manually-operated 12.7mm machine gun mountings that are shipped to counter asymmetric surface threats can also be seen immediately forward of *Hyuga*'s Phalanx system. *(Japan Maritime Self-Defence Force)*

ating electronics and machinery are contained within the base of the mounting, thereby allowing the system to be installed as a complete unit.

Phalanx has gone through several modifications since it first entered service with the US Navy in 1980. The latest Block 1B version incorporates a side-mounted infrared imaging sensor to improve tracking ability against low-altitude targets affected by sea clutter. It is therefore effective against small surface targets such as speedboats operated by terrorists or pirates. Other recent upgrades have seen changes to the gun system to reduce bullet dispersion and overall reliability, whilst heavier munitions have been developed to increase the probability of target destruction.

12.7mm Machine Gun: Although the latest variant of Phalanx has an improved performance against asymmetric surface threats, these are supplemented by additional manually-operated 12.7mm machine guns to cover the large sea area around the ship more effectively. These weapons can fire c. 450–550 rounds per minute out to an effective range of around 1.5km. It is possible that they will be replaced by more modern, remotely controlled mountings in due course.

22DDH CLASS

The successful introduction of *Hyuga* into service has seen plans advanced for a larger type of helicopter carrying destroyer. The first was authorised under the Japanese Heisei 22 year (2010) budget and is therefore referred as the 22DDH type. As for *Hyuga*, the design is focused on the operation of helicopters and the exercise of command and control functions by an escort flotilla or joint force commander. The new ship's much greater overall size means that she is more capable of multi-faceted operations, including transport, supply and disaster relief, than the 16DDH type. Standard displacement will be some 19,500 tons – increasing to 24,000 tons at full load and she will have an overall length of 248m and maximum beam of 38m. It is intended that 22DDH will replace *Shirane* in service. A second ship, authorised in 2012 as 24DDH, will replace *Kurama*, last of the first-generation helicopter-carrying destroyers.

The larger size of 22DDH is reflected in a much greater helicopter carrying capacity than her predecessor. She is designed to operate a standard air group of seven anti-submarine and two minesweeping or transport helicopters, with a

An impression of the new 22DDH type helicopter-carrying destroyer, two of which have been ordered for delivery in 2015 and 2017. Larger than the *Hyuga* class, they have a more limited armament but are capable of the deployment and simultaneous operation of more helicopters. *(Japan Maritime Self-Defence Force)*

maximum operating capacity of some fourteen machines. There are five principal helicopter landing spots on the flight deck – one more than on *Hyuga* and *Ise*. Whilst there are still two elevators to connect the flight deck with the hangar, the rear one has been shifted to a position at the edge of the deck, aft of the starboard island structure. Another change is an enlarged ramped access to the hangar on the starboard side to allow heavy vehicles to be stowed. This would permit, for example, transportation of a considerable number of heavy JGSDF trucks to assist a large-scale disaster recovery or international aid mission or even military equipment such as the Japan Air Self Defence Force's (JASDF's) Patriot surface-to-air missile batteries.

Although the starboard island and the outfit of command and communication equipment are both configured in a very similar way to the *Hyuga* class, 22DDH is also likely to see some significant differences in terms of weapons and sensors. Whilst the basic FCS-3 multifunction radar system has been retained, a decision to omit the Mk 41 vertical launch system and ESSM from the new design means that the supplementary illuminators installed in *Hyuga* and *Ise* have been made redundant. Consequently, only the large C band arrays are fitted for search, tracking and helicopter control purposes, the modified radar system being designated OPS-50 in this configuration. Close range anti-missile defence will be provided by two autonomous Sea RAM missile launchers, supplemented by two Phalanx CIWS mountings.[8] There have also been changes to the sonar system, with the OQQ-22 system selected for the design lacking the flank arrays of its predecessor. The omission of the vertical launch system also means that ASROC will not be installed. Overall, therefore, the onboard weapons outfit is substantially reduced in favour of the greater flexibility provided by the enlarged helicopter group that can be embarked.

CONCLUSION

The two *Hyuga* class vessels are now operational in the fleet, with *Hyuga* having successfully tested her surface-to-air missile system against several target drones at the end of November 2009. Their principal role is to provide flagship command and control facilities, as well as helicopter-operating facilities, to two of the four escort flotillas that comprise the fleet escort force. Consequently, *Hyuga*

Hyuga (DDH-181) pictured operating with the US Navy amphibious assault ship *Boxer* (LHD-4) during Exercise Dawn Blitz on 12 June 2013. A Chinook heavy lift helicopter is located on the forward landing spot. Although principally intended for ASW operations, the *Hyuga* class can also support amphibious or humanitarian operations, a capability which will be further enhanced in the new 22DDH design. *(US Navy)*

An aerial view of *Hyuga* (DDH-181) alongside the US Navy carrier *George Washington* (CVN-73). The difference in scale between *Hyuga* and a full-scale strike carrier is readily apparent. Whilst Hyuga's carrier-like features have drawn much attention, her aviation capabilities are designed to support a limited number of helicopters. Her ability to provide flagship command and control facilities during ASW and humanitarian operations is arguably an equally important function. *(US Navy)*

belongs to Escort Flotilla 1 (EF1) home ported at Yokosuka Naval Base whilst *Ise* belongs to EF4 and is based at Kure.

In recent years, military operations other than war have been increasing worldwide and the *Hyuga* class destroyers are expected to be very effective in supporting such deployments. This was demonstrated early in the ships' career when the Great East Japan Earthquake struck the Tohoku region of Japan on 11 March 2011. *Hyuga* subsequently departed Yokosuka Naval Base on 16 March to transport supplies to the stricken region and provide humanitarian support to the victims. This capability will be further enhanced with the planned commissioning of 22DDH – reportedly to be named *Izumo* (DDH-183) when launched in the second half of 2013 – and her sister 24DDH some two years later.

Notes

1. The Japanese Heisei era corresponds to the reign of Akihito, the current Emperor of Japan, which commenced on 8 January 1989. Accordingly, 2004 was the sixteenth year of this era and is therefore Heisei 16 year.

2. The *Shirane* class are somewhat larger than the two initial helicopter-carrying destroyers, as reflected in a full load displacement of c.7,500 tons and length of 159m. They also incorporate two funnels compared with one on the earlier ships, which lengthens their profile. The *Haruna* class were subsequently refitted to bring their weapons outfit more into line with that fitted to the two later ships.

3. The '8-8' concept has resonances with earlier Imperial Japanese Navy plans to form a fleet centred on eight battleships and eight armoured cruisers (later battlecruisers). However, its more recent formulation reflects the post-war JMSDF's focus on anti-submarine warfare. This emphasis has started to change with the growing importance of anti-air and, particularly, ballistic missile defence (BMD) and has been reflected in the subdivision of each escort flotilla into two sub-groups. One of these – centred on a helicopter-carrying destroyer – is focused on anti-submarine warfare. The other has an anti-air warfare emphasis.

4. The flight deck is designed to support the simultaneous operation of the core air group of three anti-submarine helicopters plus an additional minesweeping or transport rotorcraft. The anti-submarine helicopters are SH-60J or SH-60K variants of the US Navy's SH-60B Seahawk and are built by Mitsubishi Heavy Industries under licence. They are usually supplemented by a Kawasaki Heavy Industries MCH-101 mine countermeasures helicopter, which is a modified version of AgustaWestland's AW101.

5. Prairie-Masker technology was developed by the US Navy to reduce and distort the acoustic signature of a ship's propulsion machinery. The Prairie portion of the system acts on a ship's propellers whilst the Masker portion is usually fitted close to the hull machinery spaces. Both use air bubbles created by compressed air to create the desired effect.

6. A description of the technological development of multifunction radars is beyond the scope of this chapter. Readers wanting to read more on this subject are referred to Norman Friedman's 'Naval Multifunction Radars: An Overview of their Development', *Seaforth World Naval Review 2011* (Barnsley: Seaforth Publishing, 2010), pp.154–62.

7. FCS-3 was originally designed to operate with a surface-to-air version of Japan's AAM-4 active radar guided air-to-air missile, which carries its own active seeker for terminal guidance. When this variant was cancelled, the JMSDF had to develop a supplementary illumination system for use with the semi-active ESSM, which needs external radar illumination of the target in an engagement's final phase. It has been widely reported that Japan acquired the intermittent continuous wave illumination (ICWI) sub-system developed by Thales Nederland for their APAR multifunction radar for this purpose. ICWI is theoretically more effective than the continuous wave illumination used by, for example, Aegis, as one array can guide a number of missiles during their terminal phase.

8. Sea RAM combines the Rolling Airframe Missile (RAM) developed from the Sidewinder air-to-air missile by the United States and Germany with the radar and infrared sensors used in the Phalanx CIWS to create an autonomous point defence missile system. It can therefore be operated without RAM's need for an external guidance system whilst having a longer effective range than Phalanx's 20mm cannon.

Author:
Guy Toremans

3.2 SIGNIFICANT SHIPS

IVER HUITFELDT CLASS FRIGATES

Spearhead of the Royal Danish Navy

HDMS *Iver Huitfeldt*, the first of the Royal Danish Navy's (RDN) new frigates, sailed from her homeport of Korsør on 16 October 2012 for her maiden operational mission: a ten-month deployment to the Indian Ocean in support of NATO's counter-piracy operation 'Ocean Shield'. With the introduction of the *Iver Huitfeldt* class frigates, as well as the two *Absalon*-class flexible support ships, the RDN has been transformed from a 'small ship' navy – focused on its adjacent waters – to a small 'big-ship' force geared towards expeditionary operations at range from its home bases.

DESIGN ORIGIN AND CONSTRUCTION

In the mid-1990s the Danish Defence Commission noted that international commitments would assume higher priority for the RDN and hence have a major impact on the future size and structure of the front-line fleet. The focus had shifted towards crisis management, with an emphasis on strengthening the navy's reaction forces and their capacity to undertake international operations. This funda-

The Royal Danish Navy's new *Iver Huitfeldt* class frigate, *Peter Willemoes,* pictured during ongoing sea trials off Sjaellands Odde in August 2012. One of a class of three ships oriented towards anti-air warfare, she is derived from the earlier *Absalon* class design. *(Guy Toremans)*

mental change, aligned with the pressing need to replace the navy's three *Niels Juel* class frigates and four *Falster* class minelayers, as well as a requirement to embark the Danish Task Group staff, shaped plans for a new-look surface fleet.[1]

In August 1997, the Committee Concerning the Danish Armed Forces' Equipment recommended the construction of six new, larger standard type of ships – *Stoerre Standard Skip* – in two versions: two *Flexible Støtteskibe* (Flexible Support Ships or FSS) which were to become the *Absalon* class (partly a frigate, partly a logistic-amphibious-command platform) and four frigate variants with a similar hull – referred to as *Patruljeskibe* (Patrol Ships or PS). These latter vessels were to become the *Iver Huitfeldt* class.

Given a restricted budget, tough choices had to be made, deliberately restricting features to essential requirements and ultimately reducing the number of frigates that were ordered. Commander s.g. (senior grade) Per Bigum, the first Frigate Project Officer said that, 'there was an imperative to maximise commonality between the *Absalon* class and the frigates, trade-off certain features, maximise commercial-off-the-shelf equipment, and leverage mercantile shipbuilding standards and methods'. Another tenet underpinning the FSS/PS programme was the re-use of Standard Flex weapon modules previously procured for the *Flyvefisken* class.[2] 'We

wanted to simplify the construction of the new ships,' said Commander Bigum, 'and make best use of the logistic benefits afforded by the Standard Flex (StanFlex) concept by uplifting the existing medium-calibre gun, surface-to-surface missiles and anti-ship missile defence modules.'

The FSS/PS project was stood up by the Danish Naval Material Command (NMC) in May 2000 following approval for the FSS in the Danish Defence Plan 2000–04. In advance of the project's formal establishment, the NMC had undertaken a feasibility phase during which BAE Systems Customer Solutions & Support and DCN International both scoped possible design solutions and, using the existing *Thetis* class patrol ship as a basis, confirmed the feasibility of the concept. BAE Systems' approach was preferred and the company was subsequently retained to provide design assistance. Thereafter, NMC worked with Danyard Aalborg, MAN B&W Diesel, Odense Steel Shipyard and Orskov Yard to develop the ship specifications that would form the basis for a competitive tender. In early August 2001 parallel negotiations with Orskov Yard and Odense Steel Shipyard (OSS) commenced, with the latter selected as the successful bidder in October 2001. The following month OSS was awarded a fixed-price contract covering the detailed design phase, together with the build of the two FSS ships. It was envisaged that construction of

The *Iver Huitfeldt* class were assembled in the Odense Steel Shipyard, where these images of the construction process were taken during the first half of 2009. All three units of the class were constructed in the same giant dry dock from sections fabricated in the Baltic Republics. Most of the outfitting of military equipment was carried out after delivery at the Korsør naval base. *(DALO)*

the follow-on PS vessels at OSS would follow under the next five-year Defence Agreement.

For its *Patruljeskibe*, the RDN envisaged a multi-purpose design but with anti-air warfare being the primary role. The NMC opened up a competition for the advanced anti-air warfare suite in 2004, looking for a phased-array, multifunction radar capable of surveillance, tracking, threat evaluation, weapon alignment, illumination and missile-guidance management. This specification evolved into a requirement for a more substantial area air defence capacity capable of protecting other shipping and pushing an air defence umbrella over troops ashore, thus expanding the competition's scope. A 2005 request for information encompassed both a multifunction radar and long-range interceptor missiles. The bids for the missile package saw Raytheon face off against MBDA, offering respectively their Standard Missile 2 (SM-2) and Aster 30 systems. Raytheon was the ultimate winner. The completion for the radar system drew initial interest from Lockheed Martin (SPY-1), Raytheon (SPY-3), BAE Systems Integrated Systems Technologies (Sampson with CEAMOUNT illuminators) and Thales Nederland (APAR in combination with SMART-L). The NMC narrowed the field down to BAE Systems and Thales Nederland, before selecting the latter bid in August 2006 and inking a contract deal – worth an estimated total of around €160m (c. US$210m) – four months later. The decisive factors in this selection were (i) the Dutch system's proven capabilities (the package was already in service with the German and the Netherlands navies in combination with SM-2) and (ii) its inherent growth potential and relative ease of upgrade.

Meanwhile, approval for three PS was confirmed in the Danish Defence Plan for 2005–09, paving the way for the construction phase to start. On 20 December 2006 the Danish Ministry of Defence (MOD) awarded the construction contract for three ships, worth c. US$850m to the Odense Steel Shipyard (OSS) in Lindø; a mere US$283m per ship due to re-use of Standard Flex weapon containers, carry-through of design elements from the Flexible

Support Ships, adoption of civilian production methods; and the Danish Defence Acquisition and Logistics Organisation's (DALO's) responsibility for weapon and sensor integration.[3] 'Whilst the shipyard bore full responsibility for the design and performance of the platform itself, responsibility for all the combat system elements and their physical interface in the ships resided with DALO. To speed up construction, workers from DALO installed all navigation systems and many kilometres of cables and wires whilst the frigates were being assembled at the shipyard', Commander s.g Per Hesselberg – the current Frigate Project Officer – pointed out.

To achieve economies in the build process, OSS outsourced block construction to the Baltija Shipyard in Klaipeda, Lithuania (fabricating the lower fore and aft and keel blocks) and Loksa Shipbuilding in Estonia (fabricating the upper, central and superstructure sections), after which the blocks were shipped to Odense for assembly.

The keel for the first-of-class, to become *Iver Huitfeldt* (F361), was laid on 2 June 2008. Floated out in March 2010 and officially named by Crown Prince Frederik of Denmark in November, the frigate was officially turned over to DALO by OSS on 21 January 2011 after initial sea trials in late 2010. The handover papers were signed by Captain (N) Per Bigum Christensen – Technical Director, Naval System Division – in the presence of Rear Admiral Finn Hansen – Admiral Danish Fleet; Lieutenant General Per Ludvigsen – the Chief of Danish Acquisition and Logistic Organisation; and the commanding officer of the frigate – Commander s.g. Carsten Fjord Larsen.

THE PLATFORM

At 138.7m length and with a standard displacement of 5,900 tons (increasing to 6,645 tons at full load) the *Iver Huitfeldt* class units are somewhat shorter than the German *Sachsen* (4.3m) and Dutch *De Zeven Provinciën* (5.5m) classes but are both broader and heavier.

'The hull is based on the *Absalon* class FSS, minus the 900m[2] vehicle/cargo deck, but is optimised for twice the power. This means that the aft part of the underwater hull is modified in order to accommodate the increased propeller thrust and the flow of water it subsequently creates, as well as to encompass the larger engine rooms required for the additional prime movers,' Cdr Hesselberg explained. The funnels have also been relocated to reduce the effect of exhaust on

Table 3.2.1: *IVER HUITFELDT* CLASS COMPARISONS

CLASS:	*IVER HUITFELDT*	*DE ZEVEN PROVINCIËN*	*SACHSEN* (F-124)
Country:	Denmark	Netherlands	Germany
Full Load Displacement:	6,645 tons	6,050 tons	5,600 tons
Dimensions:	138.7m x 19.8m x 5.3m	144m.2 x 18.8m x 5.2m	143.0m x 17.4m x 5.4m
Propulsion:	CODAD, 33MW, 28+ knots	CODOG, 17MW or 38MW, 30 knots	CODAG, 39MW, 29 knots
Range:	9,000 nautical miles at 18 knots.	5,000 nautical miles at 18 knots.	4,000 nautical miles at 18 knots.
Crew:	101 (64 spare)	174 (58 spare)	185 (58 spare)
Main Sensors:	APAR plus SMART-L AS0-94 sonar	APAR plus SMART-L DSQS-24C sonar	APAR plus SMART-L DSQS-24B sonar
Armament:	2 x 76mm Oto Melara 1 x 35mm Millennium Mk 41 VLS: 32 cells MK 56 VLS: 24 cells 2 x quad Harpoon 2 x twin ASW torpedo launchers AW-101 or SH-60 helicopter	1 x 127mm Oto Melara 1/2 x 30mm Goalkeeper Mk 41 VLS: 40 cells – 2 x quad Harpoon 2 x twin ASW torpedo launchers NFH-90 helicopter	1 x 76mm Oto Melara 2 x 27mm Mauser Mk 41 VLS: 32 cells 2 x RAM 2 x quad Harpoon 2 x triple ASW torpedo launchers 1/2 x NFH-90 helicopters

the SMART-L 3D air- and surface-search radar.

Like the *Absalon* class, the design has adopted a comprehensive approach to signature reduction. The radar cross section (RCS) is reduced by flaring the hull; inclining the superstructure; and avoiding vertically aligned objects. In addition, missile launchers are installed within 'walls'; treated metalized bridge window glass is used to divert radar signals; and both the quarterdeck and forecastle are closed off in order to conceal jagged clutter that could otherwise be picked up on enemy radar. Similarly, capstans and bollards are either hidden or installed as close to the deck as possible. Significant reduction in underwater radiated noise is achieved by dampening the machinery noise through use of high-impedance multi-pole foundations; the elastic mounting of noisy machinery, equipment; and pipework and structural acoustic damping. The underwater magnetic signature is kept to a minimum by a multi-axial degaussing system. Infra-red (IR) signature is reduced through the use of cooling devices and shielding around the engine exhausts, thermal insulation around hot compartments and a wash-down system.

As for seaworthiness, the frigates are designed to maintain full operational capability in Sea State 6. A set of active stabilisers provide excellent stability. According to Cdr s.g. Carsten Fjord-Larsen, *Iver Huifeldt*'s commanding officer, 'The ships are capable of maintaining a good speed when sailing head-on into relatively rough seas and have proved even more comfortable than our *Absalon* class'. The generous dimensions of the hull aid operational effectiveness and maintainability, with increased headroom between decks, deeper and longer engine compartments and wider equipment pathways.

Two replenishment-at-sea stations are fitted port and starboard, both capable of receiving and transferring fuel and water. Although the frigates do not have the same capacity as the *Absalon* class with their 900m[2] 'flex-deck', the frigates do benefit from a mini flex-deck storage compartment which provides a number of additional capabilities. It can hold up to four 20ft (6.4m) standard containers; a decompression chamber or a medical facility. Alternatively, it can be used to embark extra supplies for longer endurance or even as a purpose-built prison, for instance during counter-piracy operations.

The frigates are built according to the Det Norske Veritas (DNV) classification society's specifications, with sixty months corrosion protection. This means that every fifth year the frigates will have to dock for between two and three weeks and undergo a two- to three-month maintenance period. Maintenance of weapons systems will not influence the operational cycle, however, because of use of the StanFlex

An overall schematic of the *Iver Huitfeldt* class ship platform, showing her overall internal layout. Of particular note is the subdivision of the hull into six main damage-control zones and the space made available for StanFlex standardised weapons containers. *(DALO)*

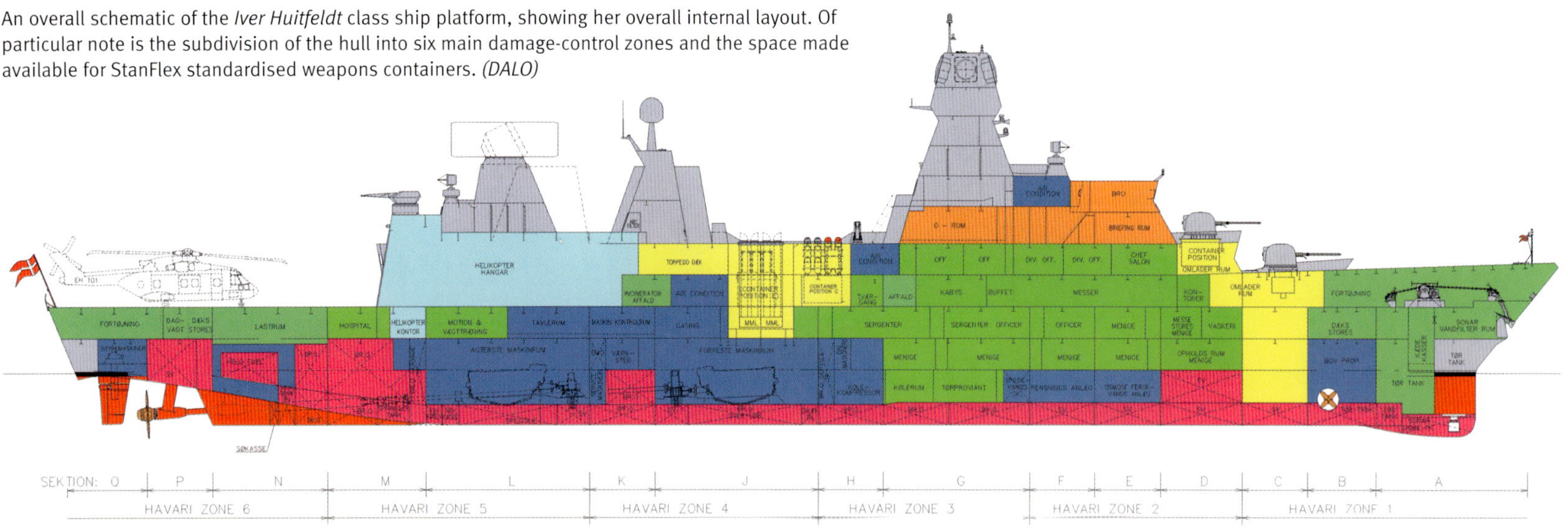

Peter Willemoes pictured whilst on trials. The hull is shorter but broader than comparable ships in the German and Royal Netherlands Navy, being derived from the *Absalon* class flexible support ship design. *(Guy Toremans)*

container system: weapon systems that need maintenance can easily be swapped for another containerised weapon system. The frigates feature one forward and four amidships StanFlex positions. The modules are craned into wells with standard interface connections, providing access to ship's services (power ventilation, communications, water, and data). 'Installation of a single container is accomplished in about thirty minutes and, depending upon the weapon and equipment, system checks are generally completed within hours', Commander Hesselberg said.

The class is certified for operations with a 20-ton helicopter and features a 600m² flight deck and a 200m² hangar. This provides sufficient margin to operate, for example, an AgustaWestland AW-101 Merlin. The helicopter deck handling system permits flight operations in up to Sea State 6, while there are engineering workshops in the hangar for operational maintenance. The spacious hangar would also come in very handy if the frigates have to deploy in support of humanitarian assistance or evacuation operations.

The *Iver Huitfeldt* class frigates are conceived with significant growth potential. Surplus space, along with extra electrical generating and cooling capacity, permits the installation of new systems and equipment during the ship's service life of c .thirty years. Potential growth could see, for example, the addition of theatre ballistic missile defence (BMD) or co-operative engagement capabilities.

SURVIVABILITY

The frigates exploit survivability studies undertaken for the *Absalon* class units. The focus is on the ships' ability to maintain combat readiness after damage. The hull is designed to remain afloat with three adjacent compartments flooded, whilst propulsion and power generation can be maintained with two adjacent compartments flooded.

The class's overall design layout is based on a structure encompassing seven decks, subdivided in fifteen water- and gas-tight compartments. There are six damage control and fire zones, along with three separate NBC citadels equipped with independent air-conditioning modules, electrical power, fire-fighting pumps and power-distribution panels. Commander Hesselberg stressed that although the ships are 'largely built to civilian standards and meet the Det Norske Veritas (DNV) ship rules, the Royal Danish Navy insisted on the application of lessons learned from former operations, such as the incorporation of lightweight splinter protection for shielding vital and hazardous areas against penetration by projectiles, as well as the addition of steel armour around the combat spaces and technical galleries. Wiring, pipes and ducts are multi-redundant and appropriately spaced in order to reduce consequences of a hit.'

Damage control co-ordination is supported by an integrated monitoring and control system centred on the machinery control room and widely accessible from the network of combat consoles distributed onboard. The system records, processes and reports specific information to the damage control teams, enabling accurate identification of the ship's platform status and situation at all times. Screens showing the ship's general arrangement plan combined with manual plotting capabilities, ship side views, alarms and warning overviews are retrievable from the various consoles. A large number of automated detectors and sensor systems (more than

The *Iver Huitfeldt* class design follows other recent warships in adopting a comprehensive approach to signature reduction, including the use of a flared hull and inclined superstructure and the avoidance of vertically-aligned objects, as evidenced in this 2012 view of *Peter Willemoes*. Survivability is also enhanced by a strong focus on damage control, including incorporation of armour and splinter protection in appropriate areas, use of multi-redundant wiring, and sub-division into multiple NBC citadels and fire zones. *(Guy Toremans)*

A Lynx helicopter conducting landing operations onboard *Iver Huitfeldt*. The 600m² flight deck is certified for operations with helicopters up to AW-101 size but can support larger, 20-ton helicopters, allowing heavy Army helicopters to land in a joint operation. *(Guy Toremans)*

6,000 sensors and fifty cameras linked to the ship's CCTV-system) are fitted throughout the ships' over 300 compartments, automatically activating a water-mist system in case of fire. The stability of the vessel in damaged conditions is assessed with computerised support, which determines the condition of the vessel from continuously updated tank level measurements and a register of damaged compartments.

PLATFORM MANAGEMENT SYSTEMS

The frigates also break new ground with regard to platform management. The electrical, propulsion and support equipment is controlled by a comprehensive integrated platform management system (IMPS) developed by Rockwell Automation. This system ensures permanent status identification and control of the ships' internal technical components relating to propulsion, the electrical network and broader ship operations. Control and monitoring can be performed from a network of consoles through the use of high-resolution colour LCD monitors. Configured in a 100 M/Bit Ethernet ring, the IPMS is equipped with a comprehensive range of user interfaces, while the subsystems are connected to a dual redundant main internet data bus.

The associated Rockwell Automation integrated

Table 3.2.2.

IVER HUITFELDT (F361) PRINCIPAL PARTICULARS

Building Information:

Laid Down:	2 June 2008
Launched:	11 March 2010
Delivered:	21 January 2011[1]
Builders:	Odense Steel Shipyard, Odense (with subsequent weapons systems outfitting at Korsør Naval Base).

Dimensions:

Displacement:	5,900 tons standard displacement, 6,645 tons full load displacement.
Overall Hull Dimensions:	138.7m (125.0m perpendiculars) x 19.8m x 5.3m (6.4m maximum).

Weapons Systems:[2]

Missiles:	4 x Mk 41 8-cell VLS modules for a total of 32 Standard SM-2 surface-to-air missiles.
	2 x Mk 56 12-cell VLS launchers for ESSM surface-to-air missiles in Stanflex container positions 'E' and 'F'.
	2 x quad Harpoon surface-to-surface missiles in Stanflex container positions 'C' and 'D'.
Guns:	2 x 76mm Oto Melara compact (one in Stanflex position 'B'). 1 x Oerlikon Contraves-Millenium 35mm CIWS. Machine guns.
Torpedoes:	2 x twin 324mm anti-submarine torpedo tubes for Eurotorp MU90 torpedoes.
Aircraft:	Flight deck and hangar for 1 x AW-101 or equivalent. Potential for UAVs.
Countermeasures:	ES-3701 electronic support measures (ESM) system. 8 x launchers for chaff/IR countermeasures.
Principal Sensors:	1 x APAR multifunction radar. 1 x SMART-L long-range search radar. 1 x Terma Scanter 6000 search radar. 1 x ASO-94 hull mounted sonar.
Combat System:	Terma C-Flex combat management system. Infocom 2000 integrated communication suite includes NATO Links 11 and 16 and provision for Link 22.

Propulsion Systems:

Machinery:	CODAD. 4 x Tognum MTU 20V 8000 M70 diesel engines rated at 33MW total produce 44,000shp through two shafts.
Speed:	Designed maximum speed is in excess of 28 knots. Range is 9,000 nautical miles at 18 knots.

Other Details:

Complement:	A typical crew comprises 101 personnel.[3] Accommodation is provided for c. 165.
Class:	Three ships have been constructed: *Iver Huitfeldt* (F361), *Peter Willemoes* (F362) and *Niels Juel* (F363).

Notes:

1 Delivery date refers to delivery by Odense Steel Shipyard to DALO. Subsequent outfitting means the ship will not be fully operational until 2014.

2 Systems refer to full class armament outfit. Armament is being installed incrementally and will vary dependent on Stanflex container outfit.

3 Encompasses 35 operational dept., 20 propulsion dept., 15 navigation dept., 15 supply dept., 15 weapons dept. and the commanding officer.

bridge system (IBS) displays all engineering control information. Providing a complete picture of the tactical situation, it allows the ship to be operated with a reduced watch-keeping team during transit cruising. There is provision for interface and information exchange between the IBS and the CMS, for example to present navigation information to the operations room or send tactical information to the bridge.

PROPULSION

The frigates are powered by four main MTU 20V 8000 M70 diesel engines. These drive twin shaft lines through a Renk reduction gearbox in a combined diesel and diesel (CODAD) configuration. Four separate diesel generators provide electricity for ship services. The CODAD configuration has a reduced maintenance workload compared with CODOG and CODAG plants because, typically,

fewer cylinders are in operation. The overall arrangement also provides potential for producing a higher speed or accommodating a greater displacement without impacting the overall propulsion or electrical systems' architecture. Generating a maximum of 44,000hp the propulsion system is capable of providing a top speed approaching 30 knots. The frigates can also achieve a staggering endurance of 9,000 nautical miles at 18 knots, which is almost

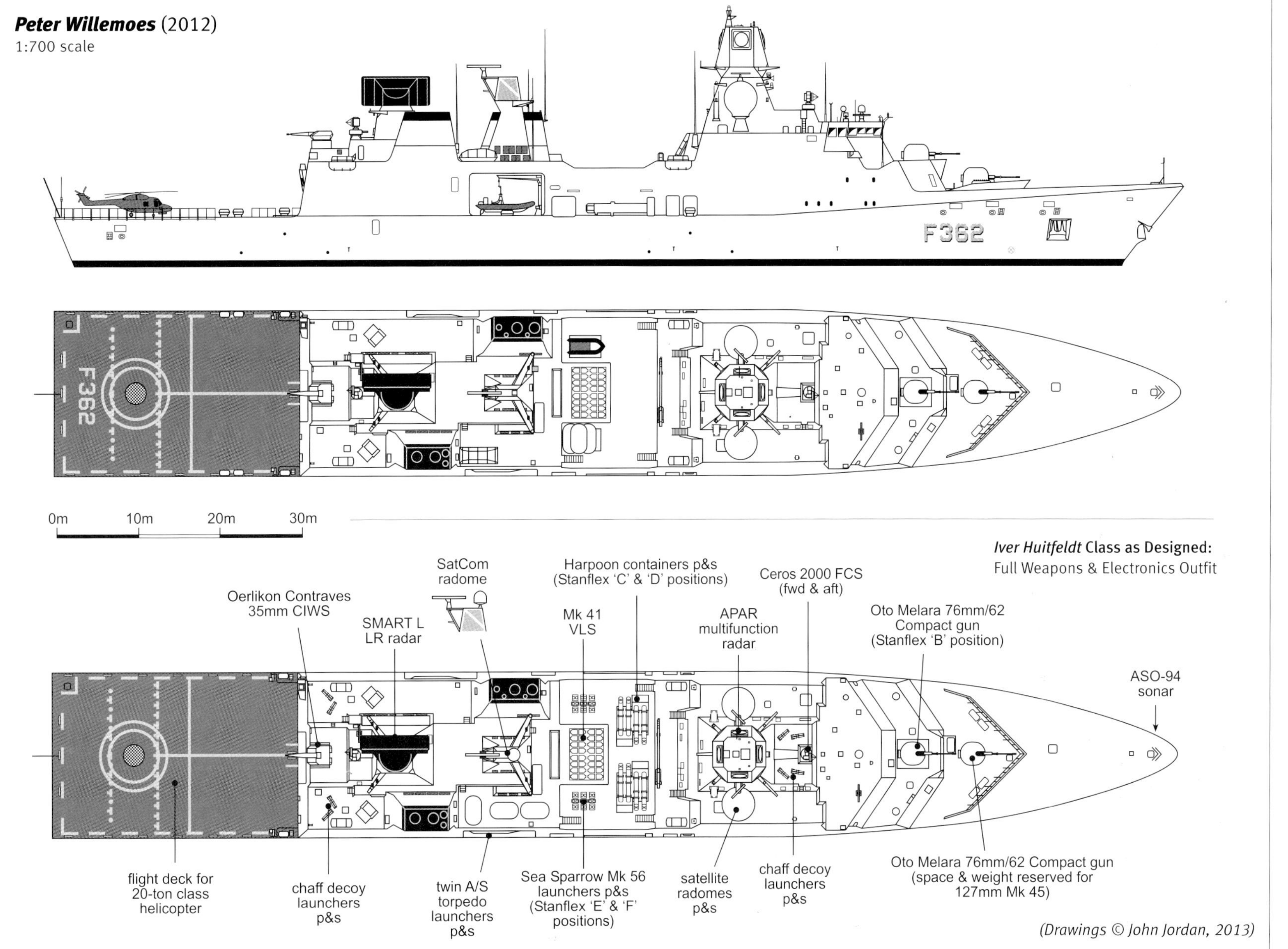

(Drawings © John Jordan, 2013)

twice as much as their German and Dutch counterparts. The frigates are fitted with a bow thruster with an output of 900kW, which provides for station-keeping and precision manoeuvring. The RDN is reportedly happy the propulsion configuration meets its specific requirements, with the diesel engines responding smoothly and swiftly during manoeuvring and with the twin MAN Alpha controllable-pitch propellers providing a good acoustic signature. However, the acoustic and vibration profile of the propeller shaft guidance systems has caused some problems.

THE COMBAT SUITE

Combat Management System: The combat management system (CMS) comprises Terma's C4I (C-Flex) command and control system based on the T-Core open architecture platform. It features a specially-designed weapons management system and incorporates commercial-off-the-shelf (COTS) equipment, including the server, console computer, interface computer, local area network (LAN) switch and universal power supply unit. The system can support up to thirty-two workstations on a duplicated one gigabyte Ethernet LAN. Modular application software is written in Java using a Windows XP operating system (planned for upgrade to Windows 7 from 2014). Sensors and C3 servers are connected directly to the intranet. Up to three additional consoles can be added to control additional weapons or other systems.

The white light operations room (CIC) features two large-screen tactical displays and thirty multi-function consoles, each with flat screens. The setup of the CIC is flexible, as each C-Flex console can be individually configured according to the system it is tasked to control. The consoles have independent processors, which allow any sea-warfare function – anti-air warfare, anti-submarine warfare, anti-surface warfare, electronic warfare, navigation, data-links or other communications – to be managed from any console. One of the consoles is dedicated to the operation of an autonomous underwater vehicle,

A view of *Peter Willemoes'* APAR multifunction radar tower being craned onto the ship at the Odense Steel Shipyard in March 2011. She was the first ship of the class to receive the system, as lead ship *Iver Huitfeldt* was completed without a full radar fit to speed trials of other systems. APAR performs search and tracking functions out to 150km as well as providing fire control guidance for the class's surface-to-air missiles. *(DALO)*

whilst the crypto and communications operators have their own dedicated operation rooms.

Sensors – The APAR and SMART-L Approach: The frigates' sensor suite provides for very good area coverage in the air, over the surface and even sub-surface environment. Targeting and missile guidance capability is entrusted to the 15-ton APAR (Active Phased-Array Radar), which operates in the I/J-band (US Navy: X-band) and provides search, tracking and fire-control capabilities. The operating band means that it has relatively limited range in search mode (reported range is in the order of 150km for aerial targets, 75km at the horizon and c. 30km for surface targets) but also that it excels in its ability to provide simultaneous mid-course and terminal homing guidance for multiple missiles, both SM-2 and ESSM. Coverage encompasses the ship's full engagement envelope and can cater for all target-approach profiles, from supersonic sea-skimming targets to incoming diving missiles. Each of the four arrays, comprising 3,424 active elements, can control the simultaneous engagement of up to four targets, manage up to eight missiles in flight and track over 200 targets at one and the same time.

The other main sensor is the multi-beam SMART-L planar-array volume search radar. Operating in the D-band (US Navy L-band) this compensates for APAR's relatively limited range by offering detection ranges out to 400km. It is capable of tracking up to 1,000 air and 100 surface targets, as well as detecting stealthy anti-ship missiles out to around 65km. Its advanced software enables it to perform well in adverse electronic warfare environments, with least-jammed frequency determination and multiple-hypothesis tracking giving a high probability that it will be able to maintain radar tracks and distinguish them from other clutter.

The fact that the *Iver Huitfeldt* class units feature the same major sensors – viz. the APAR and SMART-L radars – that are used in Germany's *Sachsen* and the Dutch *De Zeven Provinciën* class

A view of *Iver Huitfeldt* departing the Odense Steel Shipyard on 13 December 2010 to commence builders' sea trials. She was formally handed over to the Danish Defence Acquisition and Logistics Organisation (DALO) in January 2011 at which stage her SMART-L radar and Mk 41 vertical launch system were the only major weapons systems installed. SMART-L supplements APAR's relatively limited range by providing a volume search capability out to around 400km. *(DALO)*

frigates will certainly prove beneficial. As noted by Commander Fjord-Larsen, 'The Royal Danish Navy has already signed a MoU concerning joint cooperation regarding spare parts, maintenance and soft and hardware upgrades. And we are already participating in the German-Netherlands air warfare course, whilst some officers regularly embark onboard the German and Dutch counterparts to gain experience in operating these radars.'

The ships also mount a Terma Scanter 6000 surface-search navigation radar, specifically developed for surface/low-altitude surveillance in support of maritime interdiction operations, helicopter control and search-and-rescue. Other sensors include the Saab Ceros 2000 fire-control system for the guns (which can also provide secondary illumination for the ESSM missiles), two FLIR Seastar Safire III electro-optical trackers that interface with the C4I suite and a Furuno navigation radar integrated into the electronic chart display information system (ECDIS).

Weapons Systems: The frigates are capable of mounting an impressive, multi-role weapon suite.[4] The designed anti-air fit is made up of an integrated air defence system consisting of four, eight-cell Lockheed Martin Mk 41 vertical launch system modules for Raytheon SM-2 Block IIIA medium-range surface-to-air missiles and two containerised, twelve-cell Mk 56 launch units for shorter-range Evolved Sea Sparrow Missiles (ESSM) in two of the StanFlex positions amidships. As a last line of defence, the frigates also ship an Oerlikon Contraves-Millenium 35mm gun with Advanced Hit Efficiency and Destruction (AHEAD) air-burst munitions. A single system is fitted above the hangar, whilst 'B' position could also accept an additional Millennium mounting in place of the current 76mm Super Rapid mounting.

The use of the Mk 41 vertical-launch system provides the frigates with considerable flexibility for future upgrades, including the potential to acquire the SM-3 exo-atmospheric ballistic missile interceptor.[5] Tomahawk cruise missiles could also be installed for land attack missions should the Danish Government ever decide it required this capability.

The designed anti-surface warfare suite includes sixteen Harpoon surface-to-surface missiles in four quad launchers, located in the other two midships StanFlex container positions. The forward StanFlex position is occupied by an Oto Melara 76mm/62 Super Rapid gun, whilst four crew-served 12.7mm

Above, left: A view of the Mk 41 vertical launch system onboard the *Iver Huitfeldt*, which is located in the middle of the ship. Comprising four eight-cell modules, it is intended to house Standard SM-2 surface-to-air missiles but is capable of supporting a wide-range of weapons, including Tomahawk cruise missiles and SM-3 ballistic missile interceptors. Note also the space reserved alongside the launcher for StanFlex missile containers. *(Guy Toremans)*

Above, right: *Iver Huitfeldt's* last-ditch defence against anti-ship missiles is provided by the Oerlikon Contraves 35mm CIWS. One of these weapons is installed on top of the hangar, whilst it would be possible to mount a second system in the StanFlex 'B' position ahead of the bridge. *(Guy Toremans)*

The Thales Active Phased-Array Radar (APAR) tower onboard *Peter Willemoes*. Two of the system's four fixed phased-array panels – each of which has 3,424 active elements and can control the simultaneous engagement of up to four targets – can be seen. Other equipment in view includes a Furuno navigation radar above the satellite radome and a Saab Ceros 2000 fire-control system on top of the bridge. The ship's external communications include a range of satellite and radio systems that support NATO Links 11 and 16 and which are integrated with the internal network by an Infocom 2000 communications suite. *(Guy Toremans)*

The heart of the *Iver Huitfeldt* class's combat capabilities is comprised of a Terma C-Flex combat management system. The system supports thirty-two workstations, many of which can be seen in this image of the 'white light' operations room. The room's set up is flexible, as each console can be configured according to the system it is tasked to control. *(Guy Toremans)*

machine gun mounts are installed around the ship for force protection. The standard fit for 'A' position is a second Oto Melara 76mm gun, but it can take a BAE Systems Mk 45 127mm gun as an alternative.

The anti-submarine warfare system is based on the Atlas Elektronik ASO 94 hull-mounted sonar, part of the firm's Sonar 90 series, and two twin 324mm torpedo tubes for the Eurotorp MU90 lightweight anti-submarine warfare torpedoes for short range defence. These are supplemented by the capabilities of the ship's embarked helicopter.

Countermeasures: Electronic warfare systems are focused on an ITT EDO ES-3701 electronic support measures (ESM) suite. This electronic warfare system has been widely adopted by the Scandinavian (for example, in Norway's *Nansen* class frigates and Sweden's *Visby* class corvettes) and other navies and provides a broad range of surveillance capabilities. There is also a standard fit of eight chaff and IR launchers, providing 360° coverage against incoming anti-ship missiles.

COMMUNICATIONS

An Infocom 2000 integrated communications suite (ICS), identical to those fitted on board the previous *Absalon* class units, offers external communications to NATO standards, as well as providing secure internal communications, video-conferencing and real-time data exchange. The external system incorporates HF, VHF, UHF and SHF radio communications as well as a comprehensive range of satellite links such as VSAT and Inmarsat. The existing NATO Link 11 and Link 16 communications are supported, whilst there is provision for the installation of NATO Link 22 at some later date. The internal communication system comprises a tactical intercom for voice and data switching, messaging, conventional and wireless telephony, closed-circuit television, internet and intranet ports, a radio exchange, wireless communications for flight deck and machinery spaces a public address system; and sound powered telephones. The ICS also includes the infrastructure required to host joint and allied command centres during expeditionary deployments.

When roled as a command platform or principal warfare co-ordinator unit the frigates can support an embarked staff of up to forty people. Facilities provided for such a staff include dedicated multi-function consoles, planning and briefing rooms and full access to the communications network.

LEAN MANNING CONCEPT

For their size, the *Iver Huitfeldt* class units are remarkably manpower-efficient. Ships of this size have traditionally required a crew of 200 or more but, due to the 'lean manning', the new frigates have a crew of just 101 in a full operational role. This compares with the c. 230–240 found on board the comparable German *Sachsen* and Netherlands *De Zeven Provinciën* classes. Such low manning levels are achieved by means of extensive automation, as well as the adaption of innovative man-machine interfaces. The drive for manpower efficiency even extends to the stocking of supplies and stores. Gone is the need for long lines of sailors passing supplies from hand to hand, through hatches and down ladders to storerooms deep in the ship. Instead a monorail and a dedicated elevator on the main deck take supplies and pallets below decks to the store rooms and freezers.

Cdr Fjord-Larsen said that there was a steep learning curve in operating the ship with such a small crew. Relying so heavily on automated systems and fewer people requires better education and technical understanding, since operators are responsible for more than one warfare area and may have to double up as equipment maintainers. 'This high level of specialisation has potential problems because there is less slack available in the complement if someone goes sick or on leave. Personally, I think that we are at the lower end of the manning limit. During our forthcoming deployment we will certainly look into this and have confirmation [as to whether] 101 are sufficient. It will all come down to crew-endurance.' Regardless of the lean manning, the RDN may still face manpower issues once all three frigates are fully operational. This is because the current Danish defence agreement does not currently provide the resources needed for three full crews.

Given that the frigates are expected to deploy for

The *Iver Huitfeldt* class have been designed for operation by a minimal crew, with a core complement of just 101 personnel. Accommodation standards are high, reflecting the fact that the frigates are expected to deploy for extended periods. These images show a two-berth officer's cabin. *(Guy Toremans)*

Left: The Royal Danish Navy's three *Iver Huitfeldt* class frigates operating together for the first time in August 2012. Note the different weapons fits on the three ships, reflecting Denmark's decision to outfit weaponry on an incremental basis. The ships have been put through an extensive series of pre and post-delivery trials as equipment has been steadily installed. *(Royal Danish Navy)*

Below: *Iver Huitfeldt* was formally handed over to the Royal Danish Navy on 6 February 2012 – this image shows her with *Peter Willemoes* on the day of the ceremony in the ice-covered waters of Korsør Naval Base. Post-delivery outfitting of the majority of the class's weapons systems has largely been undertaken at Korsør by DALO's Forsvarets Hovadvaerksteder. *(DALO)*

extended periods, the designers paid great attention to the need to deliver a good quality of life by incorporating the latest accommodation standards. Gone are the days of cramped, heavily-populated messes, each sailor now having about forty per cent more personal space than in 1990s-vintage warships. Ratings are accommodated in four-berth compartments with *en suite* shower and toilet facilities. Petty officers enjoy four- or two-berth cabins, also with dedicated showers and lavatories, while commissioned officers are accommodated in two- or single-berth cabins. Additional accommodation for up to sixty-four personnel is provided. Furniture, bulkhead and ceiling fittings are designed for high shock resistance, easy removal, good noise insulation and high durability. The galley, wardroom and petty officers' and ratings' messes, as well as the provisions and refrigerated stores, are all located on the same deck. The onboard medical facilities allow the class to provide Role 2 medical care, i.e. general medicine, surgery and dental treatment, with one compartment serving as a surgical room and another containing three hospital beds.

OPERATIONAL EXPERIENCE

Iver Huitfeldt: As first-of-class, *Iver Huitfeldt* (F361) underwent extensive contractor trials to establish that the platform and its systems worked according to specification and met the required capabilities. 'The pre-delivery acceptance trials proved very satisfactory. Obviously, in every large and complex project, one finds deficiencies. But I am very pleased', Commander Per Hesselberg explained. 'We only found a few minor issues, which were remedied quite fast: for example, we have built water separators into the fuel system in order to protect the sophisticated common rail diesel engines; we redesigned the stern tube cooling system; and we improved some of the internal noise reduction.'

Immediately after her hand-over to DALO, the frigate went to sea to familiarise the crew and to conduct initial damage control exercises. After a week at sea she returned to the naval base in Korsør for further outfitting by the Forsvarets Hovedvaerksteder.[6] This encompassed installation of

Right: *Iver Huitfeldt* pictured in the Arabian Sea on 2 January 2013 in support of NATO's Operation 'Ocean Shield'. The frigate deployed to the Middle East in October 2012 as part of an ongoing programme of trials before becoming fully operational. *(US Navy)*

Iver Huitfeldt was subject to significant ongoing testing after initial delivery to DALO as military equipment was installed. This October 2011 image image was taken during a series of Sea Acceptance Trials between May and October of that year and shows the detonation of an explosive charge close to the hull to check the resistance of key systems to shock damage. *(DALO)*

the combat management system, military communication systems, the operational and administrative networks, the SMART-L radar, the sonar, the ESM system, an Oto Melara 76mm gun, the CEROS fire-control system, the FLIR and the surface- and heli-copter-tracking radar.[7] A second series of sea acceptance trials (SATs) commenced in May and lasted until November 2011. In the weeks between trials, the APAR mast module was installed. One of the most demanding tests was to take the ship out into a storm to see how the design would stand up to the tempestuous Baltic. It was discovered that the frigate's seaworthiness was superb, especially the ability to manoeuvre the ship precisely thanks to the rudders, the active stabilisers and the bow thruster.

In January 2012 the frigate underwent her Naval Forces Sensor and Weapon Accuracy Checks (FORACS) at the NATO site in Stavanger, with hand-over from DALO to the navy on 6 February 2012. *Iver Huitfeldt* was transferred with only 'basic frigate role' equipment. In practice, this meant that – as far as her sensors and communication suites were concerned – she was equipped in a broadly

similar fashion to the *Absalon* class; and without a functioning APAR. Commander Hesselberg explained, 'We equipped her in this "light configuration" because we decided to get the frigate out at sea quickly in order to identify any deficiencies as soon as possible, keeping in mind that the other two frigates [*Peter Willemoes* and *Niels Juel*] were to be delivered rapidly in sequence. We had to make sure that these units would not suffer any of the problems that might occur with the lead ship.'

In March 2012, *Iver Huitfeldt* took part in her first major exercise – NATO's three-week-long Cold Response 2012. 'This was a beneficial exercise because the crew got a grip on the CIC procedures and weapons and sensors systems', Commander Carsten Fjord-Larsen said. 'I was positively surprised; having expected more system integration challenges and to deal with software hitches and bugs. But everything went so smoothly. Of course we need several other exercises and situations in which we can put our sensors and weapon system through its paces.'

Upon completion of this exercise, the ship under-

went further extensive training prior to participating on the annual BALTOPS exercises in June 2012. This provided a particular opportunity to train the ship's officers-of-the-watch in close manoeuvring with other units in confined waters. Subsequently, *Iver Huitfeldt* commenced installation of mission-specific equipment in preparation for her maiden deployment in support of Operation 'Ocean Shield'. At the end of August 2012, the frigate went through a week-long period of counter-piracy training. Commander Fjord-Larsen explained, 'This was the very first time the Royal Danish Navy implemented this CP training module. In addition to the 101 core crew we embarked 46 extra personnel [a helicopter detachment, Special Forces, military policy, medical team, Somali and Arabic interpreter and a chaplain]. Throughout the training the crew had to cope with a wide range of piracy-related serials based on previous live incidents.' After final preparations the frigate sailed for Bay of Aden on 16 October 2012. 'Once in the operational area our battle-rhythm was three to four weeks 'on patrol' and four to five days 'in port' said Commander Fjord-Larsen. This deployment was also the ship's tropical-climate test.

Upon her return home in the summer of 2013, installation of the remainder of the APAR equipment and other systems will be carried out from the middle of September until the end of April 2014. The final tests will start in May 2014. It is envisaged that *Iver Huitfeldt* will then be declared fully operational around the end of 2014, with the frigate than the first in the class to have her combat management system running on the Windows 7 version software.

Peter Willemoes: Construction of the second ship, *Peter Willemoes* (F362), started in March 2009. Floated out at the end of 2010, she was officially named by Danish Prime Minister Lars Løkke Rasmussen on 13 May 2011. In March 2011, she was the first ship of the class to be fitted with an APAR tower module and subsequently commenced sea trials in June before delivery at the end of the month. Following further installation of anti-air and other systems, interspersed with trials and training, she sailed for her shakedown cruise to the Caribbean in October 2011, testing the ventilation, cooling and air-conditioning systems. Upon her return from these warm-water trials, 2012 saw the installation and live firings of the two 76mm guns and the 35mm CIWS, followed by APAR search and track tests; initially using drones and a small plane. 'With

An aerial view of *Iver Huitfeldt*. During her deployment on Operation 'Ocean Shield' she spent five months on station, disrupting a pirate attack on the Danish tanker *Torm Kristina* and assisting with the recovery of six hostages from MV *Leopard*. The class has been designed with such long-range operations in mind. *(NATO)*

An image of *Iver Huitfeldt* in August 2012. Although her APAR tower has been installed, she will not be fully furnished with her air defence system until the first half of 2014. All three sister-ships are likely to become fully operational in the course of the year. *(Guy Toremans)*

the anti-air warfare capability being "new ground" for the Danish Navy the toughest challenge will be to bring the frigates up to operational standard', Commander Per Hesselberg affirmed. Thales ultimately finalised sea acceptance trials on the APAR in March 2013, during which several air force assets such as F-16 fighters and Lynx helicopters were used for alignment and test purposes.

The remainder of 2013 is likely to see the implementation of software upgrades for the combat management system and anti-air warfare system, followed by live ESSM firings, possibly to take place off Scotland during the latter half of November. *Peter Willemoes* is scheduled to join the fleet by early 2014 and is likely to be the first of the three frigates to undergo Flag Officer Sea Training (FOST) with the British Royal Navy in 2015.

Niels Juel: The keel of the third and final member of the class, *Niels Juel* (F363), was laid in December 2009. She was floated out in December 2010 – on the same day as and slightly ahead of *Peter Willemoes* – and was named by Crown Princess Mary of Denmark on 7 November 2011. *Niels Juel* was the last vessel completed by the OSS yard before its final closure. She is currently in the trials and equipment outfitting stage and is expected to join the operational fleet during 2014.

CONCLUSION

The *Iver Huitfeldt* class frigates are well-balanced ships, whether looked at from a sensor, weapons system, ship-handling or even crew accommodation point of view. As Commander Per Hesselberg stressed, 'The Royal Danish Navy has received a "lot of ship" for the money invested in this project.' Certainly, with its three new frigates, Denmark will field a leading-edge anti-air warfare capability. Together with Germany's *Sachsen*s, the Royal Netherlands Navy's *De Zeven Provinciën*s, Spain's *Alvaro de Bazan*s, the Franco-Italian 'Horizons' and the British Royal Navy's Type 45s, they form a cohort of high-technology, European-built anti-air warfare escorts that are the equal of any comparable ships in the world.

Notes

1. All three *Niels Juel* class units were decommissioned on 18 August 2009.

2. The Standard Flex of StanFlex modular mission payload system was developed by the Royal Danish Navy during the 1980s. It consists of a wide range of weapons systems and other equipment mounted in standardised containers that can be quickly installed in pre-designated StanFlex 'slots' in appropriately-equipped warships, with the containers shipped being determined by the mission required. Typical payloads include Harpoon surface-to-surface missiles, ESSM, a variable-depth sonar module and even a hydraulic crane. StanFlex modules were first installed in the *Flyvefisken* or StanFlex 300 class of patrol vessels. Although these have now largely been decommissioned or sold, the StanFlex concept is used in a wide range of other Danish vessels.

3. The former Naval Material Command was subsumed into DALO in January 2007, which is known as the *Forsvarets Materieltjeneste* or FMT in Danish.

4. In line with the practice adopted for the *Absalon* class, the *Iver Huitfeldt* class's weapons equipment is being fitted on an incremental basis and is also subject to potential variation from ship to ship due to adoption of the StanFlex concept. As such there will be considerable variation from the design fit and the systems carried on each ship. It is also worth noting that, with the exception of the Mk 41 VLS and the SMART-L and APAR radar mountings (fitted by Odense Steel Shipyard), all combat system equipment has been installed and integrated under the direction of DALO at Korsør Naval Base.

5. An overview of recent developments in the area of ballistic missile defence is contained in Norman Friedman's 'Ballistic Missile Defence and the USN', *Seaforth World Naval Review 2013* (Barnsley: Seaforth Publishing, 2012), pp 184–91.

6. This is a branch of DALO (FMT).

7. The 35mm gun and torpedo launchers were installed after delivery to the RDN in February 2012.

8. The author wishes to acknowledge the assistance of the following Royal Danish Navy officers in the preparation of this article:
Commander s.g. Per Bigum – First Frigate Project Officer.
Commander s.g. Per Hesselberg – Current Frigate Project Officer.
Commander s.g. Carsten Fjord-Larsen – Commanding Officer *Iver Huitfeldt*.

AUSTAL
BAE SYSTEMS
SCOTT QUEST
ESCAMBIA
EVERGLADES, FL

Author:
Scott Truver

3.3 SIGNIFICANT SHIPS

USNS SPEARHEAD (JHSV-1)

'Spearheading' Joint High-Speed Vessels

Since the early 2000s, the US Navy, Army, Special Operations Command and Marine Corps (USMC) have been working to address fundamentally different ways of moving troops, vehicles and weapons, equipment and supplies at high speeds within an area of operations.[1] Bridging the gap between low-speed sealift and high-speed airlift, the US Navy's Joint High-Speed Vessel (JHSV) programme calls for ten JHSVs to be delivered by Austal USA (Mobile, Alabama) for operation by the US Navy's Military Sealift Command (MSC). Austal is teamed with General Dynamics Advanced Information Systems, which is responsible for the ship's electronic systems.

With core crews of only twenty-two civilian mariners, these 35-knot-plus ships can transport more than 300 troops and their equipment at ranges out to 1,200 nautical miles (c.2,200km).[2] At speeds of 23 knots, 4,700 nautical mile (c. 8,700km) ranges have been demonstrated, and their 12.5ft (3.83m) fully-loaded draft enables expanded access to a broad spectrum of ports and waterways denied to more traditional ship designs.[3]

The lead Joint High-Speed Vessel, *Spearhead* (JHSV-1), seen in the course of being transported out of her building hall at Austal USA's facility in Mobile, Alabama in September 2011. Austal USA is also responsible for building the *Independence* (LCS-2) variant of the littoral combat ship as well as all ten JHSVs and the yard has been subject to significant expansion to accommodate both programmes. *(Austal)*

'An evolutionary design based on mature technologies and systems, the JHSV programme has been realistic in its goals and ruthless in controlling costs,' according to Austal USA vice president Craig Hooper. 'And it got the Navy the eighty percent solution between high-speed and costly airborne transport and traditional slow-speed sealift.'[4]

'Joint High Speed Vessel, a catamaran, is about speed and volume with fuel efficiency', Chief of Naval Operations (CNO) Admiral Jonathan Greener told the US Congress House Armed Services Committee in April 2013. 'It's fast, you can put some armament on it and it can do counter-piracy operations, counter-drug operations … it can do things that we weren't sure about whenever we started. It has a good medical facility so it can do theatre security cooperation. It resonates with Southern Command, it resonates with African Command and it also can carry 300 soldiers or Marines on board with gear. Add on top of that, the backbone is in the JHSV for command and control so it can direct operations and I would see perhaps, mine countermeasures operations, counter-smuggling, that sort of thing where you bring in small boats and direct them around. It's a pretty agile vessel.'[5]

TESTING HIGH-SPEED SOLUTIONS

'Transformation' was all the rage in the US Department of Defense in the early 2000s, driving innovative ways to accomplish military roles, missions and tasks better, faster and cheaper. This desire for efficiency, speed, flexibility and agility also included military logistics. In past conflicts, US logistical efforts often had been marked by relatively slow, ponderous build-ups of supplies, ammunition and other items, often routed through a small number of vulnerable ports that were capable of handling deep-draft sealift ships. While not spurning this paradigm completely, several US military services began to look for more 'nimble' ways of moving people and material.

High-speed vessels became an important focus of the US seaborne logistics vision, shaped in part by the experience of the Australian Defence Force (ADF), which had relied upon the converted high-speed ferry *Jervis Bay* to support operations in East Timor in the late 1990s/early 2000s. In its quest for a quite evolutionary 'transformation' to complement the two conventional amphibious warships acquired from the United States that were then being refurbished, the ADF looked to seasoned suppliers of high-speed craft such as Austal located in Western Australia and Incat near Hobart in Tasmania, Australia (the supplier of *Jervis Bay*). Both of these companies had been building progressively larger, more complex high-speed ferries and other vessels since the late 1980s.

Taking a page out of the ADF's book, the US Army Transportation Corps quickly stood up the Theatre Support Vessel (TSV) programme and leased two high-speed vessels – the *Joint Venture* (IX-532, formerly HSV-X1), chartered in 2001, and

The experimental high-speed vessel *Joint Venture* (HSV-X1) pictured operating with a MH-60S helicopter in August 2002. The United States' early experimentation with high-speed vessels was significantly influenced by the Royal Australian Navy's use of the Incat-built catamaran *Jervis Bay* and *Joint Venture* herself was Incat-built. Chartered by the United States military from 2001 and seeing both army and navy use, she is now in commercial service in the Irish Sea as the Isle of Man Steam Packet Company's *Manannan*. *(US Navy)*

Spearhead (TSV-1X), chartered in 2002 – to test out high-speed intra-theatre lift operations using commercially-available ships.[6] Initially, the US Navy operated the Incat Australia-built *Joint Venture* under its High-Speed Connector (HSC) programme but later transferred HSV-X1 to the Army's TSV programme, with the ship's hull number changed to IX-532. The US Army directly leased the Incat-built *Spearhead* from the start.

Expectations for the TSV programme were high. Some projections of capabilities came close to those of the US Navy's large-deck amphibious assault ships. Observers touted the TSV's potentially revolutionary effect on US Army operations long before testing was completed. For example, a May 2002 commentary opined, the TSV '… is one of the key enablers to bring about operational throughput. It will allow commanders to operationally move and control combat power with precise sustainment into unpredictable entry points inside the theater of operations. It is the perfect complement to lighter and more agile Army forces. Combat forces can be delivered autonomously on the TSV, planning and rehearsing en route and arriving at the destination capable of immediate action. As a high-speed delivery vehicle, for example, a TSV can deliver fuel and supplies uploaded on trucks that can drive off and rendezvous with a combat force at a mission staging area.'[7]

Likewise, a December 2005 assessment concluded, 'The Army's new Theater Support Vessel … is a rapidly developed response to the transformational operational maneuver and sustainment demands of force-projection operations. The TSV is a fast-moving, shallow-draft vessel that can simulta-

The first *Spearhead* – the US Army's TSV-1X – was another Incat-built vessel chartered for three years from 2002 as part of the Theatre Support Vessel (TSV) experimental project. The US Army's positive experience with the type was a significant influence on the development of the JHSV programme. *(US Navy)*

The Austal-built *Westpac Express* formed part of the US Navy's High-Speed Connector (HSC) experimental programme and remains in service in support of the US Marine Corps in the Western Pacific. Basic design similarities with the Austal-designed JHSVs are apparent in this image. *(Austal)*

neously move troops and their equipment together as combat-ready units within theater and deploy them with little or no reception, staging, onward movement, and integration (RSOI) activities at undeveloped ports. The TSV also provides follow-on sustainment through joint logistics over-the-shore (JLOTS) operations.'8

The capabilities of the trial high-speed vessels validated much, but not all, of the hype. Any hint of a capability to conduct opposed assault, over-the-beach type operations, was out of the question, although special operations troops were inserted covertly in several instances. For example, *Joint Venture* served as a forward-staging base for US Naval Special Warfare SEAL and USMC Fleet Anti-Terrorism teams in Operation 'Iraqi Freedom' in 2003. Consequently, after three years of tests and exercises, the US Army announced its intention to acquire and operate five new-construction, new-design HSVs that would capture lessons learned from *Joint Venture* and *Spearhead*.

For its part, the US Navy's early-2000s HSC programme focused on two leased vessels, the *Westpac Express* (HSV-4676) and *Swift* (HSV-2). Built by Austal, the all-aluminium, semi-SWATH (small water-plane area twin-hull) catamaran *Westpac Express* has a length of 101m, displaces 2,100 tons full load and can carry some 750 deadweight tons; fully loaded draft is just 4.3m. Top speed is 36 knots, dropping to 33 knots when fully loaded – in which condition a range of c. 1,300 nautical miles (c. 2,400km) can be achieved. She has more than 26,000ft² (2,400m²) of space for vehicles and cargo – loaded/off-loaded using a stern ramp – and can transport 970 troops in airline-style seating.

Swift (HSV-2), which entered service with the US Navy in 2003 and took advantage of lessons learned from the earlier high-speed vessels operated by the TSV and HSC programmes. Initially used as a mine warfare command ship, she was fitted with a basic combat information centre and a defensive armament of light weapons. Her most recent use – in the first half of 2013 – has been testing the potential of small UAVs and an aerostat in anti-drug smuggling operations. *(US Navy)*

A 24 April 2013 picture of the experimental high-speed vessel *Swift* (HSV-2) taken during trials of a tethered TIF-25K 'Fat Albert' aerostat off the coast of Florida. The trials, which also involved a Puma AE UAV, were intended to assess the potential use of new systems in the fight against organised crime. *(US Navy)*

Mess facilities are available, whilst berthing is provided for the crew of civilian mariners. The ship was placed in MSC service in July 2001 and assigned to support the USMC III Marine Expeditionary Force in the western Pacific from its Okinawa home base. Naval analyst Norman Polmar notes that during an early exercise '… the *Westpac Express* carried a 400-ton load, including 370 Marines and their gear, five AH-1W Sea Cobra helicopters, two UH-1N Huey helicopters, and aviation support equipment from Japan to Okinawa in less than forty hours. (The helicopters were carried as internal cargo and could not operate from the ship.)'[9] HSV-4676 also supported disaster-relief operations in Thailand in 2005 and the Tohoku earthquake and tsunami in 2011. HSV-4676's charter has been extended several times, currently until August 2013.

This early experience with *Westpac Express* spurred further intra-theatre lift innovation. Built by Incat specifically for the US Navy, the all-aluminium *Swift* (HSV-2) was placed in service in August 2003. The ship is operated by the MSC under a five-year charter, renewed in 2008. The ship's design took into account lessons learned by the TSV and HSC programmes; construction and delivery required only ten months from contract award to ship delivery to the US Navy. *Swift* lived up to her name, again, deploying on her first voyage less than two weeks later.

Like the other ships in the trials programmes, *Swift* is a wave-piercing catamaran with water-jet propulsion. Full load displacement is c. 1,900 tons and she has a 600 deadweight ton capacity. Overall length is 97.3m and draft 3.4m. A fully automated diesel propulsion plant provides a top speed of 47 knots, falling to 38 knots when fully loaded. Range at 35 knots when fully loaded is some 1,100 nautical miles (c. 2,000km), increasing to 4,000 nautical miles (c. 7,400km) at 20 knots. *Swift* can carry c.350 people, including 128 troops in airline seating, and is operated by a joint US Navy and civilian crew. The ship has more than 28,000ft^2 (2,600m^2) of vehicle cargo space, which can accommodate vehicles up to 70 tons (e.g., an M1A2 Abrams tank). Loading and offloading is via a stern ramp and there is a 13-ton capacity crane. Unlike the other ships in the TSV and HSC programmes, *Swift* was fitted out with a combat information centre and can operate one CH-46 or two H-60 type helicopters, for which a hangar is provided. *Swift* was also initially fitted with a 25mm Mk 38 Bushmaster cannon and several machine guns, including a .50-cal Ex-45 remote-control weapon, for limited self-defence, although these have subsequently been removed.

Swift initially supported Atlantic Fleet transport requirements and served as a mine warfare command ship for the Ingleside, Texas-based Commander, Naval Mine Warfare Command (prior to the command's disestablishment and move to San Diego to the expanded Naval Mine and Anti-submarine Warfare Command). To this end, the ship embarked explosive ordnance disposal divers, marine mammal mine countermeasures systems, and naval special warfare (SEAL) forces and their supporting equipment. *Swift*'s ability to support humanitarian assistance and disaster-response needs was underscored early on. During the 2006 Israeli-Lebanon conflict, she ferried humanitarian supplies from Cyprus to Beirut. *Swift* also provided assistance in the wake of Hurricane Katrina in 2005, deployed to Caribbean and South American ports in support of Global Fleet Station theatre-engagement operations in 2007, and carried out relief efforts in Haiti in 2010.

Swift has also been involved in broader experimental roles. This experimentation has continued into 2013, with tests of a tethered scaled-down 'Fat Albert' aerostat and the Puma AE unmanned aerial vehicle, sponsored by the US Joint Interagency Task Force South. The goal is to determine how the combined systems can support Operation 'Martillo', a multinational programme to detect, engage and defeat drug and other smuggling into the United States.

Just as for the US Army, the US Navy found HSV performance to be quite satisfactory. For example, Captain Steve Parode, USN, recalls a 2003 experience related to *Joint Venture* whilst he was in charge of the Flag Watch for the Sixth Fleet in the Mediterranean, during Operation 'Iraqi Freedom':

The *Joint Venture* was making a 30-plus knot transit from ECONUS [Eastern Continental United States] to our theater for further movement east. Back then, the 'chop lines' for our AOR [area of operations] had just been reset to the west a few time zones, so the HSV 'chopped' to us just north-east of Hamilton, Bermuda, right in the middle of a deep North Atlantic winter low. NLMOC [Naval Atlantic Meteorology and Oceanography Center] had set a High Seas Warning area, with winds just about gale strength and seas greater than 12ft with a long swell. Admiral Scott Fry [then-Commander, US Sixth Fleet/Allied Forces South/Striking Forces, Europe] told me to check on the HSV to determine whether they could sustain their SOA [speed of advance] and stay on PIM [plan of intended movement] … I called the HSV's Master on Inmarsat and asked for a weather and ride report. He replied: 'Winds SE 24 gusts to 40, seas 14ft, ship steady at 34 knots SOA intending to test 40 knots SOA based on good ride.' I called the Admiral and told him that I believed the HSV would be ahead of PIM at Gibraltar, and in fact the ship was about eight hours early.[10]

Moreover, the US Navy and Marine Corps were also looking to these kinds of vessels to support their 'sea-basing' concept, under which power-projection forces would be marshalled, organised, based and sustained at sea for long periods of time, 'over the horizon' from land-based threats. 'As a result of jointly sponsored experiments,' a 2005 assessment concluded, 'the Marine Corps now requires a high-speed connector to support [the service's] expeditionary maneuver warfare doctrine and ship-to-objective maneuver [concept of operations]. The Navy's Transformational Roadmap for Sea-basing also demands high-speed, shallow-draft vessels.' Given the US Navy's interest in building a significant force of these specialised HSCs, the assessment continued, 'the Army's management of the TSV is transitioning to the Joint High-Speed Vessel Program led by the Navy. This combined approach will foster greater support for the program and is an economy-of-scale for production and sustainment.'[11] US Navy's leadership of the programme was confirmed in a January 2005 memorandum of agreement (MOA) merging the TSV and HSC projects under the US Navy's Program Executive Office, Ships.

JHSV PROGRAMME OF RECORD

The JHSV programme merged the Army TSV and the Navy HSC/HSV projects to decrease costs by taking advantage of the extensive commonality between the programmes. However, it was initially envisaged the US Army would continue to fund and acquire its own ships. Subsequently, as one outcome of the December 2011 Army-Navy War-fighter Staff Talks, the Army agreed to transfer its new-construction JHSVs to the Navy, together with all already programmed funding for the effort. A further MOA signed by the Secretary of the Army in April 2012 and the Secretary of the Navy the next month spec-

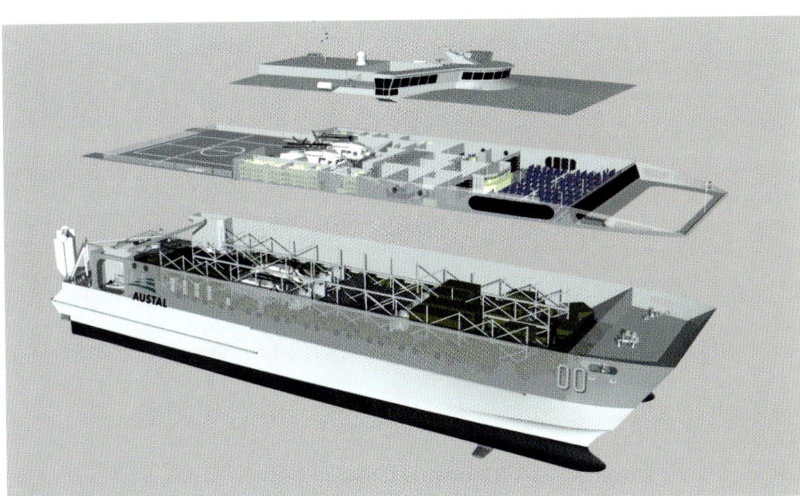

The JHSV programme resulted from a 2005 agreement to combine US Army and US Navy requirements for high-speed vessels into a joint programme under US Navy leadership. The US subsidiary of the Australian builder Austal was subsequently contracted for the detailed design and construction of the resulting ships. This early concept drawing differs from the ultimate JHSV design in a number of details but provides a good idea of the type's overall layout, combining troop and equipment transportation in a catamaran hull. *(Austal)*

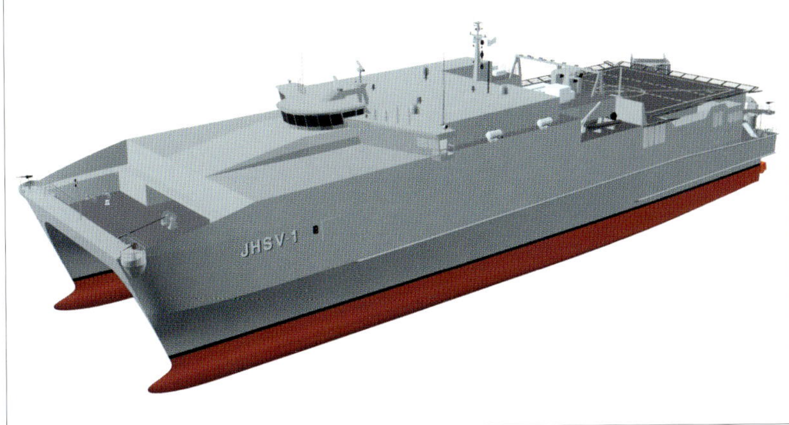

An Austal graphic of the final JHSV-1 design, which utilised the company's extensive experience of constructing civilian fast ferries to satisfy both US Army and US Navy requirements for future high-speed vessels. Key modifications from the ship's essential commercial origins include the large helicopter flight deck, the crane and loading/unloading ramp for use in ports with austere facilities and the provision for light weapons points. *(Austal)*

ified that the MSC would operate the ships, with each service reimbursing MSC for operating and maintenance costs. MSC civil service mariners will operate the first four JHSVs, whilst the rest of the JHSV fleet will be crewed by private, commercial contract mariners. This represents a change from the US Army's original plans, as they had intended to use military service mariners to crew the vessels.

The MOA also stipulated that the lead ship's name would remain *Spearhead* and, initially, the second JHSV was to be named *Vigilant*. However, in November 2011 Secretary of the Navy Ray Mabus renamed JHSV-2 *Choctaw County*, his birthplace.

Initial plans called for as many as eighteen JHSVs – thirteen for the US Navy and Marine Corps and five for the US Army. The total number was reduced to ten in 2011 as a result of increasing budget constraints and the realisation that the revised JHSV programme and projections of increased MSC ship availability would meet mobility requirements. Originally, the US Army ships were to be odd-numbered and the US Navy's even-numbered.

In November 2008, Austal USA – the Australian company's American subsidiary based in Mobile, Alabama – was awarded a US$185.4m contract for the detail design and construction of JHSV-1. The contract also included options for up to nine additional ships and associated shore-based spares. The US Navy exercised options for JHSV-2 and JHSV-3 in January 2010, JHSV-4 and JHSV-5 in October 2010, JHSV-6 and JHSV-7 in June 2011, and JHSV-8 and JHSV-9 in February 2012. The contract for JHSV-10, the final ship, was awarded on 20 December 2012 and came in at US$166.9m. Austal states that its share of overall programme contracts is potentially worth over US$1.6bn, whilst

Table 3.3.1.

SPEARHEAD (JHSV-1) PRINCIPAL PARTICULARS

Building Information:

Laid Down:	22 July 2010
Launched:	8 September 2011[1]
Delivered:	5 December 2012
Builders:	Austal USA, Mobile, Alabama.

Dimensions:

Displacement:	2,400 tons full load.
Overall Hull Dimensions:	103.0m x 28.5m x 3.8m.

Equipment:

Armament:	Fitted with 4 x weapons positions for light machine guns.
Aircraft:	Flight deck (Level 1 Class 2 certified) for one helicopter up to CH-53E Super Stallion size. Potential for future UAV operation.
Mission Deck:	1,860m² mission deck. Clear height of 4.75m. c.550 ton payload.
Loading Support:	Articulated 45° slewing stern ramp. Supports M1A2 Abrams tanks.
	Telescopic boom crane. 18.2 ton capacity to 10m.

Propulsion Systems:

Machinery:	4 x Tognum MTU 20V 8000 M71L diesels rated at 36MW total produce 49,000bhp through 4 x Wärtsilä WLD 1400 SR water-jets.
Speed:	Designed maximum speed is in excess of 43 knots, falling to 35 knots in full load condition
	Range is 1,200 nautical miles (c. 2,200km) at 35 knots in full load condition.

Other Details:

Complement:	Core crew is 22. Berthing is provided for a total of 42 crew members.
	Berthing for 104 embarked troops and airline-style seating for 312.
Class:	Ten ships have been ordered – *Spearhead* (JHSV-1); *Choctaw County* (JHSV-2); *Millinocket* (JHSV-3); *Fall River* (JHSV-4); *Trenton* (JHSV-5); *Brunswick* (JHSV-6); *Carson City* (JHSV-7); *Yuma* (JHSV-8); *Bismarck* (JHSV-9) and *Burlington* (JHSV-10).

Notes:

1. Date of rolling-out the ship from its building hall in a floating dry dock. Entry into the water was several days later; christening was on 17 September 2011.

2. Data drawn from Austal and US Navy sources.

US government figures put the total programme cost at c. US$2.1bn.

According to a March 2013 report by the US Governmental Accountability Office (GAO), lead-ship fabrication began in December 2009 with all eighteen critical technologies mature and demonstrated in a realistic environment, but without a stable three-dimensional design.[12] The shipyard did not complete the 3D design until September 2010, about nine months after fabrication began, which led to out-of-sequence work and additional rework to account for design changes. All of this contributed to cost overrun, schedule delay, and an increase in the weight of the ship. The American Bureau of Shipping (ABS) did not approve the design until May 2012. With the exception of changes to correct issues identified with the lead ship, however, the Navy does not anticipate design changes on follow-on ships, beginning with *Choctaw County* (JHSV-2).

Although the contract provided specific delivery scheduling only after JSHV-1, USNS *Spearhead* was delivered on 6 December 2012, about twelve months later than originally expected and reportedly somewhat over initial budget. Despite the challenges faced during the construction of the lead ship (e.g., hiring additional employees in skilled trades), Austal remained upbeat about its overall performance. As Austal chief executive officer Andrew Bellamy remarked in the press release issued to mark the event, *Spearhead*'s '… delivery underlines our position as a global defense prime contractor and continues Austal's worldwide legacy as the premier provider of innovative, high-speed vessels, with capabilities to construct and support these and other vessels in a global market'.

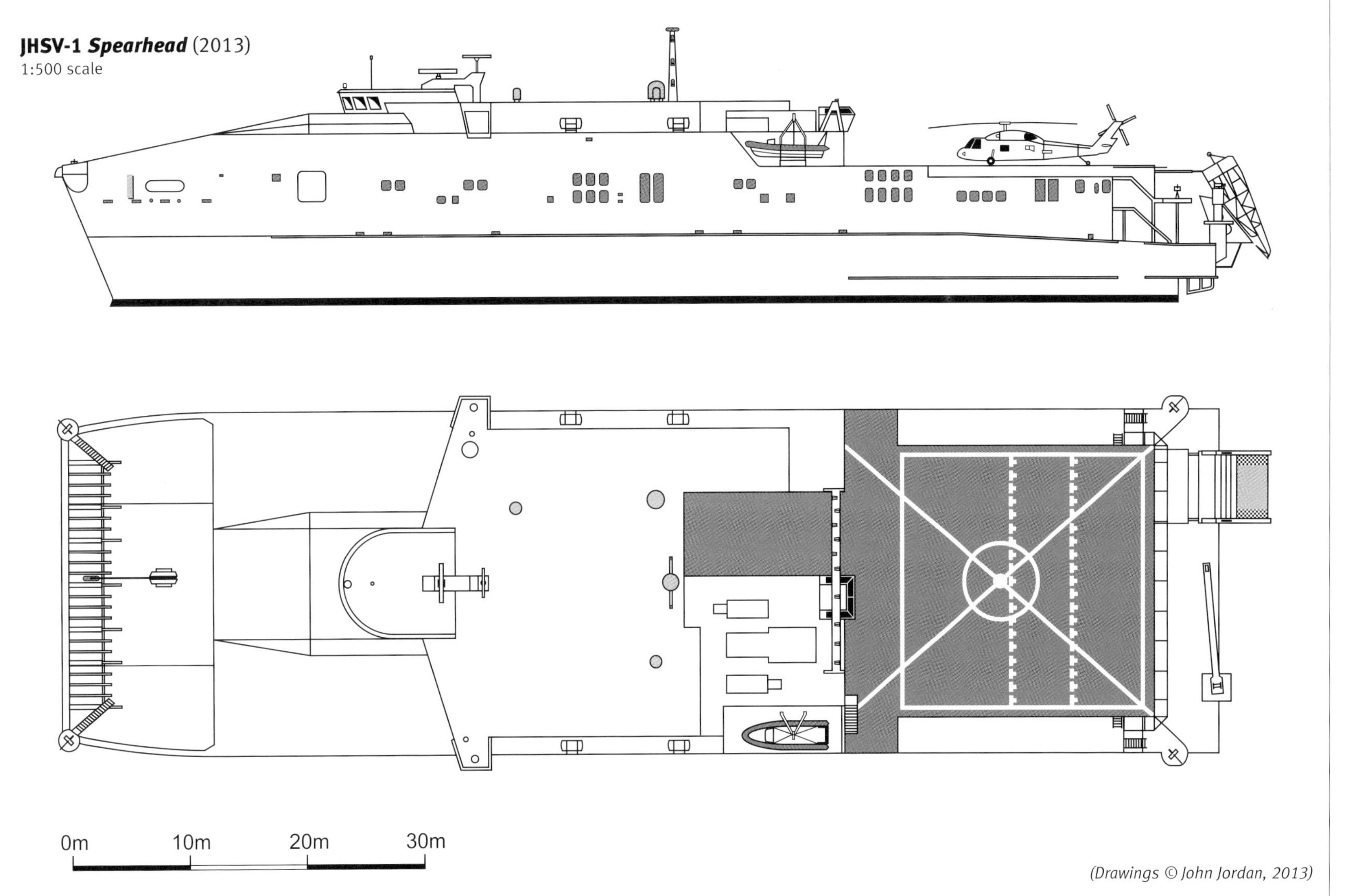

(Drawings © John Jordan, 2013)

Two images of *Spearhead* (JHSV-1) under construction at Austal's Mobile shipyard in September 2010, showing the aluminium catamaran hull structure starting to take shape. The *Independence* (LCS-2) littoral combat ship is built at the same facility and there is some commonality between the building techniques and equipment used in the two designs. Shipyard facilities and workforce at Mobile have both been expanded significantly to support the two programmes. *(Austal)*

Indeed, the GAO noted that during production of the first JHSV the shipyard initiated several facility upgrades and production process improvements, more than tripled the size of its workforce and partnered with the state of Alabama to establish a training facility, which along with its apprentice programme accounted for almost 40 per cent of Austal's new hires in 2011. With regard to other issues, the GAO report explained:

> … Navy officials noted that the Board of Inspection and Survey reported the lead ship's propulsion plant performed flawlessly during acceptance trials. Program officials said that at delivery the lead ship received interim certification from the ABS for unrestricted engine operation, and the Navy intends to hold the shipyard accountable for attaining final ABS engine certification. They noted that during pre-delivery preparations of the lead ship, the shipyard implemented modifications to the ship's cathodic protection and monitoring systems to ensure the ship met existing contractual corrosion control performance specifications. The shipyard has incorporated these modifications into the pre-launch construction scope for the remaining ships, and the Navy will monitor in-service performance of the lead ship to determine the need for other corrosion control changes.

Although it took some time to sort out 'growth issues', the programme has been running significantly more smoothly than other US Navy shipbuilding projects, something that can be attributed in part to the vessel's commercial-based design. Indeed, *Choctaw County* completed builder's sea trials during April 2013, nearly putting the programme back on the original schedule. According to Captain Henry Stevens III, the USN's Strategic and Theater Sealift Program Manager (PMS 385), 'JHSV-2 is the second ship in this class

A view of *Spearhead* (JHSV-1) at the time of her christening in September 2011. The incomplete hull of *Coronado* (LCS-4) can be seen in the building hall in the background. Although *Spearhead* was finally delivered several months late on 6 December 2012, the overall JHSV programme has been running more smoothly than many other US Navy shipbuilding projects. *(US Military Sealift Command)*

Spearhead (JHSV-1) pictured at speed during builders trials in 2012, during which time the lead ship's propulsion plant performed flawlessly. The design, intended to allow the transportation of more than 300 troops and 500 tons of equipment over distances of up to 1,200 nautical miles (c. 2,200km) at speeds of around 35 knots. *(Austal)*

to go through rigorous builder's trials testing. At this stage, JHSV-2 is more complete than the lead ship, and we are benefitting from JHSV-1's lessons learned.'[13] *Choctaw County* was delivered to the MSC on 6 June 2013, whilst third of class *Millinocket* (JHSV-3) was floated out the same month after christening on 20 April.

With all elements of the US Department of Defense continuing to wrestle with across-the-board 'sequestration' driven budget cuts, there are some fears that the US Navy might cancel the contract for JHSV-10. That said, the USN Chief of Naval Operations' fiscal year 2014 testimony and his *Navy Program Guide 2013*, released in mid-April 2013, gave no indication that the JHSV programme will be reduced in any way.[14]

EVOLVING JHSV MISSIONS

As already noted, the Navy's Military Sealift Command will operate and sustain the JHSV fleet. JHSV resources will be allocated via the US military's Global Force Management (GFM) process for use in support of theatre security co-operation, service-unique missions, intra-theatre sealift and special missions from continental US and, possibly, overseas 'layberths' as well. *Spearhead*'s layberth or homeport is at the Joint Expeditionary Base Little Creek, Virginia. Future JHSV homeports were being assessed as at mid-2013.

The CNO's 2013 *Navy Program Guide* confirmed that service thinking on JHSV's roles, missions and tasks has remained relatively constant since the early 2000s:

> The Joint High-Speed Vessel (JHSV) is a high-speed, shallow-draft surface vessel able to transport rapidly medium payloads of cargo and personnel over intra-theater distances and load/offload without reliance on port infrastructure … JHSV is an intra-theater lift capability, not an assault platform. JHSV will be capable of speeds in excess of 35 knots and ranges of 1,200 nautical miles fully loaded. In addition, the shallow-draft characteristics will enable the JHSV to operate effectively in littoral areas and access small, austere ports.

In essence, therefore, the JHSVs will transport

A February 2013 view of *Spearhead* (JHSV-1) showing her stern unloading facilities. When combined with the ship's shallow draft characteristics, they will allow the new design to unload troops and equipment in small, austere ports under non-assault conditions. *(US Navy)*

personnel, equipment and supplies over operational distances with access to littoral offload points, including austere, minor and degraded ports. They will enable the rapid projection, agile manoeuvre and sustainment of modular, tailored forces in response to a wide range of military and civilian contingencies such as non-combatant evacuation operations, humanitarian assistance and disaster relief. Generally speaking, JHSVs are designed to operate in a benign, limited-threat environment.

As Norman Polmar noted, JHSVs are in great demand by US regional combatant commanders. 'Beyond transporting troops and vehicles within theater,' Polmar wrote, 'they may also be useful for other missions, such as engagement with friendly nations (through port visits, training, and joint exercises) and some types of maritime security operations.'[15]

A direct forward image of *Spearhead* (JHSV-1) shows her catamaran design to good effect. Although displacing less than 2,500 tons, the design allows her to transport considerable volumes of equipment and unload the same in relatively shallow water. In addition to supporting military operations, potential roles include non-combatant evacuation, the provision off humanitarian assistance and disaster relief. *(US Navy)*

This observation was reinforced during a February 2013 visit by *Spearhead* to the US Naval Station Mayport, Florida. Rear Admiral Sinclair M Harris, Commander, US Naval Forces Southern Command/US Fourth Fleet, enthused, 'The joint high-speed vessel *Spearhead* is a perfect match for Fourth Fleet and we plan to use it across all of our lines of operations: security cooperation activities, maritime security operations and contingency operations.' The Fourth Fleet's area of operations encompasses South and Central America as well as the Caribbean Sea. The Fleet supports US Southern Command joint and combined 'full-spectrum military operations', with a sea-based forward presence. '*Spearhead* is critically important to Fourth Fleet's area of operations because of her shallow draft and ability to work in more austere ports that traditional warships might not be able to. We see the high-speed vessels as even more capable in terms of reaching out to our partner nations,' Admiral Harris underscored. And the 'operators' agreed. 'Flexibility may be the best attribute of this ship,' said Douglas D Casavant, Junior, *Spearhead*'s civil service master, who has been sailing for the MSC for 23 years. 'Our 20,000ft^2 [c.1,860m^2] mission bay area can be reconfigured to quickly adapt to whatever mission we are tasked with, for instance, carrying containerised portable hospitals to support disaster relief or transporting tanks and troops.'

Overall, however, thinking on the future uses of the JHSV continues to evolve. As Joseph Rella, former president of Austal USA, put it, 'When you buy a pickup truck and you ask the potential buyer, "what do you intend to do with it?" They'll have an idea, but they won't be able to fathom what you're able to do with it,' he said. 'That's what you're buying – the capability.' In his 'US Navy Posture Statement' hearing before the US Congress in April 2013, CNO Admiral Greenert agreed, noting 'During Fiscal Year 2014 [which begins on 1 October 2013] we will deploy the first JHSV, USNS *Spearhead* … We will use these deployments to integrate these new, highly adaptable platforms

Spearhead (JHSV-1) arriving at Naval Station Mayport on 14 February 2013 for a brief port visit whilst on her maiden voyage to her home base at Little Creek, Virginia. Homeports for further JHSVs currently under construction are still being assessed, although it is likely many will be assigned to ports outside the Continental United States to support locally-based US forces. *(US Navy)*

into the fleet and evaluate the ways we can employ their combination of persistent forward presence and flexible payload capacity.'

Some observers even seem to conscript these vessels into a combat role, despite their relatively light, commercially-derived features. Admiral Greenert has already identified mine-countermeasures and counter-piracy tasks. The JHSV would also allow commanders to move an entire company of Marines and their rolling stock and gear to another location quickly to surprise enemies, retired USN Rear Admiral Joseph Carnevale, senior advisor at the Shipbuilders Council of America, commented to *National Defense*. Today, commanders might have to put in a request for an amphibious ship to carry out that mission. That could take weeks to schedule. But if commanders controlled a JHSV that was stationed in the region, they could make that decision and execute it in a matter of days. 'They might think of doing things they haven't done before,' Carnevale said. 'In that regard,' Austal USA's Craig Hooper pointed out, 'the JHSV is not an amphibious replacement. It is an amphibious supplement and expeditionary strike group risk-mitigator.'

In March 2013, Admiral Greenert added the JHSV programme to the Littoral Combat Ship (LCS) Council, a three-star panel stood up in August 2012 to oversee developments of these innovative ships.[16] 'Fully exploiting the potential of the JHSV will require a similar cross-cutting effort' to the actions being taken with respect to the LCS programme, he wrote in an 11 March memo. The JHSV, he noted, has a reconfigurable payload capacity and high speed like the LCS, and 'can be employed in similar environments for similar missions'.

The next month, during a hearing conducted by the US Senate Appropriations Defense Subcommittee, Senator Richard Shelby asked the CNO, 'Given the … ship's speed, cargo-capability, and ability to maneuver in the shallow waters, would it not be prudent for the Navy to look at expanding the Joint High-Speed Vessel mission beyond theater transport?'[17] Alluding to the 'three-star' LCS/JHSV Council, Admiral Greenert called the JHSV a 'vessel with a lot of potential' and explained that the Navy and Marine Corps were indeed working to push the new ship's operational envelope.

In that regard, the *CNO's Navigation Plan 2013–2017* outlined the need to 'improve the reach of today's platforms through new payloads of more capable weapons, sensors, and unmanned vehicles'. This includes the potential to expand greatly JHSV capabilities through introduction of the Fire Scout UAV. For example, in addition to Fire-Scout's over water and land intelligence, surveillance and reconnaissance capabilities, the US Navy is looking at the potential to arm Fire Scouts with laser-guided air-to-surface missiles, providing an offensive and defensive 'punch' not envisioned originally. As the *Navigation Plan* makes clear, fielding Fire Scouts on JHSVs and other platforms like the LCS will support counterterrorism and irregular warfare missions at sea and ashore.

During the Marine Corps/Navy seventeen-nation Bold Alligator 2013 exercise, the JHSV figured prominently in what some observers called a revolution in tactical logistics support. In the synthetic Marine Expeditionary Group joint forcible-entry operation, the JHSV was a critical high-speed link between the sea-base and forces ashore in an anti-access/area-denial threat environment. The 'synthetic' JHSV was important for wounded personnel evacuation to a Level III care facility and additional intra-theatre sustainment.

JHSV DESIGN CHARACTERISTICS

The *Spearhead* design is a semi-SWATH catamaran built to commercial standards, patterned after Austal's Hawaii Superferry design (capable of carrying 900 passengers and 250 vehicles). The vessel leverages Austal's significant experience in designing commercial vessels and its state-of-market technology. Significant production and financial risks have been avoided by implementing proven technology, ensuring stable requirements and minimising change, as well as through what the company describes as 'the ruthless pursuit of cost reduction and efficiency'. For example, the JHSVs are built in a series of forty-three modules that are constructed in a covered facility and come together in a series of 'lifts'. More than half of the ship's modules are completed by the time that the ship's keel is laid.

JHSVs are being built to the American Bureau of Shipping (ABS) High-Speed Naval Craft Guide HNSC 2007. The Naval Vessel Rules (NVRs) – the approved guide for building and certifying US Navy vessels – do not apply to any part of the JHSV design.

Millinocket (JHSV-3) is pictured being rolled out of her building hall on 5 June 2013. The image provides a clear view of the JHSV's semi-SWATH (small water-plane area twin hull), catamaran design. When coupled with the ship's lightweight aluminium construction, this permits high-speed, long-endurance missions and facilitates deployment in shallow water. *(US Military Sealift Command)*

An aerial view of *Spearhead* (JHSV-1) during trials. She is powered by four Tognum MTU 20 V8000 diesel engines that drive four Wärtsilä water-jets through ZF reduction gears. Top speed in unloaded condition is reported to be in excess of 43 knots. *(Austal)*

Choctaw County (JHSV-2) pictured shortly before delivery to the US Military Sealift Command. She was handed over by Austal USA on 6 June 2013. The large flight deck can support a helicopter up to the size of the CH-53E Super Stallion and a narrow helicopter parking area is also provided immediately forward, offset slightly to starboard. *(US Military Sealift Command)*

The US Navy's requirements specifications call for a twenty-year service life for the aluminium hull.

JHSVs have no combat system capability and leverage non-developmental or commercial technology that is modified to suit military applications. Because of this commercial provenance, the JHSVs cannot sustain battle damage and this, coupled with their lack of either active or passive self-defence features, means that they are not intended to go into 'harm's way'.

JHSVs are powered by four Tognum MTU 20V8000 M71L diesel engines driving four Wärtsilä WLD 1400 SR water-jets via four ZF 60000NR2H reduction gears. Each engine is rated at 9.1MW and – combined – can generate a maximum speed of 43 knots without payload. Given that the JHSV's dominant mission characteristic is high speed, some ninety-five per cent of its fuel capacity is designated for propulsion. Only an estimated 5 per cent of total fuel consumption is used for 'hotel' and other ship services. In general, fuel consumption is dependent on a JHSV's operational speed. At low speed, the

JHSV is relatively economical but as speed – and payload – increase, fuel consumption will also rise. Economical speed management is thus an important part of JHSV mission planning.

Moreover, as a result of the lightweight nature of the vessel's aluminium construction, its short length and shallow full load draft of just 13ft (3.9m), sea state also plays a significant factor in speed and endurance compared to a steel displacement vessel. The JHSV was designed to transport 600 short tons (c.535 tons) of payload for 1,200 nautical miles (2,222km), at an average speed of 35 knots or greater, at ninety per cent of the propulsion system's rated power in calm water, and with a depth greater than 328ft (c.100m). The calm-water sea state is Sea State 3 (1.5m wave height) and below. Above Sea State 3, JHSV speed and heading become limited to reduce hull fatigue. However, as Captain Parode experienced in 2003, exceptional performance is possible: 'Winds SE 24 gusts to 40, seas 14ft, ship steady at 34 knots SOA intending to test 40 knots SOA based on good ride.'

The JHSV design features a flight deck certified to support the operations of one helicopter, and can accommodate the US Navy's heaviest helicopter, the CH-53E Super Stallion. The ship is equipped with a parking area for one helicopter, a vertical replenishment area and a helicopter control station. Kongsberg Maritime supplies the JHSV's helicopter operations surveillance system (HOSS). Operated from the control room, HOSS allows helicopter operations in very low light conditions. The system integrates a MIL-S-901D shock qualified 19in (48cm) SXGA LCD monitor suitable for night-vision device operations. And, as noted earlier, the US Navy is investigating ways to integrate Fire Scout UAVs into the JHSV. The sea state limit for safe JHSV helicopter/UAV operations is Sea State 4.

There have been very few criticisms of the US Navy JHSV design. Some observers have noted that there could be challenges associated with operating an aluminium ship, citing previous US Navy experience with aluminium-steel designs and aluminium-to-aluminium welds that are prone to cracking from open-ocean ship motions. For example, the US Navy has had a troubled history with aluminium deckhouses on steel-hulled surface warships – from frigates to cruisers – that have experienced cracking. Some US Navy officials said that the aluminium deckhouses have to contend with unusual stresses from topside equipment, such as radars and antennas, and with material problems including metallic corrosion. Others pointed to aluminium-to-aluminium weld brittleness that is prone to cracking from open-ocean ship motions.

To allay concerns, Austal engineers examined twenty years' worth of aluminium shipbuilding/operating records as they worked the JHSV design, Joseph Rella commented to *National Defense*. They completed a significant amount of computer-aided stress and dynamic-loading analysis of the hull structure to identify hotspots where there could be stress concentrations. 'That's where you add more struc-ture to distribute those stresses and potential relative motion,' he said. Moreover, the ship is being constructed out of a different grade of aluminium to withstand corrosive elements and also provide ductility, or toughness, to withstand stresses better than the brittle aluminium that was being used in the cruisers. Austal is also sequencing the welding and stress-relieving processes carefully during ship construction, he added.

MAN, EQUIP AND SUSTAIN

In order to crew the new fleet, MSC has hand-selected civilian mariners from other ships who display exceptional mariner skills and are interested in serving on JHSVs. These mariners are then provided specialised training, as required, by the US Coast Guard to operate high-speed vessels. Training consists of simulator training at the Fort Eustis, Virginia, JHSV Simulator; as well as crew familiari-sation training on board the ships and in the class-room at the Austal USA shipyard.

The MSC will schedule JHSV maintenance and updating dry-dockings annually at shipyards in the United States and in the assigned theatre on a competitive basis. The intention is that – once a JHSV is assigned to a certain geographical area – it will not return to the continental United States due to cost and time constraints. Instead, shipyards in the assigned theatre will compete for dry dock and maintenance contracts issued by the US Navy. Some of the specialised facilities required to complete a JHSV maintenance availability period include dry-docks that can accommodate a vessel with a 95ft (28.9m) beam, and shipyards that have an ABS-certified aluminium welding capability. The US Navy will award most in-service maintenance on a competitive basis. However, the MSC has entered into agreements with the original equipment manu-facturers for some key systems, including the main engines, the ship's service diesel generator sets and the water-jets.

Austal has a global network of authorised repair facilities that support the firm's commercial customers. They will have the opportunity to bid on all JHSV maintenance and repair packages issued by the MSC. Given the US Navy's shift in strategic focus to the western Pacific and East Asia, Austal is expanding collaboration with key shipyards in Singapore, Thailand and Vietnam.

One of the most unique maintenance issues for the JHSV is an annual dry-docking requirement as part of the ship's International Maritime Organization (IMO) High Speed Craft certifica-tion. This compares with a typical twice in five-year dry dock cycle for other MSC steel-hull vessels. Additionally, in a similar fashion to the littoral combat ship, the water jets on a JHSV have special maintenance requirements to control and mitigate corrosion in the propulsion tunnels during the ship's twenty-year service life.

CONCLUSION: AN EVOLUTIONARY NAVAL 'GAP-FILLER'

'The JHSV is going to be available to run missions … supporting the heavier maneuver units,' MSC Commander Rear Admiral Mark Buzby noted in an April 2013 interview.[18] 'It's very reconfigurable; you can assemble it in many different ways. It's a utility vehicle potentially for the MEU [US Marine Corps' Marine Expeditionary Unit] or for a carrier strike

An Abrams tank testing the loading/unloading ramp on *Spearhead* (JHSV-1) during post-delivery trials in March 2013. The articulated ramp is able to slew up to 45° and facilitates operations at austere port facilities. Whilst not meant to go into harm's way like traditional amphibious assault ships, the JHSVs are intended to play a significant part supporting heavier units. *(US Navy)*

Spearhead (JHSV-1) pictured at high speed during pre-delivery trials in 2012. The progressive delivery of her nine sister ships will provide the US Navy with important new capabilities, acting to bridge the traditional gap between low speed sealift and quicker – but more restricted and expensive – airlift. *(Austal)*

group depending on when they get into an area and they're operating. You have to be mindful of its capabilities and its limitations. It's not a heavy armored vessel; it's not meant to go in harm's way, particularly. But it uses its speed for survivability, its ability to move very quickly.'

Admiral Buzby's prediction was echoed by Secretary of the Navy Ray Mabus, who told the US Senate that the JHSV is one of the service's 'most flexible' platforms. For 'everything from transporting marines, soldiers, and their equipment for either combat or training or lift throughout the vast distances of the Pacific, for example, to doing partnership engagements to other missions, ... as we get these ships into the fleet [and] see their capabilities, we can expand,' he explained. In short, filling the gap between airlift and traditional sealift is at hand.

Notes

1. Dr Truver is director, TeamBlue National Security Programs, Gryphon Technologies LC, Washington DC. The discussion and conclusions presented here are his responsibility alone and should not be attributed to Gryphon or the US Navy.

2. Speed in trials of the lead ship has topped 43 knots.

3. Unless otherwise noted, ship characteristics data are from Norman Polmar, *Ships and Aircraft of the US Fleet* (Annapolis, MD: US Naval Institute Press, 2013), Chapters 23 and 33.

4. Remarks by Craig Hooper when interviewed, 4 May 2013.

5. Admiral Jonathan Greenert USN, Chief of Naval Operations, before the House Armed Services Committee, on FY 2014 Department of Navy Posture, 16 April 2013

6. The Transportation Corps is the Army's provider of intra-theatre waterborne support to service and joint forces, a Title X mission.

7. Lieutenant Colonel Zbigniew M Majchrzak, US Army (retired) and Major Charles K. Ledebuhr, US Army (retired), 'On the Spearhead of Army Transformation', *ARMY*

Magazine – May 2002 (Arlington, VA: Association of the United States Army, 2002), pp.45–6.

8. Lieutenant Colonel Stephen R Trauth, US Army (retired), et al, 'Army Transformation at Sea: The New Theater Support Vessel,' *Military Review* – November–December 2005 (Fort Leavenworth, KS: US Army Combined Arms Center, 2005), p.51.

9. Polmar, *Ships and Aircraft of the US Fleet*, p.277.

10. Based on an e-mail interview with Captain Parode, 29 April 2013. Both *Westpac Express* and *Swift* have service-area restrictions, while the *Spearhead* class JHSVs have open-ocean capabilities.

11. Trauth et al, 'Army Transformation at Sea: The New Theater Support Vessel', p.56.

12. Please refer to 'Joint High Speed Vessel (JHSV), *GAO-13-294SP – Defense Acquisitions: Assessments of Selected Weapon Programs* (Washington DC: US Government Accountability Office, 2013) pp 83–4. This can currently be found at: http://www.gao.gov/assets/660/653379.pdf

13. Captain Stevens' comments were quoted in an article entitled, 'Austal builder's trials for naval vessel' published by UPI.com on 18 March 2013.

14. Admiral Jonathan Greenert USN, Chief of Naval Operations, *Navy Program Guide 2013* (Washington DC: Office of the Chief of Naval Operations, 2013), p.160.

15. Polmar, *Ships and Aircraft of the US Fleet*, p.275.

16. Greenert created the LCS council to oversee development and fielding of the LCS ships and their mission modules. Chaired by Vice Admiral Richard Hunt, Director of the Navy Staff, the original council members were Vice Admiral Mark Skinner, principal military deputy to the Assistant Secretary of the Navy for Research, Development and Acquisition; Vice Admiral Thomas Coleman, Commander, Naval Surface Forces; and Vice Admiral Kevin McCoy, Commander, Naval Sea Systems Command. With the addition of the JHSV, the Commander of the Military Sealift Command also has a permanent seat on the council.

17. Emelie Rutherford, 'Navy Eyeing Expanded JHSV Role,' *Defense Daily* – 25 April 2013 (Rockville, MD: Access Intelligence LLC, 2013).

18. Quoted in 'Admiral Buzby on the Evolving Capabilities of a USN-USMC-MSC Enabled Fleet' in a 16 April 2013 article on the Second Line of Defense website. This can be found by searching for the article at http://www.sldinfo.com/

GERMANY'S TYPE 212A SUBMARINES

Cutting-Edge Technology Drives German Maritime Transformation

A major theme in European naval development over the past decade has been the steady metamorphosis of Germany's *Deutsche Marine* from its Cold War emphasis on Baltic and North Sea operations to a more globally deployable configuration. This trend has been clearly evident with respect to surface forces, where replacement of the previous generation of fast attack craft with the new, considerably larger K-130 *Braunschweig* corvettes is now reaching its conclusion.[1] The new F-125 stabilisation frigates of the *Baden-Württemberg* class, which are specifically designed for international peacekeeping missions, will follow before the end of the decade. If anything, however, the extent of change has been even greater beneath the waves. Here, delivery of the new generation of Type 212A patrol submarines will soon be completed with the planned acceptance during 2014 of *U-36*, the last of six German members of the class.

The new boats, which have entered service in two distinct batches since 2005, are the world's first operational submarines to be equipped with a fuel cell-based air-independent propulsion (AIP) system. AIP allows the class to remain underwater for an extended period without the need to come to the surface for air.[2] This provides a level of submerged endurance previously only available to nuclear-propelled submarines. Four further submarines of the class have been ordered for Italy's *Marina Militare*, whilst German industry has also achieved significant commercial success in exporting similar AIP systems installed in other boats, most notably in the larger Type 214 units. Although AIP propulsion is undoubtedly a key aspect of the Type 212A's superior operational capabilities, the submarines also feature a wide range of other cutting-edge advances to support builder Howaldtswerke-Deutsche Werft's (HDW's) claim that they represent 'the peak of German submarine technology'. This chapter examines the factors that influenced the Type 212A's construction and analyses the class's key design features and systems.

CLASS ORIGINS

The Type 212A class has its origins in the transfer of German submarine design efforts to a follow-on programme following the termination of the preceding Type 211 project on cost grounds in the late 1980s. The new Type 212 programme was ultimately intended to replace the existing Type 205 and 206 coastal submarines that entered service during the 1960s and 1970s and which had been largely configured for the relatively shallow waters of the Baltic. The Type 212's initial specification was therefore heavily influenced by the requirements of 'Cold War' Baltic operations, although a significant increase in overall size was envisaged to support a broader range of missions. Advances in anti-submarine detection capabilities drove a particular emphasis on stealth capabilities and were one of the main factors determining the selection of AIP technology. As in other contemporary AIP-equipped submarines, this was to supplement rather than replace the boat's primary diesel-electric propulsion system. Work on fuel cell-based AIP systems had been underway in Germany since the 1970s and a prototype alkaline-based fuel cell plant was retrofitted to the Type 205 submarine *U-1* for sea trials during 1988–9. The success of these tests resulted in the selection of Siemens' Polymer Electrolyte Membrane (PEM) fuel cells and an associated AIP propulsion system developed by HDW for the new boats.

Overall design responsibility for the Type 212 was placed in the hands of the ARGE 212 consortium of Thyssen Nordseewerke and HDW, working in conjunction with the IKL design bureau (now part of HDW). The new class drew heavily on equipment intended for the defunct Type 211 project and was also influenced by contemporary German export construction, not least Israel's *Dolphin* class.

The German Navy's Type 212A submarine *U-32* pictured running on the surface in April 2010. Delivered by ThyssenKrupp Marine System's HDW business in two distinct batches between 2005 and 2014, the class features a fuel cell-based AIP system that allows prolonged submerged operations. *(German Navy)*

At the same time, the incorporation of AIP and a new electric motor resulted in significant modifications to previous submarine blueprints. Design work was largely completed by 1992 and was followed by authorisation of a preliminary batch of four boats some two years later. At this time it was envisaged that follow-on orders would be subsequently placed for two further similar batches, giving twelve submarines in total.

By this time, however, Italy's *Marina Militare* had become interested in the Type 212 as a candidate for its own replacement submarine programme. This ultimately resulted in the signing of a memorandum of understanding between Germany and Italy in April 1996 for a common project. This was followed in August 1997 by an order with Italian shipyard Fincantieri for an initial batch of two boats. Although Italy's involvement had only limited impact on the overall Type 212 design, changes were made to accommodate specific *Marina Militare* requirements. Most notable amongst these were modifications to airlock arrangements to facilitate docking with a deep sea recovery vehicle (DSRV) and an increase in diving depth to reflect operating conditions in the Mediterranean. The designation of the class was changed to Type 212A to reflect these improvements. The changes have undoubtedly also been of benefit to the German Navy, given a steady shift in emphasis away from the class's original Baltic-centric focus to a more flexible mission profile that is unconstrained by regional restrictions.

CONSTRUCTION AND DELIVERY

With design modifications completed, the manufacturing phase of the renamed Type 212A programme officially commenced on 1 July 1998 at a ceremony presided over by then German defence minister, Volker Rühe. Key dates in the construction programme are set out in Table 3.4.1. The first boat, *U-31*, was christened on 20 March 2002 and commenced her maiden voyage just over a year later on 7 April 2003. Along with second of class, *U-32*, she was formally commissioned on 19 October 2005 after an extensive series of sea trials. All four submarines in the first German batch, along with their first two Italian sisters, had been delivered by mid-2007.

Construction work on the German submarines was shared between the Thyssen Nordseewerke yard at Emden and HDW's Kiel facility. The boats have been fabricated in five main sections, with the two

A view of HDW's construction facility at Kiel in August 2012, with part of the submarine construction hall pictured to the right of the photograph; the Type 212A submarine *U-33* seen undergoing maintenance in the middle of the picture; and the ship lift for lowering submarines into the water located on the left. *(Conrad Waters)*

Table 3.4.1: TYPE 212A SUBMARINES: CLASS LIST

NAME	PENNANT	ORDERED	CHRISTENED[1]	DELIVERED	COMMISSIONED	COUNTRY	ASSEMBLY YARD
U-31	S181	6 July 1994[2]	20 March 2002	7 September 2005	19 October 2005	Germany	HDW Kiel
U-32	S182	6 July 1994	4 December 2003	27 September 2005	19 October 2005	Germany	TNSW Emden
U-33	S183	6 July 1994	13 September 2004	20 April 2006	13 June 2006	Germany	HDW Kiel
U-34	S184	6 July 1994	1 July 2005	29 November 2006	3 May 2007	Germany	TNSW Emden
Salvatore Todaro	S526	August 1997	6 November 2003	29 March 2006	29 March 2006	Italy	Fincantieri Muggiano
Scirè	S527	August 1997	18 December 2004	19 February 2007	19 February 2007	Italy	Fincantieri Muggiano
U-35	S185	22 September 2006	15 November 2011	[Early 2014]	[Early 2014]	Germany	HDW Kiel
U-36	S186	22 September 2006	15 May 2013	[Late 2014]	[Late 2014]	Germany	HDW Kiel
Pietro Venuti	S528	21 April 2008	–	[2015]	[2015]	Italy	Fincantieri Muggiano
Romeo Romei	S529	21 April 2008	–	[2016]	[2016]	Italy	Fincantieri Muggiano

Notes

1. Christening should not be confused with the date of technical launch, which often postdates the christening ceremony. However, *U-36* was launched before her christening.

2. Although the contract for the first four German boats was authorised in 1994, design revisions relating to Italian involvement in the project delayed the start of production to 1998.

Construction of the Type 212A submarines was shared between Thyssen Nordseewerke at Emden and HDW's Kiel facility. The former yard was responsible for constructing the class's two rear modules; the sub-assembly is pictured here being delivered to HDW at Kiel for mating with the front portion of the boat. Following rationalisation of the ThyssenKrupp Marine Systems' business, all submarine manufacturing is now concentrated at Kiel. *(HDW – ThyssenKrupp Marine Systems)*

shipbuilders constructing the same parts of each submarine. More precisely, Nordseewerke was allocated responsibility for Section 10 – housing the electric motor – and Section 20 – encompassing the sound-absorbing module in which the diesel motor is installed. Meanwhile HDW constructed the forward sections – 30, 40 and 50 – as well as the hydrogen cylinders that form a key part of the AIP system. Final assembly of the first four submarines was split between the two ARGE 212 consortium yards, with HDW completing *U-31* and *U-33* and Nordseewerke assembling *U-32* and *U-34*.[3] Assembly of the two initial Italian boats was entirely focused on Fincantieri's Muggiano facility near La Spezia but they feature a significant amount of German components in addition to the core propulsion plant. For example, the torpedo release system is entirely of German origin, being manufactured by HDW in Kiel before despatch to Italy for final assembly.

A second batch of modified Type 212A submarines was ordered by Germany in September 2006, although this was limited to two instead of the expected four boats. The continued evolution of the *Deutsche Marine* towards global deployment resulted in a number of design changes. The most evident of these is a 1.2m extension in length that has allowed incorporation of an enlarged operations centre. Less immediately apparent – but equally important – modifications included:

■ Replacement of previous separate weapons and sonar command systems with an integrated sensor and weapon control suite.

A view of the submarine construction hall at HDW in Kiel, with a Type 212A boat nearing completion on the right. The facility operates on a broad production line basis. Sub-assemblies are manufactured in the area towards the top left of the image and then transported to the assembly area, where the different sections are joined together. The complete boat is then transported out of the hall for launch on the ship lift. *(HDW – ThyssenKrupp Marine Systems)*

- Replacement of one of the previous two periscopes with an optronic mast.
- Revisions to the sonar arrays.
- Enhanced communications systems.
- Increased fuel reserves and modifications to the hydroplanes for improved range and speed.
- Provision of an air-locked accommodation chamber in the fore part of the fin to assist deployment of Special Forces.
- Adaptation of systems for tropical operations.

Whilst fabrication of constituent sections for the new batch followed the arrangements implemented for the first four submarines, final assembly of both boats was carried out in Kiel.[4] The lead unit, *U-35*, was christened on 15 November 2011 and she commenced sea trials in early 2013 in advance of planned delivery by early 2014. The final boat, *U-36*, will follow before the end of 2014. No further orders are currently envisaged for the German Navy given ongoing budgetary pressures but the *Marina Militare* contracted a further batch of two boats in 2008. These will be largely identical to the existing Italian pair and are expected to be operational in the 2015/2016 timeframe.

OVERALL DESIGN

Whilst the Type 212A submarines displace almost three times the Type 206A boats that they have replaced, their dived displacement of just over 1,800 tons and overall length of c. 56m still means that they are relatively small when compared with other current-generation submarines. This is largely a reflection of the original design specification that placed emphasis on operation in the enclosed and shallow waters of the Baltic. It is, therefore, not surprising that they most resemble neighbouring Sweden's A-19 *Gotland* class in this regard.

The Type 212A class is also notably short and broad, reflecting an unusual one-and-a-half deck configuration. The broader, forward end of the pressure hull houses crew accommodation and the operations centre on its main/upper level, with much of the lower deck being given over to weapons stowage and handling. The pressure hull narrows to just one deck aft of the fin, which houses the diesel generator and electric motor. This arrangement effectively places the command centre in a dead end, preventing the potential distraction from 'through traffic' that can be prevalent in single-deck submarine designs. The commanding officer's cabin is located in close proximity to the operations room, allowing swift access should the need arise.

Fabrication of the submarines makes extensive use of non-magnetic steel. This is supplemented by the use of lightweight glass fibre reinforced plastics for some structures, including some outer hull coverings and large parts of the fin. The liquid oxygen tanks and hydrogen storage cylinders that provide fuel for the AIP system are both located outside of the pressure hull, reflecting stringent safety requirements. It

The lead member of the second batch of German Type 212A boats, *U-35*, pictured preparing to depart Kiel for sea trials on 27 March 2013. The German construction programme will be completed by delivery of her sister *U-36* towards the end of 2014. *(HDW – ThyssenKrupp Marine Systems)*

appears that this approach with respect to the oxygen tanks may have been overly cautious as the 'export' Type 214 design has its tanks located within the pressure hull.

PROPULSION SYSTEM

The Type 212A's hybrid propulsion system is probably the design feature that has attracted most attention. It combines a traditional diesel-electric propulsion plant that enables high-speed transit and deployment in lower threat locations with a supplementary AIP system for prolonged underwater operation at lower speeds in areas of greatest threat. The system comprises a balance of long-established and more recent technologies, the main elements of which are:

- A MTU 16V 396 series diesel and Piller AC generator.
- A main lead-acid battery.
- An AIP plant comprising nine Siemens BZM 34 fuel cell modules; fuel cell control boards; oxygen and hydrogen storage units and a tank for reaction waste water.
- A Siemens Permasyn electric propulsion motor.

These elements are explained in greater detail below:

Diesel Generator: A single air-breathing diesel generator is the Type 212A's primary source of electrical energy. This compact unit is built around a 16V variant of MTU's 396 series of diesel engines. They have been utilised in a wide range of land- and maritime-based applications and were first modified for underwater service in the early 1980s. Almost 250 396-series submarine engines have been delivered to date in eight, twelve and sixteen cylinder configurations, accumulating over 310,000 hours of service. It is connected to a Piller Power Systems A/C generator that can either be used to supply energy directly to the boat's electric motor or for storage in the battery for subsequent underwater operation. HDW claims that the diesel generator unit is opti-

The Type 212A programme was originally authorised as long ago as 1994. However, Italy subsequently joined Germany in the project and the basic Type 212 design was amended to meet the *Marina Militare's* requirements, delaying the start of construction. This image shows the lead Italian boat *Salvatore Todaro* in American waters on 1 August 2008. Two boats have already been delivered and a further pair are expected to become operational in the 2015/16 timeframe. *(US Navy)*

mised to facilitate short snorkelling periods, thereby supplementing the fuel cell system in minimising time spent close to the surface. It is designed to be resistant to sudden changes in air pressure and can tolerate the significant variations in pitch and heel that can characterise underwater operation.

Battery: The Type 212A uses a conventional EnerSys Hawker Varta lead-acid battery located in a compartment underneath the weapons storage spaces in the forward part of the hull. It can either be charged by the diesel generator or – in exceptional circumstances – by energy produced from the AIP system. Conventional rechargeable batteries continue to suffer from poor power density and

alternatives are being sought to enhance the underwater performance of future generations of submarines. For example, HDW has been in the lead in developing lithium-ion (L-ion) batteries for submarine use. They feature in conceptual Type 210 mod and Type 216 designs and could conceivably be retrofitted to existing boats. At this stage it is not clear whether the much-publicised problems associated with the insertion of L-ion technology in the Boeing 787 jetliner will impact its potential use in an underwater environment.

AIP Plant: The Type 212A's fuel cell-based AIP plant provides a supplementary means of producing electrical energy when access to surface air to allow

the primary diesel generator to run is not possible. The basic operating principle is based on the conversion of chemical energy produced by reactants – a fuel and an oxidant – into electricity. In the case of the HDW/Siemens AIP system, hydrogen and liquid oxygen are used. Liquid oxygen is carried in two specially insulated, shock-resistant tanks that incorporate an evaporator that uses waste heat from fuel cell operation. It is also used to supply the crew's breathing requirements. The potentially more dangerous hydrogen is stored in metal hydride cylinders specially designed by HDW, where it is bonded in the lattice structure of the host metal until released for use by the application of heat. The oxygen and hydrogen are fed to the AIP system's fuel

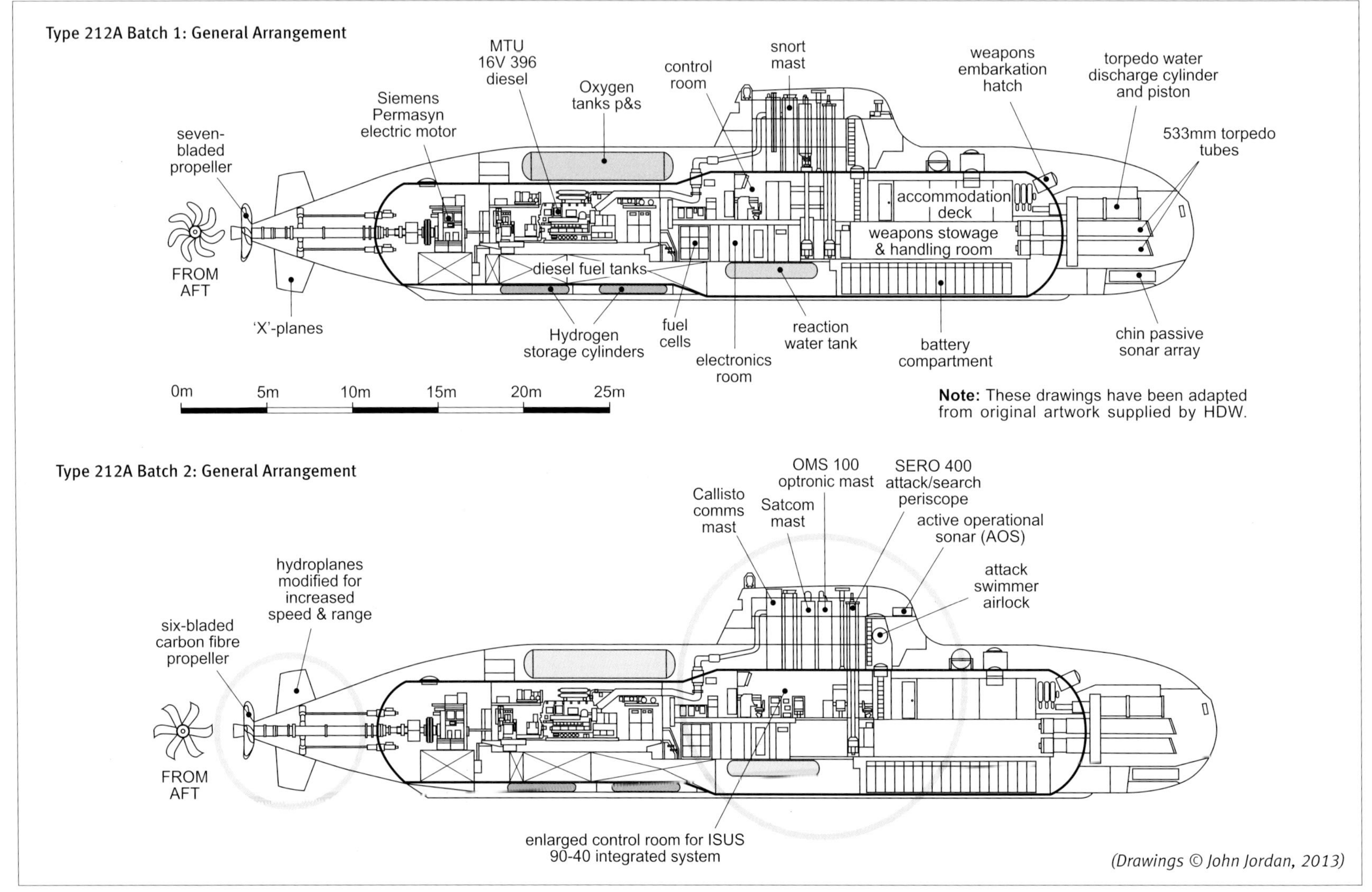

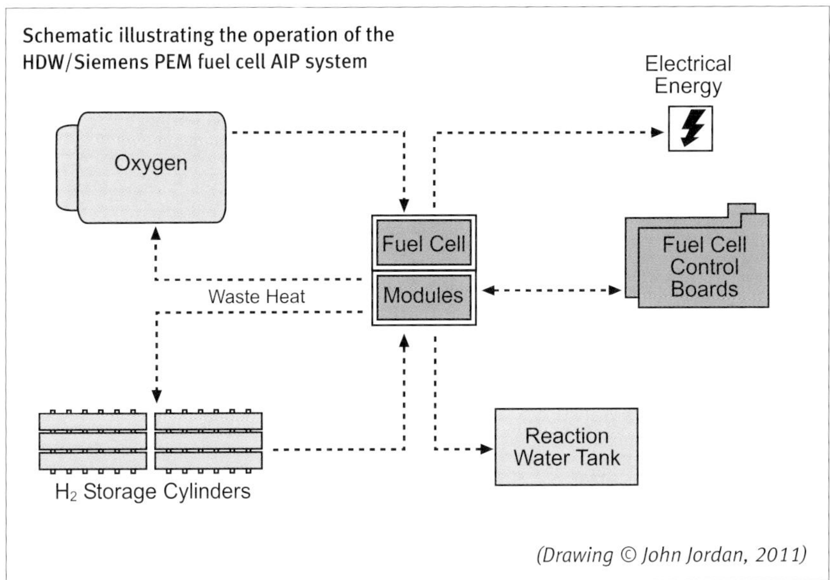

(Drawing © John Jordan, 2011)

Left: A Siemens Permasyn electric propulsion motor, which is clearly configured to use the narrow confines of a submarine's hull to maximum effect. Different sizes have been developed for the Type 212A and Type 214 submarines. The variant used in the Type 212A is reported to provide an underwater speed of at least 20 knots. *(Siemens)*

cell modules in separate, double-walled pipes.

The heart of the AIP system in the Type 212A comprises its Siemens BZM 34 PEM fuel cell modules.[5] Each of these weighs just 650kg and is capable of producing 34kW of energy from seventy-two individual cells. The pressure-resistant modules are encapsulated in a nitrogen-filled container that assists early identification and prevention of potential safety issues such as chemical leakage. Each submarine is equipped with nine individual modules – one of which is a spare that engages automatically in event of a failure – that are connected to the boat's main electrical switchboard. They are located on the lower deck just forward of the sound-absorbing module housing the diesel generator. The only by-product of the process is distilled water, which is fed into a tank and counterbalances the weight of the reactants used.

During normal AIP operation, the AIP system's fuel cells and the conventional battery are both permanently connected to the propulsion system and operate in conjunction with each other. The fuel cell system essentially provides power for low-speed operations. It is supplemented by the battery if the electrical requirements of the propulsion system exceed its electrical capacity and the battery has sufficient charge remaining to assist. It is also possible to use the AIP fuel cells to produce energy

This detailed view of *U-33* under maintenance shows one of the two shock-resistant tanks for liquid oxygen, which are located side-by-side outside of the pressure hull, aft the fin. Hydrogen is stored in specially-designed metal hydride cylinders wrapped round the aft hull. Some of these can just be seen behind the scaffolding. *(Conrad Waters)*

The German Navy's Type 212A submarine *U-33* is seen passing the mine-countermeasures vessel *Hameln* in September 2011. The image gives a good impression of the Type 212A's diminutive size, which was driven by an original design specification placing emphasis on operation in the enclosed and shallow waters of the Baltic. This operational requirement is also reflected in the selected 'X' rudder configuration, which facilitates operation in minimal water depths. *(German Navy)*

An image of the first Type 212A submarine *U-31* pictured during sea trials. The forward hydroplanes are located on the fin to reduce the impact of noise on sonar operation. *(HDW – ThyssenKrupp Marine Systems)*

in isolated operation, although this would only be relevant in cases of equipment failure. Starting the fuel cell plant in isolated operation requires use of an auxiliary power supply from an independent source.

The PEM AIP system is regarded as being highly successful in practice, offering several advantages in securing stealthy operation in high threat areas. The fuel cells themselves do not generate any noise; there is no requirement to release any waste products that might assist detection and impact diving depth, whilst a relatively low operating temperature (c.80°C) minimises infrared signature. Fuel cell-based AIP systems are also regarded as more efficient than competing technologies – HDW claims by a factor of at least two – allowing greater underwater endurance for a given quantity of stored oxygen. The class is capable of operating underwater for considerably in excess of two weeks, albeit at low speeds.

Electric Propulsion Motor: The development of the Siemens Permasyn motor that equips the Type 212A class started in the early 1980s. The overall aim was to develop a submarine drive system that combined efficient and reliable operation with minimal noise, heat and magnetic signatures. The resultant design utilises permanent magnets to produce alternating current (AC) and is more compact and efficient than equivalent conventional DC motors. Key control and cooling functions are integrated into the unit, providing further economy of space. The variant fitted in the Type 212A boats weights approximately 28 tons, operates in the c.2MW power range and is constructed of non-magnetic steel. A particularly noteworthy design feature is the motor's ability to achieve the same torque at much lower revolutions than previously, permitting the use of slow turning propeller with enhanced hydro-acoustic properties.

The Type 212A's Permasyn motor is connected directly to a seven-bladed, skewback propeller. This design is intended to reduce cavitation – and hence noise generation – whilst maintaining efficiency. The blades are tilted rearward along the longitudinal axis, with the blade tips swept back against the direction of rotation. Published data suggests that the class can achieve a maximum underwater speed in the region of 20 knots, reducing to 12 knots on the surface. HDW is developing a new carbon-fibre propeller to achieve further efficiencies and this might be fitted to the second batch of boats. Published information suggests that this will incor-

A view of the operations centre in one of the German Navy's first batch of Type 212A submarines. Four, two-screen consoles for the Norwegian Kongsberg MSI-90U weapon-control system can be seen in the foreground, whilst the three consoles for the Atlas Elektronik DBQS-40 sonar are covered to the rear. The Batch 2 German boats feature an integrated sensor and weapon-control system of purely German origin with eight consoles. The MSI-90U weapon control system is fitted to the first batch of German Type 212A submarines and all the Italian boats. *(HDW – Thyssen Krupp Marine Systems)*

porate a six-bladed form. However, the design characteristics of propellers remain subject to significant secrecy. Hence, this is one area where published information and reality can differ significantly.

OTHER ENGINEERING ASPECTS

The initial focus on Baltic operations means that good manoeuvrability in shallow waters was a key design consideration. This is reflected in selection of an 'X' rudder configuration. No distinction is made between the boat's aft hydroplanes and rudder, with all four hydroplanes being used to steer and dive the boat. In addition to facilitating operation in minimal water depths, this arrangement is also claimed to lower overall water resistance. The forward hydroplanes are located on the fin to reduce the impact of noise on sonar operation. Further enhancements are being made to the hydroplanes to improve water flows in the second Type 212A batch. The aim is to improve underwater speed or endurance by around 5 per cent.

In line with efforts to minimise crew size, propulsion and other electrical systems are controlled by an integrated platform management system. This is referred to as the EMCS (Engineering Monitoring and Control System) in HDW documentation. EMCS permits centralised performance of propulsion and steering functions, as well as controlling and monitoring a wide range of other equipment. It operates by means of a duplicated data network. The system is controlled from two separate one-man consoles. One of these is for steering and the other for engineering control.

COMBAT SYSTEMS AND WEAPONRY

The heart of the Type 212A's war-fighting capability is provided by its command and weapons control system. In the four original, Batch 1 boats, this comprises the Norwegian Kongsberg MSI-90U weapon control system. This operates in conjunction with the Atlas Elektronik DBQS 40 sonar and

with other sensors, most notably the two periscopes.

MSI-90U was the result of German-Norwegian collaboration in submarine design during the 1980s and was first installed in Norway's German-built *Ula* class (Type 210) boats. It uses the same data network as EMCS to collect and process informa-

tion from the submarine's sensors and communications system. The resultant situational position is displayed on four, two-screen multi-function consoles located in the command centre. These are linked with the submarine's weapons, principally its torpedoes, to allow hostile tracks to be engaged.

A detailed view of a Kongsberg MSI-90U weapon-control system console. The screens display information gathered by the submarine's sensors and allow system operators to select hostile tracks for engagement. *(HDW – Thyssen Krupp Marine Systems)*

MSI-90U is designed to support multiple engagements in quick succession: published data suggests an ability to track twenty-five targets and control up to eight weapons simultaneously.

DBQS-40 is an integrated sonar system that encompasses:

- A passive cylindrical array sonar (CAS) in the submarine's chin.
- A mine avoidance sonar (MAS) above the torpedo tubes.
- Flank array sonars (FAS) and passive ranging sonar (PRS) panels port and starboard.
- A cylindrical intercept array (CIA) on the aft of the fin.
- A towed array sonar (TAS) operated by a winch located outside of the pressure hull aft.
- Three operator consoles.

There are also additional sensors for own noise analysis, encompassing hydrophones on the outer hull and internal structure noise sensors. The various arrays are linked to three consoles, which display the results on colour screens and can also support target sound analysis. The identification of potentially hostile submarines and other vessels by operators trained to distinguish their acoustic signature still remains important in spite of ongoing advances in other technology.

The Batch 1 submarines also house two conventional periscopes manufactured by EADS' Cassidian Optronics subsidiary.[6] These comprise a SERO 15 attack periscope with an optical and laser

Table 3.4.2.

U-31 PRINCIPAL PARTICULARS

Building Information:

Fabrication Commenced:	1 July 1998
Christened:	20 March 2002
Commissioned:	19 October 2005
Builders:	ThyssenKrupp Marine Systems at its HDW yard in Kiel from sections built at HDW and TNSW in Emden.

Dimensions:

Displacement:	1,500 tons surface displacement, 1,800 tons dived displacement.
Overall Hull Dimensions:	56.0m x 7.0m x 6.0m. Height to top of fin is 11.5m. (**Batch 2:** 57.2m x 7.0m x 6.0m).

Weapons Systems:

Armament:	6 x bow 533mm torpedo tubes. Space for up to 12 torpedoes or equivalent. Potential weapons outfit includes:
	Atlas Elektronik DM2 A4 Sea Hake heavyweight torpedo. Active/passive homing and fibre optical guidance to 50km (27nm) at speeds of up to 50 knots.
	Diehl BGD Defence IDAS missile. IR seeker & fibre optic guidance for underwater engagement of air, surface and land-based targets to 20km (11nm).
	Quad packed launch canister. System currently under development.
	Minelaying capability.
Countermeasures:	FL1800 U ESM system. TAU 2000 torpedo countermeasures system (**Batch 2:** Fitted for, not with).
Principal Sensors:	Atlas Elektronik DBQS 40 integrated sonar suite. EADS Cassidian SERO 14 and SERO 15 periscopes. Navigation radar.
	(**Batch 2:** Atlas Elektronik ISUS 90 integrated sensor and weapon control system. SERO 400 periscope. OMS 100 optronic mast).
Combat System:	Kongsberg MSI-90U weapon control system. (**Batch 2:** Atlas Elektronik ISUS 90 integrated sensor and weapon control system. Improved communications systems including Links 11 and 16).

Propulsion Systems:

Machinery:	Diesel-electric with auxiliary AIP propulsion. 1 x MTU 16V 396 series diesel with Piller generator rated at 1.2MW. 1 x Siemens Permasyn electric motor. HDW/Siemens PEM AIP system. 8+1 spare BZM 34 fuel cell modules for 272kW.
Speed and Range:	12 knots surfaced, 20 knots submerged. Over 2 weeks underwater endurance on AIP.
Diving Depth:	Over 250m.

Other Details:

Complement:	Accommodation is provided for 27 personnel.
Class:	Four Batch 1 submarines ordered for Germany in 1994, with two additional Batch 2 submarines ordered in 2006.
	Italy has ordered a further four submarines in two batches, all of which are broadly identical to the Batch 1 specification.

rangefinder; and a SERO 14 search periscope with an optical rangefinder, thermal imagery and a combined electronic support measures (ESM) and GPS antenna. The ESM system is the 'U' version of the Germany Navy's standard FL1800 series. The fin also houses a navigation radar and a hoistable mast for radio communications for use whilst on the surface.

The Type 212A submarines are equipped with six torpedo tubes and associated handling and storage arrangements. The automated storage system is located on the lower deck and operates on a revolver principle, with spare torpedoes housed in six separate chambers. The appropriate chamber is aligned with the relevant inner tube door to transfer a weapon into the torpedo tube. Discharge is by means of a HDW-designed water pressure expulsion system, which uses two water cylinders and associated water pistons to allow the silent release of weapons. Each cylinder operates three torpedo tubes, with release implemented from a weapons control system console or from the torpedo storage system's central operating station. The need to find space for the water cylinders has resulted in an asymmetrical arrangement of the torpedo tubes, which are aligned slightly to port.

Up to twelve Atlas Elektronik DM2 A4 series Sea Hake heavyweight 533mm torpedoes can be shipped. Incorporating fibre optical guidance and active/passive homing, these weapons feature a modular battery system. More battery modules are used dependent on the range and speed required, with public sources suggesting a c. 250kg warhead

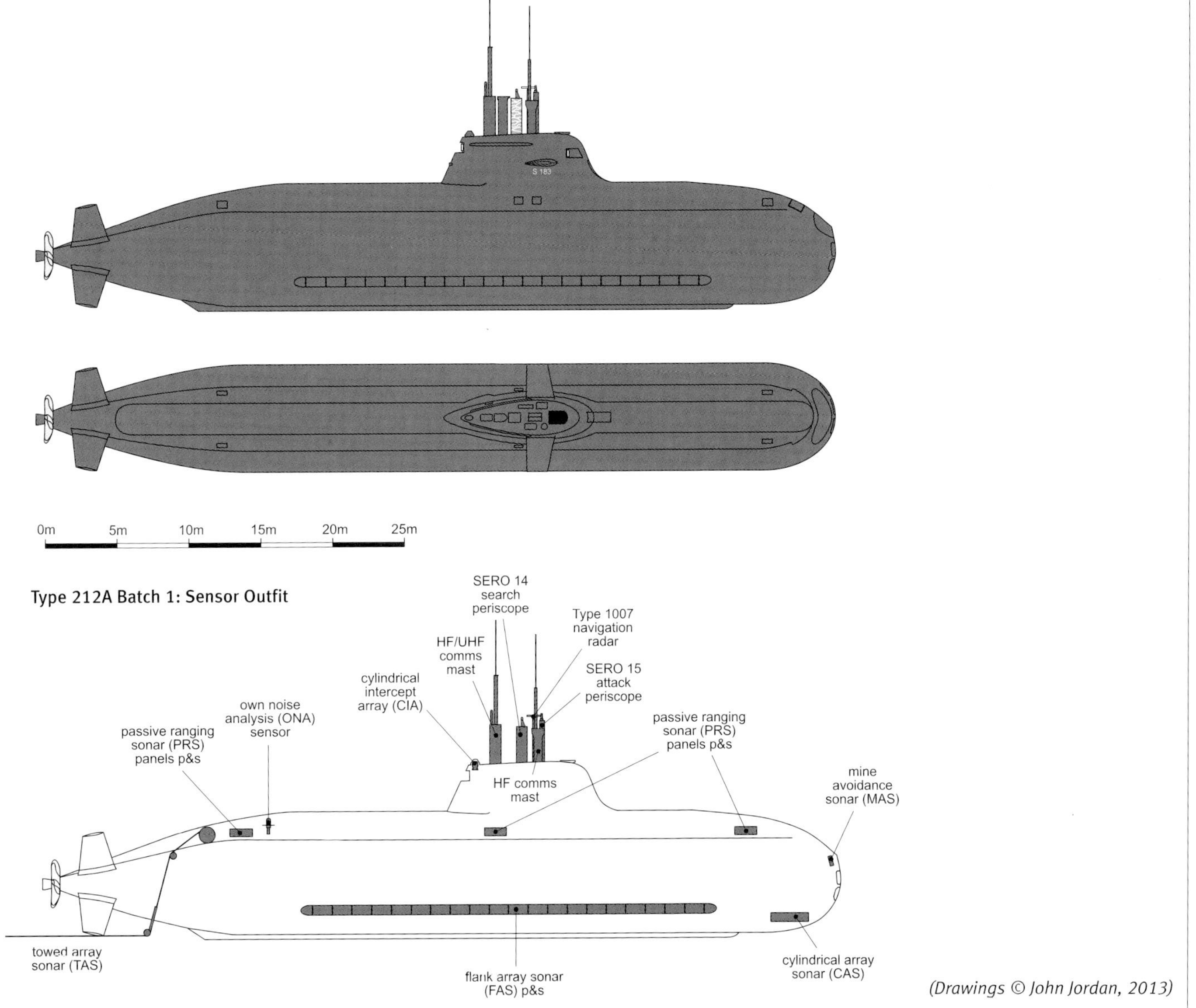

(Drawings © John Jordan, 2013)

Above, left: A close-up picture of *U-34*'s fin taken whilst she was transiting the Kiel Canal. Sensors pictured (forward to aft) include a Type 1007 navigation radar on a narrow hoist. A SERO 14 search periscope with a much broader trunk is located immediately forward of the snort mast. A communications mast is located aft. Also visible is the shark fin like cover of the cylindrical intercept array. The Batch II German boats feature significant differences, including installation of an OMS 100 optronic mast in place of one of the periscopes and provision for a CALLISTO communications system. *(Arne Lütkenhorst)*

Above, right: The Type 212A's torpedo discharge system is one of the more complex pieces of engineering equipment installed in the class. It incorporates two large cylinders containing water pistons that allow silent torpedo discharge from the six smaller torpedo tubes. Each water cylinder controls release from three of the tubes, with the space taken up by the lower, starboard cylinder requiring the torpedo tubes to be offset to port. *(HDW – Thyssen Krupp Marine Systems)*

Left: The lead Type 212A submarine *U-31* pictured on HDW's ship lift. The asymmetrical arrangement of the torpedo tubes is apparent. Principal armament comprises Atlas Elektronik DM2 A4 series torpedoes, although the IDAS air defence weapon has also been trialled. *(HDW – ThyssenKrupp Marine Systems)*

can be delivered up to 50km at a speed of more than 50 knots. Type 212A submarines are also able to carry out minelaying operations and have trialled the Diehl BGT Defence IDAS Interactive Defence and Attack System for Submarines. This features a rocket-propelled autonomous missile with an infrared seeker which can be used to engage surface or air targets. They are housed in a quad-packed launch container and fired from one of the torpedo tubes. Passive defence is provided by the TAU-2000 torpedo countermeasures system, with four self-contained launchers deploying jammers and decoys against incoming torpedoes.

The Batch 2 submarines ordered for the German Navy incorporate a number of combat system modifications in comparison with their Batch 1 counterparts, most notably the replacement of the separate MSI-90U and DBQS-40 systems with an integrated sensor and weapon control system of purely German origin; Atlas Elektronik's ISUS 90-40. A variant of the modular, open architecture system already installed in a number of export submarine classes, ISUS 90-40 incorporates an additional eighth multi-function console, whilst upgrades to sonar hardware encompass enhanced flank arrays and an active sonar in the forepart of the fin. ISUS 90-40 is also integrated with an electronic chart display and information system. More negatively, funding issues meant that additional towed arrays were not purchased for the last two submarines meaning, in practice, that the existing systems have to be shared across the total fleet.

Other enhancements to the second batch of Type 212A submarines includes the installation of a SERO 400 combined attack/search periscope and the replacement of the second periscope with an OMS 100 optronic mast. The former offers 1.5x, 6x and 12x magnification and is equipped with high-resolution video and still cameras. It is used for both combat and navigation purposes. The optronic mast can be operated remotely from one of the combat system's multi-function consoles and can provide pre-settable and automatic search and observation duties. In contrast to a normal periscope, it does not penetrate the pressure hull. There have also been significant upgrades to communications systems, most notably the addition of NATO Link 11/16 tactical data capabilities for exchange of information with allied units. Another important enhancement is provision of the CALLISTO communications system, which uses a hoistable mast and buoy attached to a cable to allow contact to be maintained with a deeply submerged submarine.

OTHER KEY DESIGN FEATURES

The Type 212A has been designed with high levels of survivability and damage-resistance in mind. The first line of defence is clearly the consistent attention paid to stealth throughout the design process. This includes the mounting of the diesel generator in a sound-absorbing module, the extensive use of non-magnetic materials, the inherently low signatures of much of the propulsion equipment and the freedom of operation provided by the AIP fuel cells. The submarines also have significant resistance to shock damage, most notably in the raft mounting of the command centre, the use of flexible flooring in the accommodation areas and the use of elastic mountings in the torpedo tubes and associated storage system. A comprehensive fire detection and fire-fighting system includes the use of nitrogen fire-fighting units in the machinery spaces. Oxygen breathing points are also provided around the interior of the boat to assist crew survivability in situations where there is smoke contamination or flooding.

German submarine operating philosophy is focused on safe recovery of the boat to the surface in the event of a critical accident, reflecting the enhanced range of options this provides. However, the *Marina Militare* mandated an ability to dock with a DSRV when they joined the Type 212A project, leading to the incorporation of a second airlock in the design. A range of options to recover the crew is therefore available should a worst-case scenario arise. The Batch 2 boats also benefit from improved capabilities to deploy Special Forces, most notably through the provision of an air-locked accommodation chamber in the fore part of the fin. Removable pressure-proof containers for Special Forces' equipment have been developed for attachment to the outer hull.

Less critical crew considerations are also evident

U-31 pictured running on the service on 31 October 2005, shortly after being delivered to the German Navy. German operating philosophy dictates all possible efforts should be made to recover boats to the surface in the event of a critical accident but other means of crew escape are possible. *(HDW – ThyssenKrupp Marine Systems)*

U-32 is seen running at speed on the surface in this 2010 photograph. In April 2006 she undertook a two-week underwater voyage from the German Bight to the Bay of Cadiz operating on AIP alone. *(German Navy)*

in the Type 212A class. Notable amongst these is the almost total abolition of the previous practice of 'hot bunking' under which a single berth was shared by more than one crew member.[7] Perhaps conversely, the class has introduced an arrangement under which each submarine is allocated two crews, maximising utilisation of the capital invested in the design. The Batch 2 boats feature tropicalisation to assist global deployment.

TRIALS AND ENTRY INTO SERVICE

Whilst submarine operations are inevitably subject to a degree of secrecy, the Type 212A class seem to have been a clear success since first entering service in October 2005. The second member of the class, *U-32*, was quickly used to demonstrate the efficiency of the fuel cell-based AIP system. Whilst sailing for Taranto in Italy for operations with the *Marina Militare*'s first Type 212A boat, *Salvatore Todaro*, she undertook a well-publicised two-week underwater voyage from the German Bight to the Bay of Cadiz from 11 to 25 April 2006 on AIP propulsion alone. In addition, both *Todaro* and her sister-boat *Scirè* made early transits of the Atlantic to provide the US Navy with an insight into the new technology, a voyage which *U-32* has also made in 2013. *Todaro's* deployment in 2008 was reportedly the first time since the Second World War that an Italian submarine had operated in American waters. In spite of the design's initial development for Baltic operations, it is clear that they are well-suited for international deployment.

The most potent evidence of the Type 212A's success, however, is probably demonstrated by HDW's ability to win repeat orders from both Germany and Italy, as well as the use of similar technologies in the larger Type 214 export design.[8] Approaching fifteen submarines equipped with HDW/Siemens PEM fuel cell-based AIP systems are now in service, whilst additional boats either under

The Italian Navy's two serving Type 212A submarines have both crossed the Atlantic for operations with the US Navy, representing the first time Italian boats have been seen in these waters since the entirely different circumstances of the Second World War. *(US Navy)*

Right: *U-34* transiting the Kiel Canal on March 2011. The Type 212A's successful introduction of PEM-based fuel cell AIP has cemented HDW's market position in submarine construction. This has been particularly evident in export sales of the larger Type 214 submarines. *(Arne Lütkenhorst)*

construction or on order will more than double this total. This track record is considerably greater than competing systems, probably reflecting the attractions of fuel cell-based AIP's inherent efficiency and its positive stealth characteristics.

CONCLUSION[9]

It is now over ten years since *U-31,* the first Type 212A submarine, departed Kiel on its maiden voyage. Since then, the economic environment in Europe has changed dramatically and the defence policies of many of its constituents have been adapted to match. The final members of the class that are now entering service are therefore being delivered in very different circumstances from the first boats. Certainly, Germany's initial intention to operate as many as twelve members of the class is little more than a distant memory. In spite of this, the design has had immense significance, both for the *Deutsche Marine* and for Germany's shipbuilding industry.

From a purely naval perspective, the Type 212A

Below: Although the German Navy originally planned to buy twelve Type 212A submarines, defence cutbacks mean the two Batch 2 submarines will be the last German boats. This view of *U-35* shows some of the changes to the enlarged fin, including the new optronic mast and the CALLISTO communications system aft. *(HDW – ThyssenKrupp Marine Systems)*

provides the German Navy with a state-of-the art underwater flotilla that has a submerged endurance bettered only by those few navies able to afford nuclear-propelled boats, as well as an overall level of stealth that is perhaps second-to-none. The development and introduction into service of submarines with an effective AIP plant means that the navy has been able to significantly reduce the vulnerability of its boats whilst operating in littoral or otherwise confined waters. They are able to loiter underwater on AIP propulsion for many days without draining the main battery, only resorting to the electric motor's full capacity for limited periods of high-speed activity. This confers a significant advantage during, for example, the performance of defensive missions in the class's originally intended primary operating theatre in the Baltic. However, AIP's stealth characteristics – bolstered by other stealth technologies incorporated in the design – also facilitate forward deployment in surveillance and other covert roles. This is a capability particularly relevant in supporting the global stabilisation mission the *Deutsche Marine* is steadily transitioning towards. Although still some distance away from furnishing the true offensive oceanic proficiency of high-speed attack submarines powered by high-capacity nuclear reactors, the enhancements such as tropicalisation being introduced in the Batch 2 submarines provides further potential for global operation.

Industrially, the Type 212A's successful introduction of PEM fuel cell AIP has cemented HDW's market position in submarine construction at a time when export contracts are increasingly important for European naval shipbuilding's survival. The rather bespoke nature of the Type 212A design, including its limited size and use of expensive, non-magnetic materials, has restricted direct overseas sales. However, this has been more than counterbalanced by the adoption of much of its technology in the Type 214 and other boats, where it has secured broad worldwide acceptance. This success is, in turn, spurring further investment in research and development. This includes the Type 210 mod and Type 216 concepts aimed at future Norwegian and Australian requirements, the construction of a demonstrator plant for onboard production of hydrogen by means of a methanol reformer to extend AIP range, and investigation of new acoustic coatings and use of alternative construction materials. In short, the Type 212A's successful adoption of cutting-edge technology has driven the transformation that has ensured the continuation of Germany's traditional position as a global leader in submarine design.

Notes

1. A full review of the K-130 class was contained in Guy Toremans' '*Braunschweig* Class Corvettes: Eagerly awaited by the German Navy', *Seaforth World Naval Review 2013* (Barnsley: Seaforth Publishing, 2012), pp.128–47.

2. The development of AIP technology and the different competing systems currently available is beyond the scope of this chapter. Readers interested in exploring the subject in more detail are directed towards the editor's 'Modern Air-Independent Propulsion Equipped Submarines', *Warship 2012* (London: Anova Books, 2012), pp.65–80.

3. The two separate halves of each boat were transported to the relevant assembly yard by barge.

4. The acquisition of HDW by ThyssenKrupp, owners of Nordseewerke, in January 2005 and the resultant creation of ThyssenKrupp Marine Systems meant that the two shipyards involved in the Type 212A programme became part of a common industrial structure encompassing a number of other shipbuilding facilities. Subsequent rationalisation of the ThyssenKrupp Marine Systems business has included the disposal of much of the Nordseewerke yard and consolidation of German submarine manufacturing on the HDW site at Kiel. The facility at Kiel essentially operates on a construction line principle, with component units fabricated at one end of the main construction hall and then moved to a construction area for assembly into a complete boat. The completed unit is transported out of the construction hall and onto a ship lift for 'launch'.

5. Various types of fuel cell have been developed since their use was first driven by the US space programme. However, all comprise three main elements, viz: (i) an anode, (ii) a cathode and (iii) an electrolyte that allows charges to move between the two sides of the fuel cell. The Siemens PEM fuel cell sees hydrogen channelled into the anodic side of the membrane where it is divided into its electrons and protons with the assistance of a platinum catalyst. The PEM polymer electrolyte membrane allows the protons to pass directly to the cathode but prevents the passage of the electrons. These are forced to travel to the cathode via an external circuit that creates an electrical load. The electrons subsequently combine with oxygen – and the protons – on the cathode catalyst to produce water. The conversion process – cold combustion – is shown in the diagram below.

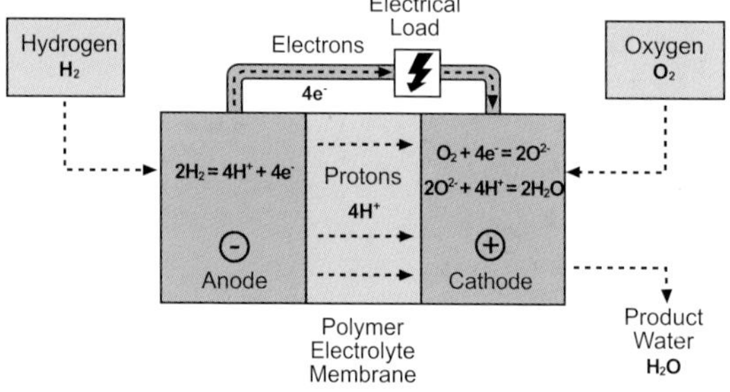

(Drawing © John Jordan, 2011)

6. Cassidian Optronics is the former defence and security division of Carl Zeiss Optronics, which Cassidian has controlled since October 2012.

7. The Type 212A design was originally intended to be operated by twenty-seven crew and twenty-seven berths are provided in the design. However, current complement is understood to be twenty-eight personnel.

8. The Type 214 submarine is based on the design principles of the well-established Type 209 series of diesel-electric submarines but incorporates technologies developed for the Type 212A programme, most notably the AIP system. This AIP plant shares a common architecture with that installed in the Type 212A boats but utilises two larger, 900kg BZM 120 PEM fuel cell modules, each of which produces 120kW of electricity from 320 cells. The design has been sold to Greece, South Korea and Turkey, as well as to Portugal under the Type 209PN designation.

9. This chapter has drawn heavily on contemporary industry and other press releases to support its preparation. The additional sources listed below provided additional information:

– Martin Driver, 'Holding breath on AIP', *Jane's Navy International* – June 2005 (Coulsdon: IHS Jane's, 2005), pp 20–5.
– Peter Hauschildt & Albert Hammerschmidt, 'PEM Fuel Cell Systems – An attractive energy source for submarines', *Naval Forces* – October 2005 (Bonn: Mönch Publishing Group, 2005), pp.30–3.
– Jan Wiedemann (Editor-in-Chief), *Naval Forces: Subcon 2011 Conference Proceedings Special Issue; Submarines – Unseen but on Scene* (Bonn, Mönch Publishing Group, 2011).

Given the secrecy that still surrounds submarine design and operation, hard facts about technical specifications and performance are limited and potentially subject to distortion. This chapter needs to be read with this in mind.

Author:
David Hobbs

4.1 TECHNOLOGICAL REVIEW

WORLD NAVAL AVIATION

An Overview of Recent Developments

INTRODUCTION

Budget problems in 2013 have had a dramatic impact on naval aviation in several leading navies, with measures aimed at achieving short-term savings leading to shutdowns, delayed projects and the prospect of capability gaps from which it will not be easy to recover. The US Navy has suffered a particularly damaging series of funding cuts and the British Royal Navy faces a growing number of embarked aviation gaps during the remainder of the decade. At this stage, however, it is too early to analyse the full impact of the measures that have already been announced or to predict what might happen next in other nations that are still considering deep reductions in their defence budgets. Conversely, India and China both had 'new' carriers at sea during 2013 and Australia and Russia both have big-deck ships under construction. These latter vessels will have impressive multi-role capabilities even if they are not, at least initially, used to their full potential.

CARRIER AVIATION

The US Navy already expected its carrier force to be stretched to meet all its commitments in 2014. The world's first nuclear-powered aircraft carrier *Enterprise* (CVN-65) was withdrawn after fifty-one years of service at the end of 2012, implementing a temporary reduction in the carrier fleet to ten ships. This situation was exacerbated by commencement of a planned four-year refuelling and comprehensive overhaul (RCOH) for the *Abraham Lincoln* (CVN-72) in March 2013.[1] However, the failure of the US

The development and deployment of unmanned aerial vehicles is starting to have a marked impact on world naval aviation. This image shows Northrop Grumman's X-47B demonstrator during initial handling trials on the US aircraft carrier *Harry S Truman* (CVN-75) during December 2012. *(Northrop Grumman)*

Senate to agree a budget deal by March 2013 and consequent imposition of the 2011 Budget Control Act – requiring automatic, government-wide cuts under a process known as sequestration – has made the situation far worse. Given the reality of the Act's implementation and the associated uncertainty over future budgets, the US Navy was forced to make

preparations for immediate reductions that – if implemented in full – would have a serious long-term impact on force levels and plans.

The advent of sequestration compounded problems arising from the failure to agree the FY2013 US budget that had already delayed *Abraham Lincoln*'s refuelling and caused a last-minute cancellation of a

The first US Navy nuclear-powered aircraft carrier *Enterprise* (CVN-65) seen transiting the Strait of Gibraltar in October 2012 towards the end of her final deployment. Her withdrawal from the fleet after fifty-one years of service is one of many factors putting US carrier aviation under pressure. *(US Navy)*

scheduled deployment by the *Harry S Truman* (CVN-75) and her battle group to the Persian Gulf. Subsequently, on 1 March, Ray Mabus, the US Secretary of the Navy, announced further cost reductions including plans to shut down Carrier Air Wing 2 (CVW-2) based at Naval Air Station (NAS) Lemoore, California in April 2013 and initiate preparations to shut down at least a further three CVWs later in the year. These were subsequently identified as CVW-7 in the *Dwight D Eisenhower* (CVN-69), CVW-9 in the *John C Stennis* (CVN-74) and CVW-17 in the *Carl Vinson* (CVN-70). Two further unidentified CVWs were to be reduced to minimum safe levels of flying. In total, therefore, the announcement heralded steps to reduce over half the US Navy's carrier air wings to a non-operational status by the end of 2013.

A spokesman for the Commander Naval Air Forces in Coronado, California stated – after the measures were announced – that 'shutting down a Carrier Air Wing did not imply that the unit was being disestablished or disbanded'. He explained that during the shutdown period aircraft would be prepared for long-term storage, minimising the amount of maintenance they required and no flight training would take place. Air Wing personnel would perform administrative and other duties and conduct other general military training that did not involve flight. That said, it is clear that a shutdown cannot be sustained indefinitely and regeneration of the air wings to full operational capability will not be a simple task; aircrew will have to re-qualify on type and regain day and night deck landing qualifications; maintenance teams will have to restore the aircraft to full flying status; squadrons will have to be assessed as fit to embark and whole air wings will have to undergo operational readiness inspections (ORI) after working up before they are considered ready to deploy. Air Wings usually undergo requalification and ORI at a measured pace, tied in with carrier deployment cycles but regenerating four from 'shutdown' will be a big ask. The wings that have continued to fly at minimum safe levels will be easier, but still not easy, to recover and they will also have to regain their operational status.

Other measures announced impacting US naval aviation included cancellation of displays by the 'Blue Angels' aerobatic display team for at least the month of April 2013 to give public visibility to the scale of the cutbacks. Less evident – but more significant – was reduction of training not related to the

An EA-18G Growler electronic warfare aircraft pictured in 2009 whilst operating with the VX-9 Air Test and Evaluation Squadron. The FY2014 US Presidential budget envisages the final contracts for this type, a variant of the F/A-18F Super Hornet for which concluding US orders were authorised in FY2013. *(Boeing)*

readiness of deployed or next-to-deploy forces and curtailment of depot-level maintenance.

The Secretary of the Navy made it clear in his signal to the Fleet that these actions had been taken to preserve support for forces that were already forward-deployed and that they had been considered carefully with the hope that they could be reversed or restored quickly if funding was restored. Shutdowns will buy time to consider the next step but, if they continue for months, the disbandment of some air wings may become inevitable as personnel move further away from their previous proficiency; replacement personnel will find themselves in non-operational units and block regeneration of a number of air wings will become increasingly impractical. The carefully worked-out maintenance programme for carriers will also have been disjointed by the deferred work and it is likely that several ships may have to be laid up in long-term reserve. As carrier air wings shut down there will be no outlet for graduates from the training squadrons, some of which will have to shut down. The effect on depot level maintenance has already been dramatic and immediate.

The longer-term funding situation remains unclear as of June 2013. The enactment of Public Law 113-6 on 26 March 2013 brought an end to the stand-off on the FY2013 budget and greater short term clarity to naval finances, allowing projects such as *Abraham Lincoln*'s refuelling to progress. However, the debate over sequestration remains unresolved. As such, the presidential proposals for the US Navy's FY2014 budget announced on 10 April 2013 need to be viewed with even greater circumspection than usual. Planned aircraft procurement is, however, set out in Table 4.1.1.

Although the FY-2014 budget proposal slows down procurement of smaller unmanned aerial vehicles (UAVs), it includes US$21m to continue Northrop Grumman's X-47B UAV development programme, which successfully completed carrier compatibility tests in *Harry S Truman* (CVN-75) during the latter part of 2012. The prototypes also carried out catapult launches and arrested landings ashore at NAS Patuxent River in preparation for sea trials on *George H W Bush* (CVN-77), which took place in May 2013. These are to be followed by an announcement about the development of the unmanned carrier-launched airborne surveillance and strike system (UCLASS) which is intended to put a squadron of unmanned aircraft to sea in an operational carrier by 2020. As of mid-2013,

Table 4.1.1: US NAVY PLANNED AIRCRAFT PROCUREMENT: FY2013–FY2018

TYPE	MISSION	FY2013[1]	FY2014[2]	FY2015	FY2016	FY2017	FY2018	FYDP 2014–18[3]
Fixed Wing (Carrier-Based)								
F-35B Lightning II JSF	Strike Fighter (STOVL)	6	6 (6)	6 (6)	9 (9)	14 (14)	20	55 (41)
F-35C Lightning II JSF	Strike Fighter (CV)	4	4 (4)	6 (6)	9 (9)	14 (14)	20	53 (37)
F/A-18E/F Super Hornet	Strike Fighter	26 +11	0 (13)	0 (0)	0 (0)	0 (0)	0	0 (39)
EA-18G Growler	Electronic Warfare	12	21 (0)	0 (0)	0 (0)	0 (0)	0	21 (12)
E-2D Advanced Hawkeye	Surveillance/Control	5	5 (5)	5 (7)	6 (6)	8 (7)	8	32 (30)
Fixed Wing (Land-Based)								
P-8A Poseidon	Maritime Patrol	13	16 (17)	16 (20)	16 (20)	14 (13)	10	72 (83)
C-40A Clipper	Transport	0 +1	0 (0)	0 (0)	0 (0)	0 (1)	1	1 (1)
KC-130J Hercules	Tanker	0 +3	2 (2)	1 (2)	1 (2)	1 (2)	2	7 (8)
UC-12W Huron	Transport	0	1 (0)	0 (0)	0 (0)	0 (0)	0	1 (0)
Rotary Wing								
AH-1Z/UH-1Y Viper/Venom	Attack/Utility	28 +3	25 (27)	26 (27)	27 (26)	28 (31)	30	136 (139)
CH-53K Super Stallion	Heavy-Lift	0	0	0	2 (2)	4 (2)	7	13 (4)
MV-22B Osprey	Transport	17 +1	18 (18)	19 (19)	19 (19)	18 (18)	4	78 (91)
MH-60R Seahawk	Sea Control	19	19 (19)	29 (31)	29 (38)	0 (0)	0	77 (107)
MH-60S Seahawk	Multi-Mission	18	18 (18)	8 (8)	0 (0)	0 (0)	0	26 (44)
Unmanned Aerial Vehicles								
MQ-8 Fire Scout/Fire-X	Reconnaissance	6	1 (7)	5 (7)	8 (8)	2 (6)	2	18 (34)
MQ-4 BAMS Triton	Maritime Patrol	0	0 (3)	3 (4)	4 (4)	4 (5)	6	17 (16)
STUAS[4]	Tactical reconnaissance	5	0 (5)	0 (5)	0 (0)	0 (0)	0	0 (15)
Training								
T-6A/B Texan II	Training	33	29 (31)	0 (0)	0 (0)	0 (0)	0	29 (64)
Totals:		192 +19	165 (175)	124 (142)	130 (143)	107 (113)	110	636 (765)

Notes

1 FY2013 base numbers relate to that year's Presidential budget request with additional '+' numbers reflecting the actual programme authorised by PL 113-6.

2 Numbers for 2014 to 2018 relate to FY2014 budget plans; numbers in brackets reflect purchases for that year previously envisaged in the FY 2013 budget request.

3 Future Years Defence Programme; numbers in brackets reflect FYDP for 2013–17.

4 Small Tactical Unmanned Aircraft System.

however, a decision on the way forward appears to be finely balanced. Further development could be cancelled or deferred to give an immediate cost saving before any contract had been signed or, alternatively, continued because the technology holds the promise of reducing air wing operating costs dramatically in the years after 2020. A derivative of the X-47B has obvious advantages as a UCLASS air vehicle but its selection is by no means certain if the programme goes ahead. Other contenders include the Boeing X-45C Phantom Ray; the General Atomics Avenger developed from the earlier Predator C design; and Lockheed Martin's Sea Ghost. The Avenger is less complex and stealthy than the X-47 and cheaper but it may not be viable against sophisticated opposition. Current plans envisage proposals from manufacturers being studied in 2013 after issue of a request for particulars (RFP) from the four companies on 10 June, followed by a contract with one during 2014.

UCLASS has the potential to change carrier operations dramatically by allowing far longer sorties with no need for pilot proficiency flying during non-operational periods. Apart from reducing cost, these attributes will reduce the number of airframes that need to be embarked to achieve operational effect. Aircraft systems will be as sharp at the end of a nine-hour sortie as they were at the beginning and human controllers can work in watches to stay 'on the ball'. Whole-life flying hours will be reduced because UCLASS airframes will not be restricted to a particular group of pilots and will not need to return to base at the end of a deployment to maintain currency. Instead they can be flown onto a replacement carrier to remain on station, if necessary for years. Should one become so unserviceable as to require depot level maintenance it can be shipped back to the USA and a replacement flown directly to the carrier, given the range of which UCLASS is to be capable.

Budget issues have taken the spotlight off the F-35C, carrier variant of the Lightning II Joint Strike Fighter but it continues to have its problems.

A replacement tail hook has been designed and was being tested in mid-2013 ahead of projected sea trials in 2014. The reduced number of carrier hulls may impact these and, with new F/A-18E/Fs now being delivered into long-term storage, the US Navy is not desperate to absorb the new type. Arguably the F-35C has missed its 'window of opportunity' with UCLASS likely to be a better stealth option soon after 2020 if it goes ahead. However, the US Navy is caught in an impossible situation over its variant of the Lightning since every cancellation will decrease the total buy and put up the unit cost of the remaining aircraft. If the US Navy were to pull out of the F-35C altogether, a not-unlikely hypothesis given the impact of sequestration, the financial impact on the remainder of the programme would be significant. In any event, F-35Cs are unlikely to reach a unit with real operational capability before 2018 at the earliest.

The US Navy air wing shutdowns, if implemented, may also have an effect on the British Royal Navy which has a number of fighter pilots embedded in USN F/A-18E Super Hornet squadrons to maintain skills until the first British F-35B Lightning II unit is formed. With its own fighter force effectively halved, the US Navy is likely to want all the flying slots it can maintain for its own pilots to maintain their own operational skills. By late 2013, the United Kingdom will have three pre-production F-35Bs operating within the US Marine Corps' VMFAT-501 at Eglin Air Force Base in Florida, itself part of the joint 33rd Fighter Wing. The British aircraft are being used for pilot and technical training together with development work. In a statement to the UK Parliament in March 2013, Andrew Robathan, the Minister for the Armed Forces, shed some light on the next British steps. He confirmed that development Lightnings would not leave the USA but front-line Lightnings would be received from 2015 'with an initial operating capability from land in 2018'. Whether any significance can be drawn from his choice of the word 'operating', implying little more than the ability to fly training sorties, rather than 'operational', implying the ability to mount combat missions, only time will tell but a significant operational capability by that date seems optimistic. Robathan did not say whether the 'land' in question would be in the USA or the UK, or whether the shore-based unit would be a naval squadron preparing for sea trials or a Royal Air Force unit dedicated to other tasks. He did say that

An X-47B UCAS demonstrator flys over the carrier *George H W Bush* (CVN-77) during trials of the new unmanned combat air system in May 2013. The aircraft made a first successful catapult launch on 14 May 2013 and was scheduled to carry out trial arrested landings in the second half of the year. A RFP for an operational UCLASS follow-on was issued on 10 June 2013. *(US Navy)*

Two F-35C carrier variants of the Lightning II Joint Strike Fighter pictured undertaking aerial refuelling trials in January 2013. Initial carrier trials of the type are currently scheduled for 2014. *(US Navy)*

The French Navy's possession of the nuclear-powered *Charles de Gaulle* leaves it with the most effective carrier force outside of the United States. This image was taken when the French carrier was operating with the US Navy's *Dwight D Eisenhower* (CVN-69) in the Mediterranean on 1 July 2012. *(US Navy)*

first of class flying trials on *Queen Elizabeth* would follow in late 2018, however, but gave no indication of a date by which an operational naval squadron of whatever size could be embarked in her.

Robathan confirmed that Lightning II would be operated jointly by the Royal Navy and Royal Air Force but said that RAF Marham had now been selected as the main base for the type rather than RAF Lossiemouth as announced in 2005 and that 'further work will now be carried out to determine the precise investment requirements as the base transitions to support Lightning II'. The statement was not full of detail and leaves vague the number and capability of production aircraft to be ordered, although previous reports suggest an initial buy of forty-eight aircraft is contemplated.[2] The 'precise investment requirements' presumably include procurement of the F-35 autonomous logistic information system (ALIS), without which the F-35 is inoperable. Similarly, the purchase of US weapons seems likely unless funding is allocated for the development of software or interfaces to enable the F-35B to carry British weapons. The need for development of a 'rolling vertical landing' capability to be funded and developed was once considered essential to allow the STOVL variant to land-on with unused weapons in hot conditions but is no longer mentioned. The UK Government appears to be wary about making statements that might be criticised by the National Audit Office but it cannot be criticised for failing to meet a delivery schedule that has not been announced or exceeding a cost that has never been publicly stated.

Other western nations are suffering the effects of economic difficulties and Spain paid off its only carrier, *Principe de Asturias*, on 6 February 2013 leaving the LHD type amphibious assault ship *Juan Carlos I* which is capable of embarking different mixes of AV-8B Harriers and helicopters for the sea control or amphibious roles. The Italian Navy carrier *Giuseppe Garibaldi*, completed in 1985, must be approaching the end of her practical life with little chance of an immediate replacement in prospect, given Italy's financial problems.[3] Her withdrawal would leave the Italian fleet with the multi-role *Cavour* which was completed in 2009. Like the

Financial austerity forced Spain to decommission her sole aircraft carrier *Principe de Asturias* on 6 February 2013 after a previously-planned refit was cancelled. Spain continues to maintain a fixed-wing aviation capability through operation of the new LHD type amphibious assault ship *Juan Carlos I,* which can embark the navy's small fleet of AV-8B Harriers. *(US Navy)*

Spanish LHD she is capable of operating in either the sea control or amphibious roles with a mixed group of AV-8B Harriers and helicopters. Both the Spanish and Italian ships are fitted to act as fleet flagships.

Brazil continues to operate the elderly *São Paulo* with an air group of up to thirty Skyhawks and helicopters, the latter including Sea Kings and Super Pumas. Designated the AF-1M and AF-1AM in Brazilian Naval service, twenty-three of the former A-4KU Skyhawks are undergoing a modernisation programme by Embraer with the first example delivered in 2013. The modified aircraft are fitted with Israel Aerospace Industries' Elta 2032 radars capable of both air-to-air and ground-mapping modes, HOTAS controls and new communications and navigation systems. The resulting aircraft are both affordable and effective. The French Navy has continued to operate *Charles de Gaulle* effectively and is making progress towards an all-Rafale air wing with the third Flotille due to re-equip with the type in 2015. Individual Rafales are being brought up to F3 standard and new production examples are fitted with the active electronically scanned array (AESA) version of the Thales RBE2 radar, which was tested in 2013. The financial crisis in the Eurozone has resulted in plans to build a second strike carrier being deferred indefinitely.

Only India and China have acquired 'new' carriers recently; both are based on elderly Russian hulls that have undergone extensive reconstruction. The Indian *Vikramaditya* was due to be handed over from the Russian Sevmash Dockyard after sea trials in December 2012 but problems with seven of her eight boilers were discovered during sea trials which necessitated repairs. These will delay her entry into service until late 2013 and initial operational capability until 2014. The problems were attributed to the Indian decision to replace asbestos in the machinery's thermal insulation system with firebricks which proved unable to withstand the temperatures generated at high speed. Once delivered the Indian Navy intends to operate an air group of single-seat MiG-29K and two-seat MiG-29KUB fighters together with Ka-31 RLD airborne surveillance and Ka-29 'Helix' sea control helicopters. The Mig-29s carried out sea trials in both *Vikramaditya* and the Russian *Admiral Gorshkov* in 2012. The first operational squadron, the 'Black Panthers' of Indian Naval Air Squadron 303, subsequently commissioned at INS Hansa in Goa on11 May 2013 prior to arrival of the new ship. *Viraat* (formerly *Hermes* in

the Royal Navy) continues in service with an air group of Sea Harriers and Sea King helicopters. The Sea Harriers have been upgraded with the same Israel Aerospace Industries' Elta 2032 multi-mode radar that is being fitted to the Brazilian AF-1M fighters and give the type a viable capability despite the limited number now in service.

China's first aircraft carrier was named *Liaoning* and commissioned in September 2012 after which she carried out successful sea trials which were well covered in the Chinese media. Her arrival dispelled mistaken early reports about her name and rumours that she had not been fitted with arrester wires. The latter were very much in evidence when Shenyang J-15 fighters carried out successful sea trials in November 2012 and she has also operated Z-9C helicopters, a licence-built version of the Eurocopter AS365 Dauphin. Her air wing is still being developed and it is unlikely that the ship will be fully operational before the end of 2014 but she already shows considerable potential. It will eventually comprise up to twenty-six J-15s and twenty-six Z-9Cs. There have been claims by some sources that two further conventionally-powered carriers are being built for completion by 2020, both slightly larger than *Liaoning* but these have not yet been substantiated. Beyond that, some sources believe that an even larger nuclear-powered carrier is being designed. The Russian Navy continues to show interest in new carrier construction but there is, as yet, no report of an order for a strike carrier. However, the potential licensed construction of two *Mistral* class ships would help with the design process whilst providing a multi-role capability.

BIG 'FLAT-TOPS' WITH DUAL CAPABILITIES

Whilst the US Navy's nuclear carriers remain the most capable aviation assets yet put into service with any navy, the budgetary crisis in 2013 showed that even the US Navy may find it too expensive to operate them all, let alone replace them on a one-for-one basis, in the future.

A number of nations have already invested in 'carrier-shaped' ships that are capable of operating in both amphibious and sea control roles, depending on the size or composition of the aircraft and military forces embarked. The ability to 'swing' between roles had already given these ships the potential to become the capital ships of the twenty-first century but the decline in the number of strike carriers may

accelerate the process. The Spanish *Juan Carlos*, mentioned above, is a good example of the new trend. She is capable of deploying an air wing containing a mix of AV-8B Harriers, Chinook, NH-90 transport and Sea King airborne surveillance and control helicopters; she is also potentially capable of operating the F-35B STOVL variant of the Lightning II Joint Strike Fighter as an AV-8 replacement although the Spanish economy is unlikely to permit funding for such a procurement in the short term. Garage decks and the docking area under the flight and hangar decks can take up to 150 vehicles including main battle tanks and the four LCM-8 landing craft are capable of landing them 'over the beach'. She has extensive communications to support her use as a command centre and, in addition to the basic ship's company of c. 245 personnel, there is accommodation for 100 flag staff, c. 170 air group technicians and aircrew and up to 1,000 military personnel. Two very similar ships, *Canberra* and *Adelaide*, are being built for the Royal Australian Navy with the first due to enter service in 2014. As light carriers these ships could operate an air wing of STOVL strike fighters and airborne surveillance and control helicopters giving a powerful air dimension to naval task forces. No physical alterations are needed to enhance the number and type of helicopters embarked; to load bulk stores in the vehicle decks for operation as a disaster relief ship; or to enhance the medical facilities to provide many of the features of a hospital ship.

Different nations have arrived at similar solutions evolved from other directions. Design work on the British 66,000-ton *Queen Elizabeth* class began with the intention of producing strike carriers able to operate up to thirty-six fighters, four airborne surveillance and control aircraft, and helicopters for anti-submarine warfare and SAR tasks. The design process was tortuous, unnecessarily expensive and lacked focus but is about to produce big ships capable of a variety of important uses. By 2013 the design envisaged the regular embarkation of Lightning IIs plus a number of helicopters in the sea control, amphibious or humanitarian relief roles. The class makes an interesting comparison with the new 45,000-ton *America* (LHA-6), a gas-turbine powered evolution of the *Makin Island* (LHD-8), last ship of the *Wasp* class. Enhanced aviation arrangements, including a larger hangar and greater stowage for aviation fuel and weapons, have been provided by removing the earlier ships' well deck and docking arrangements. She has no landing craft but can use her greater number of MV-22 Osprey tilt-rotors to carry out 'over the horizon' assault operations. A re-configurable software C4ISR suite can be used for sea control, amphibious warfare and humanitarian relief operations as well as the command of national and international forces. In the sea control role she can operate over twenty F-35B Lightning Joint Strike Fighters; in other roles she can operate a smaller number of jets with a mix of MV-22 Osprey tilt-rotors and CH-53E Sea Stallion, UH-1Y Huey, AH-1Z Super Cobra, MH-60R and MH-60S Seahawk helicopters. Her ship's company of c. 1,050 is relatively large and expensive but she can carry an embarked marine

force of nearly 1,700 plus almost another 200 under surge conditions. *Queen Elizabeth* is expected to be handed over for Royal Navy trials in 2016; *America* was originally due to be completed in 2013 but this may be slightly delayed and her operational date is uncertain. A second ship, *Tripoli* (LHA-8) was laid down in April 2013 and more are planned.

The three French *Mistral* class LHDs are proving to be capable amphibious ships, one of which demonstrated an ability to operate army attack helicopters in a light strike role off Libya in 2011. The Russian Navy signed a €1.2bn (US$1.6bn) deal for two ships of this class, to be named *Vladivostock* and *Sevastopol*, in June 2011. They are being built in sections in France and Russia: the official keel laying

ceremony took place at the French STX Shipyard at Saint Nazaire in February 2013. Despite some questions over the ships' ability to operate in the low temperatures found inside the Arctic Circle, the project seems to be working well.[4] The Russian Navy made several revisions to the design, specifying a thicker grade of steel for the hull to allow passage through light ice and a strengthened flight deck to accommodate Russian naval helicopter types. Other changes have been made to improve capability in the sea control mission, including a taller hangar to accommodate high Kamov helicopters and support for a larger air group. Two helicopter types are to be embarked initially, a navalised version of the Kamov Ka-52 designated the Ka-52K (with the NATO

Canberra, the first of two type *Juan Carlos I* amphibious assault ships being built by a consortium of Navantia and BAE Systems for the Royal Australian Navy, is due to enter service in 2014. This picture, taken in August 2012, shows the ship onboard a heavy lift vessel off Navantia's Ferrol yard prior to transportation to Australia for final fitting out. *(Navantia)*

Right: The French Navy's *Mistral* class of amphibious assault ships are smaller than those operated by the United States and Spain but are proving to be capable in service. A contract for the construction of two modified variants for Russia was finalised in June 2011 and the official keel laying ceremony for the first took place at Saint-Nazaire in February 2013. This image shows *Mistral* during a deployment to the United States for exercises with the US Navy in early 2012. *(US Navy)*

Below: An image of the new US Navy amphibious assault ship *America* (LHA-6) shortly after launch in June 2012. She makes an interesting comparison with the Royal Navy's new *Queen Elizabeth* class. *(Huntington Ingalls Industries)*

An E-2C Hawkeye early warning aircraft assigned to the 'Tigertails' of VAW-125 operating onboard the US Navy's *Carl Vinson* (CVN-70) in April 2012. The squadron is scheduled to be the first operational unit to convert to the new E-2D Hawkeye, which was cleared for full-rate production in February 2013. *(US Navy)*

reporting name 'Hokum' B) and the Ka-29 ('Helix' B) assault helicopter. The ships are also perfectly capable of embarking Ka-31 RLD airborne surveillance and control helicopters when employed on sea control operations.

Thailand, South Korea and Japan continue to operate small carriers that can operate in the sea control, amphibious, anti-submarine or disaster relief roles with embarked helicopters. The Royal Thai Navy retains the ability to operate a small number of AV-8A Harriers from *Chakri Naruebet*.

BATTLESPACE MANAGEMENT AIRCRAFT

The US Navy announced that the Northrop Grumman E-2D Hawkeye had been declared 'suitable and effective' in February 2013 at the end of a period of operational test and evaluation by VX-1 Squadron, the 'Pioneers', at NAS Patuxent River and the Defence Acquisition Board has authorised a transition to full-rate production by the manufacturer. The US Navy plans, eventually, to order seventy-five examples of the type of which twenty had already been delivered or were in production under low rate initial production (LRIP) contracts in mid-2013.

Under present plans, which may change, the E-2D is to achieve initial operational capability (IOC) in 2015 and several squadron moves are underway or scheduled to prepare for it. In 2013 VAW-116, the 'Sun Kings' moved to CVW-17, later identified as one of the units that might be stood down, to replace VAW-125, the 'Tigertails', which is to become the first operational E-2D unit. Late in 2013 the fleet replacement squadron, VAW-120 at NAS Norfolk, Virginia, is scheduled to complete its own transition to the new type and then train VAW-125 up to operational standard. After the latter unit has passed its operational readiness inspection and achieved IOC, it will deploy forward to the Naval Air Facility Atsugi in Japan during 2015, replacing VAW-115, the 'Liberty Bells' in CVW-5. VAW-115 is then due to return to NAS Norfolk where it will begin its own transition to the E-2D, after which

A British Royal Navy Sea King ASaC7 airborne surveillance and control helicopter operating from the flight deck of the Type 45 destroyer *Diamond* in late 2012 whilst the destroyer was deployed to the Arabian Gulf. The capability they provide will be 'gapped' for around four years after the Sea King is withdrawn from service in 2016 due to delays in funding replacements. *(Crown Copyright 2012)*

units are planned to transition at the rate of a squadron per year.

A report by the UK National Audit Office in early 2013 highlighted concerns for the British Royal Navy following the failure of the UK Ministry of Defence (MOD) to identify a replacement for the Sea King ASaC7 airborne surveillance and control helicopter which is due to be withdrawn from service with all other UK Sea King variants in 2016. The Audit Office warned that the role will have to be gapped with the loss of 'perishable skills' built up by aircrew over decades with the consequent loss of capability for *Queen Elizabeth*. It stated that it may be necessary to retain the ASaC7 in service by a further four years to give time for an adequate replacement to be procured. The ASaC7 airframes are over forty years old and have been worked hard in Afghanistan so, while such an extension may be technically feasible, it would need to be carefully planned and funded. For some years the MOD 'planning assumption' envisaged conversion of the twelve Merlin airframes that were not to be upgraded to HM2 standard being refurbished with the Searchwater 2000 radar and Cerberus mission system removed from ASaC7s. This seems to be an affordable and sensible short-term solution but no action has been taken by the MOD in time to be effective. Current plans, reiterated in April 2013, confirm the new Crowsnest programme will not deliver new airborne early warning helicopters until 2020, coinciding with the entry of *Queen Elizabeth* into operational service. The Lockheed Martin podded 'Vigilance' system appears to be the front-runner for the contract, although Searchwater 2000 may still win through as a low-cost alternative. Meanwhile, the Royal Navy continued to operate one of its two front-line ASaC7 units ashore in Afghanistan during 2013 but the type will be withdrawn from this theatre of operations in 2014.

In the rest of the world, France still intends to upgrade its E-2Cs with improved IFF and ESM systems under a US$180m foreign military sales contract first reported in late 2013. The purchase of a fourth aircraft has been ruled out in the recent Defence White Paper. Meanwhile, Russia, India, Spain and Italy also continue to operate helicopter-based systems.

AMPHIBIOUS WARFARE AIRCRAFT

The helicopter carriers at the core of amphibious capability were described among the dual-purpose ships above. The F-35B continues to make the head-lines and much was made of the formation of the first 'operational' Marine F-35B Lightning II unit at MCAS Yuma at the end of 2012. VMFA-121, the 'Green Pawns', received three F-35s and continued to receive new aircraft through 2013 with the intention to build the unit up to an eventual sixteen aircraft. Despite its designation, however, the unit is far from operational in reality and its aircraft only have an elementary software release that limits their ability to deliver weapons and which allows the pilots to do little more than fly simple familiarisation sorties. Operational software is still some way from accept-ance and VMFA-121 will not begin its initial operational assessment until 2017. Meanwhile, in July 2013 an AV-8B squadron, VMA-513, the 'Flying Marines', stood down leaving only six operational USMC Harrier squadrons in service. Their aircraft are undergoing upgrades, known as the future airborne capability environment (FACE), however, which comprises the installation of a second open-system processor into the mission computer to provide enhanced navigational performance.

Modernisation of the US Marine Corps heli-copter fleet has continued with the steady replace-ment of the CH-46E Sea Knight by MV-22B Ospreys at the rate of two squadrons per year. The last CH-46 unit in Okinawa, HMM-262 the 'Flying Tigers', was to be re-equipped by the end of 2013 leaving only two active CH-46 units at Camp Pendleton. The future replacement of two reserve CH-46 units is in some doubt but by 2014 MV-22s will have replaced the CH-46Es in Marine Squadron 1 that provides support for the President. Marine light attack squadrons continue to be re-equipped with the Bell UH-1Y Venom and the Bell AH-1Z Viper. Fabrication and development of the new CH-53K heavy-lift helicopter has continued and it is scheduled to fly in 2014.

Amphibious assault is another British Royal Navy capability facing a gap after 2016 when Sea Kings are withdrawn from service. In 2013 naval aircrew and maintenance personnel continued to train on RAF Merlin HC3 helicopters in preparation for the type to be handed over to the Commando Helicopter Force as a Sea King replacement, but the 2013 National Audit Office Report noted that the planned upgrade of the Merlin to HC4 standard with power-folding main rotors and other changes needed for embarked operation cannot produce operational aircraft in the required numbers before 2018. There

The first 'operational' US Marine Corps F-35B squadron has been formed at Marine Corps Air Station Yuma in Arizona, albeit it will be some years before it has a true war-fighting capability. This picture depicts the first short take-off and vertical landing (STOVL) operations at the base on 21 March 2013. *(Lockheed Martin)*

A prototype military variant AW159 Lynx Wildcat helicopter on troop trials. Entry into service has been delayed until August 2014. *(AgustaWestland)*

The British Royal Navy helicopter carrier *Illustrious* pictured on exercise in the Mediterranean during 2012 with Apache, Merlin and Sea King helicopters visible on her flight deck. She will be replaced by a newly refitted *Ocean* during 2014 but withdrawal of the Sea Kings will limit the latter's capability for amphibious missions. *(Crown Copyright 2012)*

will, thus, be at least a two-year gap in embarked helicopter assault capability between the withdrawal of the Sea King HC4 and the introduction of its replacement. Some consideration has, apparently, been given to using the main rotor gearboxes of the Merlin HM1s that have not been upgraded to HM2 standard as a 'quick fix' but this would still be expensive and the aircraft would need a life-extension programme to remain viable beyond 2020.

The military version of the new AW159 Lynx Wildcat helicopter has been delayed. It will not enter service with its first unit, 847 Naval Air Squadron in the Commando Helicopter Force until August 2014, eight months later than originally planned. In 2014 *Ocean* is due to complete a major overhaul and upgrade and will return to service, replacing *Illustrious* as the operational LPH. However, her precise role is uncertain given the lack of amphibious helicopters for her to operate.

Delays with the NH-90 and its derivatives have continued in several navies but it is slowly moving towards widespread operational capability. The Royal Australian Navy version, designated the MRH-90, is to be operated by 808 Naval Air Squadron, which is expected to be formally recommissioned in July 2013.

Meanwhile, the development of the Ka-52K attack helicopter in Russia will give its fleets a combination of submarine-, ship- and air-launched missiles, offering a wide range of strike alternatives that are relevant in both low-intensity littoral warfare and the kind of surface action that is a possible consequence of the territorial disputes over sea resources in the Pacific rim that are a developing feature of this decade. The ability to deploy the right mix of force to flashpoints where and when they can create the maximum effect underpins most national maritime strategies and the expansion of amphibious forces appears to be far from over.

The Ka-52K has been equipped to carry out close air support and land attack missions in support of an amphibious force and is unusual for a helicopter in having two pilots seated side-by-side on Zvelda K-37-800 ejection seats; the rotor blades are blown off before the seats fire when ejection is initiated. It has folding stub wings with four hard points capable of carrying a total of up to 3,000kg (6,610lbs) of weapons. For these roles it can carry AT-6 anti-tank guided weapons, 80mm and 122mm rocket pods, AS-12 anti-radiation missiles and AA-11 air-to-air missiles. It also has a fixed forward-firing 30mm cannon in the starboard side of the fuselage. Reportedly the Ka-52K has also been designed to carry AS-17 and AS-20 anti-ship missiles giving it a viable surface attack capability in littoral and 'blue water' operations. The major sensor is a Zhuk-A phased-array radar based on the type used in the Mig-35 fighter. It can detect both air and surface targets and is one of the most sophisticated radars produced in Russia to date with a reported range of 130km against a small warship head-on and the ability to track thirty targets automatically while engaging up to six. The Ka-29 that will join it onboard the new *Mistral* type amphibious assault ships is the Russian Navy's standard assault helicopter, developed from the Ka-27 anti-submarine type that first entered service in the 1980s. It can carry sixteen marines, an internal load of 2,000kg or an external load of 4,000kg. It can be armed with anti-tank missiles, rockets and machine guns.

SEA CONTROL HELICOPTERS

US Navy helicopter force modernisation continued at a steady pace until March 2013 when sequestration complicated the issue. Sikorsky MH-60R and MH-60S Seahawk variants are displacing SH-60B, SH-60F and HH-60H units at the rate of about two squadrons of each new type per year. As the US Navy emerges from sequestration-related stand downs in 2014 there may be a significant reduction in the number of active squadrons but it is too soon to tell. Meanwhile, Northrop Grumman is working towards the first flight of the upgraded MQ-8C version of the Fire Scout rotary-wing UAV in 2014. The programme continues to feature in the FY2014 presidential budget proposals but acquisition plans appear to have been significantly revised. The 'C' retains the avionics of the 'B' but fitted into a larger airframe based on the Bell 407. This would allow a greater payload including more fuel to increase endurance and radius of action and more capable sensors. Earlier problems with the MQ-8B recovery system appear to have been resolved and the type resumed deployments in frigates during 2013. An embarkation in the littoral combat ship *Freedom* (LCS-1) during its deployment to Singapore is planned for the latter part of 2013.

The British Royal Navy has fewer problems with helicopters in this category than with respect to other types. However, the upgrading of Merlin HM1s to HM2 standard has proceeded more slowly than planned and, whilst deliveries are underway,

NH industries is struggling to meet production targets for its NFH-90 sea control helicopter, although the Royal Netherlands Navy embarked the type in its frigate *De Ruyter* for an operational deployment to the Indian ocean in early 2013. *(AgustaWestland)*

the projected in-service date has been delayed from February to June 2014. The new Wildcat is still expected to be in service from January 2015, however, despite the delay in getting the military version into service. During 2013 the South Korean Navy selected the Wildcat naval variant as a Lynx replacement with an order for eight. This showed that the type does have export potential against the SH-60R and NFH-90 and counterbalanced the disappointment of losing a November 2012 contract for nine helicopters for Denmark to the American type. NFH-90 variants have made gradual progress in a number of navies and Germany has ordered eighteen of the type following a broader restructuring of helicopter purchases. By contrast, Norway had yet to receive an operational frigate version in mid-2013 and is considering alternatives. NH Industries has continued to have difficulty in meeting its production targets and the aircraft delivered so far have not all been brought up to a full operational capability. However, in early 2013, the Dutch Navy carried out its first operational deployment with the type in *De Ruyter,* in which it was embarked for anti-piracy duties off Somalia in the Gulf of Aden.

SHORE-BASED NAVAL AVIATION

The Boeing P-8A Poseidon continued to make progress within predicted time and cost limits into 2013. A training squadron, VP-30 the 'Pro's Nest', formed in 2012 at NAS Jacksonville in Florida.

When its instructors qualified on type they began to train aircrew for the first operational unit, VP-16 the 'War Eagles', which had recently returned from deployment with its P-3C Orions. The type's initial operational capability was defined as VP-16 having six aircraft capable of deployment and it was due to take its new P-8As to the Naval Air Facility at Kadena in Okinawa in late 2013. Subsequently, the US Navy plans to transition two squadrons per year from the P-3C to the P-8A until all twelve VP squadrons have moved onto the new type.[5] Each squadron is to comprise six aircraft and twelve crews. Production deliveries were originally planned to continue until 2019 with a total of 117 aircraft but the FY2014 budget suggests a slight re-profiling of the production run to meet new cost realities. By early 2013 the flight test programme was largely complete and initial operational evaluation included a deployment to RAF Leuchars in Scotland for participation in UK Joint Warrior exercises alongside USN and NATO P-3s. The P-8 design was 'frozen' before flight test began and a number of follow-on capability increments are planned to bring the aircraft up to the latest 'post-freeze' standard; the first two involve software improvements to be implemented in 2016. They have not been funded and, as with so much else, the plan may have to change.

In US Navy service the P-8A Poseidon will operate alongside the broad area maritime surveillance system (BAMS) which will use unmanned MQ-4C aircraft, recently given the appropriate name Triton,

P-3C Orion and P-8A Poseidon maritime patrol aircraft at the US Navy's Naval Air Station Jacksonville in Florida in January 2013. A training squadron has been formed at the base to assist the transition from the former to the latter type. *(US Navy)*

The MQ-4C Triton unmanned aerial vehicle is scheduled to operate alongside the P-8A Poseidon in the surveillance role. Two units were delivered for ground testing during 2012 before a first flight that took place on 22 May 2013. *(Northrop Grumman)*

to maintain orbits over large sea areas to transmit real-time data to control bases in the USA and task forces at sea. The first unit, VUP-19, is due to form in October 2013 at NAS Jacksonville in Florida. When it reaches operational maturity it is to provide aircraft for deployment to forward operating bases which will maintain orbits in support of the US Fourth, Fifth and Sixth Fleets; Fleet Forces Atlantic Operations and the Commander Task Force 20. It will also support the United States Northern and Southern Commands when required. A second unit, to be designated VUP-11, is to be formed at NAS Whidbey Island in Washington at a later date to provide Tritons to forward operating bases that will support the Third and Seventh Fleets. The forward bases will launch and recover MQ-4Cs but their control, while they carry out their orbits, will be exercised from the main bases. The first MQ-4C flew on 22 May 2013 and initial operational capability, defined as the ability to sustain the first orbit, is to be achieved by VUP-19 in 2016 after the completion of development, demonstration and training work. Tritons are expected to transform both the ability to provide persistent coverage of significant sea areas and reduce the cost of long-range patrol missions over the sea by the end of the decade.

The Indian Navy was the first international customer for the P-8; it has procured eight P-8Is to date and holds options to buy four more. The first was handed over in December 2012 but remained in the United States temporarily for testing, evaluation and crew training. As such, official induction did not take place until May 2013. The P-8I will replace Tu-124s in the Indian Navy and it differs from the USN 'A' variant in having an additional radar facing aft to provide full hemisphere coverage, a magnetic anomaly detection system plus Indian data links and communications. Australia has signed a memorandum of understanding to procure the P-8A as a replacement for its AP-3Cs but has yet to place firm orders for aircraft. It – as well as India – has also expressed interest in purchasing a batch of Tritons for operation alongside its P-8As but has not yet ruled out the possibility of buying a cheaper alternative as well as or instead of the MQ-4C. Boeing estimates that there is a market for about eighty further P-8s and has had discussions with several countries including the United Kingdom. However, there seems little prospect of the British Government reversing its decision to delete maritime patrol aircraft from its inventory

Many nations continue to operate maritime patrol aircraft and low-cost replacements are attractive during an age of austerity. Airbus Military is heavily promoting its C295 transport aircraft for this role, for which it can be fitted with anti-submarine torpedoes and air-to-surface missiles. These images show successful release trials with the Marte Mk2/S anti-ship missile in March 2013. (*Airbus Military*)

before economic recovery becomes a reality.

Meanwhile, Japan has gone its own way in developing a new maritime patrol aircraft, with the first Kawasaki P-1 being delivered to the Japan Maritime Self-Defence Force (JMSDF) on 26 March 2013. Intended to replace Japan's existing P-3Cs, the new aircraft is powered by four IHI Corporation XF7-10 jet engines, has a Toshiba active scanned radar and can deploy a powerful array of air-to-surface missiles, torpedoes and sonobuoys. Ten aircraft have been authorised to date out of a planned total buy of over fifty aircraft.

Many other nations continue to operate fleets of maritime patrol aircraft and Russia is upgrading its fleet of Il-38 'May' aircraft with new sensors and avionics. Russian aircraft began to patrol the Arctic Ocean on a regular basis in 2013 with both Tu-142 'Bears' and Il-38 'Mays' from the Northern Fleet flying over sea routes 'to monitor pack ice and assist navigation for civilian shipping' according to a Northern Fleet spokesman. He added that the flights were conducted according to international regulations and without over-flying the borders of other nations. Others may see the situation differently: for example, during 2012 Norwegian fighters were 'scrambled' forty-one times in northern latitudes and identified seventy-one Russian aircraft of interest in flight.

Notes

1. *Abraham Lincoln* was originally scheduled to arrive at Huntington Ingalls Industries' Newport News facility on 14 February 2013 to commence her RCOH but her arrival was delayed by the uncertainties related to the failure to agree a FY2013 budget. She finally arrived on 29 March after the enactment of Public Law 113-6 on 26 March 2013 provided the financial framework for the work to commence.

2. The figure of forty-eight is derived from comments made by British Secretary State for Defence, Philip Hammond, in July 2012 and is a significant reduction from original plans for 138 aircraft. Whilst additional orders are likely in the longer term, these may be F-35A conventional variants for use solely by the Royal Air Force. Meanwhile a single United Kingdom F-35C order is envisaged under low rate initial production (LRIP) lot 7, increasing to four aircraft under LRIP lot 8 as part of a planned fourteen-airframe order.

3. With the arrival of *Cavour*, it is envisaged that *Giuseppe Garibaldi* will be operated largely as a helicopter carrier. Her replacement is increasingly linked to recapitalisation of Italy's amphibious fleet, currently centred on the three *San Giorgio* class LPD-type amphibious transport docks.

4. The acquisition of French-designed ships has not been well-received in all parts of the Russian defence establishment and has resulted in somewhat bizarre claims that the class will not be able to operate in northern Russian temperatures or use Russian-grade fuel oil. The claims appear to relate to internal debate within the Russian defence ministry as to whether an option for two additional ships – to be assembled in Russia – should be exercised.

5. The replacement of P-3C aircraft – and the availability of stored airframes from redundant earlier variants – is resulting in sales prospects for refurbished aircraft. For example *Jane's Defence Weekly* has reported a potential sale of non-weapons carrying P-3s to Vietnam: see Gareth Jennings' 'US considering sale of P-3 MPA to Vietnam' *Jane's Defence Weekly* – 17 April 2013 (Coulsdon: IHS Jane's, 2013), p.8.

6. This chapter has been compiled from a wide range of periodicals, of which *Air International, Flight, Jane's Defence Weekly, Warship World* and *The Navy* (the journal of the Navy League of Australia) provide particularly good sources of further reading. Reference should also be made to the following publications, as well as to the websites of relevant aircraft manufacturers and navies:

– Gunter Endres and Michael J Gething, *Janes's Aircraft Recognition Guide- Fifth Edition* (London: Collins-Jane's, 2007).
– Norman Friedman, *The Naval Institute Guide to World Naval Weapon Systems – Fifth Edition* (Annapolis, MD: Naval Institute Press, 2006).
– *Jane's Fighting Ships* – Various Editions (Coulsdon: IHS Jane's).

Author:
Norman Friedman

4.2 **TECHNOLOGICAL REVIEW**

CURRENT AND FUTURE TORPEDOES

In 2014, as in the past, the great divide in torpedoes is between full-size weapons for submarines and lightweight ones for surface ships and for anti-submarine aircraft, rockets and missiles. There are also the special super-cavitating torpedoes introduced decades ago by the Soviets, and purchased in small numbers by a few other countries, such as China and Iran. Another great divide is between weapons intended primarily to hunt and destroy submarines and those used against surface vessels. This chapter looks at these factors and a number of others impacting current and future torpedo design.[1]

TORPEDO SIZE

Torpedo shape is defined by torpedo tubes. In practice, it is seemingly difficult to enlarge the tubes on board submarines, so their tubes define the standard 53cm (21in) calibre of full-size weapons; the Russians were unique during the Cold War in adopting 65cm (25.6in) calibre for some torpedoes, whilst the three US Navy *Seawolf* class submarines have 30in (76cm) tubes. It is easier to change out surface ship tubes. However, the 12.75in (32.4cm) US Mk 44 and Mk 46 torpedoes were so widely made that this has become a standard small-torpedo calibre, although the Swedes have long used 40cm (16in) submarine-launched ASW torpedoes. Stowage space onboard submarines is particularly limited. *If* torpedoes swim themselves out of tubes, then short torpedoes can be loaded end-to-end and, of course, smaller torpedoes can be packed a lot more densely in a torpedo room.

The argument against small torpedoes is that they carry small warheads, but lightweight torpedoes seem to be powerful enough to sink even large submarines, mainly because at depth any hole in a pressure hull is likely to be fatal. During the Cold War, at least three torpedoes (the British Sting Ray, the EuroTorp MU 90 and the US Mk 50) had shaped-charge warheads intended to smash through

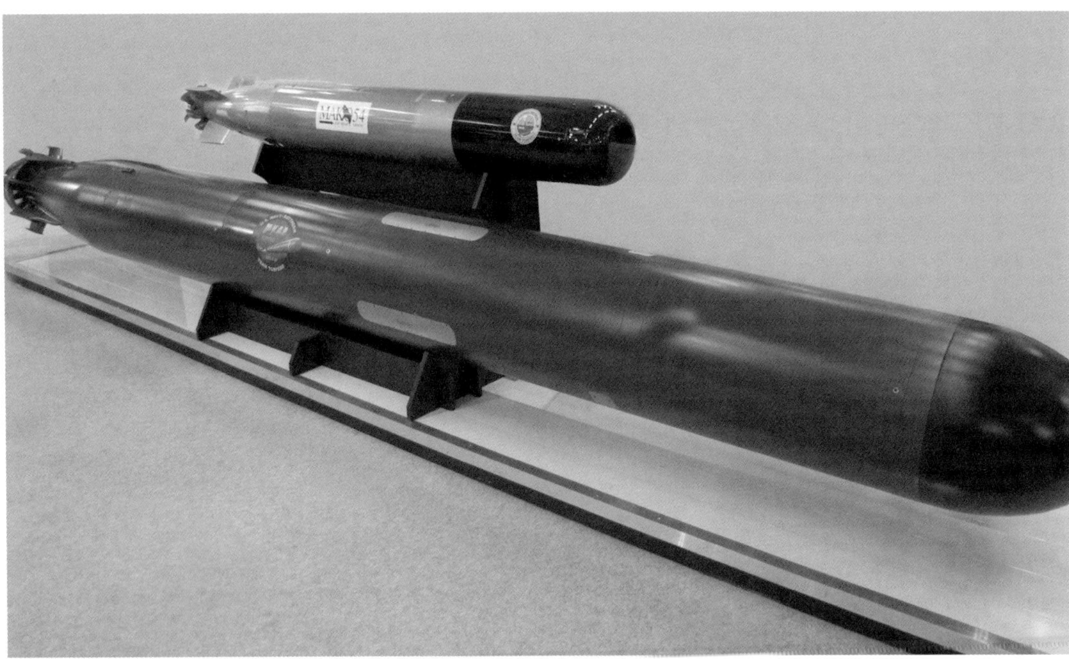

The great divide in respect of torpedoes is between full-size weapons for submarines and lightweights fired from ships, dropped by aircraft or forming missile payloads. This image shows the two torpedo sizes side by side: a US Mk 54 lightweight torpedo is located above the US Navy's standard Mk 48 heavyweight. The Mk 54 combines the propulsion end of a Mk 46, a widely-used lightweight, with the front end of the Cold War Mk 50. *(Norman Friedman)*

the double hulls of large Soviet submarines, and there were probably others as well. As the Soviet threat subsided, it seemed that the future threat would be confined mainly to smaller diesel-electric submarines, against which the 100lb warhead of a lightweight would be quite enough. Even a much smaller warhead might suffice, as in the new US multi-purpose 6.75in (17.1cm) torpedo.

For some time there has been another possibility. About a decade ago there were claims that new more energetic materials offered as much as ten times the effect per pound of explosive. The head of British torpedo development went so far as to say that in future the Royal Navy might neck down to a single standard torpedo for all purposes: a lightweight with the punch of a modern heavyweight. Punch would not be the whole story. If the torpedo was intended mainly for anti-submarine work, a lightweight warhead might already suffice; the question would be whether the requisite speed and endurance could be packaged in a lightweight body. If most surface targets are relatively small (frigates and small destroyers), a lightweight warhead exploding in the right place may be enough. Standardising on a single universal torpedo would offer real advantages. Not only would submarines have many more shots, but surface ships would have the flexibility of a dual-purpose weapon. That might be consistent with a shift from Cold War submarine defence towards something more like classic naval surface operations. Anti-submarine missiles and anti-submarine aircraft would also be given an effective anti-ship weapon.

ACOUSTIC CONSIDERATIONS AND PROPULSION

Because submarines are generally fairly quiet and because torpedoes generally do not listen at the low frequencies at which their sound is easiest to detect, anti-submarine torpedoes generally rely on active terminal homing. Late in the Cold War, when the Soviets fielded new quiet submarines, the US Navy became interested in small arrays which torpedoes could tow to listen at low frequencies, but they never seem to have become operational. These arrays

A view of the Royal Canadian Navy's patrol submarine *Chicoutimi* (the former British Royal Navy's *Upholder*) loaded on a semi-submersible transport vessel in January 2005 after her return to Canada was disrupted by a fatal fire on 5 October 2004 which left her immobilised. Her six 21in (53cm) torpedo tubes, which drive the 'de facto' standard size for submarine torpedoes across the world, are clearly visible. *(Canadian Forces Combat Camera)*

A Mk 46 exercise torpedo being fired from a Mk 32 torpedo tube mount on the US Navy destroyer *Truxtun* (DDG-103). Whilst it is easier to deploy different diameter torpedo tubes on surface warships than on submarines, the prevalence of 12.75in (324mm) calibre Mk 44 and Mk 46 torpedoes has made this a standard for small torpedoes, at least in Western navies. *(US Navy)*

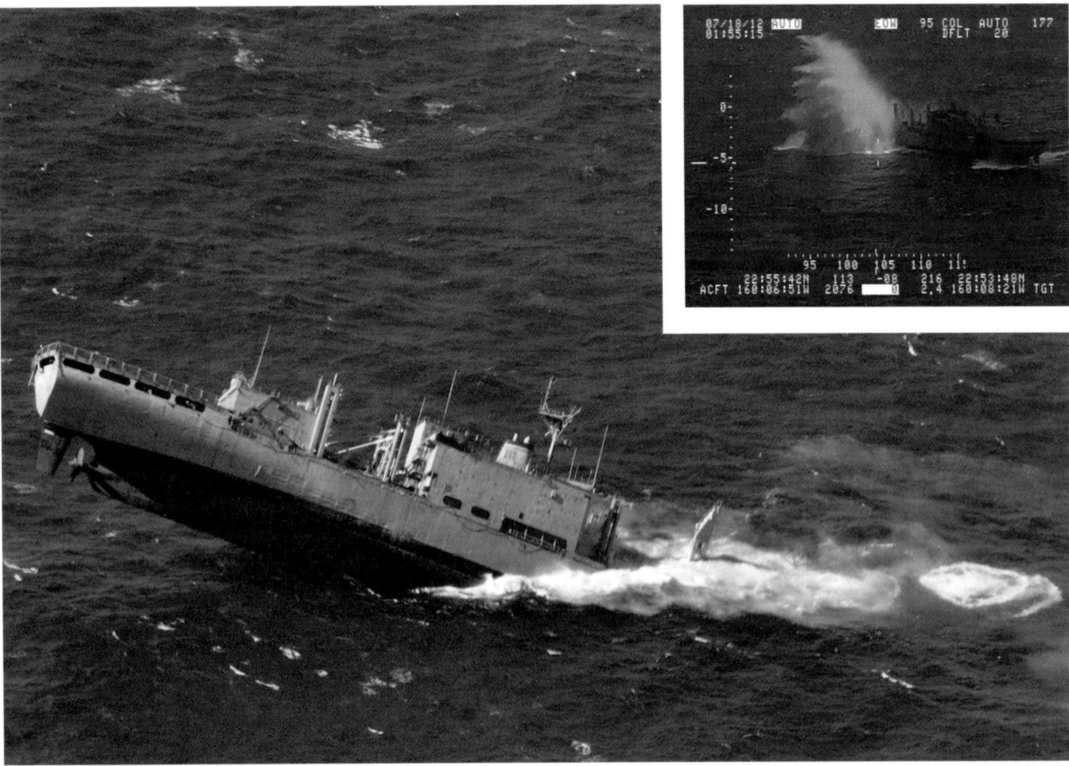

The tremendous power of a modern heavyweight torpedo is apparent in these photos of the former US auxiliary *Comfort* (T-AFS-5) which was sunk off Hawaii by a US Mk 48 weapon fired by the Canadian submarine *Victoria* in a SINKEX during the 2012 Rim of the Pacific (RIMPAC) war games on 17 July 2012. The Mk 48 is powered by an internal combustion engine, originally to provide sufficient speed to catch fast Soviet submarines, but this carries a noise penalty compared with quieter battery-driven types. *(Canadian Forces Combat Camera)*

would have bridged a gap between presetting or mid-course guidance and self-homing. The Russian APR series of air-launched weapons, developed during the Cold War, also employ passive sonar as their initial sensor.[2]

Diesel-electric submarines are inherently quiet when they run on batteries (and advocates of air-independent propulsion claim that they are no noisier); nuclear submarines are inherently noisy but can be silenced. Many modern submarines have coatings which substantially reduce the strength of pings echoing from them, although they cannot eliminate those echoes altogether. These factors have made it more and more important to silence torpedoes, both to avoid warning the target (until the torpedo begins its attack) and to reduce any noise which might interfere with what the torpedo picks up.

The quietest form of torpedo propulsion is electric, using a battery which may become active only after the torpedo takes seawater on board. However, even the most efficient battery has limited capacity. A torpedo of a given size with a given warhead and a given guidance system has only so much volume and weight left over for propulsion. In the past, the choice was between a quiet torpedo with relatively low performance or a higher-performance but noisier torpedo with an internal combustion power plant (as in the US Mk 46 and Mk 48 and the British Spearfish). For internal combustion, the issue was then generally whether the torpedo traded off speed for range at depth. Thus the US swash-plate engine, as in Mk 46 and Mk 48, kept its speed but lost range. The British turbine (Spearfish) lost speed (in theory a Spearfish could run out at maximum speed by adopting an up-and-over trajectory under wire control).

An internal combustion engine is relatively heavy, but its fuel (typically Otto monopropellant) has high

A British Spearfish heavyweight torpedo store, showing the torpedoes packed in storages cases. The size of a modern heavyweight torpedo is readily apparent, driven by its need to carry a heavy payload and be capable of travelling long distances at speed. In common with the USN, current British heavyweight torpedoes rely on an internal combustion engine to achieve the required performance but advances in battery technology – and, possibly, the greater significance of slower diesel-electric submarines as targets – mean that the most recent battery-powered heavyweights may provide a better balance between self-noise and performance. *(BAE Systems)*

energy density. Thus it is arguable that – for a heavyweight torpedo – the best way to achieve power as well as endurance in the available space and weight is internal combustion. However, the smaller the torpedo, the smaller the engine has to be. Therefore, the much smaller weight per horsepower may favour an electric motor in a small torpedo. Electric propulsion also avoids the danger inherent in a monopropellant. In particular, once it begins to burn, it is difficult to extinguish, because it carries its own oxidant. Current European lightweight torpedoes are all electric, as are many of their heavyweights. The more recent incorporate new battery technology which, their manufacturers claim, has greatly reduced the advantages enjoyed by internal combustion engines. High speed is less important if the targets are slower; a rule of thumb is that a torpedo should be 50 per cent faster than its target. It is one thing if the target is a nuclear submarine capable of 30 knots or more, and quite another if it is a 20-knot (or slower) diesel submarine.

Silencing also involves the torpedo's propulsor. Many recent torpedoes, going back to the US Mk 48, have pump-jets rather than conventional propellers. Propellers create an undulating stream of water passing over the fins of the torpedo. When a fin hits an undulation, it vibrates, and that vibration typically passes up the propeller shaft and through the nose of the torpedo. Propellers can be shaped to reduce these undulations, and contraprops also smooth the water flow. A pump-jet smooths it much further. This issue was first important not for torpedoes but for full-size submarines; the problem was discovered during tests of the first fast single-screw nuclear submarines about 1960 (this is why British nuclear submarines have pump-jets).

WAKE HOMING

The surface-ship situation is more complicated. The surface reflects pings, so there is little point in direct active homing (the torpedo may find itself colliding with the surface instead). However, a surface ship leaves a wake which an active pinger can detect from below. For example, a torpedo crossing a wake can detect both edges of the wake. As it emerges from the other side of the wake, it can make a programmed turn back into the wake, but further up (closer to the target). A series of such programmed turns brings it to the target. After the Cold War ended, it became clear that the Soviets had adopted wake-homing in the mid-1960s and that, consequently, anyone buying a 'Kilo' class submarine was also buying wake-homing anti-ship torpedoes. It is also now evident that every major navy has tried some form of wake-homing since the Germans invented it as a variation on patternrunning during the Second World War.[3] The sheer variety of possible wake sensors, both active and passive, is remarkable. Most current Western torpedoes now incorporate wake-homing in some form, either as wake-crossing or as guidance which keeps the torpedo within the wake. The latter is more complicated, but it also requires less endurance on the part of the torpedo before it reaches its target. Wake-following is probably inherent in any modern torpedo with an electronically-steered acoustic array.[4]

Wake homing is attractive because it is extremely difficult to counter. No known single decoy looks like a wake to the torpedo. It seems likely that a string of underwater explosions or bubble-makers could create a false wake, which might seduce a wake-follower. That may be current practice. However, the problem is that wake-following generally requires considerable endurance on the part of the torpedo. The false wake does not end in a false target against which the deluded torpedo explodes. Instead, it just peters out. The torpedo probably has lost-contact routines which cause it to begin searching for a real wake as it emerges from the false one. Presumably the hope is that a false wake can be directed so far from the target ship that a re-attack is unlikely – but in that case it may still bring the torpedo too close to an accompanying ship. Wakefollowing and straight-running (unguided torpedoes) have inspired attempts to build anti-torpedo torpedoes. The most important current example is the US Navy's 6.75in weapon, which is envisaged both as an anti-torpedo and as an ultra-lightweight torpedo.

Perhaps it was significant that at the Euronaval 2012 exhibition the Italian torpedo maker Whitehead displayed the dual-purpose lightweight

A graphic of a BAE Systems Sting Ray Mod 1 lightweight torpedo. Developed during the Cold War, Sting Ray was one of a number of torpedoes fitted with a shaped-charge warhead to smash through the double hulls of large Soviet submarines. In common with other European lightweights, the British Sting Ray is electric-powered. *(BAE Systems)*

BAE Systems Spearfish torpedo tails, showing the pump jet propulsor unit. Pump jet propulsion is used in many modern heavyweight torpedoes as it has a significant silencing benefit, thereby making the torpedo seeker more effective and also reducing the probability that the torpedo will be detected. *(BAE Systems)*

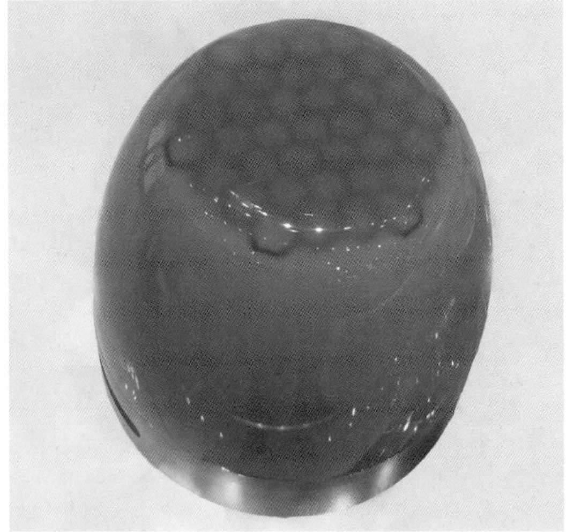

The homing head of the Italian Flash Black lightweight torpedo. In a digital torpedo, such a panel of sensors is the equivalent of the fixed array of a phased array radar: the torpedo computer can create beams pointing ahead or up or down to track a target. In the past, a key distinction between anti-ship and anti-submarine torpedoes was that the former homed passively and the latter actively, as active pings would bounce misleading off the surface. However, an active beam pitched up at a steep enough angle can detect the edge of a ship's wake. In this way active sonar can be used both to home on a submerged submarine and to detect (and hence follow) the wake of a surface ship. *(Norman Friedman)*

The Aegis-equipped cruiser *Vela Gulf* (CG-72) conducts high-speed turns during a torpedo evasion exercise. However, the development of wake-homing torpedoes can make it difficult to counter a torpedo attack. *(US Navy)*

The Royal Navy *Astute* class nuclear-powered submarine *Ambush* undergoing berthing trials alongside the forward support vessel *Diligence* in Gareloch, Scotland in April 2013. Much Cold War era torpedo development was directed towards countering high-speed nuclear boats but the post-Cold War environment has meant that littoral operations against slower but stealthier diesel-electric submarines are more in focus. *(Crown Copyright 2013)*

Flash Black torpedo, the first of its type. It combined the usual active homing of an anti-submarine torpedo with wake homing to attack surface ships.

POST-COLD WAR INFLUENCES

Torpedoes have had to adapt to the post-Cold War environment. That has meant greater emphasis on diesel-electric submarines rather than on nuclear ones, although the nuclear submarine club is expanding and the balance may well shift back. It has also meant greater emphasis on operations in littoral waters. They tend to be much busier than deep water, and a shallow bottom reflects sound in confusing ways.

For example, imagine a torpedo pinging at a fixed frequency in deep water. Unless the torpedo is near the surface, only the target is likely to reflect that ping. To detect the echo at longer ranges, the torpedo emits more energy, generally in the form of a longer ping (if it emitted more frequent pings, it would be operating at shorter unambiguous range).[5]

In shallow water, the torpedo easily receives reflections off the bottom and the surface, and it may even receive multiple bottom reflections from different bits of topography. How can it distinguish a real target? It can begin by shifting frequency on a pulse by pulse basis, to distinguish long- from short-range reflections. It can subject what it receives to multiple types of processing to distinguish submarine-like trains of echoes from what look like static ones (although the submarine may survive by sitting still on the bottom). It can operate in multiple acoustic modes simultaneously, to strip as much information as possible from the train of pulses it receives, and also perhaps from what it can hear on a passive basis. For example, it may monitor the acoustic background, and speed up or slow down to maintain the requisite signal to noise ratio. The torpedo may also manoeuvre (and thus physically manoeuvre its fixed acoustic array) to clarify what it is hearing. For example, EuroTorp, which makes the MU 90 lightweight torpedo, claims that its torpedo uses onboard signal processing applied to its guid-

ance and control system to define the apparent length and shape of the target submarine. The smarter the torpedo, the better. Of course, the advance of micro-processors makes it relatively easy to upgrade existing torpedoes.

MID-COURSE GUIDANCE

A torpedo is probably best seen as an underwater guided missile, facing all the requirements of other missiles. With a few exceptions, the torpedo homes independently once the guiding fire control system places it in a basket close enough to its target. It generally faces countermeasures, typically decoys. Its target may also evade and torpedo speed is not so high (except for the super-cavitators) that it can always overcome evasion. Like other missiles, torpedoes can have both mid-course and terminal guidance modes. Mid-course guidance places the torpedo as close as possible to the target, based on whatever long-range sensing its launch platform can do. For example, the lower-frequency sonar on board a submarine will generally be able to detect

Two views of a Mk 48 ADCAP (Advanced Capability) torpedo being loaded on the nuclear-powered attack submarine *Oklahoma City* (SSN-723) at Guam in November 2012. Conceived in the mid-1950s in the pre-digital age the Mk 48 was the first torpedo in the world to use multi-speed propulsion, with a wire-guided high transport speed carrying it to a point where it would slow and begin homing. Once the torpedo began to 'ping', it had to slow to distinguish echoes from the noise of water flowing around its acoustic array. However, as the torpedo came closer to the target, it would accelerate again because the echoes were stronger. *(US Navy)*

and track another submarine at much greater range than the higher-frequency homing head on a torpedo.

In the mid-1950s the US Navy faced the prospect of fast Soviet nuclear submarines. Its particular problem was that the noise of water flowing over the nose of any really fast torpedo would drown out the echoes the torpedo might use to home on an enemy submarine. The interim solution was the nuclear-tipped Mk 45 (ASTOR). Its warhead gave it a lethal range comparable to the homing range of existing torpedoes. In its case, mid-course guidance brought it within lethal range of its target. That was never entirely satisfactory (among other things the shock of its explosion might well damage or even destroy the launching submarine), so from the outset the US Navy sought some means of solving the flow-noise problem. By the late 1950s it had hit on an answer. The submarine would wire-guide the torpedo into position at high, albeit noisy, speed, what the US Navy called transport speed. Once close enough to the target, the torpedo would slow down to homing speed. At low-enough speed it could pick up strong-enough echoes to complete its mission. As long as homing speed was not too low, and as long as it was brought close enough, it would be effective. Once the torpedo was close enough, listening was no longer so important, so it could accelerate again to make evasion difficult. This idea was and remains the basis of the Mk 48 torpedo. When the lightweight Mk 46 was modified to deal with more sophisticated targets, which might have echo-deadening coverings, it was given a new variable fuel valve and its power plant and propeller were made quieter. The variable fuel valve allowed it to slow down once in position to home (its mid-course guidance amounted to pre-setting on the basis of its ship's sonar data).

A US Navy Orion P-3C maritime patrol aircraft. Whilst lightweight torpedoes deployed from ships and aircraft are not subject to further guidance once the weapon is launched, an aircraft can compensate for this by deploying the torpedo close to the target. *(US Navy)*

A MQ-8B Fire Scout UAV operating from the frigate *Simpson* (FFG-56) in March 2012. The deployment of unmanned aerial vehicles has spurred investment in ultra-lightweight torpedoes such as the CVLWT (common lightweight torpedo), although these may have more potential as an anti-torpedo weapon. *(US Department of Defense)*

Including the mid-course element of torpedo guidance emphasises the way in which the torpedo is integrated into a larger weapon system, whose quirks may determine whether features inherent to the torpedo are worthwhile. Note that a submarine can provide continuous mid-course guidance up to the point where the seeker on the torpedo takes over.[6] For an aircraft or a surface ship, mid-course guidance ends at the moment of launch. To the extent that data are stale by that time, the homing load on the torpedo increases. The longer the torpedo has to run between the last input of information and the homing phase, the worse the chance that it will connect with the target. That is a matter both of range and of the target's speed. That explains torpedo-carrying ASW missiles. Conversely, to the extent the nuclear submarine threat declines, these missiles become less important. In the US Navy, for example, vertical-launch ASROC competed for space in vertical launchers with both anti-aircraft missiles and Tomahawk cruise missiles.

For aircraft, the associated factor is the height of release. The higher the aircraft, the larger the field of sonobuoys it can monitor and, probably, the greater its ability to track a submarine through that field (as long as the sonobuoys are passive, the submarine is unlikely to change course or speed as it passes through the field). On the other hand, the higher the plane, the less precise the torpedo's placement (i.e. the worse the mid-course guidance). In recent years there have been several projects for submarine-borne anti-aircraft missiles, which may also force an aircraft to stay high. A current solution is a torpedo equivalent of the guidance in a JDAMS bomb, using a retractable wing to gain range.

ULTRA-LIGHTWEIGHT TORPEDOES

Conversely, the better the initial target location, the less the torpedo has to do. If it does not need much in the way of endurance, it can be smaller even than a lightweight. The US Navy became interested in a form of shallow-water operation it described at one time as precision ASW, in analogy to precision strike. In precision strike, an external system decided what had to be struck so precisely that a GPS-guided bomb could be dropped on the target. The bomb was precise, but precision was worthwhile because of how well the target could be located. The ASW equivalent of the targeting network was a collection of bottom arrays. Each could detect a submarine as it passed overhead. No single array could track the submarine, but the combined arrays certainly could. If the arrays were emplaced accurately and their product was processed well enough, the submarine could be tracked and its future course predicted precisely. A torpedo could be dropped very close to its expected position; it would not have to do much to get to its target. The concept was associated with the Fire Scout UAV, which can be flown very precisely to drop first the arrays and then a small torpedo. The associated torpedo is half the diameter of a standard lightweight, 6.75in (105in [2.7m] long, 200lbs [441kg]). It looks like a miniature, stretched-out Mk 48. The same device is being developed as an anti-torpedo weapon, and it is understood now to be in limited service for that purpose.

In the past, other NATO navies have been interested in an ultra-lightweight torpedo, but for another purpose. The weapon was intended to deal with diesel-electric submarines which might sit on the bottom. Because torpedoes typically use Doppler to distinguish real submarines from the bottom, they are ill-equipped to handle static targets (nuclear submarines are not potential static targets, because if they bottom they risk taking mud or sand into their condensers, putting their powerplants out of action). The idea was that a submarine detecting something coming near her would find it necessary to run, and thus would open herself to a more conventional attack.

ONBOARD PROCESSING

Like any other missile, the torpedo can simply head for the strongest active or passive signal (pursuit path). A more sophisticated torpedo tracks its target and calculates a collision course. This is equivalent to proportional navigation by a missile. It is much more efficient, and it works even if the torpedo is not too much faster than the target. More importantly, if it is tracking the target on which it is homing, the torpedo can try to decide whether that is a realistic target. For example, DCNS, which makes the new French F21 torpedo, claims that it can simultaneously track many different targets, rejecting those it decides are decoys. Other torpedo builders make similar claims. Such decoy-rejection technology forces a decoy maker towards greater realism, which means greater size and cost. Given the limited space on board a submarine, which is the usual target for a torpedo, decoying becomes more and more difficult.

Moreover, if the torpedo can manoeuvre as it analyses the pings it receives, it may be able to measure the length of the target submarine. It can

then attack as close as possible to the centre of the target, or perhaps to the control room, which is usually directly below the sail. This capability is claimed for some current lightweight torpedoes, such as the EuroTorp MU90.

ROCKET TORPEDOES

One other kind of torpedo deserves mention: the rocket, exemplified by the Russian Shkval. Shkval offers extraordinary speed, 200 knots (with a range of 12,000 yards [10,900m]). Its gas generator forms the super-cavitating bubble in which it runs. It might be likened to a bullet fired from a gun, four times as fast as a conventional torpedo, hence, it would seem, far more difficult to evade. However, a bullet has to be aimed precisely, and a submarine's sonar system is typically credited with fifteen degree accuracy. That would seem to equate to 500 yards at 12,000 yards maximum range. When Shkval was designed, that was no problem: it carried a nuclear warhead set to burst deep. A 500-yard miss would have been as good as a hit. It might be added that super-cavitation probably works a lot better at a considerable depth than near the surface. Perhaps, therefore, Shkval is not the ultimate anti-carrier weapon, after all. The Russians have been offering a

The brains of a modern torpedo: a circuit board from the Italian Flash Black lightweight torpedo. *(Norman Friedman)*

guided version for years but it seems not yet to have materialised. Its absence is probably one of many consequences of the crash in Russian military R&D since the end of the Cold War.

Notes

1. All views expressed in this article are the author's own, and do not necessarily reflect the views of the US Navy or of any other organisation with which he has been associated.

2. The Russians think of APR (Yastreb) as a cross between a bomb and a torpedo. It was introduced in 1981, but was unknown in the West until it was displayed (in poster form) at the 1992 Moscow Air Show. It is the payload of Russian ASW missiles and is also dropped from aircraft. The object was to achieve the quickest response in the target search and detection mode, with a high enough attack speed that the target would not have time to take countermeasures. The torpedo listens as it sinks in a spiral path (in more or less horizontal attitude, for maximum array gain in the horizontal plane). Once it detects a target, the torpedo ignites and starts for it, using an active seeker with a maximum range of 1,500m (1,640 yards). Maximum speed is comparable to that of a US Mk 46 torpedo: 80km/hour (44 knots).

3. A US study of wake-following, conducted in the 1960s, concluded that the method was extremely reliable but that it should not be pursued because there was no obvious countermeasure. By that time, unknown to the US Navy, the

Soviets had already adopted wake-following in preference to their previous passive anti-ship homing technique. Probably the first public discussion of wake-following was in the context of a modified Mk 45 torpedo offered by Westinghouse to Turkey in 1973 (the project died due to the Turkish attack on Cyprus in 1974). There was speculation that the Soviets had learned about wake-following by careful reading of the US patent literature. The reality was that nearly every major post-war navy had already experimented with some form of wake-following, often in conjunction. For example, in 1946 the US Navy and the Royal Australian Navy pursued a co-operative programme in which the wake was detected using photocells in the torpedo (the wake is whiter water). The victorious Allies all gained access to the earlier German work.

4. The Soviet wake-followers had separate active pingers on top of their bodies, typically one per torpedo. That made it possible for them to identify the onset and end of the wake as they crossed, but not to wiggle up the wake itself. If the target was fast enough, and if the torpedo entered the wake far enough back, the target could probably escape. For these torpedoes, the great advantage of wake-following was that the sensor was far enough from the nose of the torpedo not to be unduly affected by flow

noise. However, modern Western torpedoes credited with wake-following capability do not seem to have separate upward-looking arrays, because they do not need them. The flat or wrap-around acoustic arrays in their noses are steered electronically in two directions (right-left and up-down). Tilted up at a steep angle, they can detect the edges of the wake, and they may often be able to detect both at the same time. In that case they can remain within the wake, following it up to the target as it narrows. Given the ability to steer the array, all that is needed in addition is some software (the earlier Soviet wake-followers were hard-wired, as are probably the current Russian ones).

5. As with radar, unambiguous range is set by the interval between pings. Unless it has some way of distinguishing one ping from another, the receiver cannot distinguish between a ping received after the next has gone out, and a ping received back at short range. In radars this is the 'Second Time Around Effect' (STAE).

6. The wire can carry messages back from the torpedo to the firing ship. German ASW torpedoes carry back data from their own sonars to the controlling submarine combat system, acting as probes which complement the low-frequency sonars of the submarine.

Authors:
Ian Johnston
Paul Sweeney

4.3 TECHNOLOGICAL REVIEW
FROM DARING TO DUNCAN

Building the Type 45 Destroyers

With the completion and departure of the last British Royal Navy Type 45 destroyer, *Duncan*, from BAE Systems' Scotstoun shipyard, there is no significant shipbuilding work there until decisions regarding construction of the Type 26 Global Combat Ship are finalised. This is, therefore, an appropriate point to review the Type 45 programme from a construction perspective, with a particular focus on the significance of Scotstoun shipyard, known for the greater part of its long life as Yarrows.

THE ORIGINS AND HISTORY OF SHIPBUILDING AT SCOTSTOUN

The Yarrow business was established by Alfred Fernandez Yarrow on the Thames at the Isle of Dogs in 1865. Humble beginnings as engineers soon gave way to the building of steam launches and, in the 1870s, spar torpedo boats. Whitehead's self-propelled torpedo of 1877 resulted in the development of the torpedo boat and – later – destroyers, the design and development of which Yarrow was intimately involved with. Together with his superior design of marine boiler, this allowed the business to thrive as a designer and builder of high-speed naval craft. At this time, the Thames was declining as a major shipbuilding and marine engineering centre, primarily because of the rise of the great northern shipbuilding industries on Clydeside, Tyneside and elsewhere. There, lower costs and access to large pools of skilled labour and nearby steel mills, coupled with an ever-increasing accumulation of supply industries, made relocation inevitable. In 1906, a greenfield site at Scotstoun on the Clyde was acquired. Over the course of the next two years the business was transferred to the new Clyde yard and the first destroyer launched from there in July 1908.

Yarrow was immediately in good company, with over fifteen other shipyards in the upper Clyde alone. Timing was good too, with the Anglo-German naval race about to move into high gear. This ensured a plentiful supply of orders for the Admiralty. During the course of the First World War, twenty-nine destroyers and various other vessels were built at Scotstoun.

The collapse of the market for warships after the war, together with the depressed 1920s, closed the yard briefly at the end of 1922. Although reformed a few months later, land boiler manufacture was initially pivotal. It was not until 1924 that the first post-war destroyer was ordered, the 37-knot *Ambuscade*. From 1931 onwards the order book began to grow, especially after rearmament began in 1936. From then until the end of the Second World War, Yarrow produced a large number of destroyers and frigates, despite being bombed during the Clydeside blitz of March 1941. After the war the company opened YARD, Yarrow Admiralty Research Department, with a remit to look at the propulsion systems envisaged for new frigates where the weight, size and fuel efficiency of steam machinery were crucial. YARD also played a significant part in developing gas turbine installations as well as diversifying into a broad range of marine related areas.

By the 1960s the British shipbuilding industry was in straightened times in the face of foreign competition and the general reduction in naval strength. Government attempts at reorganising the industry saw Yarrow Shipbuilders Ltd become part of Upper Clyde Shipbuilders in 1968, although the company was demerged in 1970 before the group collapsed in spectacular fashion. At the same time, the failure of adjoining shipyards enabled a major expansion of facilities through the acquisition of the Blythswood shipyard on the eastern boundary in 1965 and of Barclay Curle's Elderslie Dockyard to the west in 1974. This brought three dry docks under company control and allowed the construction of a covered building hall within the by now 62-acre yard. In 1977 the yard was nationalised, only to be de-nationalised eight years later when it was sold to GEC Marconi to become Marconi Marine (YSL). In 1999 BAE Systems was created out of the merger of GEC Marconi and British Aerospace, with the shipyard becoming part of BAE Systems Marine. Throughout this period the Scotstoun yard was heavily involved in all classes of frigate construction from the Type 12 and 14s of the 1950s up to the Type 23s of the 1990s, as well as the six Type 45 destroyers.

The launch of the sixth and final Type 45 destroyer, *Duncan*, took place at Govan on 11 October 2010. Her subsequent delivery in March 2013 marked the end of a highly successful programme for the British shipbuilding industry in general and BAE Systems' Clyde yards in particular. *(BAE Systems)*

THE TYPE 45 DESTROYER PROGRAMME AND BLOCK-BUILD

Intended to renew the British Royal Navy's air defence capabilities, the Type 45 destroyer programme emerged from the collapse of the Common New Generation Frigate project with France and Italy in April 1999 and an associated decision to develop a new national design.[1] This decision was to have significant implications for British naval shipbuilding in general and the Clyde yards in particular, not least through the adoption of a block-build strategy for the new ships.

Block-build is a widely-adopted contemporary shipbuilding method where each block is, in turn, assembled from a number of prefabricated units. Each block is designed and constructed in a manner that enables a high level of fitting-out to take place without reference to adjoining blocks. This permits the simultaneous construction of several blocks,

speeding overall build time. In the case of Type 45 it also created scope for geographically-dispersed construction which, although not an essential part of a block-build strategy, served political considerations in terms of maintaining key skills and levels of employment in the few shipbuilding sites remaining across the UK. In this respect, the UK Ministry of Defence's (MOD's) use of this method echoed earlier Admiralty strategies aimed at maintaining warship building capacity in shipbuilding centres during periods of cyclical downturn in commercial ship demand.

Because of its origins as part of the Franco-Italian Common New-Generation Frigate programme, the design of the Type 45 destroyer was not optimised from the outset for a multi-site, modular block-build strategy. Despite several inherent design challenges – such as the ship's operations room straddling the boundary of Blocks C and D – block-build

would rapidly evolve to form the defining characteristic of the Type 45 construction programme; with the ship ultimately sub-divided into six discrete hull blocks (see Figure 4.3.1).

The origins of the block-build strategy for the Type 45 destroyer programme can be traced back to the integration of the last two shipyards on the upper Clyde – Govan and Scotstoun – into a single operational unit, BAE Systems Marine, on 4 May 2000.[2] This enterprise also included the BAE-owned shipyard at Barrow in Cumbria. From the outset, a key priority for this combined entity was to bring together the operations of the two Clyde yards – with their different facilities, expertise and operational cultures – to form an integrated operation that best utilised their respective complimentary capabilities and yard capacities. Together with Barrow, they accounted for approximately eighty per cent of the UK's warship design, build and integra-

Figure 4.3.1 Type 45 Blocks
Breakdown of blocks showing units per block, block tonnage and build location. Note that, for *Daring*, some Govan fabrications and sub-assemblies were integrated into blocks and mega-blocks at Scotstoun. Tonnages refer to steelwork only and not the all-up weight of blocks as fitted-out.

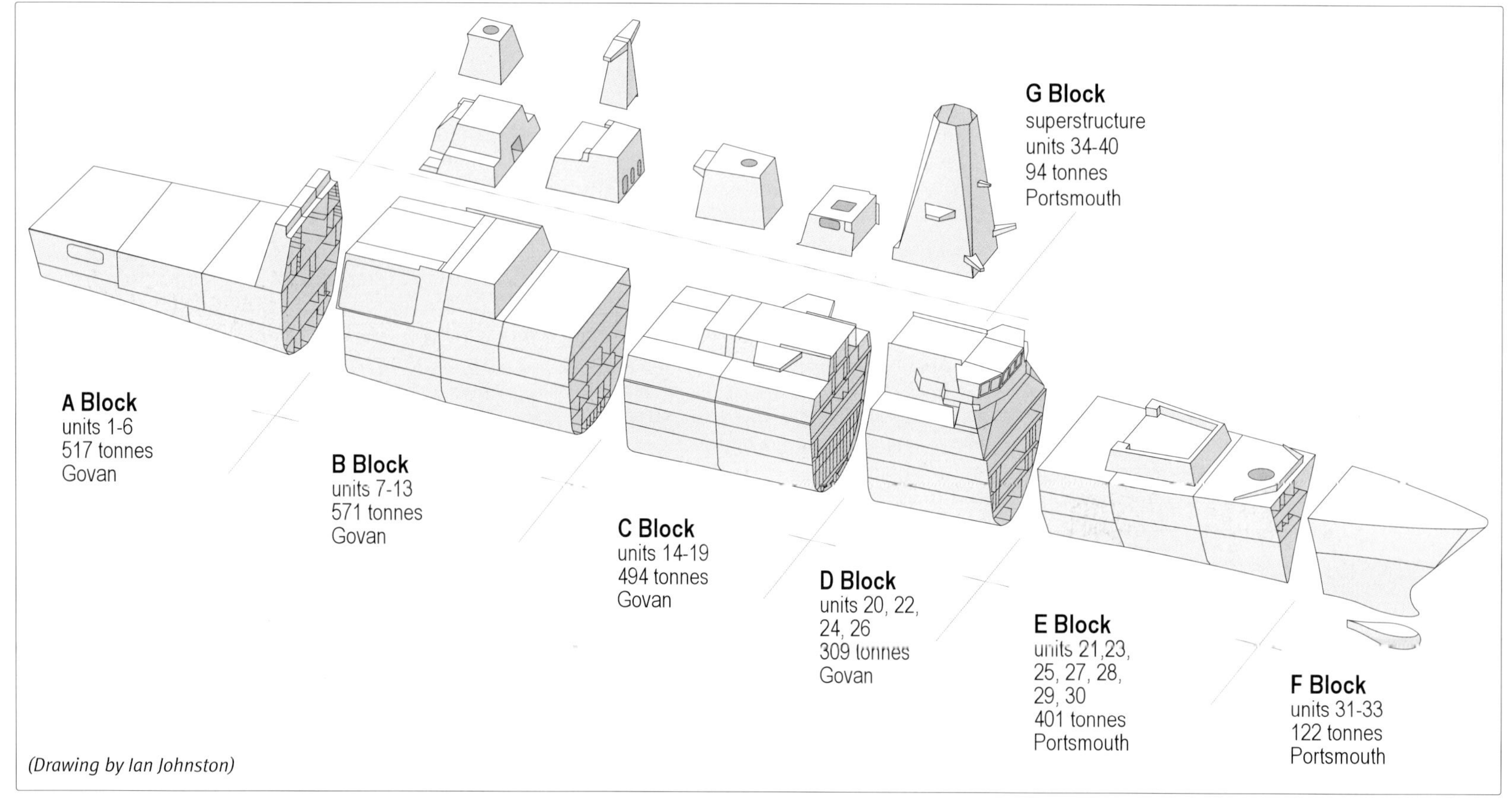

(Drawing by Ian Johnston)

tion skills base. The balance at that time was made up by Swan Hunter on Tyneside and Vosper Thornycroft (VT) at Southampton.

BAE Systems Marine was placed in the vanguard of the Type 45 build programme with the award of a £1.2bn 'Demonstration for Manufacture' (DFM) contract for the first batch of three ships to BAE Systems' Type 45 Prime Contract Office in December 2000. The initial concept of the build strategy envisaged that the first of class, *Daring*, would be assembled in the covered berth facility at Scotstoun. *Daring* would be the largest vessel ever launched from the Scotstoun shipyard and this resulted in a number of key differences in her build strategy from subsequent vessels. The critical factor in this was the enclosed covered berths, originally completed in 1970 and the largest in the world when opened. The 150m long building was originally designed for the construction of the considerably smaller *Leander* class frigates. Despite inherent advantages in building under cover due to the elim-

ination of risk from adverse weather conditions, it would also present certain constraints on the build of the first Type 45, particularly in terms of headroom, with a clearance of only 22.5m at the berth door portal. This prevented the installation of the masts and other superstructure elements, therefore limiting fitting-out during the pre-launch stage of construction.

Despite these constraints, Scotstoun was favoured on account of the significant experience it had accumulated since the establishment of YARD in 1949; a key consideration given that the first of class is generally where most of the design and production problems are encountered and contained. This expertise included its recent role with respect to the preceding Type 23 frigates, for which it had acted as lead yard for design and manufacture and had built twelve out of the sixteen vessels in the class. This established centre of excellence in complex warship design was capitalised upon with the opening of the Type 45 'Platform Design Centre' in the refurbished

Technical Office Block at Scotstoun in May 2001, incorporating engineering staff from both BAE Systems and VT. This facilitated the creation of a close working relationship between the design and manufacturing teams working on the project, which was ultimately intended to ensure that the ship's design was fully optimised for manufacture. At this time, it was envisaged BAE Systems and VT would each be responsible for the assembly of one follow-on ship in a first batch of three vessels. There was also significant interest from the MOD in utilising the inherent flexibility afforded by the block-build method to facilitate both a general industry-wide competitive tendering process for steel unit fabrication and modular sub-assembly work on the Type 45 and also between BAE Systems Marine and VT for the subsequent assembly, fitting-out and commissioning work.

Type 45 was not the first class of UK surface combatant to utilise the block-build method, with many of the latter Yarrow-built Type 23s adopting a

Block C of the final Type 45 destroyer *Duncan* seen in the Ship Block and Outfit Hall at BAE Systems' Govan facility in January 2010. The wholesale adoption of block build for the Type 45 programme was an important step forward for British naval construction. *(BAE Systems)*

An image of the constituent Block C of *Duncan* in the block transition area of No. 1 berth at Govan in January 2010. Block D can be seen immediately behind. The Type 45 destroyer's origins in the tripartite Common New Generation Frigate programme meant the design was not optimised for block production and caused several challenges: for example the ship's operation room straddles the boundary of Blocks C and D. *(BAE Systems)*

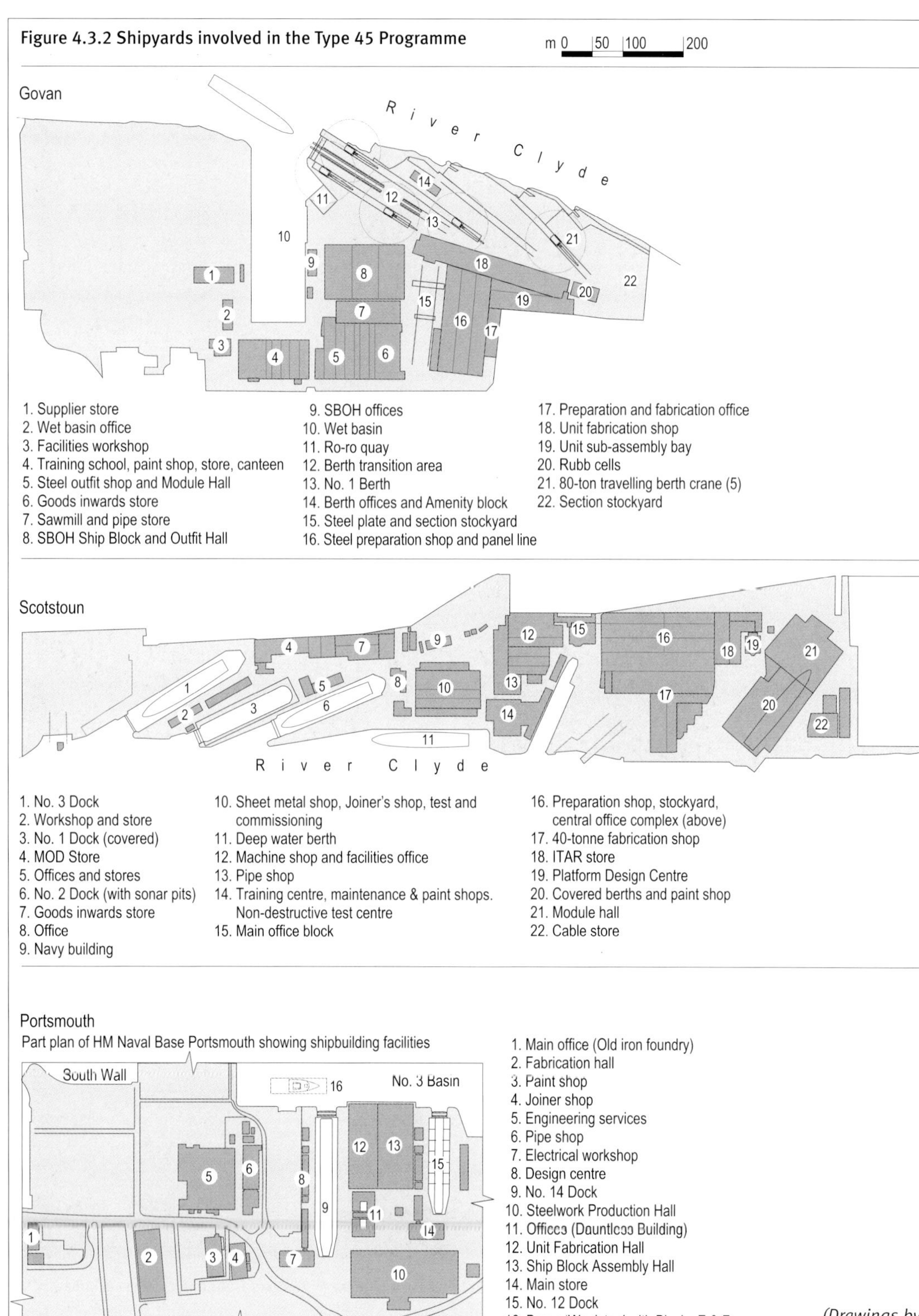

Figure 4.3.2 Shipyards involved in the Type 45 Programme

m 0 | 50 | 100 | 200

Govan

1. Supplier store
2. Wet basin office
3. Facilities workshop
4. Training school, paint shop, store, canteen
5. Steel outfit shop and Module Hall
6. Goods inwards store
7. Sawmill and pipe store
8. SBOH Ship Block and Outfit Hall
9. SBOH offices
10. Wet basin
11. Ro-ro quay
12. Berth transition area
13. No. 1 Berth
14. Berth offices and Amenity block
15. Steel plate and section stockyard
16. Steel preparation shop and panel line
17. Preparation and fabrication office
18. Unit fabrication shop
19. Unit sub-assembly bay
20. Rubb cells
21. 80-ton travelling berth crane (5)
22. Section stockyard

Scotstoun

1. No. 3 Dock
2. Workshop and store
3. No. 1 Dock (covered)
4. MOD Store
5. Offices and stores
6. No. 2 Dock (with sonar pits)
7. Goods inwards store
8. Office
9. Navy building
10. Sheet metal shop, Joiner's shop, test and commissioning
11. Deep water berth
12. Machine shop and facilities office
13. Pipe shop
14. Training centre, maintenance & paint shops. Non-destructive test centre
15. Main office block
16. Preparation shop, stockyard, central office complex (above)
17. 40-tonne fabrication shop
18. ITAR store
19. Platform Design Centre
20. Covered berths and paint shop
21. Module hall
22. Cable store

Portsmouth
Part plan of HM Naval Base Portsmouth showing shipbuilding facilities

1. Main office (Old iron foundry)
2. Fabrication hall
3. Paint shop
4. Joiner shop
5. Engineering services
6. Pipe shop
7. Electrical workshop
8. Design centre
9. No. 14 Dock
10. Steelwork Production Hall
11. Offices (Dauntless Building)
12. Unit Fabrication Hall
13. Ship Block Assembly Hall
14. Main store
15. No. 12 Dock
16. Barge 'Woolston' with Blocks E & F

(Drawings by Ian Johnston)

nascent form of this approach, particularly after the completion of a 8,400m^2, three-bay Module Hall facility, immediately to the north of the covered berths, in 1987 (see Figure 4.3.2). However, this was not as integral to the design of the Type 23s as it would become on Type 45. For this new class of destroyer, a particular driver of the block-build philosophy was the MOD's commitment to a geographically-dispersed block-build strategy, requiring the transportation of blocks by barge around the west and south coasts of Britain to the designated assembly yard. This required the construction of a 1,350-ton, 90m long barge, *Woolston*, at VT's new £50 (c. US$75m) million shipbuilding hall at Portsmouth Naval Base. On completion in May 2004, it was the first vessel to be built in Portsmouth for thirty-seven years, being used to test the operational capability of the new 'ship factory' facility, prior to the commencement of work on the Type 45 programme proper.

DEVELOPING BUILD PROPOSALS

The cost-effectiveness of such a risk-sharing partnership approach to the block-build of the Type 45 class had initially been the subject of dispute between VT and BAE Systems Marine. This had culminated in the latter submitting an unsolicited proposal to build the entire projected class of twelve vessels itself during December 2000, based on the arguable greater cost-effectiveness of such an approach.[3]

Eventually a compromise build strategy solution was agreed in July 2001. The number of vessels initially contracted for was extended from three to six; with four sites intended to participate in the build programme, Barrow, Portsmouth and Glasgow; the latter comprising the Scotstoun and Govan shipyards. Blocks A to F (see Figure 4.3.1) were to be distributed as follows:

A and D – Glasgow.
B and C – Barrow.
E and F – Portsmouth (where main mast and other superstructure units would also be built).

It was intended that the first of class, *Daring*, would continue to be assembled and fitted-out at Scotstoun under this arrangement, while the remaining five contracted ships would be assembled, fitted-out and commissioned at BAE Systems' largest single shipyard site, Barrow-in-Furness. VT at Portsmouth would no longer function as an assembly and integration yard for any ships in the class but would, instead, be subcontracted to supply two pre-outfitted hull blocks and other modular superstructure elements for each ship, in particular the distinctive forward mast, which carries the Sampson multifunction radar. VT's overall contribution to the build of the Type 45 class would amount to approximately fifteen per cent of each ship. The DFM contract was revised to reflect this new arrangement in February 2002.

The planned switch to Barrow for assembly in the Devonshire Dock Hall (DDH) of the remainder of the class was largely determined by the greater flexibility afforded by the 25,000m² DDH facility and associated cost savings, where the overheads were correspondingly lower. However, by the end of 2002, as the Type 45 design process was approaching completion, it was apparent that this strategy would not work in terms of risk. This was principally because design and project management problems of the *Astute* class nuclear submarines at Barrow had become acute; resulting in serious cost overruns and programme delays of three years.[4] This prompted a decision to remove Barrow from the compromise Type 45 build strategy in favour of the Clyde. This was almost immediately followed up by the split of BAE Systems Marine into separate Naval Ships and Submarines business units; the latter based at Barrow and the former on the Clyde. This approach was intended to allow the Barrow shipyard to concentrate exclusively on recovering the issues concerned with *Astute* and the completion of the two *Albion* class LPDs, leaving all Type 45 shipbuilding operations focused on the two BAE Systems Clyde yards and VT at Portsmouth.

FINAL BUILD STRATEGY

This final revision of the Type 45 build strategy was announced by BAE Systems on 21 January 2003, a mere two months prior to cutting the first steel plate on 28 March at Govan for the pilot unit of Yard No. 1060, comprising the forward machinery room (FMR) of *Daring*. This unit was used to test the new manufacturing methods devised for Type 45. In order to achieve the high level of design definition required by the Type 45 programme, CADDS5 computer aided design software was used to develop a highly mature 3D model of the internal arrangements of the ship. The intention behind this process was to achieve a target of 100 per cent completion of 'hotwork' (structural welds and penetrations) at the

An aerial view of *Daring* being fitted-out in Scotstoun's No. 2 Dock in the summer of 2006. Scotstoun's extensive expertise in surface warship design and manufacture meant that it was always earmarked for construction and delivery of the first Type 45 destroyer, although subsequent changes in build strategy driven by problems with *Astute* class submarine construction at Barrow also meant it was involved in fitting-out all class members. *(BAE Systems)*

unit fabrication stage of build, with a target of eighty per cent of fitting-out work to be achieved on each block before it was moved to the berth for assembly. This was a stark contrast with an average of thirty-five per cent on the previous Yarrow-built Type 23s. The model was also used to optimise the build sequence in conjunction with the specialised ship production planning software, MLCC (Marine Life Cycle Catalogue) in order to mitigate the risk of rework. This was particularly important given that some ninety-seven per cent of the approximately 425,000 component parts on the engineering bill of materials (EBOM) for each ship were new to the Royal Navy, with around seventy per cent of the value of the ship derived from the supply chain. Full-scale Main Build operations on Type 45 began on 11 August 2003 and ramped up through September of that year.

GOVAN SHIPYARD

By far the greatest amount of steelwork for the entire programme was completed at the Govan yard, which has the most extensive steel preparation and fabrication facilities of any shipyard in the UK. The Govan yard, with a long and eminent history in commercial and naval shipbuilding, had been extensively modernised in the 1990s during its ownership by the Norwegian Kværner Group (1988 to 1999), who used the yard primarily for the construction of commercial LPG carriers. Where previously prefabricated units weighing up to 120 tons were transported from the unit fabrication shop by transporter directly to the berth, the Norwegians introduced the block-build concept to Govan. This was centred on a new 10,000m², three-bay Tank Assembly Shop (TAS) where a liquid gas tank or complete hull ring segment could be built up in each bay from units delivered from the fabrication shop by Self-Propelled Modular Transporters (SPMTs), which each have a maximum capacity of 400 tons. By this method, blocks of up to 1,600 tons could be assembled and then transported to the berth. The TAS was subsequently re-named the Ship Block & Outfit Hall (SBOH) by BAE Systems to reflect its new role in the block-build of the Type 45 programme.

Block D of the Type 45 destroyer *Duncan* being moved out of the Ship Block and Outfit Hall at Govan by Self Propelled Modular Transporters. The Type 45 programme benefitted considerably from investment made by the Norwegian Kværner Group in Govan during the 1990s, when it used the yard for LPG carrier construction. *(BAE Systems)*

The bow section of a Type 45 destroyer arriving at the Ro-Ro quay at Govan. The creation of the new 1,152m² quay to facilitate the transfer of blocks was a key part of a capital investment programme amounting to £57m in total aimed at improving the infrastructure supporting Type 45 construction. *(BAE Systems)*

CAPITAL INVESTMENT

The new six ship contract and projected decade-long build programme for Type 45 was an unprecedented order for an industry that had become notorious for unstable 'feast and famine' cycles in demand. It afforded sufficient confidence for BAE Systems to embark upon an extensive programme of capital investment at its Govan and Scotstoun shipyards. This investment strategy reflected Govan's strength in steelwork; with the shipyard being formally designated as the company's 'Steelwork Centre of Excellence'. Similarly, Scotstoun's long-established expertise in the fitting-out, testing and commissioning of complex systems for Royal Navy warships – that account for over seventy per cent of the finished value of the ship –

saw it designated as the 'Design Engineering, Fitting-out and Manufacturing Centre of Excellence'. The total capital invested in renewing the physical infrastructure of the shipyards over the course of the Type 45 programme totalled some £57m (c. US$85m).

At Scotstoun (see Figure 4.3.2), initial investments were made to improve access to the Module Hall and to create an adjacent Ro-Ro quay to enable the block-build of the first of class. Further investments were made in reconfiguring and re-tooling the on-site manufacturing areas that supplied the ships throughout their build lifecycle; the Pipe Shop, Machine Shop, Sheet Metal Shop and Joiner Shop. The identification of Scotstoun as the hub for post-launch fitting-out was in part due to its extensive

complex of three graving docks to the west of the site. Although the covered No. 1 Dry Dock was precluded from involvement in the Type 45 programme due to its restricted headroom of 25m, Nos. 2 and 3 Dry Docks underwent a comprehensive reconditioning of the dock gates and dockside services to support the fitting-out, testing, system integration and compartment completion process for all six ships in the class. Key improvements at Govan (see Figure 4.3.2) included a 12m extension to the north of the SBOH facility to accommodate larger blocks for the Type 45 programme, the creation of a 1,152m² Ro-Ro quay to permit the transfer of blocks, and the installation of a dock gate on No. 1 berth. The last step eliminated tidal restrictions on working at the stern of ships on the berth,

Blocks from *Dragon* being positioned on the building berth at Govan in March 2008. Blocks D, E and F have already been joined together whilst Block C is being transported into the block transition area, comprising a reinforced hard standing and a 39m removable section of the ways. A dock gate was fitted to this berth as part of the capital investment programme supporting Type 45 construction, eliminating tidal restrictions on working at the stern of ships being assembled. *(BAE Systems)*

particularly during the critical operation of boring the A-brackets and installing the drive shafts and bearings. Other work at Govan involved a significant refurbishment of the steel preparation and fabrication shops; including the procurement of new plasma plate burning machines, a robotic bar cutter, plate seam welding equipment and a new integrated panel production line.

BLOCK-BUILD AT SCOTSTOUN

The first blocks to be assembled and fitted-out for *Daring* were A and D. These were fabricated and fitted-out in Govan, before being barged 3km downriver to the covered berth at Scotstoun. The first 700-ton stern Block A was positioned on No. 6 berth at Scotstoun in December 2004. Block D arrived from Govan as a 'half-block' comprising just the hull units and was positioned in Bay 2 of the Module Hall in order to have additional superstructure units – also supplied from Govan's unit fabrication shop – lifted into place and integrated.

A notable feature in the build strategy for *Daring* was the construction of the 'mega-block' B/C, weighing over 2,500 tons. This block was built-up in Bay 3 of the Module Hall from a series of Govan supplied steel units in an 'open canoe' manner, in order to incorporate major 'lock-out items' which primarily comprised both the forward and aft Wärtsilä 12V200 diesel generators, the Rolls-Royce WR-21 gas turbines and the 20MW Converteam propulsion motors associated with the Type 45's innovative Integrated Electric Propulsion system.[5] This system – the first of its kind to be fitted to a warship – drives the ship's twin shafts as well as supplying power to on-board services. The combined B/C 'mega-block' was transported the short journey from Bay 3 of the Module Hall to link up with Block A on the berth during March 2005.

The VT element of the build, Block E/F, comprised of the bow section forward of the bridge screen, which incorporated an enclosed forecastle, space for the Sylver A50 vertical launch system (VLS) and 4.5in (114mm) Mk 8 Mod 1 main gun housing. The E/F bow block was also designed with redundant space to accommodate an additional, multi-role VLS silo or a larger-calibre (155mm) main gun. This combined block left VT's Portsmouth facility on-board the *Woolston* barge in June 2005.

On arrival at Scotstoun the block was offloaded via the new Ro-Ro quay facility and transported via a specially constructed door to the Module Hall. It was temporarily positioned on the footprint previously occupied by Block B/C at the top of Bay 3, which allowed sufficient space for the Govan-built Block D to be manoeuvred from the adjacent Bay 2 and onto the berth. This bow Block E/F was linked up with the rest of the ship on the berth by the end of June 2005, enabling the process of aligning, welding and integrating the four discrete block sections to form the complete hull. The process of welding the blocks together was completed in November of 2005 with the welding of the butt weld of Block D to Block E/F.

Two images of *Daring* pictured during and just after launch from Scotstoun on 1 February 2006. 700 tons of drag chains were used to arrest the ship's 5,222-tonne launch weight in the relatively narrow confines of the River Clyde. As the image shows, computer simulations designed to ensure the hull would be stopped soon after leaving the ways were successful. *(Conrad Waters)*

By the end of 2005 some sixty-three per cent of pipework and over twenty-five per cent of cable reeves had been installed; both milestones were achieved by utilising the large technical galleries situated along the flanks of the hull. The weight of the ship at launch was 5,222 tonnes, almost at the maximum loading of the covered berth, the concrete foundations of which could handle a weight of up to 5,306 tonnes, including the launch shoring, ways and poppet supports.

The Clyde is a relatively narrow river and launching incidents, particularly collisions on the opposite bank, are not an unknown occurrence. Despite tens of thousands of dynamic launches on the river, they are regarded as the single greatest operational risk undertaken during the build process as the hull is essentially not under control once the launching triggers are released. At the same time an unusual load is experienced by the structure of the ship as its weight is transferred from the ground ways to the buoyancy of the water. To mitigate any possibility of collisions with the larger Type 45 hull, computer simulation was undertaken to ensure that the hull would be stopped soon after leaving the ways. The method used to arrest hulls is by attaching drag chains to either side of the hull. Calculation determined that 700 tons of drag chains would be required for *Daring*, where a mere 300 tons had been sufficient for the Type 23 frigate *St. Albans*, launched from the adjacent berth some six years earlier. At Govan, with a much longer launching run, 320 tons of drag chains were sufficient to arrest subsequent Type 45s.

BLOCK-BUILD AT GOVAN

With the last of the two 'Bay' class Landing Ship Dock (Auxiliary) vessels for the Royal Fleet Auxiliary, *Mounts Bay* and *Cardigan Bay*, having been launched in April 2005, the 216m long No.1 berth at Govan was released for use by the second of class, *Dauntless*, and all subsequent vessels. Although the first steel for *Dauntless* was cut in August 2004, the high level of block fitting-out being undertaken in the large SBOH facility meant that the first block was not skidded into position on the berth until March 2006.

The build sequence at Govan involved units, delivered to the SBOH from the fabrication shop, being lifted from the transporters by two 80-ton overhead travelling cranes and positioned in place to form a block. During this process 'lock-out items' including gas turbines, diesel generators and HV

An image of *Duncan*'s launch. Govan has a much longer launching run than Scotstoun, meaning only 320 tons of drag chains – as opposed to 700 tons for *Daring* – were needed to arrest her launch. (*BAE Systems*)

Figure 4.3.3 *Duncan*: movement of blocks and unit composition

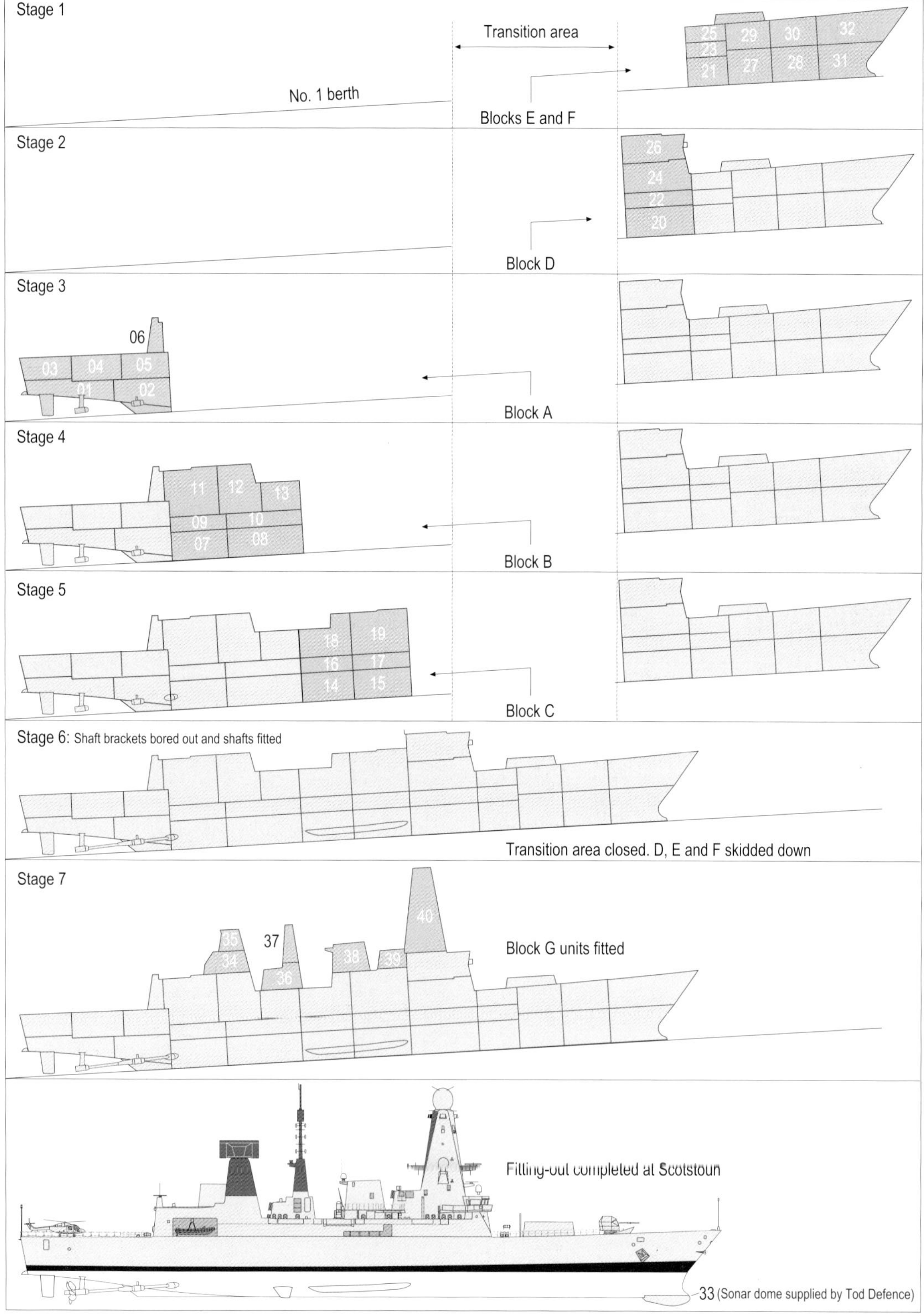

switchboards were installed. At any one time, two bays in the SBOH were utilised for block-build, with the third bay used for preparing the units and supporting blocks in the adjacent bays. The location and position of each block was determined by the planned sequence of block movement onto the berth. Structurally complete and highly fitted-out blocks of up to 1,600 tons in weight were then transported directly from the SBOH to the fixed concrete No. 1 berth using SPMTs and then hydraulically skidded into position via a block transition area, comprising a reinforced hard-standing and a 39m removable section of the concrete ways. The only divergence from this was for Blocks E/F, which were delivered to the Ro-Ro transfer quay at Govan from Portsmouth by the *Woolston* barge, manoeuvred to the transition area and skidded up the fixed ways into position (see Figure 4.3.3). The shell plate seams at the respective block butts were faired and welded together using the automated KAT carriage and track method to form the complete hull, with deck seams joined using a combination of metal inert gas (MIG) and submerged-arc welding. Once the hull structure was complete, the superstructure elements were then lifted into position using the four 80-ton luffing cranes servicing No. 1 berth, while the twin propeller drive shafts were installed and aligned using chain blocks attached to the shell plate. The structurally complete ship was then dynamically launched.

Although *Dauntless* was, in many respects, a new first of class due to the different build method employed, lessons learned resulted in *Dauntless* rapidly improving the maturity of the build process, expending only sixty-five per cent of the man-hours required to build the first of class.

FITTING-OUT AT SCOTSTOUN

At Scotstoun, the post-launch fitting-out, testing and commissioning process was largely common to both the Scotstoun-built first of class and the subse-

There was variation in block assembly across the class depending upon block availability. With *Duncan*, conjoined Blocks E and F from Portsmouth were brought to the transition area, jacked-up and moved to the head of the berth. Block D was similarly lifted and joined to E and F. Block A and later Blocks B and C were moved through the transition area to the bottom of the berth and the transition area closed. D, E and F Blocks were then skidded and joined to the other blocks. Block G units were fitted and the ship brought to the launching stage.
(Drawings by Ian Johnston)

Two images of the final Type 45 destroyer, *Duncan*, in the process of fitting out at Scotstoun, where key items of combat equipment such as the Sampson radar and Mk 8 Mod 1 4.5in gun were installed. *(BAE Systems)*

quent vessels launched from Govan. The only major difference was in the case of *Daring*, where the constraints of the Scotstoun covered berth required her Block G superstructure units to be fitted in dry dock. This was followed by installation of equipment supporting the combat and navigational systems, notably the Sampson multifunction radar, the S1850M long range radar, the Sylver A50 vertical launch system and the 4.5in main gun. The 185m long Dry Dock No. 2 at Scotstoun is fitted with two recessed pits at either end of the dock floor to enable fitting the sonar dome and propeller blades. Prior to fitting the fixed-pitch blades however, the propeller hub was first fitted with dummy 'paddles' and the ship manoeuvred into the

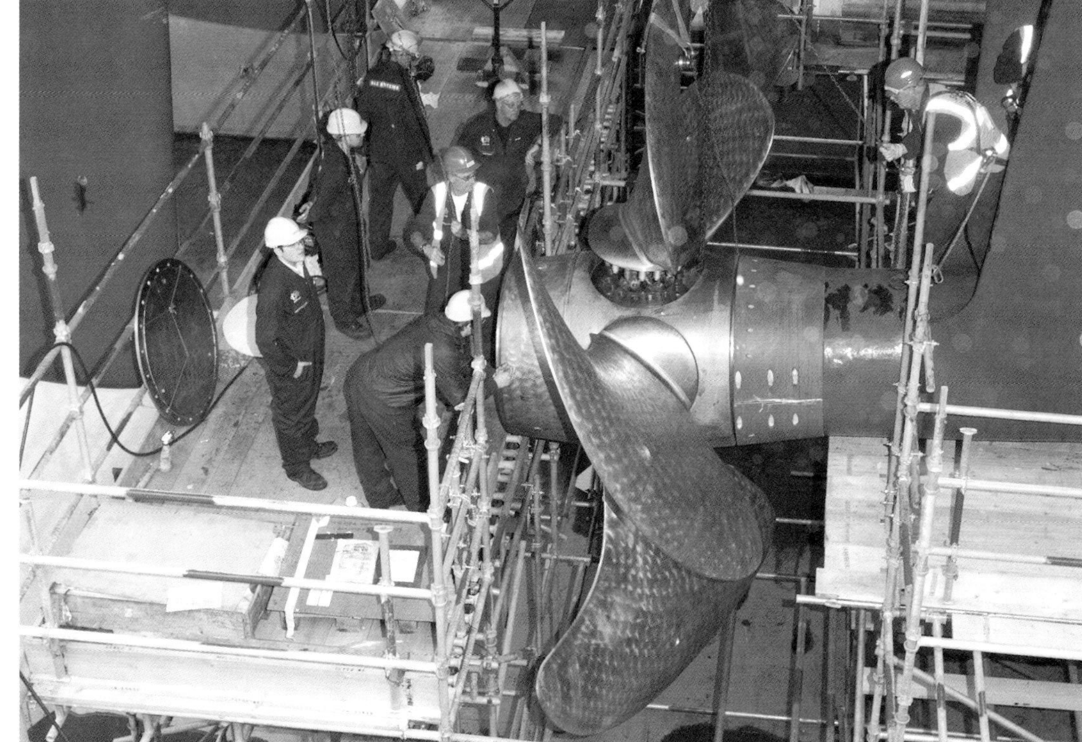

A detailed view of the propeller blades being attached to a Type 45 destroyer. The process took place in the 185m long Dry Dock No. 2 at Scotstoun, which is fitted with recessed pits to aid the process. *(BAE Systems)*

Dauntless pictured during full power trials in Scotstoun's No. 3 Dry Dock in 2008. Fitting the ship with dummy 'paddles' instead of propeller blades allowed a large proportion of the machinery trials to be carried out within the confines of the shipyard. *(BAE Systems)*

207m long No. 3 Dry Dock to undertake dynamic basin trials in the flooded dock.

The basin trials were an innovation on Type 45, particularly as they allowed a large proportion of the machinery trials – including full-power running of the gas turbines, diesel generators and propulsion motors – to be carried out in conjunction with the subcontractor within the confines of the shipyard, rather than at sea. This realised considerable savings, in terms of both time and expenditure, on contractor sea trials (CST). After the basin trials were completed, the ship was transferred back to Dry Dock No. 2 where the propeller blades were fitted, Intersleek anti-fouling paint applied, and the ship readied for its first stage CST, with the primary focus on undertaking completion, joint inspection and acceptance of the ship's 800 compartments and numerous systems by the customer during both the docking periods and at sea. Due to maturity and change issues, *Daring* undertook three CST periods of approximately four weeks. This was subsequently stabilised to two CST periods of the same length; the first focused on a shakedown of the ship's machinery and 'hotel' functions, along with testing of the ship's guns. The second CST period was heavily orientated towards testing the ship's combat systems. After a further period alongside at Scotstoun's Deep Water Berth, to complete the acceptance process, a delivery voyage to Portsmouth Naval Base was undertaken; averaging four days for each ship. At that point the ship was accepted off contract by the Royal Navy and the build programme formally concluded.

Throughout the Type 45 build programme, best practice continued to be effectively transferred across each ship in such profusion that the final ship in the class, *Duncan*, achieved a state of sixty per cent completion prior to her launch on 11 October 2010, with total man-hours expended at final acceptance off contract by the Royal Navy in March 2013, a mere sixty per cent of that used to achieve the same milestone on *Daring* in December 2008 (see Figure 4.3.4).[6]

CONCLUSION

The Type 45 programme, involving the design and construction of what is claimed to be the world's most advanced class of air defence destroyers, has been a highly successful achievement for the British shipbuilding industry. The complexity of its design, coupled with the block-build strategy, encouraged significant collaboration and innovation between the

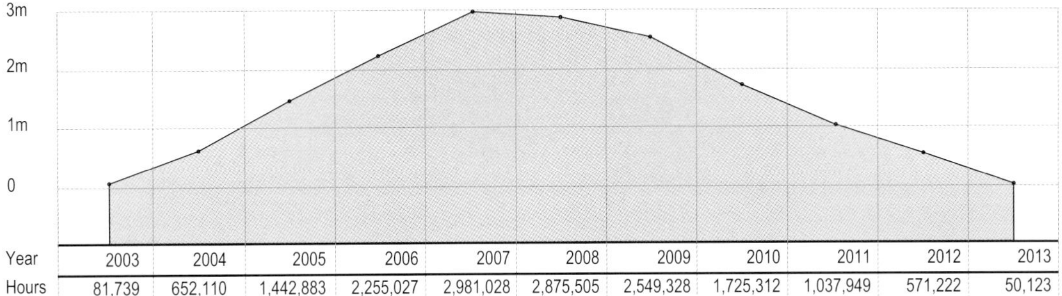

Figure 4.3.4 Type 45 Man Hours
Expressed annually over the class by year and by individual ship

Daring	3,866,929	Diamond	2,505,401	Defender	2,353,652
Dauntless	2,552,103	Dragon	2,349,056	Duncan	2,365,330

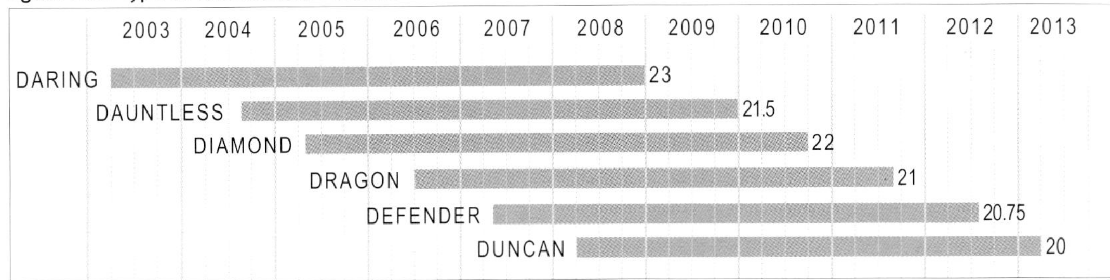

Figure 4.3.5 Type 45 Construction Timeline

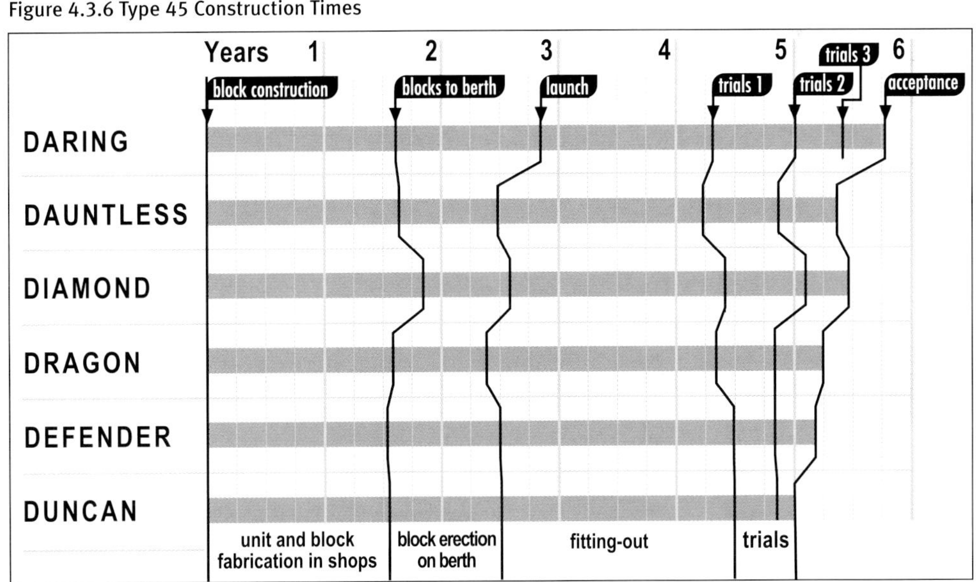

Figure 4.3.6 Type 45 Construction Times

Block construction - period begining with first steel cut date, unit production and integration into block
Blocks to berth - period begining when the first block was placed on the building berth
Launch - launch of the hull
trials 1 - commencement of first sea trials
trials 2 - commencement of second sea trials
trials 3 - commencement of third sea trials (Daring only)
Acceptance - date of handover to RN

(All drawings by Ian Johnston)

Above: *Dauntless* pictured in the course of contractor sea trials during 2009. All ships except *Daring* (which had three trials periods) underwent two periods of contractor sea trials of c. four weeks each; the former being focused on the machinery and 'hotel' functions and the latter on testing the ship's combat systems. *(BAE Systems)*

The final Type 45 destroyer *Duncan* pictured sailing down the Clyde to start her first sea trials on 31 August 2012. She departed Scotstoun for the final time on 19 March 2013 prior to delivery to the Royal Navy. *(Crown Copyright 2012)*

shipyards involved, as well as their extensive supply chains. In 2005 this principle was extrapolated into the formation of a full alliance structure for the build of the *Queen Elizabeth* class aircraft carriers, the largest naval vessels ever built in Britain. Subsequently, in July 2008, this unprecedented approach to shipbuilding in the UK culminated in the full operational merger of VT's Portsmouth ship-building and support operations with BAE Systems' Glasgow-based Surface Fleet Solutions to form a joint venture, BVT Surface Fleet Ltd, at the behest of the MOD. All parties signed a Terms of Business Agreement guaranteeing a stable demand for complex warship procurement in UK over the following fifteen years. Further consolidation occurred with VT exiting the joint venture in October 2009, leaving BAE Systems Surface Ships Ltd. as the sole complex naval surface shipbuilding firm in the UK.

This industrial strategy – effectively to maintain

Table 4.3.1: BAE SYSTEMS SURFACE SHIPBUILDING: NOMENCLATURE AND TIMELINE

1985:	Yarrow Shipbuilders Ltd at Scotstoun acquired by GEC. Name retained.
1995:	Vickers Shipbuilding & Engineering Ltd at Barrow bought by GEC. Name retained.
1996:	GEC Marine Group formed including VSEL (Vickers Shipbuilding & Engineering Ltd) and YSL (Yarrow Shipbuilders Ltd).
1998 – September:	GEC Marconi renamed Marconi Electronic Systems Ltd. GEC Marine becomes Marconi Naval Systems.
1998 – November:	Yarrow Shipbuilders Ltd renamed Marconi Marine (YSL) Ltd. VSEL renamed Marconi Marine (VSEL) Ltd.
1998 – December:	Marconi Naval Systems becomes Marconi Electronic Systems Operating Group.
1999 – April:	Kvaerner Group put Kvaerner Govan yard up for sale. Agreement reached on merger of Marconi Electronic Systems Ltd and British Aerospace (BAe).
1999 – July:	GEC announces intention to acquire Govan.
1999 – November:	Marconi Electronic Systems Ltd and British Aerospace (BAe) merge to form BAE Systems plc.
1999 – December:	Govan purchased by Marconi Electronic Systems Ltd and managed from Scotstoun yard which is now part of BAE Systems Marine (YSL) Ltd.
2000:	All three shipyards (Barrow, Govan and Scotstoun) merged as BAE Systems Marine Ltd.
2002:	BAE Systems Marine Ltd. becomes part of the Sea Systems sector within BAE Systems Programmes.
2003:	BAE Systems Marine Ltd split to form BAE Systems Submarines (Barrow) and BAE Systems Naval Ships (Govan and Scotstoun) within BAE Systems Programmes. Sea Systems disbanded.
2007:	Surface Fleet Solutions formed incorporating Naval Ships and subsequently consolidated into BAE Systems Surface Fleet Solutions Ltd.
2008:	BVT Surface Fleet Ltd formed as a joint venture with Vosper Thornycroft (BAE Systems 55 per cent, VT 45 per cent).
2009:	BVT Surface Fleet Ltd renamed BAE Systems Surface Ships Ltd on outright purchase of business by BAE Systems.
2011:	BAE Systems Surface Ships Ltd merged with BAE Systems Submarine Solutions Ltd. to form BAE Systems Maritime.
2012:	Surface Ships element of Maritime renamed BAE Systems Maritime – Naval Ships.

the 'sovereign capability' to design, build and support complex warships in the UK – has built upon the preceding decade of stability in the industry engendered by the Type 45 programme. At the height of the programme in 2008/09, the Type 45s contributed some £231m (c. US$345m) of direct Gross Value Added (GVA) to the UK economy, with an additional £366m (c. US$550m) created as an indirect multiplier, via the effects of wage and supplier payments. It has encouraged investment not only in the shipyards, but in the shipbuilders too. Approximately 6,700 direct and 8,200 indirect jobs have been sustained by the Type 45 programme; including over 600 apprentices and graduates employed in the shipyards during the build of the six vessels.

When *Duncan* departed the Scotstoun shipyard on 19 March 2013, it marked the first occasion that a full ship had not been in some form of build at this famous shipyard since the 1920s. Despite that, the on-going build of the two *Queen Elizabeth* class aircraft carriers, and design work on the Type 26 Global Combat Ship underpinned by the strategic fifteen-year agreement with the MOD, gives reason to be optimistic about British shipbuilding in the way that Alfred Fernandez Yarrow was in 1906, when he first acquired his Scotstoun shipyard to build destroyers for the Royal Navy.

Notes

1. Greater detail on the origins of the Type 45 programme can be found in the editor's 'HMS *Daring*: The Royal Navy's Type 45 Air-Defence Destroyer', *Seaforth World Naval Review 2010* (Barnsley: Seaforth Publishing, 2009), pp.132–49.

2. BAE Systems' shipyard at Govan was better known for the greater part of its life as the Fairfield Shipbuilding & Engineering Co Ltd., one of the classic names in British heavy industry. The Govan yard was the first large private integrated shipyard in the United Kingdom, laid out by marine engineer John Elder in 1864. It became a world leader as the Fairfield yard, building record breaking North Atlantic liners in the 1890s. In common with most British shipyards, Fairfield built ships of all types including the capital ships *Indomitable*, *New Zealand*, *Valiant*, *Renown*, *Howe* and *Implacable*. From the 1960s onwards lack of competitiveness forced many British yards out of business and the Govan yard is now one of only a handful of shipyards in the UK and the last of the big yards building surface ships to have worked continuously since inception.

3. The original MOD planning assumption was for a class of up to twelve Type 45 vessels but the 2003 Defence White Paper subsequently revised this to a class of eight ships, of which six had been contracted. The announcement that an option for the seventh and eighth vessels was not going to be taken up was eventually made in June 2008.

4. The issues that emerged with the *Astute* build programme are covered in depth in Richard Beedall's '*Astute* Class Submarines: A Quantum Leap in Capability for the Silent Service', *Seaforth World Naval Review 2011* (Barnsley: Seaforth Publishing, 2010), pp.84–101.

5. 'Open canoe' refers to the deck-head of a compartment not being fitted in order to facilitate the installation of large items of equipment. 'Lock out' generally refers to a large item of equipment (such as a gas turbine) that – due to physical constraints – requires installation at an early stage of build via 'open canoe' access and is then temporarily sealed off as the rest of the build progresses.

6. Figures 4.3.5 and 4.3.6 provide additional information on the construction times for each member of the Type 45 class.

7. The authors would like to thank BAE Systems Maritime – Naval Ships for their cooperation in writing this article and, in particular, the following individuals:

Jennifer Osbaldestin, Type 45 Programme Director.
Derek McCaffrey, Type 45 Project Manager.
Simon Murphy, Type 45 Project Controls Manager.
David Connelly, Type 45 Ship Manager.
Tony Hepburn, Type 45 Ship Manager.
William Smithyman, Production Planning Manager.
Gordon McLeod, Lead Production Planner.
Bill Cullen, Senior Photographer.

Contributors

Richard Beedall is an IT Consultant with a long-standing interest in the Royal Navy (RN) and naval affairs in general. He served for fourteen years in the RNR as a rating and officer, working with the USN and local naval forces in the Middle East and around the world. In 1999 he founded one of the earliest naval websites on the RN – now called *Navy Matters*. He has contributed to *Seaforth Naval Review* since the initial 2010 edition, and has written extensively on naval developments for many other organisations and publications, including *AMI International*, *Naval Forces*, *Defence Management* and *Warships IFR*. He currently lives in Ireland with his wife and two young daughters.

Norman Friedman is one of the best-known naval analysts and historians in the US and the author of over thirty-five books. He has written on broad issues of modern military interest, including an award-winning history of the Cold War, whilst in the field of warship development his greatest sustained achievement is probably an eight-volume series on the design of different US warship types. The holder of a PhD in theoretical physics from Columbia, Dr Friedman is a regular guest commentator on television and lectures widely on professional defence issues. He is a resident of New York.

David Hobbs is a well-known author and naval historian. He has written fouteen books and co-authored many more. He writes for several periodicals and in 2005 won the Aerospace Journalist of the Year, Best Defence Submission. He lectures on naval subjects worldwide and has been on radio and TV in several countries. He served in the Royal Navy from 1964 until 1997, and retired with the rank of Commander. He qualified as both a fixed and rotary wing pilot and his log book contains 2,300 hours with over 800 carrier landings, 150 of which were at night.

Ian Johnston has a long interest in the growth and decline of shipbuilding, especially on the Clyde. He has written a number of books on this subject including histories of the William Beardmore shipyard at Dalmuir and John Brown's at Clydebank. Most recently he has written *Clydebank Battlecruisers* and *The Battleship Builders*, the latter co-written with Ian Buxton. He is a member of the HMS *Ramillies* Association and hopes to publish a book on that ship soon. Currently he is involved in a project to establish a heritage centre dedicated to the Fairfield shipyard in Govan, Glasgow.

Ross Gillett joined the RANR in 1982 and served on full time duties for five years. He completed his twenty-two year career with the RAN as the Senior Public Affairs Officer at Garden Island in Sydney. Ross also edited three Australian magazines, *The Navy* (1978–1999), *Australian Sea Heritage* (1986–88) and *Australian Warship* (2011–13). He has authored seventeen major naval/nautical books and edited a further ten. He has also written extensively for other Australian and international naval magazines. He is now a full-time author/editor, currently working on his eighteenth naval book. Ross who lives with his wife in Sydney, NSW, also serves as volunteer guide for the Naval Historical Society around the historic Garden Island Naval Dockyard.

Paul Sweeney was educated at the University of Glasgow prior to joining BAE Systems in 2011 on the company's graduate programme. Most recently he was a team member on the last of the Type 45s, HMS *Duncan*, taking her through a critical phase of the fitting-out programme and Contractor Sea Trials prior to acceptance off-contract by the Royal Navy in March 2013. From a family of Clyde shipbuilders, his passion for the shipbuilding industry, historical and contemporary, was fostered from childhood. He is actively supporting a number of initiatives aimed at conserving shipbuilding heritage on the Clyde; combining these activities with service as a Territorial Army reservist.

Tomohiko Tada was engaged in the development, design, manufacture, quality control and project management of defence equipment for the JMSDF at a major Japanese electronics firm for more than thirty years. After retirement, he has studied the history, current status and future trends of defence technology. He is now a defence technology researcher and writer for the magazines *Japan Military Review*, *Ships of the World*, *MARU* and *World Weapons*. He is author of *The World's Warship Catalogue* and co-author of the *United States Navy Handbook*, *The World's Near Future Weapons*, *21st Century Weapon Technology: Naval Ships and Aircraft*, the *Review of Today's European Navies*, the *Japan Maritime Self Defence Force Destroyer Perfect Guide* and others. He is a guest commentator on television and lectures on naval defence issues and ballistic missile defence.

Guy Toremans is a Belgian-based maritime freelance correspondent and a member of the Association of Belgian & Foreign Journalists, an association accredited by NATO and the UN. His reports, ship profiles and interviews are published in the English language naval magazines *Jane's Navy International*, *Naval Forces* and *Warships IFR*, as well as in the French *Marines & Forces Navales* and the Japanese *J-Ships*. Since 1990, he has regularly embarked on NATO, Asian, South African and Pacific-based warships, including aircraft carriers, destroyers, frigates, mine-countermeasures vessels and support ships.

Scott Truver is Director, Team Blue, at Gryphon Technologies LC, specialising in national and homeland security, and naval and maritime affairs. Since 1972 Dr. Truver has participated in numerous studies – most notably the inter-agency task force drafting the US *National Strategy for Maritime Security* (2005) – and has written extensively for US and foreign publications. He has lectured at the US Naval Academy, Naval War College and Naval Postgraduate School, among other venues. Further qualifications include a PhD degree in Marine Policy Studies and a MA in Political Science/International Relations from the University of Delaware.

Conrad Waters is a lawyer by training but a banker by profession. Educated at Liverpool University prior to being called to the bar at Gray's Inn, his interest in naval affairs was stimulated by a family history of officers in merchant navy service. A long-standing writer on naval affairs, his work includes six years producing the 'World Navies in Review' chapter of the annual *Warship* before joining for *Seaforth World Naval Review* as founding editor. Managing Director for Credit Analysis at the European arm of one of the world's largest banks, Conrad lives with wife Susan and children Emma, Alexander and Imogen in Haslemere, Surrey.